THE
PAWNEE
GHOST DANCE
HAND GAME

THE PAWNEE GHOST DANCE HAND GAME

Ghost Dance Revival and Ethnic Identity

Alexander Lesser

The University of Wisconsin Press

Published 1978

The University of Wisconsin Press
Box 1379, Madison, Wisconsin 53701
The University of Wisconsin Press, Ltd.
70 Great Russell Street, London

Wisconsin edition
First printing, 1978

Originally published in 1933
by Columbia University Press as Volume XVI in
Columbia University Contributions to Anthropology

Printed in the United States of America
ISBN 0-299-07480-3 cloth, 0-299-07484-6 paper
LC 77-91056

TO

FRANZ BOAS

CONTENTS

AUTHOR'S FOREWORD

I

The *Pawnee Ghost Dance Hand Game* was written in 1932, based on field research among the Pawnees in 1929-31. It was first published in 1933 by the Columbia University Press as a volume in its series of Columbia University Publications in Anthropology. In 1969 it was republished by the AMS press in New York, which took over the republication of that entire Columbia series. The book was well received in reviews and in the field of American Indian studies, but neither of its earlier publications gave it wide circulation or readership. The present edition, which has added this foreword and an expanded bibliography to the original text, may reach a larger audience.

My field research in the 1930s was primarily devoted to intensive study of traditional Pawnee religion, in which I had an opportunity to use for descriptive detail a large manuscript by James R. Murie and Clark Wissler entitled "Ceremonies of the Pawnee," then awaiting publication by the Bureau of American Ethnology. With this in hand, I could largely disregard recording descriptive ritual detail and concentrate on understanding Pawnee theology and philosophy. It was while I did this day after day with many informants that I discovered the tremendous impact of the Ghost Dance doctrines of the 1890s on the Pawnee people, and the creative emergence in those years of the Pawnee Ghost Dance Hand Games. Postponing work on the traditional religious theology in the expectation that the Murrie-Wissler manuscript would be published shortly, I wrote my first book to tell the story of the Ghost Dance years and the Pawnee Ghost Dance Hand Games. Publication of the "Ceremonies of the Pawnee" unfortunately languished for these many years. Only now or in another year, with special linguistic editing by Douglas R. Parks, is the Smithsonian Institution expected to publish it.

It was possible in 1929-31 to recapture events of the 1890s because a great deal about Ghost Dance times was known and remembered by Pawnees of those years. It would be impossible to do this study today among living Pawnees.

The book showed that the Ghost Dance was more than a period of religious excitement for the Pawnee. Its doctrines and activities involved individuals, families, and traditional groups in efforts to remember and

ix

carry out again traditional ways that were on the verge of extinction. The Ghost Dance was a *nativistic* revival. Its reassertion of Pawnee values was an experience of Pawnee ethnic identity—a renewed awareness for some, a new experience for others. In our time, ethnic identity, often with goals of political autonomy, is being reasserted by submerged, repressed peoples in many parts of the world. In relation to this widespread phenomenon, the Ghost Dance of years ago among the Pawnee and other Indian Americans can now be understood as the same kind of reassertion of ethnic identity. In fact, it now raises a fundamental question: Is not this the meaning of *any* nativistic revival which occurs under nationalistic assimilation programs of dominant peoples?

The excitement of the Ghost Dance years among the Pawnee continued into the early twentieth century. Indian Affairs officials were concerned in those years to quiet down, if possible, Pawnee Ghost Dance activities, and especially the playing of Ghost Dance Hand Games; they wanted to continue the allotting of land units to individuals and the persuading of Pawnee families to settle on their allotments and farm them. That was the program of assimilation with which Pawnee Ghost Dance excitement interfered.

By the 1930s, when I was among the Pawnee, most revivals of traditional forms were gone again. Life in and around Pawnee, Oklahoma, provided no meaningful basis for sacred bundles and rituals or for men's military societies, and few of the traditional personnel to carry them out survived. The Hand Games lost their religious meaning and became occasions for fun and recreation. They still are in 1977. But the tribal sense of being Pawnees, of having values of their own, of having a history, a language, and traditions from a remote past, remained. In fact, during years of change, from the 1930s to the present, some events have strengthened the Pawnees in their tribalism and in their tribal pride.

The Pawnee population in 1930 was 844, up from its all-time low of 600 in 1900. Actually, the population was steadily increasing, year by year. It numbered 977 in 1938, the year in which the Pawnees established their present tribal organization under the Indian Reorganization Act of the 1934 Indian "New Deal." By 1940 the Pawnee roll was 1,017; and in 1964, 1,898 Pawnees shared in the per capita distribution of a judgment recovered by the tribe from the United States through the Indian Claims Commission. It compensated for inequities in nineteenth-century treaty settlements for their former lands in Kansas and Nebraska. Today, in 1976-77, there are 2,213 Pawnees on the tribal roll.

Although Pawnee life is still related to the town of Pawnee and the county of Pawnee, the relationship has changed fundamentally over the years. In 1930 virtually all Pawnees lived in or near the town, perhaps three-fourths of the 844 members of the tribe within a radius of four or five miles, visiting town constantly by horse and wagon. On Saturdays the town square around the courthouse was a gathering place for families who came to spend a good part of the day, and many walked about in the main streets throughout the day, meeting one another. The official Pawnee Agency of the Bureau of Indian Affairs was at that time about a mile out of town on tribal-owned land.

In contrast to the 1930s, by 1967 less than one-fourth of the tribe lived near Pawnee. Today, in 1977, Pawnee families are much more widely dispersed than ever, and the town itself is no longer a tribal center. On weekends it is as deserted by Pawnees as it is by others. Saturdays are no time to meet people in town, and on Sundays everything in town is closed, including eating places.

Several factors account for this change. The car is one. Increased education and technical training of Pawnees have led any number of families to live where they find jobs and career opportunities. A good many live in other Oklahoma towns and the cities of Oklahoma City and Tulsa. Many Pawnees live outside the state, numbers in the Southwest and California.

The political situation is the most striking factor in the changed political relationship of Pawnees to the town and to themselves as a tribe. The Bureau of Indian Affairs Pawnee Agency, which manages the Bureau affairs of five tribes—the Ponca, Oto, Kaw, and Tonkawa, besides the Pawnee—formerly located on Pawnee lands out of town, is now in Pawnee itself, in rented quarters. The Pawnee Tribe, by contrast, as a phase of its steadily developing tribal self-government, conducts most of its business in a Pawnee Tribal Business Building on Pawnee tribal lands in the area where the Agency once was. Both the Pawnee Agency and the Pawnee Tribal Office are open weekdays only.

For recreational gatherings larger than families-at-home, the Pawnee reserve lands out of town provide facilities, some in use and more being developed. There are camp grounds and fair grounds, and room for the annual July pow-wow, considered by many Pawnees, even families living at a distance, an annual homecoming.

The changes have made the Pawnees less and less concerned with the town of Pawnee. The tribe is thinking today much more in terms of itself, of the tribal center developing on Pawnee lands, including the Pawnee Tribal Business Building and the Pawnee Hospital, already operating, the Round House recreation center in process, a Pawnee Industrial park, well advanced in planning, renovated housing, and many other projects already part of tribal approved plans.

In the early 1930s the Pawnee tribe was not organized politically. The tradition of hereditary chiefs provided a mechanism still respected by Pawnees, and the chiefs acted for the people in dealing with United States officials. When the Indian New Deal of President Roosevelt's administration offered for the first time, in the Indian Reorganization Act (IRA) and supplementary legislation, a nonassimilation program in Indian Affairs, the Pawnee supported it early. The program accepted the existence of Indian communities and attempted to provide them with the legal status and machinery and the economic resources needed to continue their tribal existence as long as they chose. Tribal self-government and tribal business corporations were authorized, and provisions were made for an adequate land base, financial credit, and adequate training and education.

The Pawnees began drafting a plan for a tribal constitution in 1936, although they could not adopt it until 1937 when the Oklahoma Indian Welfare Act became part of the IRA body of legislation; the original IRA did not include Oklahoma tribes. In the draft, the traditional status of Pawnee chiefs was recognized by establishing a Chiefs Council as one of two governing bodies of the tribe. In January 1938, the Pawnees voted to adopt the proposed Tribal Constitution and By-Laws. Their support was substantial. Of 460 eligible to vote, 257 (56 percent) participated and voted 197 to 60 (3.5 to 1) in favor of the plan. A Pawnee Tribal Business Council of eight members was established, to be elected every two years by vote of all Pawnees twenty-one years old or older, and a Nasharo or Chiefs Council of eight, to be elected every four years. Chiefs could not be members of the Business Council, and only chiefs, with inherited rights of chieftainship, were eligible for election to the Nasharo Council. The Business Council was to be the active governing body of the tribe, to speak and act and transact tribal business for the tribe, and to appoint subordinate functionaries. The Nasharo Council had the right to review all Business Council actions concerned with tribal membership and tribal claims and rights under treaties. All tribesmembers were guaranteed full rights of citizenship under the United States and Oklahoma constitutions. Although men and women voted, only men were initially eligible for positions on the Business Council; a constitutional amendment making both men and women twenty-five years old or older eligible was ratified December 17, 1974.

In its structure and principles, and in the spirit of the Indian Reorganization Act behind it, the 1938 Pawnee Indian tribal organization was a further step in the realization of Pawnee identity. It strengthened tribal confidence and pride. It offered a framework on which Pawnees could structure an improved life and a Pawnee future.

First, of course, the Pawnees, like other tribes organized under the

IRA, had to learn the ordinary day-by-day business of operating government agencies of their own, of all the details of budgeting, managing funds and paying bills, hiring and firing, and complicated routines of programming and making decisions and plans that could become realities. In all this, which had for so many years been handled by the Commissioner of Indian Affairs, the Bureau of Indian Affairs, and their local Pawnee officialdom, the Pawnees found that they could not exercise tribal authority freely. There were strong habits not easily shaken of turning to the Agency for advice and decisions; and, on the other side, the Bureau of Indian Affairs and its representatives were not able to end automatically their practice of running the lives and business of Pawnee individuals and the Pawnee Tribe. Learning by doing was difficult under these conditions.

But a larger difficulty for the Pawnee Tribe, from 1938 to the late 1950s, was that the philosophy and the principles of the IRA did not have steady majority support in Congress, and after Roosevelt's administration, in the Executive Branch. Quite the opposite. The view that assimilation of the American Indians should be the goal in Indian Affairs remained a commitment of many, and legislative enactments and resolutions, as well as executive actions, expressed that repeatedly.

In the early 1950s, for example, the Commissioner and Bureau of Indian Affairs promoted a program of relocation of reservation Indians into urban centers. The theory was that Indian areas, predominantly rural, could not be developed to support their Indian population, that these areas were in fact overpopulated. Even if unskilled, Indians should be helped to find jobs in and settle in industrialized areas. Those who did, it was expected, would leave Indian reservation life behind and prefer to live permanently in cities as part of the American labor force. The program opposed any plans, by Indian tribes or others, to bring industry or business onto Indian-owned lands and thereby create new economic opportunities for Indians at home. In the end, the relocation program proved a relatively weak threat to Indian tribal existence or development; it failed to achieve its goals. Most Indians who were persuaded to try relocation, unskilled as they were and offered virtually no technical training, met unemployment in the cities if it occurred by returning home to rejoin their kinfolk.

More threatening to Indian community development and even to the continued existence of IRA tribal organization was the commitment of Congress in the mid-1950s to a program for termination of federal responsibility for Indians as rapidly as possible. The theory behind this, given support even in some anthropological studies, was that it was the federal status of Indian tribes which was responsible for their continuing separateness and rejection of assimilation—a federal status which went back to colonial times when colonists made treaties with Indian tribes as they found them, autonomous and self-governing. House Concurrent Resolution 108 put into words the congressional determination to terminate the federal status and rights of Indian tribes, and for years it was quoted as a national commitment by assimilationists in Congress and in the Bureau of Indian Affairs. Indian tribal opposition to termination, along with the strong support of public organizations concerned with Indian rights and liberal members of Congress, was not able to prevent all legislative termination efforts. After general termination legislation was defeated, the Congress shrewdly adopted a course of enacting termination bills tribe by tribe, multiplying the difficulties of opposing them. Some tribes were terminated despite powerful opposition, including, in 1954, such notable cases as the Klamath Indians of Oregon and the Menomini Indians of Wisconsin. The Menomini case proved so conclusively a failure after a few years that the Menominis and their friends were able, in 1973, to get their status reversed and return the tribe to federal status and jurisdiction.

The Pawnee Tribe was not directly attacked by termination legislation. Assimilationists did not claim that the Pawnees were "ready" for such a drastic change. Even for assimilationists, to be "ready" meant more advanced economic development than the Pawnee Tribe had yet achieved. But termination as a threat and the practical obstructions of tribal self-government by bureaucratic Bureau of Indian Affairs paternalism continued. They were actually ended only in the 1960s by a fundamental change in national Indian policy. Termination was put aside or conceptually postponed, with the thought that economic development and improvement of Indian life with federal help must precede any idea of ending Indian federal status.

The 1960s, under President Kennedy and President Johnson, were years marked by a national recognition of widespread chronic unemployment, poverty, poor housing, and poor health, especially among deprived minority groups, and equally marked was a determination to do something about such conditions. A whole body of corrective legislation was enacted, dealing with area redevelopment, public housing, a youth conservation corps, the war on poverty, civil rights. New in the history of Indian Affairs was the inclusion of Indian communities among minorities to be helped by these programs.[1] A good many involved Indian Americans with government agencies or departments other than the Interior Department and its Bureau of Indian Affairs (traditionally their only jurisdiction). Prominent

1. See Richard Schifter, "Trends in Federal Indian Administration," *South Dakota Law Review* 15 (Winter 1970).

among these new jurisdictions were the Department of Commerce, the Department of Labor, and the Department of Health, Education, and Welfare. In some cases also, new federal directives added new obligations toward Indian Americans to the responsibilities of the Bureau of Indian Affairs.

The new opportunities in all areas required a procedure new to most tribes. Grants or loans, to be secured for approved purposes, called for applications, often complex and varying from case to case, made directly by recognized government units to appropriate agencies. The organized Pawnee Tribe was a recognized local government unit. But in understanding requirements and procedures, the tribe had virtually no experience, and little or no preparation by education or technical training. In a few cases, Congress tried to provide that needed experts from Washington visit Indians to help. But more frequently, even to make initial program applications, Pawnees found it necessary to send delegates to Washington for help. It took a good many years, especially as additional federal programs developed, to learn by trial and error, and only in the 1970s had the Pawnee Tribal Business Council reached a mature degree of outlook and performances.

This maturity appears in a devotion to Pawnee needs and goals shown by the core of tribal leadership. Improvement of economic conditions and opportunities, education, health, and the Pawnee future as Pawnees get their continuing attention. When the American Indian Movement (AIM) enlisted Pawnee adherents and led a protest in Pawnee, Oklahoma, in 1972, the tribe looked beyond AIM's pan-Indian philosophy and action methods, and any important influence of AIM was short-lived. Most Pawnees saw the Pawnee future in Pawnee ethnic terms, different in important ways from a generalized pan-Indian American movement, requiring separate and independent planning on its own. The Pawnee Tribal Business Council concerned itself even more intensely with education and technical training for immediate and future opportunities, with economic planning to improve conditions of Pawnee individual, family, and tribal life, with social planning for better recreation and enjoyment for all, and with cultural possibilities of holding and recovering Pawnee ethnic history and the Pawnee language.

Education has been and is vital to individual and tribal development in dealing with the alien, non-Indian world. Special technical training for technical jobs is of course chosen by many. But others, and their number is increasing, elect to study at advanced institutions along professional and career lines. This trend somewhat parallels the needs of the Pawnees for specialized experts and long-term thinking.

By 1976-77, virtually all Pawnee children were finishing public school.

This has meant that an increased number have gone on to public high school, and today, according to the chairman of the town school board, 95 percent of Pawnees in high school complete their studies and graduate. Perhaps a third of the high school graduates go on further into advanced technical training or into college. Informed estimates are that thirty to sixty Pawnees were enrolled in 1975, 1976, and 1977 at institutions of higher education.

Among college majors, behavioral sciences—sociology and social work, psychology, educational counseling—along with business and law, are increasingly popular. Many women have chosen nursing as a career. Short-courses in mechanics and welding have been popular among men, in clerical skills and cosmetology among women. Clerical work has usually been with the local agency of the Bureau of Indian Affairs or other BIA offices, or with the tribal administration. The Tribal Business Council sets up additional opportunities when it can. For example, in May 1975 the Council contracted with the Bureau of Indian Affairs for an instructor to train tribal employees in bookkeeping, payroll procedures, state and federal withholding taxes, and the like, and in June of that year arranged through the Comprehensive Employment Training Act (CETA) for five on-the-job training openings: three security officers, a jailor, and a cook.

Financial help for education, a vital factor in the Pawnee educational development that has occurred, is increasingly available through government agencies. A Higher Educational Grant Program through HEW has assisted high school students for many years; these grants are at most $1400 a year. For the past four years Basic Educational Opportunity Grants, based on need, have supplemented HEW grants for high school and beyond. Loan programs, more widely available, have helped Indians and non-Indians alike. Short vocational technical training courses, usually at Indian Meridian in Stillwater, get CETA assistance. College work is principally at Oklahoma State University, but other Oklahoma institutions are attended as well. In summary, Pawnee Indians are now making use of the whole range of public schools and high schools, trade schools, colleges, and universities.

Although general economic conditions have improved over the years since the 1930s, Pawnee Indians are still, in 1977, a poor people. Income of individuals and families is primarily from land rented to non-Indian farmers, supplemented by income of those who work. Few have business enterprises of their own in Pawnee or elsewhere. Many skilled and professional Pawnees live and work away from the Pawnee area. Pawnee, Oklahoma, offers limited employment for Indians, principally through the

Bureau Agency or the Pawnee Tribe itself. The town of Pawnee is a declining area economically. The development of Stillwater, about thirty miles away, as the University of Oklahoma center with a student population of 10,000 to 15,000, and as a commercial and industrial center, has made Pawnee and its commercial activities peripheral, showing few signs of business progress over the past forty years. The non-Indian residential area of Pawnee has grown considerably, as many who work or do business in Stillwater live in Pawnee and commute, but business has shrunken.

Unemployment among Pawnees has been and is high. In 1967, Pawnee median income in the Pawnee area was about three-fourths of that of local non-Indians, and the latter was low. A 1972 survey showed that more than 50 percent of the potential Pawnee labor force was unemployed. In 1977 unemployment is considered to be as high as 75 percent, and as having been more than 60 percent over the last several years. The Pawnees are, of course, eligible for social security programs, and the unemployed have recourse to unemployment insurance. But the economic needs of the area and of the Pawnees are obvious, and the tribal leadership is deeply concerned with this in tribal programming.

The efforts of the Pawnee Tribal Business Council to manage Pawnee affairs effectively and to promote Pawnee development are supported, even financially, by present federal policy. The Bureau of Indian Affairs administers a Tribal Government Development Program under which the Business Council can make contracts for needed personnel and equipment, and an Office of Native American Programs (ONAP) in Washington funds special tribal program needs, including employment of required specialists. Under the latter, the Pawnee Tribe added to its active staff certified public accountants, an engineer, an attorney, and a program specialist, as well as necessary secretaries for them. The tribal attorney completed action last year which added to the tribal reserve forty acres of Pawnee land that had come under the control of the town of Pawnee. In legal action with the Arkansas Riverbed Trust Authority, he recovered for the Pawnee the value of their interest in the Arkansas and Cimarron riverbeds. The engineer helped the Pawnee plan construction projects and determine site locations for future construction. And for special help, the tribe was able in 1977 to ask BIA land specialists to appraise all Pawnee tribal land, and to turn to the Oklahoma Indian Affairs Commission for assistance in preparing a Comprehensive Land Use and Economic Resource Plan.

Health and housing developments are a steady part of Tribal Business Council discussions and planning. The tribe is trying to keep the Pawnee Indian Hospital exclusively Pawnee, and in long-range planning seeks to establish a new health center on the Pawnee tribal reserve, to provide comprehensive health services. In housing, the Pawnee Tribal Housing Authority, established under the United States Public Housing Administration, is planning, where possible, rehabilitation of old housing on the tribal reserve (once offices and homes of BIA teachers and officials), and planned in 1977 to build twenty-five new low-rent housing units.

Different proposals, submitted as separate units to appropriate agencies for funding, require that the tribe have an overall development program in mind into which each proposal fits as a part. Such a program was drafted in December 1975 and discussed by the Business Council in the early months of 1976. It states in an integrated way the series of numbered and titled projects which, taken together, are visualized by the Pawnees today as their way to achieve progress toward better Pawnee individual and tribal life. As proposed, it is known as the Pawnee Heritage Program. Its project themes are Heritage House, Elders Council Center, Youth Council Center, Job Opportunities Office, Pawnee Tribal Industrial Park Authority, and Pawnee Tribal Finance Office.

The Elders and Youth Council centers virtually describe themselves. Each proposes a facility for an age group, to provide a broad range of services. There are 30 to 50 elderly Pawnees now served meals twice a month at the Pawnee Tribal Community House; the project envisages staffing a facility for 30 to 100 elderly Pawnees who live in and around Pawnee County. It would provide, besides nutrition, continuing education, health services, and needed transportation, recreation, and counseling. The Youth Center would service 150 Pawnees now twelve to eighteen years of age. Besides sports facilities and equipment, it would provide supplemental education, counseling, and training in leadership and community services. Both programs were visualized as requiring a year to be ready to begin operation.

The Job Opportunities Office, the Finance Office, and the Industrial Park Authority, taken together, constitute a fundamental economic development program. The Industrial Park on the Pawnee reserve is designed to bring new industries into the tribal world, with new employment for Pawnees; they would have the competitive advantage of paying no state or local taxes. The Job Office is to provide information on skills needed for the new employment to come; and the Finance Office is to develop a program to meet all the fiscal needs of individuals, small businesses, and new industries.

Heritage House is the most ambitious and idealistic of the projects. It is conceived as a centralizing force for the tribal organization, the Youth Center, the Elders Center, and the Pawnee people at large. It would provide a museum for the Pawnee cultural and historical heritage, and facilities and staff for bilingual, bicultural, and supplemental education. Its major subject areas are language, art, music and dance, and tribal history. It is central to the overall program effort to develop Pawnee confidence and pride of origin, to strengthen motivations and drives toward Pawnee self-determination.

By 1977 only a few parts of the bold Heritage Program were achieved, or in progress, or fully approved. The most prominent achievement was the building of a Pawnee Administration Building on tribal land by renovation of the old Indian School. A grant of $300,000 from the Economic Development Administration (EDA) met most of the cost; work was begun in mid-1976 for completion by January 1977. The exterior was finished and about one-third of the interior rooms, and in 1977 the Pawnee Tribal Business Council was working in its own modern quarters. The original plan was to relocate the entire Bureau of Indian Affairs Agency—now in rented office space in Pawnee—in the larger facilities of the new Pawnee Administration Building. The Pawnee planned to finance the work of completing the interior for the BIA with EDA loans, and expected to carry the loans with the rent to be paid by the BIA. This plan is at an impasse, because the other tribes serviced by the BIA Agency—the Ponca, Oto, Kaw, and Tonkawa—claim the right to share in the BIA rent payments. The Pawnee Tribe, which owns the land and building and would be responsible for the EDA loans, denies any legal right of others to share the rents. Despite this situation, the Pawnee Tribe is extremely proud of its achievement and of its own Pawnee Tribal Business Building, the center of Pawnee self-government and business activity now. Pawnee officials must, on occasion, meet with Agency officials in town; but there are important Pawnee business occasions when Agency officials have to join Pawnee officials at the new Pawnee offices.

The Pawnee Industrial Park has made important headway in planning but in 1977 is not as yet funded. The Pawnees report that two industrial concerns want to locate in the Park. According to Pawnee projections, these, if successful, could provide employment for as many as 600 in three to four years. Such a development is seen as primary by Pawnee leaders, who consider improved economic conditions and reduction of Pawnee unemployment a precondition for all other goals. But a strong desire among the people for more immediate satisfactions gave a recreation center, the Round House as central to the camp grounds, greater priority. By 1977 it had been approved and work had begun. Tradition in fact won in its design—round and built of wood, instead of oblong and made of metal, the latter preferable from a technical viewpoint.

The language program made a beginning in 1977. The Pawnee language had been described as gradually disappearing. A 1974 count showed 190 speakers, most of them over forty years of age. The plan of the program began in September 1977 by recording the speech and songs of older Pawnees. It looks toward the preparation of a bilingual source book, and the stated goal is the teaching of Pawnee in school, and in the end bilingual, bicultural education for all age groups. Most important, it is understood in discussions among Pawnee leaders as a program that can bring young and old together in reviving what is almost a lost part of Pawnee culture.

The Pawnee language program, with other commitments of the Heritage House plan, reaffirms the continuing determination of many Pawnees to maintain Pawnee identity into the future. The past fifty years of Pawnee life, despite the confusions and changes of federal Indian policy over the years, are putting assimilation and loss of Indianism aside and structuring Pawnee definition of Pawnee individual and tribal destiny.

To add a subjective note of personal observation: Talking with Pawnee adults in 1977 was a different experience from that of 1930. Today, Pawnees seemed ready and eager to raise questions about Pawnee origins and history and to expect help in finding answers. Individuals spoke of themselves as Pawnee Indians with a deep pride that seems new and that I had not found in them years ago.

II

In the perspective of the many years since the *Pawnee Ghost Dance Hand Game* was written, it was and is unique and in important ways ahead of its time. The study of culture change among Indian Americans was considered at the time to be primarily a description and analysis of how Indian people had adapted to the white man's superior technology and ways of life. In acculturation, when two peoples of different culture met, there was a giving of culture between them and a receiving of culture. But, in the case of the Indian Americans, the culture of European peoples who met them was assumed to be the giving culture, that of the Indian Americans the receiving culture. The *Pawnee Ghost Dance Hand Game* rejected this view and showed that in the conquest of Indian peoples by Europeans, the colonialism and nationalism of the Europeans made the *assimilation* of the aborigines, for purposes of exploitation, the primary European concern. Assimilation meant that the Indianism of the engulfed peoples would be wiped out, that Indians would become like others of the American population. This study of the Pawnees showed that the Ghost Dance revival movement was a vigorous rejection of the fate that assimilation had in store for the Indians, and the summary of what has happened during the decades since the original study is continuing proof of that interpretation.

In later years it became evident that the rejection of assimilation shown in this study was not exceptional but was characteristic of most Indian American peoples. I summarized the facts in a paper which has become best known under the title "The Right Not to Assimilate."[2]

The Pawnee Ghost Dance Hand Game showed, however, more than rejection of assimilation, as I pointed out in the beginning of this foreword. The Ghost Dance years among the Pawnee were a time of reassertion of Pawnee values, a revival of Indianism and Indian identity. During decades of the twentieth century, the Pawnee tribe has maintained the essentials of that Indianism and takes pride today in being Pawnee. This case, as I have pointed out, raises the broad general question of whether any nativistic revival under such assimilation conditions is not a reassertion of native identity.

The Pawnee Ghost Dance revival was a time not only of excitement but of joy. After the sadness and losses of nineteenth-century Pawnee experience, the 1890s inspired among the Pawnees a revival of play, of games. Intertwined with their faith in a new coming of old ways and a return of their lost kin was a happiness that made their old games new experiences to enjoy. The Hand Games, based on a traditional men's gambling game, became sacred ceremonies for men, women, and children, and today, no longer rituals, the games are played for fun and recreation.

The empirical method of study and presentation, with Pawnee history and traditions as an integral part of the context, made the analysis of the Hand Games an exceptional opportunity to achieve an understanding of Pawnee ritualism. The traditional Pawnee ceremonies are complex and involve an intricate interweaving of symbols in their formal offerings. In the Hand Game rituals the powers involved are limited, although the ritual formalism followed is consistent with traditional procedures. It was therefore possible to reduce the forms in the Hand Games to the limited abstraction basic to all Pawnee rituals. Moreover, the comparison of the several offerings—the tobacco and smoke offerings and the food offerings—showed that the order and form of the offering with pipe and tobacco was the definitive structure of other offerings in the same ritual; so that the handling of the pipe, when analyzed, proved the key to the entire ritual. In the study of Doctor Dances in the 1930s, along with other traditional ceremonies, this discovery of structure in the Hand Games

2. "Education and the Future of Tribalism in the United States: The Case of the American Indian," Phelps-Stokes Fund, 1961. Republished in the *Social Service Review,* June 1961, and reprinted in vol. 2 of Morton H. Fried, *Readings in Anthropology,* 2d ed. (1968), pp. 583-93.

proved true in the traditional forms. In this sense, the Hand Game study was and remains an important contribution to the study of Pawnee religion in all its complexity, and I believe to the analysis of ritual in general.

The most important contribution of the *Pawnee Ghost Dance Hand Game,* however, is methodological. This was recognized in its initial review in the *American Anthropologist* by William Duncan Strong, who wrote, "This study is a forceful demonstration 'of the inevitability of founding ethnological methodology on a metaphysic of history.' "[3] In the book itself I wrote, page 336, that it was an "illustrative case" in terms of which "I would contend that methodologically, time perspective or historicity is essential to an understanding of culture, whatever special approach is undertaken. Culture is not a static content but a dynamic continuum like the rest of the universe. Its state at any moment, like the condition of any element within it, has multitudinous associations, affects and effects, and has been determined by many factors of which the greater part have not determinately but accidentally come to play a part." A footnote added, "From the standpoint taken herein functionalism in social anthropology which is divorced from time perspective is metaphysically false."

Functionalism, with a denial of the relevance of history to an understanding of functional relations within culture, was at that time becoming an insistent approach in ethnology and anthropology. Two years after the *Pawnee Ghost Dance Hand Game* was written, with that study and other data as a basis, I challenged the antihistorical functional position in a paper read at joint sessions of the American Anthropological Association, the American Folk-Lore Society, and Section H of the American Association for the Advancement of Science.[4] In it, basing my view on the meaning of functional relations in mathematics and the natural sciences, I stated that "a genuinely functional relation is one which is established between two or more terms or variables such that it can be asserted that under certain defined conditions . . . certain defined expressions of those conditions . . . are observed."[5] To indicate the way in which time perspective is essential to establish such functional relations, I offered a description of the meaning of history in the study of culture, as follows:[6]

3. *American Anthropologist* 38 (1936), 112-13.

4. A. Lesser, "Functionalism in Social Anthropology," *American Anthropologist* 37 (1934), 386-93.

5. See also on the scientific meaning of functional relations, Ernest Nagel, *The Structure of Science* (1961), pp. 520-34.

6. Quoted with approval by Sidney W. Mintz in his "History and Anthropology: A Brief Reprise," a chapter of *Race and Slavery in the Western Hemisphere,* ed. Stanley L. Engerman and Eugene D. Genovese (1974).

"We see such and such events going on. Many things are always happening at the same time, however. How are we to determine whether or not those things which happen at the same time are related to one another? For it is obvious that they may be contemporary events, or even serial events, not because they are related to one another but because their determinants, unknown and unobserved, have caused them to happen at the same or subsequent times. In short, contemporary or associated events may be merely coexistences. Culture, at any one time, is first and foremost a mass of coexistent events. If we are to attempt to define relationships between such events, it is impossible, in view of the known historicity of things, to assume that the relations lie on the contemporary surface of events. Whatever occurs is determined more by events which happened before the occasion in question than by what can be observed contemporaneously with it. As soon as we turn to prior events for an understanding of events observed, we are turning to history. History is no more than that. It is a utilization of the conditioning fact of historicity for the elucidation of seen events."

In a lengthy discussion which followed my presentation, A. R. Radcliffe-Brown, a prominent functionalist, took issue with my position, and many rose to defend it. Among them, William Duncan Strong, in his remarks, called attention to my *Pawnee Ghost Dance Hand Game* as an empirical study in which I had demonstrated the reality and validity of my thesis. In a publication in which Radcliffe-Brown was invited to summarize his comments on my paper, he said in a foreword, which has never been republished with his article: "I do not define 'function' in the same way as Dr. Lesser. In the circumstances I cannot offer any real criticism of his paper."[7]

Nonhistorical functionalism is associated with studies of peoples and cultures which are presented *as if* a cross section of time—a single moment in the stream of time—had been captured and put on paper. Such ethnologies describe a people or a culture without recognition of its existence in time and place, or of its relations with other peoples. The result is a picture or a configuration that is false to reality. The concept which has been used for such studies is that they are *synchronic,* analyses of pure contemporaneity, and they are distinguished from studies which take the historical context into account by calling the latter *diachronic.* It is an essential meaning of the *Pawnee Ghost Dance Hand Game* that the distinction between synchronic and diachronic is artificial and makes no contribution to the study of human cultures and human history or evolution. Any attempt at synchronic analysis inevitably leads the analyst into con-

7. *American Anthropologist* 37 (1935), 394.

PREFACE

Acculturation, though a recent term which has yet to establish itself in dictionary usage, is a useful term for the processes by which aspects or elements of two cultures mingle and merge. Within this broad meaning, however, we should distinguish assimilation as of a separate character. Acculturation may be taken to refer to the ways in which some cultural aspect is taken into a culture and adjusted or fitted to it. This implies some relative cultural equality between the giving and receiving cultures. Assimilation, however, is the process of transforming aspects of a conquered or engulfed culture into a status of relative adjustment to the forms of the ruling culture. The problem of acculturation, when we are considering the American Indians in relation to their adjustment to European culture, is a problem of assimilation.

Assimilation and acculturation differ in another important way. In acculturation the cultural groups involved are in an essentially reciprocal relationship. Both give and take. As a result it is a valid problem to consider what is adopted and what not, and the whys and wherefores. In assimilation the tendency is for the ruling cultural group to enforce the adoption of certain externals, in terms of which superficial adjustment seems to be attained. The adopting culture is not in a position to choose. Its forms are often technically so inferior, particularly in material culture, that they tend to be obliterated at once by the technical products of the culture which engulfs them. In addition the ruled are generally ordered to do so and so, and to stop doing so and so. In this situation the only possible reactions are passive acceptance or active resistance and rejection. The study of assimilation of the American Indian must take into consideration the fact that American Indian culture has not met a culture of the same order of complexity or technical advancement, and that in the methods which have been used to assimilate the Indian, neither individually nor collectively as tribal groups were the natives brought into direct contact with our culture as such. They were offered, here and there, certain obvious externals. These externals are relatively superficial in relation to the values and standards of our culture, and could not replace the essential values of American Indian culture which were meanwhile destroyed.

In 1930 and 1931, while engaged in the study of Pawnee and Wichita ethnology in Oklahoma, I found it necessary to control the recent changes in religion and ritual. In doing so, the story of the renaissance of culture which took place among the Pawnee under the stimulus of the Ghost Dance was pieced together. In presenting this material I have described the developments against the background of Pawnee history since white contact. This serves to bring to light the motivations and influences which were stimulants of change. And in reference to the new forms which developed I have concentrated on the Ghost Dance Hand Games, the most important in terms of the emphasis made by the Pawnee themselves. The controlled consideration of the games in their changing forms has made it possible to consider the meaning of processes of change, and the inevitability of founding ethnological methodology on a metaphysic of history.

The field work among the Pawnee, of which this study is a specialized part, was carried out under a project supported by the Columbia Council for Research in the Social Sciences. This manuscript was in part prepared while I was Fellow of the American Council of Learned Societies. In addition to published material, I have had the use of unpublished materials of James R. Murie, in the form of a manuscript by George A. Dorsey and James R. Murie, which was made available to me through the courtesy of Dr. Dorsey and Dr. Berthold Laufer of the Field Museum of Natural History; and I was also able to refer to a Bureau of American Eth ology manuscript on the ceremonies of the Pawnee, by James R. Murie, which was at the time being linguistically revised by Dr. Gene Weltfish. The use of these materials proved invaluable, not only for the work which has resulted in the present study, but also for the consideration of Pawnee religion which I hope to present in another year.

I cannot close these remarks without acknowledging my indebtedness to Professors Franz Boas and Ruth Benedict of Columbia University, who gave me the opportunity to make the field studies on which this work is based. I am also obligated to many Pawnee friends, and particularly to my chief informant, Mark Evarts, a rare mind and a hearty friend, and Henry Chapman, whose help was important in this and other work. My wife, Dr. Gene Weltfish, has cooperated with me in countless ways. But most of all, I must express my intellectual obligations to Professors Franz Boas and John Dewey. For many years I have believed their conceptions of method to be basically in harmony, and in my own thought and work I have leaned heavily on their teachings.

Alexander Lesser

October, 1932

THE
PAWNEE
GHOST DANCE
HAND GAME

Part One

I

THE PAWNEE
IN THE NINETEENTH CENTURY[1]

FIRST PERIOD: TO 1833

The Pawnee enter the perspective of American governmental
Indian affairs after the purchase of the Louisiana Territory in 1803
by which their traditional territory, ranging from the Missouri
indefinitely westward between the Niobrara River and the Arkansas,
became a part of the United States. Lewis and Clarke, on their
explorations of the newly acquired domain, met the Pawnee on the
Platte River in Nebraska in 1804. In 1806, Major Pike visited the
villages of the Kitkahaxki[x] band of Pawnee on the Republican fork
of the Kansas River. But the first government treaties with the
Pawnee were not concluded until 1818. At that time the four bands
were politically independent of each other, and lived apart, and
four separate treaties, embodying the identical articles, were
drawn up at St. Louis. By these treaties the government secured
for the American people the peace and friendship of the Pawnee,
while the tribes acknowledged the "protection" of the United
States. All past acts of hostility were to be mutually forgiven and
forgotten, and future violations of the treaty were to be dealt with
according to the laws of the United States. These objectives were
further defined by the treaty of 1825 at Ft. Atkinson, at which
time the government dealt with the Pawnee as one tribal or national
unit composed of four federated bands. In this latter treaty the
Pawnee acknowledged the supremacy of the United States, and
the United States received the Pawnee under their protection.
Specifically, the function of this treaty was to establish rules for
the trade of the Indians with the whites, and to limit such trade to
citizens of the United States. The Pawnee also gave a guaranty in
this treaty that they would refrain from selling or trading arms
and ammunition to hostile Indian tribes.

---

[1] The historical account which comprises Chapter I, as well as parts of
the second section of Chapter II, and the last section of Chapter III, are
founded on:

1

The first period of Nineteenth Century Pawnee relations with
the white man and the United States government begins with the
first contacts following the Louisiana Purchase and ends with the
treaty of 1833. The population of the tribe during this time is
open to dispute, as no accurate figures are available. In 1804,
Lewis and Clarke estimated the tribe at 4,000, but they were unacquainted with the Pitahawirat[a]. According to these explorers
the tribe had suffered terribly from a smallpox epidemic the previous
year which had greatly reduced their numbers. Pike in 1806 gave
a count of 6,223 for the same three bands. Major S. H. Long, who
visited the tribe on his travels in 1819, estimated their number at
6,500, still without knowing the Pitahawirat[a]. The first government
figure appeared in 1834, just after the treaty of 1833 brought an
agent, Dougherty, in contact with the tribe. He numbered the
Pawnee at 12,500. This figure was carried on the government
records for years, occasionally displaced by the estimate of the

----

United States. Indian Affairs Office. Annual Reports of the Commissioner
of Indian Affairs. Washington, 1824 to date. The series has been consulted
throughout its entire run. Details of importance on the Pawnee begin with
the report of 1837. Referred to in footnotes as Annual Reports.

Kappler, C. J. (Compiler). Indian Affairs, Laws and Treaties. 2 volumes.
Washington, 1903. 57 Congress, First Session. Document 452.

Royce, C. C. Indian Land Cessions in the United States. 18th Annual
Report, Bureau of American Ethnology.

I have also consulted:

Dunbar, J. The Pawnee Indians. Magazine of American History.
4 : 241—281; 5 : 321—385; 8 : 734—756.

Grinnell, G. B. Pawnee Hero Stories and Folk Tales.

Irving, J. T. Indian Sketches Taken during a U. S. expedition to make
treaties with the Pawnee and other tribes of Indians in 1833. 1838, reprinted
1888.

Murray, C. A. Travels in North America, including a summer residence
with the Pawnee tribe of Indians in the remote prairies of the Missouri.
2 volumes. 3rd. revised edition, London, 1854.

Oehler, G. F. and Smith, D. Z. Description of a Journey and visit to the
Pawnee Indians. April 22-May 18, 1851. Reprinted from Moravian Church
Miscellany of 1851—1852.

Tuttle, Sarah. History of the American Mission to the Pawnee Indians.
Boston, 1838.

Williamson, J. W. The Battle of Massacre Canyon. The unfortunate
ending of the last buffalo hunt of the Pawnees. Republican Leader, Trenton,
Nebraska, 1922.

Where differences on dates and other important data have been encoun-
tered, the account presented has taken the information in the reports, year
by year, as the final arbiter. All basic concrete data and interpretations
are essentially restatements of source material; it has seemed unnecessary
to introduce minute footnotes. Interpolated interpretations of the writer
are few and obvious.

missionaries, Dunbar and Allis, who were first with the tribe from 1835 to 1837, and considered the government estimate too high, offering 10,000 as approximating the true population more closely. The discrepancies between these various figures are not severe. That of Lewis and Clarke, in spite of the decimation of the Pawnee the previous year, is probably too low, and may not have been intended to include all villages of all four bands. The computations of Pike and Long, based upon three of the four bands, indicates a total of close to 9,000 for the whole tribe. This last figure represents the approximate "normal" figure for the Pawnee tribes during the first period of the Nineteenth Century. There were without doubt major fluctuations in the numbers of the Pawnee during this period, and the trend of the tribal population was to diminish rather than increase. One general consideration, however, can hardly be open to question. At the opening of the Nineteenth Century, the Pawnee bands together constituted one of the five or six large Indian tribal groups between the Mississippi River and the Rocky Mountains. They maintained themselves in spite of the hostility of practically every tribe in the region. In their aboriginal state their trade must have been severely limited by tribal feud. It is unlikely that they had economic dealings of any importance with tribes other than the Arikara, Mandan and Wichita. All the major indigenous peoples around them were continually in a state of conflict with them: the many groups of the Dakota Sioux on the north and northwest, the Kiowa, Comanche, Cheyenne and Arapaho to the southwest, the Osage and Kansa to the south and southeast. Immediately to their east were the Omaha, Ponca and Oto, with whom a state of partial amity prevailed, born of the fear they had inspired in these tribes. Later in the century the Pawnee became close friends of the Omaha and Ponca. The Oto, given opportunity as the Pawnee declined, assaulted small parties of Pawnee on occasion, but later became friends of the Pawnee.

In the period which closed with the treaty of 1833 changes were taking place in the basic conditions of life of the Pawnee which were only to appear in their fullest effect in later periods. A tide of white emigration and transcontinental travel began to appear, moving westward, and swelling with the years. These emigrants brought white diseases into the midst of the Indian tribes, trampled their fields, hunted the buffalo for sustenance and pleasure, and keeping the herds of the plains in constant fear, limited the natural range and increase of the buffalo.

The diseases which the Pawnee acquired from white contact included, besides infantile diseases, venereal diseases, small-pox and cholera. The small-pox was particularly deadly. It had already afflicted the tribe in 1803, and in 1825 a serious epidemic again broke out, with great mortality. Small-pox in the years 1829 to 1833 was so serious in the Indian population, that the government spent large sums annually for vaccination among the Indians who were already "wards" of the government. This did not include the Pawnee, as yet only "peaceful friends."

The white emigration was not the only condition which began to effect the gradual extinction of the great buffalo herds of the western plains. Traders came in, ready to barter white goods for hides and skins, and the normal Indian use of the buffalo herds was increased. Finally the Indian population of the plains was suddenly enlarged by the United States policy of removing Indian tribes from east of the Mississippi to the west, and settling them among the indigenous tribes. This policy of removal was designed to eliminate the friction between the tribes in the east and the white settlers of their localities, as well as to avoid abuse of Indian rights by State governments. In addition, of course, their lands were wanted east of the Mississippi by white people. These removals were not an inconsiderable shift of population. By 1836, 51,327 Indians of eastern tribes had already emigrated, and 39,950 were waiting to remove, a total of over 81,000. Government calculations of the same period placed the indigenous population of the region from the Mississippi to the Rocky Mountains at 231,806, so that the actual increase by removals was an addition of 35 per cent to the population of the plains. The Plains tribes lived primarily by hunting the buffalo, while on the eastern fringe of the Plains the village tribes, of which the Pawnee were one, combined hunting in the summer and winter, with the cultivation of corn, beans and squash. This increase of the Indian population affected the food supply in two ways: greater demands were made upon the animal resources of the region, and the free range of the vast herds of buffalo began to be more and more restricted. This closing in of the populations around the buffalo range, by Indian removals, white settlement and white emigration, prevented the natural maintenance of the herds, and as the herds became increasingly smaller, the pressure of the surrounding populations increased as hunters came further and further into the buffalo range to find herds. All of these factors, the demands of a larger Indian population, the requirements of trade, the use of the buffalo by the emigrants, and the interference with the wide range of the herds, were cumulative, interdependent and interactive, and beginning in this period, continued until in the latter part of the century the buffalo was practically extinct.

The increase of population and the decrease of the herds led to greater conflict between the native tribes west of the Mississippi for control of the hunting range. Tribes traditionally hostile to one another met oftener on the more restricted hunting grounds, had more frequently to penetrate each other's terrain after the vanishing herds, and became increasingly resentful of intrusions and trespass. Tribal warfare became bloodier with the years. The Pawnee, always at odds with their neighbors, found themselves in this period increasingly attacked. They had dominated one of the richest parts of the buffalo range; now they resented and resisted the incursions of their ancient enemies. There is little doubt that the Pawnee suffered a heavy mortality in these years through death in battle, although we have few records of their encounters. But in 1832 they suffered a major defeat at the hands of the Comanche on the Arkansas River, involving sufficient slaughter to have been retold and reported. It is a fair estimate that the death rate in Plains warfare in the years from 1820 to 1850 was from four to five times the rate of mortality in the Eighteenth Century.

In the process of removing the Indian tribes of the east across the Mississippi, the government was not overcareful to consider the territorial rights of the indigenous peoples of the Plains. After tribes had been removed and settled in western locations, their eastern lands ceded to the United States and already overrun by settlers, it was discovered that the removed tribe was being rapidly exterminated by its neighbors, the indigenous tribes of the region. Such was the case with the Delaware who were located west of the Missouri, between the Kansas River and the Platte, only to find themselves involved in continuous and bloody warfare with their neighbors, particularly the Pawnee, then dominant in the region. It was to remedy this condition that the Commissioner of Indian Affairs went to the Pawnee in 1833, and there at the Tcawi village on the south side of the Platte River, drew up the treaty of 1833.

The short-sighted policies of the United States government in its dealings with the Indians is aptly illustrated by this whole affair. To get the eastern Indians out of the way of American citizens, they were removed westward, persuaded that the government could assure them agreeable living conditions in the western territorial regions as yet under the direct control of the federal government. In the west, however, in most cases the government had merely treaties of peace and friendship with the indigenous tribes, and had acquired no right to settle other Indian groups on tribal lands. When the emigrant tribes were settled in the west, conflicts inevitably followed. The Pawnee, finding their lands en-

croached upon and their hunting territories trespassed upon by
new invaders from east of the Mississippi, actively defended their
rights. When large numbers were killed in these conflicts between
the emigrant Indians and the indigenous peoples, and between
indigenous peoples who found their hunting grounds crowded and
narrow, the government was compelled to interfere to stop the
slaughter, ostensibly in order to protect their wards, the "removed"
Indians, but actually in order to safeguard the whole policy of
removal, since with the unsettled conditions and continous conflict west of the Mississippi it was impossible to carry forward the
emigration of the eastern Indians still in the way of the white man.
The only course to follow was to secure large cessions of land
from the indigenous tribes, on which the government could then
locate the emigrant tribes.

SECOND PERIOD: 1833 TO 1857

The second period of Pawnee history in the 19th Century begins
with the treaty of 1833, and closes with the treaty of 1857. By the
treaty of 1833, the Pawnee ceded land in return for compensation,
but were left an independent people; with the treaty of 1857 they
relinquished all their lands to the United States, abrogated their
freedom, and became wards of the government. The period of
twenty-four years from 1833 to 1857 falls naturally into two parts:
the Pawnee removal to the north side of the Platte, and their
attempt there to develop agricultural settlements, which terminated
in 1846 with their retreat to the south side of the Platte River; and
the residence of the Pawnee on the south side of the Platte, in
violation of their treaty agreement, which continued until execution
of the provisions of the treaty of 1857.

The treaty of 1833 was the second step in governmental procedure with the Indian tribes. From treaties of peace and friendship
and amicable trade, the government had advanced to one of
acquisition. By it the tribe was restricted within narrower boundaries in return for a consideration. The Pawnee ceded and relinquished all right to their lands south of the Platte River, a provision
which they were to rue for years to come. In return for this cession
they were to receive an annuity of $4,600 for a period of twelve years,
to be given regularly stated amounts of agricultural implements,
and to be supplied with blacksmiths, demonstration farmers, mills
and a school.

Instruction in farming was intended to civilize the Indian and
so to open the continent to white settlement. The nomadic hunting

life of Plains tribes was considered wild and barbaric by a people whose culture for centuries had been grounded on an agricultural economy. To tame and civilize the savage it was necessary to make them an agricultural people; and this was the more essential in that an agricultural economy would locate the tribes permanently in restricted areas and release wide reaches of land for the uses of the white man.

The Pawnee do not seem to have been in agreement about the removal. While the provisions of the treaty made the lands south of the Platte River ceded by the Pawnee a common hunting ground, still open to them, it confined their villages and farm lands to the north side of the river. Prior to this time the three bands of Tcawi, Kitkahaxki[x] and Pitahawirat[a] had maintained their permanent village settlements south of the Platte, while only the Skiri band resided on the north. The Kitkahaxki[x] and Pitahawirat[a] accepted the terms of the treaty and removed, as well as some of the Tcawi, but most of the Tcawi refused to leave their homes on the south side of the river. This main Tcawi village was below the Platte some miles west of the Bellevue settlement on the Missouri River. It was to this group that the other bands removed in 1846.

The exact year of final removal is not certain. In 1839 the bands asked aid in locating their permanent settlements on the north side, inasmuch as the land was to be cultivated according to white methods of farming, and must be suitable for such purposes. By 1841 all the Pawnee who accepted the treaty provision had removed. One large village was built together by the Pitahawirat[a], Kitkahaxki[x], and those Tcawi who removed. The Skiri are not mentioned as building a new village from which we may infer that they probably continued at their old location.

In the midst of the difficulties attending the removal, the Pawnee were afflicted again by the smallpox. An epidemic broke out in 1838 and did not subside until a year and a half later. It is said to have been communicated to the Pawnee by some Dakota women captured by them in the spring of 1838. Great numbers of children perished in the epidemic, while the mortality rate among the adults was perceptibly lower. Nevertheless the total deaths must have considerably exceeded five hundred in the period of the

---

[1] Dunbar, in Magazine of American History, 4 : 257, places the Kitkahaxki[x] 18 miles northwest of the mouth of the Loup River on the north side of the Loup, and the Pitahawirat[a] 11 miles above the mouth on the same side, as early as 1834. I have not found evidence to validate the location of these bands north of the Platte at this early date.

epidemic, in view of the census figure reached by Dunbar and Allis
in the summer of 1840 of 6,787, exclusive of some detachments of
the tribe then absent, who could at most bring the total to 7,500.

With the organization of the Department of Indian Affairs
by act of Congress in 1834, an agency was established for dealings
with the Oto and Missouri, Ponca, Omaha, and Pawnee tribes,
located for many years at Council Bluffs. An agent does not seem
to have taken active charge of the affairs of these tribes until 1836.

Missionaries had worked among the Pawnee for about two years
just prior to the removal of the South Bands. Dunbar was among
the Tcawi, Allis with the Skiri, and Satterlee with the Kitkahaxki[x].
Satterlee was murdered in 1837 by a white trader, but Dunbar and
Allis helped the bands locate their settlements, and accompanied
them in the removal. At the time of the removal a location was
chosen on Plum Creek for the site of the government establishment
and a mission; but on account of the disturbances caused by
Sioux raids, execution of the plan was delayed until 1844.

With the removal north of the Platte, resident farmers settled
with the Pawnee, and Samuel Allis was appointed government
teacher and opened a school. Nevertheless, the period from 1841
to 1847 was one of breakdown and chaos in Pawnee life, rather
than progress.

Once on the north side of the Platte, the Pawnee were exposed
more than ever before to remorseless attacks of the Dakota who
had been increasing in numbers and boldness for some time. This
constant threat hung over every month of the year.

The intention of the government in sending farmers among the
Pawnee was to teach them plough agriculture. Their old methods
of digging-stick cultivation while they had yielded relatively
large crops had never been sufficiently productive to permit the
Pawnee to rely completely on their fields. In the summer, observers
reported, they succeeded in raising but little more corn, beans and
squash than they consumed by the time the cold weather set in.
Occasionally their crops were more plentiful but any drought
threatened to leave them without a subsistence minimum.

The farmers were indefatigable in breaking up virgin soil for
cultivation. The school teacher, finding it impossible to carry out
any genuine instruction the first years, joined in, and helped with
the agriculture. All reports indicate that the Pawnee themselves
showed commendable zeal in their efforts to learn and gave
promise of becoming successful farmers more rapidly than other
tribes. Nevertheless the farming operations, in the long run, were
a failure. The Pawnee did not take to productive farming. The

reason is not far to seek. Successful farming required the working of isolated plots, and meant the scattering of the people over the land. This was to court death at the hands of the Sioux raiding and attacking parties. To keep the people together in the village, united against an assault, was their only safety.

"From the exposed position of the Pawnee they are compelled to guard their women while engaged in cultivating their corn, digging roots and collecting wood, yet with all their vigilance there is scarcely a month that passes (unless in the extremity of winter) that some of their people do not fall to the tomahawk of their enemies."[1] On June 27, 1843, the Sioux attacked the South Band village killing sixty-seven Pawnee, wounding twenty-six, many of whom later died. They burned twenty of the forty-one lodges in the village. They captured nearly four hundred horses. From March to August of the same year sixty-nine Pawnee while away from the village met their death at the hands of war parties, making a death total of one hundred thirty-six in one short season. From the standpoint of the government's policy the worst phase of the Sioux attack of June was that it fell primarily upon that part of the Pawnee, who, loyal to the plans and purposes of the United States government, were assembled around the agency location learning to become tillers of the soil.

This disaster stayed the rest of the Pawnee who had held back from farming, but were on the verge of taking it up. The government officials wrote that all hope of civilizing the Pawnee through farming must be given up unless the people received protection from the Sioux. Reports had come that the Sioux vowed a war of extermination against their traditional foe, the Pawnee. The Pawnee asked arms and ammunition to protect themselves, and remuneration for their losses. According to their treaty arrangements, they were to have had twenty-five guns with suitable ammunition in their villages, in the hands of the government farmers, to be used in self-defense, but these had never been turned over to the farmers. By treaty they were not to retaliate upon their enemies. Without suffering through retaliation, the Sioux became bolder with each year. The agent wrote in September of 1843, that the Pawnee had decided to persevere at their new locations in spite of their misfortunes.

In the following year there were further Sioux attacks, and the Superintendent at St. Louis commented that the Pawnee lost a great number, and had at hand but one gun and an old pistol for

---

[1] Supt. Harvey, writing from St. Louis, Sept. 10, 1845. Annual Report of 1844—45.

defense. As a result of such raids, when the Pawnee left for the summer or winter buffalo hunts, every man, woman and child would go along for safety. The fields and farms were left deserted and the crops untended. It was on such an occasion in the summer of 1846 while the tribe was away hunting that the Sioux came down upon the village. The white people hid the Pawnee school children in cellars while the Sioux were destroying the village, then evacuated the place with the children and crossed the Platte to Bellevue. When the Pawnee returned from the hunt to their village they found it burned to the ground, and they too crossed the Platte to the south side and joined their kinsmen there who had never accepted removal across the Platte.

During this same period, prior to the retreat across the Platte, it was not alone in their villages that the Pawnee were annoyed by Sioux raids. On the hunt they found their hunting territories more crowded than ever before, the buffalo herds scarcer and smaller, and the Sioux war parties larger and bolder. Often their hunt became a battle and they returned to their villages almost empty-handed. It was during this time that the slaughter to which the buffalo herds were subjected by the tide of emigration and travel across the plains was beginning to have a telling effect.

By 1847, with the Pawnee again settled on the south side of the Platte River, it was apparent that all the government objectives had failed. The farming demonstrations were a failure, the school had accomplished little more than to assist in farm work, missionaries could do little, and the tribe was again placed squarely in the way of the white movement of western emigration.[1]

---

[1] The viewpoint taken herein by the writer is that the Pawnee were entitled to the protection of the United States government against the Sioux, and that by failing to provide such protection the government failed to carry out its treaty obligations. This is not only the viewpoint of the Pawnee, but also the conception of the matter revealed in the reports of all the agents and superintendents who were in charge of the Pawnee during this period; and there can be no question that it was an indispensable measure if the government was to succeed in its policy of education and civilization.

John Dunbar, writing in the Magazine of American History, for April, 1880 (volume 4, p. 255), states: "The treaty of 1833 contains no direct provision that the United States should protect the Pawnees from the Dakotas on the north, and the Comanches and other tribes on the south. But unfortunately the Pawnees distinctly understood that this was the case, i. e., that so long as they did not molest other tribes, such tribes should not be allowed to trouble them. Accordingly for several years they scrupulously refrained from any aggressive hostilities, though meantime suffering severely from their various enemies. It was only after a final declaration from the Government in 1848 that it had no intention to protect them that they at last attempted to reassert their prestige..."

The Pawnee school was continued at Bellevue. Some reading was taught the children, and the girls learned to sew. The schooling was out of touch with the needs of Pawnee life, and under the hazardous physical and economic conditions very little could be hoped for from its instruction to a handful of children. The pupils for some time were dependent on the generosity of the teacher for sustenance, since after the retreat to the south of the Platte government farming operations were suspended.

Let us consider what basis the Pawnee had for an expectation of protection, and why the officials of the Indian service agreed with them.

The treaty of 1825 reads in part (italics mine):

"For the purpose of perpetuating the friendship which has heretofore existed, as also to remove all future cause of discussion or dissension, as it respects trade and friendship...

"Article I. It is admitted by the Pawnee tribe of Indians, that they reside within the territorial limits of the United States, acknowledge their supremacy, and *claim their protection.*

"Article II. The United States agree to receive the Pawnee tribe of Indians into their friendship, and *under their protection,* and to extend to them, from time to time, such benefits and acts of kindness as may be convenient, and seem just and proper to the President of the United States."

In the treaty of 1833 we find (italics mine):

"Article IX. The Pawnee nation renew their assurance of friendship for the white men, their fidelity to the United States, and their desire for peace with all neighboring tribes of red men. The Pawnee nation therefore agree not to molest or injure the person or property of any white citizen of the United States, wherever found, *nor to make war upon any tribe with whom said Pawnee nation now are, or may be, at peace; but should any difficulty arise between said nation and any other tribe, they agree to refer the matter in dispute to such arbiter as the President shall appoint to settle the same.*

"Article XII. In case the Pawnee nation will remain at home during the year, and give the protection specified, the United States agree to place twenty-five guns, with suitable ammunition, in the hands of the farmers of each village, to be used in case of an attack from hostile bands."

These provisions seem adequate guarantee of some kind of protection against their enemies. It is true that the provision of article IX above refers to those tribes with whom the Pawnee are at peace. From the Pawnee standpoint they are at peace when no aggressive attacks and counter attacks are going on, and it would be a shoddy avoidance of the issue if the government contended that since the Dakota and Comanche were traditional enemies the provision did not apply. It should be again noted that the guns referred to in article XII were never furnished the Pawnee villages. Here again there is a legal loophole, since the provisions of the article imply that the government is not bound by it unless the Pawnee give up their buffalo hunting. But they would certainly have been a sorry spectacle without buffalo during this period, when at least three-fourths of their food supply came from the hunt, as well as their major requirements in robes and tent-covers, and while the government agricultural scheme failed and the government supplied practically no food.

It has also been suggested, relative to the Sioux conflicts of this period,

The position of the Pawnee on the south of the Platte was directly on the transcontinental route to Oregon. During the period from 1841—1847, the Pawnee group who remained in their old haunts had become a considerable annoyance to white travel. With the whole tribe after 1847 in the way of emigrant movements the situation forced itself upon the attention of the Commissioner of Indian Affairs, who took cognizance of the necessity of establishing military garrisons in the region to prevent the Sioux from terrorizing the northern plains. The intention was to recolonize the Pawnee north of the Platte after affording them such protection. Other tribes were to be removed southward, and with the Pawnees

---

that the account herein overemphasizes the destructiveness of the warfare, inasmuch as the type pattern of culture in the Plains, which the Pawnee shared, made warfare the great game of life for men. This criticism requires comment from several points of view.

In the first place, Plains warfare as carried on by the Sioux in the latter half of the Nineteenth Century was not the typical pattern of Plains warfare. Typically, a warparty consisted of a handful of youths to raid primarily to secure horses, and to achieve renown. Killing and securing scalps was often subordinated to touching the enemy in the midst of the enemy village and escaping unharmed, or to stealing ponies out of the enemy village unharmed and even undetected. The Sioux developed war expeditions on a much larger scale, and intended virtual extermination of the Pawnee, something quite different from the "war game" of the Plains.

In the second place, recent archaeological evidence, as uncovered by W. D. Strong[1], has demonstrated that the Pawnee, and probably the other "village" tribes of the Plains, had been horticultural people in the region for centuries before the incursion of the Plains hunting peoples, and the typical development of Plains warfare and buffalo hunting. From this standpoint the combination of hunting and horticulture by the village tribes must be considered an adjustment of horticultural peoples to the changing conditions of life around them (Strong); and it may be doubted if the adjustment brought economic security. With the decline of horticulture among the Pawnee as the demands of warfare and hunting increased, we find in the nineteenth century that even a successful crop was not on a large enough scale to secure a supply of corn, beans and squash ample to supply the tribe during a subsequent period of failure on the hunt or on the land. It may also be doubted whether the Plains war-psychology was ever the core of Pawnee culture, as it was of the typical Plains tribes.

In the third place, the account of these years is not based on a reading-in of Sioux destructiveness. It reproduces merely the comment, made year after year, in the government reports, of a succession of agents, superintendents, teachers, farmers and missionaries, — men who were eyewitnesses of the assaults and their effects upon Pawnee life and assimilation. Whatever judgment be passed upon the Pawnee for not maintaining themselves as a warlike people, the fact that the Sioux raids were the chief cause of Pawnee failure during this period cannot be doubted on the basis of the historical records which are available.

[1] Strong, Plains Culture in the Light of Archaeology.

north, and the Sioux restrained from coming south of the Platte, it was hoped that a wide and safe passage could be opened for the Oregon emigrants.

In how far even the theory of civilizing the Indians through agriculture dominated government policy may be judged from the statements of the Commissioner in his annual report for 1848. The Superintendent of the Central Superintendency, located at St. Louis, had recommended the necessity of providing the Indian tribes of the prairie with suitable land for agricultural purposes, where these tribes had none of their own. This was Superintendent T. H. Harvey, who, judging from his reports, was sincere in his efforts to carry out the professed governmental Indian policy. He contended that the buffalo were approaching extinction, and that plans should be made in advance of that event for settling the tribes as farmers on lands suitable for farming. This policy according to the Commissioner, was contrary to his own recommendations "of procuring and keeping open these lands [viz. good agricultural lands] for the egress and expansion of our own population." He was of the opinion that the Indian tribes would gradually move westward after the disappearing buffalo, and so keep out of the white man's way.

The annuities of the treaty of 1833 had run out their term by 1845; and the aid to Pawnee agriculture by supplying implements, farmers and mills was subject to the Pawnee locating north of the Platte. As a result, in the period from 1847 to 1857 the tribe was practically without government aid. In 1848 at Fort Childs, the United States government purchased Grand Island from the Pawnee for $ 2000 in merchandise, which was of incidental aid to a tribe numbering over 4,000. The acquisition of Grand Island was part of the program for the establishment of military posts on the route to Oregon.

While the school was maintained at Bellevue as a nucleus for future operations, all other civilizing activities in the tribe were practically suspended. Even the missionaries gave up, because of the hazard. South of the Platte the Pawnee claimed the land was unproductive with their methods of planting corn, and there was no available timber for building lodges. The three bands who had been north of the Platte professed in the fall of 1848 their willingness to return there, if the Tcawi who had been living alone south of the Platte were made to accompany them so as to increase their military strength for defense against Sioux assaults.

The government purchased some corn for the Pawnee in the summer of 1848, but that fall they were in a miserable condition, their crops having failed because of drought. Apparently the tribe was not successful in their winter hunt, since we find that in June of 1849, agent John Barrow found two hundred aged and infirm Pawnee, left behind when the tribe went on the summer hunt, starving around the agency. Cholera had broken out among them and before it subsided, eighty-four were dead. When the bands returned from the hunt, he found that the rest of the tribe had also been decimated by cholera while away, a condition brought on by their lack of proper nourishment. His estimate, after talking the matter over with the chiefs of the tribe, was that no less than 259 men and 900 women and children had fallen victims of cholera while the tribe had been away; making a total of 1234 deaths that summer from the epidemic. Barrow seems to have been astoundingly callous. He reports the Pawnee deaths and their condition quite objectively, and treats as incidental that in the midst of their other misfortunes, the Oto, spurred by white traders who gave them guns, had attacked the Pawnee and killed eleven. The Oto shrewdly claimed that their Great White Father had told them to protect and assist the whites, and Barrow reports that he assured the Oto that if their story was true — to the effect that the white traders had been robbed by the Pawnee — their Great Father would forgive them.

In spite of this disastrous season which wiped out a fourth of the tribe, the Pawnee had made a successful hunt, but without a harvest upon their return to the village, they would soon again be destitute.

The Pawnee school was disbanded in 1851 when the treaty arrangements for a term of schooling ran out. Samuel Allis, making his final report, admits his failure, but remarks, "I still consider the Pawnee an interesting tribe, capable of great improvement could they be protected from their enemies and brought under proper subjection themselves."

Pawnee conditions of life gradually became worse. The tide of emigration increased, and between 1847 and 1859, was literally "pouring through and into the very midst of their corn fields, their villages and their hunting grounds," referring to the tribes of the Council Bluff Agency, the Oto, the Omaha and the Pawnee. The Pawnee along with these other tribes were forced into a position where they became more and more anxious to make some further trade of land with the white man in return for a guaranteed sustenance. This was reported to the Commissioner of Indian Affairs year after year. The advisability of carrying out the third step in the government program for dealing with Indian tribes, the purchase of their lands, and the settlement of the tribe on a limited reservation, was clear. This was the surest method of avoiding the increasing conflict between the starving Indians and the white settlers and emigrants. Driven by necessity, the proud American Indian had become a petty thief and beggar along the highways. Nevertheless governmental inactivity seems to have prevented action until 1853, when the Commissioner of Indian Affairs visited many of the western tribes and executed treaties with them. The Pawnee, however, were avoided at this time although their needs, as reported to the authorities, were as great as those of other tribes. In fact, it appears that to an observer on the spot, James Gatewood, agent at the Council Bluffs Agency, writing October 16, 1853, "these Indians (the Pawnee) have suffered perhaps more than any single tribe by emigration. All of the roads on the north side of Nebraska River pass through their country, and on the south side of that river pass through their hunting ground; and more of their wood and grass are consumed and more game run off, than there is from the bands of any other nation, and yet they receive no compensation; whilst others that suffer much less in that way are liberally compensated..."

In the same year the Pawnee were reported destitute. Their numbers had been reduced to fifty per cent of their former strength in four years. Responsible for this great mortality were the relentless assaults of the Dakota and Cheyenne; and disease, a major small-pox epidemic in 1852 again decimating the tribe. In 1854 the Commissioner of Indian Affairs recommended the tribes of Nebraska to the attention of the government. He considered it "very important that arrangements be made as soon as practicable with the Pawnee and Ponca Indians... by which their limits may be restricted and defined, and their assaults upon emigrants... terminated." He further pointed out that "the roads on the principal routes to the Pacific Coast have become very important thoroughfares. Thousands of emigrants and many merchants who with their property to the amount of several millions in value pass annually over the plains are entitled to the protection of the government."

While the government was still inactive the Pawnee suffered further heavy losses. One of the major disasters occurred when in 1854 a party of 113 Pawnee were cut off and surrounded by an overwhelming force of Cheyenne and Kiowa and killed almost to a man.

In 1856 the Pawnee were thoroughly depressed. They were not able to cultivate successfully where they were south of the Platte, white settlers being all about them. The whites were encroaching on their lands north of the Platte. The buffalo was scarce. Disease had reduced them to a handful. Their pleas to the government to make some arrangement for their future were unanswered. At intervals they did not have the representation of an agent. Samuel Allis wrote on behalf of the Pawnee to the Superintendent at St. Louis. The document credits him with being "interpreter," but there was no official status to such a position among the Pawnee at that time. The truth is there was neither agent, nor missionary, nor teacher, nor farmer, among the Pawnee officially, and that Allis, faithful to the people among whom he had worked, took the matter into his own hands. He wrote that the whites were settling close around the Pawnee and using up their timber, and that the Pawnee deeply resented the government purchase from the Omaha of lands along the Platte River from Shell Creek to Beaver Creek, which had from ancient times been Pawnee territory. He advised that they be met in council the next spring.

THIRD PERIOD: 1857 TO 1876

The treaty which was drawn up with the Pawnee on September 24 of the following year at Table Creek in Nebraska Territory, ushered in the third period of Pawnee history in the 19th Century, which closes with the removal of the tribe from Nebraska to Oklahoma in 1874 to 1876. During this period the Pawnee were again settled north of the Platte River, this time on a reservation, as wards of the government.

This treaty was the third step in governmental Indian procedure. The conditions initiated by the original treaties of "peace and friendship," and the first cessions of land, had now brought results favorable to the needs of the white men. The treaty of 1857 ended the independence of the Pawnee forever. They yielded their roving freedom, ceded their lands, and acknowledged in the treaty their "dependence" on the United States. These things they did willingly enough; they had been petitioning the government for years to effect such an arrangement. But it was a willingness born of desperation, born of the necessity of extricating themselves from a network of conditions which made existence well nigh impossible. By the treaty of 1857 the Pawnee admitted their cultural and economic defeat, and resigned themselves to the inevitable guardianship of the government. The provisions of the treaty were many and detailed; its major objective is rendered, however, in the first two articles. Article one provides that the Pawnee cede all their lands to the United States government, retaining a reservation thirty miles by fifteen at the Loup fork of the Platte River, or at any other location in their traditional range more suitable as a permanent home, and remove to it within a year. Article two provides that the United States government pay the Pawnee for their lands $ 40,000 yearly for five years, and $ 30,000 yearly in perpetuity thereafter, subject to commutation by the President. Other articles provide for two manual labor schools to be provided by the government, blacksmith shops, farming implements, grain and lumber mills, and laborers. The Pawnee agreed to send their children between the ages of seven and eighteen to school nine months of the year.

In this treaty the Pawnee inserted some provisions of their own. By article nine, they saw to it that half-breeds were provided for, whether they wished to live with the tribe, or with the white men. By article ten, they asked that the United States government share with them in the payment of $ 2,000 to Samuel Allis, as a recompense for his good services to the tribe. In their last smallpox epidemic he had vaccinated 2,000 and saved their lives; and when they were starving they appropriated his property and used it as their own. By article eleven, the Pawnee asked that a chief and four braves who had guided an American army expedition against the Cheyenne and nearly lost their lives returning alone to the tribe be compensated by the United States government with $ 100 each, or a horse worth $ 100.

According to the terms of the treaty the Pawnee were to make a final selection of their reservation and remove to it within one year of the date of ratification by the United States Senate, until which time the tribe was to remain unmolested in the villages south of the Platte. Ratification took place March 31, 1858. By the fall of that year the Pawnee "were almost entirely surrounded by settlers, a majority of whom, as the more worthy settlers have testified, are less civilized than the Indians."[1] By 1859 the Pawnee had accepted the reservation for which they had originally asked, the territory embracing both banks of the Loup fork of the Platte River, and had removed to it. It was a fertile land, which it was expected would by proper cultivation make them in a few years independent of buffalo hunting. On their reserve the Pawnee were free from the increasing pressure of the white occupation, their eastern boundary being the only point accessible to white settlements.

[1] Agent W. W. Dennison, writing September 22, 1858, from the Council Bluff Agency. Annual Reports, 1857—1858.

The whole tribe removed, abandoning their old settlements, ready to attempt to build a new home above the Platte, but not without misgiving. The Dakota tribes now outnumbered them eight or nine to one. The "Indians appeared to consent reluctantly to a settlement upon their reservation, returning with gloomy foreboding to the country where in days past they had lost in battle many of their sages and warriors. They appeared satisfied, however, after an assurance from their agent that they should receive the protection guaranteed in the late treaty."[1]

In the period from the Pawnee settlement on reservation sites in 1859 to 1873, when the question of removing the tribe to the Indian Territory of Oklahoma became immediate, the major effort of the government was directed toward accustoming the tribe to a farming life. The policy initiated by the reservation system was to eventuate in locating individual families on individual farms, to be allotted in severalty. Since this was not practicable until the Pawnee men had learned the white man's methods of cultivation, no immediate attempt was made to survey allotments. Instead, the government initiated farming among the Pawnee by locating a government or agency farm close to the school and agency buildings. This was worked and managed principally by government farmers sent for that purpose, who made periodic reports to the agents and superintendent. On this farm the Pawnee men and boys who were willing to learn were persuaded to labor, and it was expected that they would then be anxious to locate farms of their own and work them.

During the whole period the Pawnee also continued to cultivate and plant corn, beans and squash, after their traditional methods. This agricultural work was done by the women. In the old way of life, the men did the hunting and fighting, the women the planting, the skinwork and the housework. Since working the land was women's work, it was not to be expected that the Pawnee men would take to farming eagerly. Those young men and boys who did were taunted continually by others.

The activities of the government farm on the Pawnee reservation were initiated as soon as possible after the removal. In 1860 a grist and saw mill to be run by steam was erected, and a corn granary nearly completed, to be used for storing the produce of the farm. The work was continually interrupted by attacks of the Dakota. A farmer was on hand and raised one hundred and sixty acres of corn, oats and wheat. The same year, the Pawnee women

---

[1] Superintendent of the Central Superintendency, writing in 1859. Annual Report, 1858—1859.

cultivated eight hundred acres of corn, beans and squash in their old manner. The farmer duplicated his effort in 1861, but not until the summer of 1862 did he give any actual instruction to the Pawnee in farming. That year the agency farm crops and the Pawnee native crops both suffered from a grasshopper pestilence. It was planned that summer to proceed as rapidly as possible to break up enough land for cultivation, so that the head of each Pawnee family could take over a plot and learn by actively operating it.

In 1863 the government farmers had ploughed up for this purpose 725 acres. Meanwhile the native women had a bountiful crop, for the first time in years a surplus. In 1864 and 1865 the government demonstration proved a failure; drought and severe grasshopper pestilences destroyed the greater part of the crop. But the Pawnee crop of corn, beans and squash was much less affected in these years. In 1867 the government farm consisted of 114 acres in corn, wheat, oats and potatoes, while the Pawnee had 1000 acres under cultivation, mostly in corn, with patches of beans and squash. That year saw a bountiful crop all round, with so large a surplus for the Pawnee that they gave food to the Ponca, whose crop had failed, sold a considerable amount, and still retained a store. The following year misfortune visited the whole land in the form of a grasshopper plague of such severity as had never been known. "They came in a cloud so thick as to obscure the sun." They left not a green thing.

In spite of the fact that the government farming demonstration was not strikingly successful during these years, the Pawnee were becoming increasingly conscious of the gradual disappearance of the buffalo, and the need for basing their economic life on a sure agricultural supply. They observed the value and usefulness of wagons, plows, mowing machinery and the like, and in 1868 began to request that large sums of their annuity payment be spent for the purchase of such things. Part of the annuity was being paid to them in merchandise. Inasmuch as no attempt was made to send the people what they specifically needed, a great part of the goods annuity was waste; the Pawnee would sell off most of it to traders for things they needed more, losing considerably in the exchange. The agents pointed out that along with their purchase of agricultural implements, wagons and harness, the Pawnee from 1865 on were asking for cooking stoves and household articles, and began to take an interest in houses.

Building on the reservation had not been active. In addition to the farm buildings erected in 1860, a number of buildings were taken over which had been erected by the Mormons during their two year stay in the region on their movement westward. A brick school building planned in 1860 was finally in service in 1862. By 1867 the agency structures included eight frame houses and three log houses. But throughout this period and until the removal to Oklahoma practically no Pawnee family lived in a house. All still used the traditional earth lodge and the tipi. The only exceptions seem to have been the children who lived at the school and the Pawnee who were employed at or around the agency and lived in agency buildings.

Considerable blundering handicapped the use of the mills on the reservation. Hardly a year had passed after the installation of a steam grist and saw mill in 1862 before it was noticed that wood, the only fuel available, was scarce, and that most of the timber of the region was being eaten up by the mill. Recommendations that it be changed to one run by water power, which was available three-fourths of a mile from the agency, were made over a period of years. Finally in 1869 and 1870 a mill dam and raceway were installed at Pawnee expense, the tribe appropriating $ 7000 of their annuity funds for the purpose and themselves doing the labor. Unfortunately the spring and summer floods of the region had not been considered. The Beaver River overflowed so frequently in the next two years, ruining the dam and raceway, that by 1873 the decision had been reached to abandon the attempt to use water power, and substitute wind power.

Civilization of the tribe by means of education in farm life was accompanied during these years by demonstration in certain useful manual arts and by an attempt at schooling. Blacksmith and tinsmith shops were set up on the reservation and equipped by the government. The government furnished the blacksmiths, but in order to teach the Pawnee, the strikers were Pawnee youths, employed at fair pay. From this period on, the interest of government policy became increasingly centered on teaching trades to the Indian, and a constant attempt was made to employ Pawnee apprentices in all the government or agency managed activities. The blacksmith and tinsmith shops were flooded with work by the Pawnee, more than they could handle.

The first school on the Pawnee reservation was established and began functioning July 16, 1862. The teacher with the agent's help succeeded in persuading parents of sixteen children, eight boys and eight girls, to send them to school. They were supplied with suitable clothes. The boys were taught some farming and mechanical pursuits, the girls instructed in varied household duties. Both were instructed in reading. The first reports indicated that the Pawnee children were quick and eager to learn, and the results promising. By the next year, the chief handicap to the education of the girls began to come to attention. In the old traditional way of life girls were married off by their parents when about fourteen or fifteen. Family considerations were usually paramount and neither the girl nor the boy was officially consulted. Now the teacher found that girls of fourteen were being taken away from the school to be married. The agent was in no position to enforce the compulsory education which was stipulated in the treaty of 1857, since the government had as yet provided meager and inadequate facilities for schooling, with a handful of children at school out of a population including many hundreds of school age.

The boys meanwhile were getting ahead. For the first time, in 1863, the school teacher was able to clip off their scalp locks without their attempting to conceal the change under hats. The boys were learning manual arts, were enjoying the work and activity and were unashamed to be seen at labor by older and conservative tribesmen.

The third year of the school, 1864, was an unfortunate one. Epidemics of measles and diptheria broke out in the school, and carried off a number of children. The children seem to have offered little resistance to these diseases and those who recovered were low in vitality for some time, and subject to other ailments. The school teacher found himself handicapped by the fact that parents began taking away from school the children who had been there since its inception. While he was able to secure others to take their places, the impetus of the instruction was lost, and work would have to start over again from the beginning. Health conditions were better in 1865, when new buildings were put to use, and the crowding avoided. The school attendance was only twenty-two, but agent and teacher subscribed to a program of raising it to at least a hundred, a number for which facilities were now adequate. In 1865 the staff consisted of six. The political changes of agency control were however interfering with the work of instruction, and the teacher advised the government to take the school out of politics by having the instruction turned over to a missionary board. Two school buildings were in use after 1867, with attendance increased to sixty-eight and two teachers of the Episcopal denomination in charge.

With these government activities leading the Pawnee away from their old customs, why is it that by 1872 the whole program had essentially failed ? No allotments had been made. The tribe still clung to its village life. The people lived in earth-lodges, several families to a lodge. Their basic agriculture was still the native cultivation of corn, beans and squash, though here and there a man could be seen using his own plow. They were still dependent upon the buffalo to a great extent.

It is easy to put this Pawnee conservatism down to "cultural lag," and to speak of the slow transformation that takes place in cultural impact. It is tempting to claim that what we have here is a conflict between two basically divergent systems of economy. But these concepts introduce no intelligible determinants; they merely replace the descriptive facts with verbal phrases. What evidence we have indicates that the Pawnee attitude at this period was favorable to the principal part of the government program. The Pawnee chiefs and leaders are reported eager to have the tribe settle down to a farming life, and many of the chiefs led the way, themselves working lands with the plow. The rank and file were convinced that white methods of cultivation gave a larger yield. All knew that buffalo hunts were more difficult and hazardous each year, and are said to have been aware that the buffalo were rapidly becoming extinct. Adults and children alike are reported alert and intelligent, quick to learn, anxious to master mechanical arts and the agricultural technique. Of a conflict between economic ideologies of individual enterprise and communal effort there is no sign. There is no indication that the government was concerned with how individual Pawnee cooperated with one another in farming or how they distributed the produce. Individual skill and enterprise were not unfamiliar to Pawnee men. Warfare and the hunt emphasized these very traits, and renown in Pawnee life was individual renown.

To understand such problems of cultural assimilation and adjustment as concerns us in this period of Pawnee life we must consider the actual conditions and determinants as we find them. Were the conditions of life on the Pawnee reservation favorable to their transformation into peaceful farmers ? The answer to this question is no. Quite apart from any natural disinclination of the people to break up village life, or of the men to take up a kind of activity which in earlier generations was women's work, throughout this period remorseless and continous attacks by Sioux made the defense of their lives the first consideration of the Pawnee.

The Pawnee were hardly established in their new reservation homes before they again felt the Sioux cloud hanging over their lives. In 1860 Dakota war parties, accompanied by Cheyenne and Arapaho, attacked the Pawnee on the Pawnee reservation, on April 10, May 19 and May 21, June 22, July 5 and July 11, September 1 and September 14. "In these several attacks they killed thirteen Pawnee, wounded many others, carried off over thirty horses, and burned over sixty lodges, all on the reservation where the faith of the government is pledged by treaty for their protection. These lodges, if built by white people, would be attended with great expense."[1] The attacks of September occurred while United States troops were on the reservation. All the activities of the year were continually interrupted by this stream of assaults. Military authorities recommended that a block house be built, which they claimed with one large gun and a handful of men could permanently put a stop to these raids.

In 1862 the Dakota attacked the villages early in June and on August 27; in each attack sixteen Pawnee were killed or wounded. In May 1863 the Brulé Dakota attacked, and returned in larger numbers on June 22 of the same year. On the latter occasion several Pawnee women working in the fields within a few yards of the agent's residence were killed and scalped. A company of Nebraska cavalry drove the Sioux off.

By the fall of 1863 the Pawnee were living in a continual state of alarm. Sioux scouts were seen lurking on the reservation, and at times when the Pawnee did not see them, reports reached them that they were close at hand. The Pawnee could not be induced to go into their fields to work, because of the danger. When the tribe left for the buffalo hunt, not one could be induced to remain behind to attend to the farm.[2]

The Pawnee were not alone in suffering heavily from the Dakota war parties. To the north their kinsmen the Arikara, along with the Mandan and Hidatsa of the Fort Berthold Agency, were at this very time holding council, sending messages to the government asking protection and redress. They had lost heavily in numbers, had lost thousands of horses, and repeatedly their corn fields had been burnt. Failing to get government aid, the Arikara wrote to the Pawnee asking the whole tribe to move north and join them; and the Mandan asked the Winnebago to move to the North Dakota country. The Indian councils had decided that their only resource lay in numbers, and with the Pawnee and Arikara, along with the Mandan, Hidatsa and Winnebago on one reservation, they felt competent to cope with the numbers of the Sioux. The Pawnee however declined to join them. In 1832 the Arikara had lived with

---

[1] J. L. Gillis, from Pawnee Agency, October, 1860. Annual Report, 1859—60.

[2] B. F. Lushbaugh, agent, Pawnee Agency, Sept. 21, 1863. Annual Report, 1862—63.

the Pawnee for a brief period and disagreements had resulted; and from a Pawnee standpoint the Ft. Berthold country was if anything more exposed to Sioux assault than the Pawnee reservation in Nebraska.

The Pawnee summer and winter buffalo hunts were hampered and obstructed during this time by the Dakota. The summer of 1859, at the time of their removal to the Nebraska reservation, they were driven from their hunting fields by superior numbers of Brulé and Oglalla Dakota, and left in want of adequate meat provisions. Nevertheless, during the following years, with the farming and agricultural activities of the Pawnee and the government farmers on the reservation yielding less than a maintenance, the buffalo hunt was of necessity the great reliance of the Pawnee for adequate sustenance, The Pawnee persevered, going regularly on fall and winter hunts. The herds were smaller and further away, and the journey to the distant hunting grounds hazardous. When they overtook the herds, as in the summer of 1864, they were likely to be driven from the hunting grounds by superior forces of the Dakota.

Some protection was afforded the Pawnee on several occasions from 1865 on. Accompanied on their summer hunt in 1865 by a squad of soldiers, they were unusually successful. The tribe killed and secured the hides and meat of 1600 buffalo, antelope, elk and deer, on a hunt of fifty days duration which brought them back to their reservation villages the ninth of August. Throughout the year a company of cavalry was stationed at the Pawnee Agency, and there were no Sioux attacks in 1865. Crops were plentiful, and a feeling of security spread. The winter hunt of 1865 was a success, and again in the summer of 1866 the Pawnee were successful on a buffalo hunt from July 6 to August 25.

The Pawnee Scouts were organized in 1864 under Major Frank North for a year of service, but their term had expired and they were mustered out of service (later to be reorganized) after the campaigns of 1865. This, with the removal of troops from the Pawnee Agency, left the tribe without guns or protection, and in early May a raid was made upon the agency in which eighteen horses were stolen. Up to this time, it was often impossible for the government officials to determine accurately what hostile bands were responsible for the attacks. On this occasion one horse which was too weak to run rapidly was shot with an arrow which proved to be Dakota.

Raids interrupted cultivation in 1866 and 1867, and on the hunts in the winter of 1866 and the summer of 1867 the Pawnee were annoyed by the Dakota. On July 19, 1867 the Pawnee left for the hunting grounds in company with the Omaha and Ponca. They intended to remain out hunting until near the end of September. The Dakota were in the hunting territory in large numbers, but did not offer to meet the Pawnee in open battle. They kept under cover until the Pawnee had made a surround, and as soon as the men were scattered out over the hunting field chasing the buffalo, the Sioux appeared, fell upon small parties of Pawnee hunters in different quarters of the field, and attacked the Pawnee camp. The Pawnee returned to the camp to defend their families, and after hours of fighting drove back the Dakota. In this way the day was spent in fighting, and the meat of the slain buffalo spoiled before it could be secured. Repeatedly this performance was carried out by the Dakota, and although the Pawnee and their allies found large herds, they secured little meat. Six Pawnee and two Ponca were slain in these encounters, and the tribes finally became discouraged at the continuous annoyance of these attacks, abandoned the hunt, and returned to their reservations with what they had.

The Union Pacific Railroad crossed the state of Nebraska at this time, and by railroad and highway the tide of emigration to the west was bringing settlers to all the watercourses in the buffalo country, cutting off the buffalo herds from their natural watering-places and limiting their range. The Pawnee observed these conditions when they went hunting, and were aware of the pending inevitable abandonment of the chase.

The Pawnee Scouts were reorganized under Major North in 1867, and cooperated with the United States Army forces in policing the line of the Union Pacific Railroad and in campaigning against hostile Indian tribes. Pawnee readily chose such service because the tribe considered itself an ally of the United States. But there were also strong cultural and economic incentives. The youths exchanged a life of relative inactivity on the reservation, with an insecure food supply, for the active life of a frontier soldier, which more nearly resembled the warrior life of old, and which offered regular rations and good pay. While the campaigns against the Dakota and other hostile Indian tribes were in progress, the Pawnee in the summer of 1869 were persuaded by military authorities to forego their usual hunt. The officials feared that the armies who ranged the buffalo country in pursuit of hostile Indians might mistake the Pawnee for the enemy.

In spite of the army campaigns the Pawnee suffered in 1870 from raids by small Dakota war parties, which stole a number of horses, and killed six Pawnee. An attempt was begun in this year to bring about a treaty of peace between the Pawnee and the Dakota tribes. Red Cloud and Spotted Tail, however, chiefs of bands of Teton Dakota, contended that they could not enforce peace unless all the Dakota bands came to agreement. By the following year it was clear that the overtures made to these chiefs were a failure. There were so many large bands of nomadic Sioux that concerted action was difficult to obtain. Five Pawnee were killed on the Pawnee reservation in 1871 by war parties from Spotted Tail's band.

By this time the practicability of cultivating individual farms, according to report, had impressed itself upon the leaders of the Pawnee people, but they expressed themselves as unable to consent to disruption of village life while the threat of death at the hands of marauding war parties continued. Agents, superintendents and investigating officials concurred in believing that the Pawnee could readily be transformed into peaceful farmers if security was assured them. In 1872 a new instrument for the defense of the Pawnee was utilized, the telegraph service. The agents of the Dakota bands cooperated with other officials of the government service in sending warnings whenever they had reason to believe that war parties had left to plunder neighboring tribes. As a result no successful raid was made upon the Pawnee reservation in 1872. Two war parties of Dakota started for the reservation; the first found the season too early for pasturing their ponies and gave up the expedition, while the second was overhauled by United States cavalry and turned from its purpose of attacking the Pawnee only to fall upon the Ponca on their reservation, run off stock, and kill a Ponca medicine man. The Pawnee Agency had been informed of each of these raids in advance by telegraph and the entire Pawnee tribe had been on guard and in readiness. This was a method useful in saving the Pawnee from sudden and unexpected death while on their reservation, but during the suspense, while they awaited an expected attack, their energies were paralyzed, and they could not make an effort to carry on their labors. And the telegraph service was not available to them when on the hunt, as they were soon to find out.

The success of the various government agencies in preventing Dakota attacks in 1872 was but a lull in the storm. Accompanied by officials on their summer hunt in 1872, the Pawnee were successful. While on the hunt they ranged for weeks with the Brulé Sioux camped often as close as eight or ten miles away, and although each tribe was aware of the other's presence, neither molested the other. By the winter of 1872 it was felt on the Pawnee reservation and in the surrounding country that the worst was over.

"A feeling of perfect security pervades the whole community for many miles around, and the citizens who were clamorous for the removal of the Indians from the State are now satisfied that they shall remain . . ."[1]

This feeling of security was shaken by a Sioux attack upon the Pawnee winter hunt of 1872—73, in which on January 10, 1873 one Pawnee was killed and 100 horses captured. All thought of security was shattered in the summer of 1873 by what took place in Massacre Canyon, Hitchcock County, Nebraska, which took its name from the event.

A Pawnee hunting party left the reservation on the second of July, 1873, with full permission from government officials for the hunt, and accompanied by a white man. Its numbers have been variously placed at 700 including 350 men; 400, including 250 men; and 300. Significant about these figures is the fact that the "security" of the previous year had so lulled the Pawnee that on this occasion we find only a small part of the tribe organized for the hunt. If danger were expected, it is likely that, as in days past, the whole tribe would have organized, in order to present a united front to their common enemy. Most of the men were armed merely with bows and arrows, but here and there warriors carried muzzle-loading rifles or carbines. The intention of the party was to hunt in the valley of the Republican River. They were unusually successful and had found several herds and made killings, when they started back toward the reservation with their hundreds of pack horses loaded with meat. On August 4 rumors reached them through white men that Dakota scouts were spying upon them, and that large war parties were not far off. It is said that the Pawnee chiefs put little credence in these reports, claiming that they were intended only to scare the Pawnee out of the country so that the white man could have the hunting grounds to himself. On the morning of August 5 a buffalo scout sighted a large herd, and the Pawnee hunters rode for the herd, and were scattered out making their kills when word spread that the Sioux were coming. The numbers of the attacking party have been placed at 600 warriors and at 1200 to 1500 warriors, but the latter is undoubtedly too large a figure. They were Oglalla and Brulé Dakotas, said to have been under Chief Snow Flake. The surprise of the Pawnee was so complete that Sky-Chief, in charge of the Pawnee hunting party,

---

[1] Agent J. M. Troth, from the Pawnee Agency, September, 1872. Annual Report, 1871—72.

was killed while in the act of skinning a buffalo. The Pawnee
rallied and made a brief stand, but finding themselves outnumbered
three or four to one, attempted a retreat through a narrow canyon,
their women and children fleeing before them. It was apparently
while the press of the retreat was forcing its way through this
canyon to the river that the worst episodes of the massacre took
place. The Dakota warriors rode past the retreat on both sides
firing at the Pawnee.

The Pawnee escaped complete annihilation when their retreat
reached the river and there came upon United States cavalry. The
tribal party refused, however, to return after the wounded and
the buffalo meat. Overcome with grief the Pawnee camped that
night to mourn the dead, and returned in scattered groups to the
reservation, broken, depressed and empty-handed.

The mortality in the massacre was great. The figures available
are open to dispute. The official agency report placed the dead
at 69, with a dozen wounded; Dunbar records the total as 86; while
Williamson, the white man in charge of the hunting party, claims
a total of 156 casualties.[1]

The government took cognizance of the severity of the conflict
between the Dakota and the Pawnee following the massacre of 1873.
Negotiations were begun with the Dakota looking toward the
abrogation of their right to hunt south of the Niobrara River. When
by their treaty of 1867 the Dakota relinquished all claim to lands
south of the Niobrara, they retained the right to hunt in that territory. In 1874, the bands of the Red Cloud Agency were offered
$ 25,000 to forego that hunting right forever. This would obviate
conflict with hunting parties of the Pawnee and other tribes then
located in Nebraska, and also confine them in the north out of the
way of white emigrants and settlers. An agreement was drawn with
these Dakota bands June 23, 1875, by which they relinquished their
hunting rights south of the Niobrara River. By this time the
Pawnee had taken matters into their own hands.

From the Pawnee standpoint the massacre of 1873 ended all
indecision and hesitation. It brought forcibly to the native mind
the necessity of taking measures of their own to preserve their
very lives.

In the fall of 1873, within weeks of the return of the remnants
of the hunting party which had escaped death in the massacre, a
group of Pawnee families evacuated their homes and travelled

---

[1] J. W. Williamson, The Battle of Massacre Canyon. This account was
written from memory years after the event, and is doubtless colored by
romantic exaggerations.

southward to Indian Territory. They had a long-standing invitation from their kinsmen the Wichita, which they now took advantage of. Thirty lodges of families, numbering about 360 individuals went; most of these were members of the Kitkahaxki[x] band. They were received heartily by the Wichita, and settled themselves among the Wichita on the Wichita reservation. Through the leader of this party an invitation was extended to the rest of the Pawnee still in Nebraska to remove to Indian Territory and settle with the Wichita. Reports sent back were glowing with the promise of the land in the south, and the Pawnee in Nebraska, accustomed to struggling against drought and the grasshopper pestilence to secure a crop, believed that the country in the south offered not only a haven from extermination at the hands of the Sioux, but a life of plenty.

This migration of part of the Pawnee was not only conceived by the people themselves, but was undertaken and carried out in spite of the remonstrances and objections of their agent and other officials. Once they were settled with the Wichita, however, there was nothing for the government officials to do but to accept the situation. Since they could not compel them to return to Nebraska, they were "allowed to remain." They drew rations at the Wichita Agency along with the tribes located there, and joined the Wichita in farming.

In Nebraska the government gave the Pawnee partial indemnification for the losses sustained in the massacre by expending $ 9,000 for cattle and supplies, with which aid the bands in the north were made comfortable during the winter of 1873. The desire to move to Indian Territory was not as yet general that winter: the promise of the south had not yet reached them. The tribe in council, assuming that they were to continue to struggle in Nebraska, asked that $ 10,000 of their annuity be spent the next year for agricultural implements and labor. In the spring of 1874, the agency officials made a herculean effort on their behalf. The government farmers broke 350 acres for the Pawnee to farm, while the Pawnee cultivated 1,000 acres on their own behalf; in addition the agency farm of 315 acres was planted, and the school farm of 25 acres, a total of 1,690 acres in cultivation. The Pawnee were said that year to show a greater willingness to labor than ever before. Unfortunately, the prospects of a fine crop were destroyed by drought, Colorado beetles and grasshoppers, and the harvest yielded only 1,400 bushels of wheat, less than half a crop, and a few beets and potatoes. By fall the destitution of the people was great, and the officials reported to the government that aid must be given them.

It was this complete failure of their best efforts in Nebraska, while they were receiving word from their kinsmen of the plenty of the Indian Territory, that spread the desire to remove southward among them like a fever. The Pawnee made it plain to the officials in charge that they could live in Nebraska no longer, and that they would remove with or without permission immediately. They refused to consider waiting until the government could carry out official arrangements. The tribe asked that their lands in Nebraska be sold for the best price they would bring, and the funds used to locate them on suitable lands in the Indian Territory. The white settlers around them, realizing the rich harvest in land for settlement that the removal of the Pawnee promised, spurred them on, and argued to the agent that they failed to see why, in view of the desire of the Pawnee to remove, the government did not let them go.

The Pawnee were excited, and emergency measures were taken. October 10, 1874, Barclay White, the Superintendent of the Northern Superintendency in which the Pawnee Agency was then located, William Burgess, the Pawnee agent, and other officials held a council with the Pawnee to discuss their wish to remove. The Department of Indian Affairs had drawn up a plan, practically equivalent to a new treaty, which the Pawnee in council considered for two days, accepted and signed. The tribe was not altogether satisfied with the provisions, but it was more important to them to manage the removal expeditiously.

In accordance with the government plan, the vanguard of the Pawnee tribe, consisting of the abler men and leaders, left Nebraska shortly thereafter, proceeding to the Wichita Agency in Indian Territory, where they arrived in December. The main contingent of the tribe migrated a month later accompanied by agency employees. The agent, Burgess, had left Nebraska with his son in November, and examined different portions of the Indian Territory available for reservation settlements. The rest of the tribe, to the number of some four hundred, consisting of the aged and infirm, and small children, were left at the old reservation in Nebraska, and were only to be removed after the tribe had chosen its new reservation in the Indian Territory, removed to it, and made some beginning in the erection of their new homes.

Burgess reached the Wichita reservation early in January of 1875, before the main body of the tribe had arrived. He waited until the two parties, the pioneer group and the general tribal contingent, were reunited at the Wichita Agency. With a delegation of forty he left for the northern part of the territory to allow the Pawnee to inspect for themselves the land to be turned over to them as a reservation. The tract chosen was south of the Osage Agency and north of the Sauk and Fox reservation in the forks of the Cimarron and Arkansas Rivers. The Pawnee agreed upon the location, finding the land apparently a fertile and hospitable home. In late June of the same year the main body of the Pawnee removed from the Wichita reservation to this new location, leaving a body of 374 Pawnee with the Wichita to harvest the Pawnee crop from the fields planted by the Pawnee that spring on Wichita land.

In Nebraska during 1875 the Pawnee remnant who were left behind consisted of that part of the tribe who were least able to defend themselves against attack. A company of infantry from Omaha were stationed at the old Pawnee Agency at Genoa in Nebraska during the spring and summer to protect them. With the summer well advanced, and no untoward events having occurred or being anticipated, they were withdrawn. On August 23 the wife of Eagle Chief was shot and killed while she was drying corn in the early morning. Marauding white men or Indians were suspected. Again on the morning of August 30, a raid was made at sunrise by party of fourteen Indians on fleet horses. Unable to capture a small herd of horses, they shot the Pawnee boy who was herding them. The Pawnee men available made an unsuccessful pursuit, and from that day until the removal of this last remnant of the Pawnee guarded the village by day and night. These were parting blows of the Pawnee enemy. This last contingent of the Pawnee were removed with all their movable effects by wagons and teams in November of 1875. After the harvest on the Wichita reservation that year, the Pawnee who had remained behind a few months also moved to the new reservation in northern Indian Territory, and by the spring of 1876 the entire tribe, which then numbered 2,026, were collected together and settled on the new reservation south of the Arkansas River.

The most striking characteristic of this entire period from the treaty of 1857 to the removal, completed in 1875, aside from the failure of the government program for transforming the tribe into individual families of farmers, is the steady and rapid decrease in Pawnee numbers. There is reason to believe that the Pawnee population for the four bands was close to 4,000 when they removed to their reservation north of the Platte River in 1859. The census of 1861 listed them at 3,414, from which total their numbers fell steadily to 2,026 in 1876, when they were together again in Oklahoma. The official report for the year 1875 to 1876 recorded 95 births and 150 deaths. This is some indication of the steady decrease. This decrease is to be accounted for by two continuous factors, the mortality inflicted upon the Pawnee by the Dakota and other hostile tribes, and the continuous inroads which diseases, particularly pulmonary diseases, were making upon the tribe. The mortality in warfare is only partly represented by the recorded incidents mentioned herein; the worst phase of the continuous marauding strife was the annihilation here and there from time to time of small parties of Pawnee cut off away from the reservation, or on the hunt, for whom no accounting has been made. In the removal itself there is reason to believe that many perished; all the separate contingents of the tribe were removed in the late fall and winter months over open country in wagons and on horseback. Not the least of the Pawnee difficulties was the sudden change of climatic conditions from Nebraska to Oklahoma, which was to have its effect upon the health of the tribe for some years.

The removal of the Pawnee to Oklahoma was carried out by the tribe and the Department of Indian Affairs before legal arrangements could be made. Expenses incurred were met as best they could be by executive order and appropriation. A bill had been introduced in Congress in 1875, but in the press of the closing days of the session no action on it was taken. It was not until the spring of 1876, when the tribe was together in Oklahoma, that Congressional action for the sale of the Pawnee reservation in Nebraska and for the appropriation of an advance against the proceeds of that sale was obtained. These provisions were included with the stipulations for the purchase and authorization of the new reservation in Indian Territory, in the Act of the Forty-Fourth Congress, First Session, April 10, 1876, "an act to authorize the sale of the Pawnee Reservation."

With the decline of Pawnee numbers in Nebraska before the removal and the increasing pressure of white settlers demanding land, the Department of Indian Affairs had concluded an agreement with the Pawnee in 1872 by which the tribe accepted the Congressional authorization of the sale of 50,000 acres of surplus land of their reservation, taken from that part lying south of the Loup fork. This act was repealed by that of 1876, which provided for the sale of the entire reservation. After due advertisement the land was to be sold in separate tracts of 160 acres for not less than $ 2.50 an acre. Meanwhile the government appropriated $ 300,000 for use by the Pawnee, to be reimbursed to the United States Treasury from the sale of the Nebraska reservation. Half of this sum was to be used to settle claims for expenditures involved in the removal and maintenance of the Pawnee up to the date of the act, the other half for necessary expenditures on behalf of the tribe until they could become self-sustaining in Indian Territory. The reports of agents and superintendents during the period of the removal were to the effect that the entire movement had been carried out under the supervision of agency employees on their regular government salaries, and without major expenses of any kind, which makes this handsome provision by Congress seem rather startling.

The income from the sale of the Nebraska lands was also to be used in part for the purchase of the lands forming the Pawnee reservation in Indian Territory. The new reservation consisted of 283,020 acres of land, of which about four-fifths was Cherokee land, in accordance with the Cherokee treaty of 1866, and the other fifth Creek land ceded to the United States by the Creek treaty of June 14, 1866. The Cherokee were to be paid not more than seventy-five cents an acre by the Pawnee; while the United States agreed to accept thirty cents an acre for the land formerly held by the Creek.

The Pawnee lands in Nebraska with improvements thereon were appraised by special government officials in 1877 at $ 761,800.21. Their sale took place in the years following, although some plots for which payment was not made as required had to be resold as late as 1890. The balance in favor of the Pawnee from the sale, after the government had been reimbursed for its advance and the cost of the new reservation had been deducted, was placed to the credit of the Pawnee tribe in the books of the United States Treasury. On this, their first trust fund, the Pawnee were to receive interest at five per cent, payable per capita, semi-annually.

FOURTH PERIOD: 1876 TO 1892

The fourth period of Pawnee history in the Nineteenth Century begins with their settlement on the reservation in Indian Territory, and closes with the break-up of their reservation and allotment of lands in severalty to them in 1892, the year in which the Pawnee took up the Ghost Dance.

The government program during this period of Pawnee life was a continuation and gradual expansion of the plans and policies attempted in Nebraska. To civilize the tribe and adjust them to citizenship they were to be made farmers, cultivating individual tracts of land which they fenced and on which they lived in frame houses. They were to be stimulated to labor in the white man's way, in lumbering, carpentry, freight-hauling, and other pursuits. They were to be made self-sustaining by means of cattle-herding and the cultivation of fruit trees, in addition to farming. Education in the rudiments of common schooling, along with training in manual arts, was combined later with an effort to stimulate self government. Finally a persistent campaign was instituted against forms of the old Pawnee life which were considered barbaric and detrimental to their new life as citizens; their unsanitary mode of life, the methods of the medicine men, their polygamous marriage customs, their wasteful mourning customs, their Indian clothing, their religious dances and ceremonies, their indolent social gatherings for dancing and gambling, their intemperate feasting.

The major objective of the government, however, was directed toward the division of the tribal lands into tracts held in severalty, which would introduce individual property ownership and inheritance, and break down the communal forms of life around which centered, from the white man's standpoint, the barbaric tribal customs which barred the Indian from an imperceptible and gradual absorption into the white population of the United States.

The government program could not be initiated upon the arrival of the Pawnee. They came in several contingents during winter months to a territory uninhabited and still virgin to the plow. The first Pawnee to arrive, including by arrangement the strongest men and women, taking new heart with the possibilities of peaceful and secure life in their new home, began at once to build their settlement close to the agency location on Black Bear Creek. Accustomed still to the tipi and the earth-lodge, the former for temporary shelter on the march and the hunt, the latter for more permanent habitations, they built villages in their old way. The first winters were difficult, the Pawnee suffering severely from exposure, after their long migration, and from the changed climatic conditions. The building of frame houses with government aid and direction was contingent on the settling of individual families on individual tracts of land, a condition which could not be met immediately upon arrival.

It was essential to begin cultivation at once. Large sums had been expended to provision the tribe during the years of removal, and they had to become self-sustaining soon. Government farmers began the agency farm. The bands chose the locations in which they would settle, and as rapidly as possible the government farmers broke land for them to cultivate.

The Pawnee camped around the agency until land was ready for them. Two bands removed to land broken for them in 1877; the other two the following spring. By the summer of 1888 all were cultivating their lands.

As they removed, the bands transferred their village encampments to their separate tracts. The land broken for each band was but a small part of their sector; it was neither large enough nor so situated as to make practicable a division of it into individual tracts for family groups. Each band therefore began to farm the band tract cooperatively. In theory each man did his share of the work and each took his share of the harvest. The band lived together on the tract, and their encampments rapidly became permanent villages of tipis and earth-lodges.

This redevelopment of village life, instituted by the Pawnee as an adjustment to the conditions of their settlement in Indian Territory, and intentionally overlooked by agency officials, who considered it a temporary expedient, was to continue for some years. To the Pawnee it was a satisfactory adjustment, approximating as it did their accustomed way of life. In these villages something of the old tribal life continued; the chiefs, priests and medicine men functioned, the old social gatherings and ceremonies were possible.

The produce of the band farms, together with that at the agency, constituted the basic food supply of the Pawnee. For years this was inadequate and insecure; the people suffered greatly for lack of food, and some of the mortalities of the period were due to starvation and malnutrition. The principal crop was corn, supplemented by some beans and squash, and increasing cultivation of wheat, oats, potatoes and other vegetables. Most of the farms were in the bottom lands and along the streams, and yet the usual hazards of cultivation caused crop failures a number of times. The country in which the Pawnee had settled is in a belt which is subject to periodic hot, dry summers, when rain is at a premium. Droughts were severe in 1880, 1887, and 1890. On occasion bugs destroyed much of the crop, while once, in 1885, a terrific hailstorm broke the stand of grain. Crop failures left the Pawnee dependent on government aid, in the form of rations, or food purchased for them with money from their annuity funds.

For a meat supply the Pawnee had to depend primarily on government rations. The first winter the Pawnee were together in Oklahoma, that of 1875 to 1876, the tribe attempted a buffalo hunt, but the herds were too remote to be reached with the limited preparations the Pawnee were able to make. While the buffalo were reported on the plains in considerable numbers the next summer, only occasional buffalo were captured by straggling parties of Pawnee. In a few years the tribe was persuaded to forego the hunt; they talked of it the winter of 1878, but did not go. From this time on we hear of no buffalo hunting. The organized tribal hunt was a thing of the past.

The meat rations supplied the Pawnee by the government were until 1880 delivered on the hoof, and the Indians, gathered round the agency to receive their oxen, would turn the day into one of carnage and slaughter, killing and dressing their own beeves. The "oxy kill 'em day," as this was known to the Indian service, ended in 1880 after which the rations were turned over to the tribe in the form of dressed meat.

Not more than one-third of the Pawnee reservation was suitable for farming, but there was a great deal of good pasture land. Cows and calves were issued to the Pawnee in 1878, and received such good care that with the Indians asking for cattle the government made an attempt to develop stock-raising. In the summer of 1880 four hundred head of two-year-old heifers and bulls were brought from northern Texas and distributed among the Pawnee. The tribe hailed their coming with delight. Unfortunately a scourge carried off many oxen the first winter. The Pawnee were not yet free of their hunting complex. When they wanted meat, they killed cattle, and finding that traders would buy the hides, so many were slaughtered that by 1882 only a few head of the cattle issued to the tribe remained. Stock-raising by the Pawnee was admittedly a failure.

A great need in the food supply was fresh fruit, for want of which various ailments afflicted the Pawnee. To obviate this fruit trees were bought and small orchards planted on the reservation, but they did not flourish.

The food rations, supplies, and implements distributed to the tribe had to be shipped to the reservation by freighting from the nearest railroad point. At first this was at Coffeyville, Kansas, a distance of one hundred miles; the route went northward through the Osage Agency. Later there was a shipping point at Arkansas City, a distance of seventy miles. The agent turned the freighting over to the Pawnee, who handled it with wagons and teams on their own responsibility.

As conditions on the reservation became more settled, the government farm program was renewed. A major provision of the Congressional Act of 1876 which established the Pawnee reservation applied to allotments in severalty. Each head of a family, or single person over 21 years of age, who so desired, was to be allotted 160 acres of land. Certificates were to be issued by the Commissioner of Indian Affairs recognizing the individual ownership of such tracts. An allotee occupying and cultivating his land for five successive years, who had at least twenty-five acres fenced and in crop, was to be entitled to receive a patent in fee simple for his allotment, inalienable for fifteen years thereafter. In this way the Indians were to be transformed gradually into individual holders of land.

Enterprising Pawnee, young and progressive, had taken over individual farm lands as soon as these could be surveyed and made available for them. For such families frame houses were erected on their allotments, the agency carpenter managing the work, assisted by the Pawnee. This development was sluggish before 1880, owing partly to indolent management on the part of the agents. Families who chose tracts of land often camped for long periods near them in tipis, before the surveying and alloting could be done, and aid given them in house-building. By 1881 only forty such houses had been built and occupied by Pawnee families; and the allotments seem not to have been officially registered.

The main body of the tribe, however, continued to reside in the band villages. Once established in villages the Pawnee were loath to break up their social life for a life on scattered farms. The agents found stubborn resistance to their program of change. From the official standpoint village life was the center of stability for the old barbaric customs. Polygamous marriage, gambling, inveterate dancing and indolence, superstitious awe of the medicine men, were aspects of Pawnee life which could not be eliminated unless the villages were broken up. The conditions of band farming which were natural to the Pawnee were obnoxious from the white standpoint. In the native view the chief controlled the farm in the interest of the general welfare, and all shared its produce according to need. In the agent's view the chief was an exploiter, and under his rule indolence flourished and individual initiative was submerged. The indolent and lazy, supported by the labor of others, could hang out around the agency waiting for the distribution of rations and goods, and money payments.

While after 1881 the agents were making a concentrated drive to get the Pawnee on individual allotments, there seem to have been two extreme parties in the tribe, a radically progressive group who were in favor of separate farms and homes, and the conservative majority content with band village life. The chiefs, priests and medicine men of the tribe seem to have been in the main opposed to a change to individualized farming. The government agents claimed their obstructionism was born of a desire to maintain their own power and influence, which would fade with the people scattered in isolated homes. But it was more than this. The Pawnee had been accustomed to sedentary village life as far back as tradition could go. Recent archaeological evidence indicates that they had been a basically horticultural people in the plains of North America even before the buffalo hunting era.[1] The whole round of life, with its conceptual and religious meanings, was to the Pawnee bound up with group life in a village. Their ceremonies were village rituals in intent and action; their dances called for gatherings on a large scale. In opposing a destruction of the village communities, the chiefs were supporting traditional Pawnee values. In addition, it must not be forgotten that even after the settlement of the Pawnee on a Nebraska reservation in 1859 the tribe had been permitted to continue the old village organization. To be sure, it was not in line with government policy that they did so, but because, as we have seen, the government failed to give the tribe protection and did not dare to scatter the people and render them defenceless. Nevertheless, the effect was the same. The Pawnee were not opposed to farming. They were proud in 1884 of their independence of government aid, of their ownership of horses, cattle and farming implements. What was good and useful to a productive and happy life was not lost on the Pawnee. But their past experience inclined them to the belief that reservation life, based on farming, could be carried on successfully without the break-up of their villages. In dealing with such village tribes as the pueblo peoples, the United States government did not destroy the village organization and settlements; as a result, much of value and significance in their ancient culture has continued into the present among the south-western Indians. The implication here is that the Pawnee chiefs were right; and that in the case of their tribe the government was attempting a more violent and rapid change than was good for their cultural health.

In 1880 there were only a few individual farms held by Pawnee. The government reapers and mowers were used on these as well as on the band farms. The band farms were still cooperatively planted and worked. In 1882 the concerted drive of the officials persuaded a number of enterprising families to locate. With a family on an allotted tract, the agent proceeded to build a frame house for them. The Indians hewed logs and brought them to the saw-mill. The government carpenter directed the work of erecting the house, with Pawnee men assisting. The latter did a good share of the work, and as time went by put up their own houses. From 1886 on, all the frame houses built on the Pawnee reservation are reported to have been erected by the Pawnee themselves.

Until 1884 there was a scarcity of timber and cut wood for building, and many families camped on allotments. Those who

---

[1] W. D. Strong, Plains Culture in the Light of Archaeology.

were comfortably settled in homes on individual plots remained on them and worked them faithfully. Living in houses, they were soon asking for tables and chairs and bedsteads. Ponies being their chief form of property, the homesteaders would offer ponies for cooking stoves and culinary implements. Some exchanged ponies for hogs. A great change was coming into Pawnee life.

The chiefs, priests and medicine men stubbornly opposed the change. Their resistance was strengthened by lax and inefficient methods of government officials. Agents were political appointees, subject to the changing winds of political control. In the eight-year period from 1876 to 1884 seven agents were successively in charge of the Pawnee. The indications are that often they were lax and indolent, occasionally viciously dishonest. The great suffering for lack of adequate provisions in the early years was in part a result of such maladministration. In 1883 supervision became worse, when the independent Pawnee Agency was merged into a combined agency for the Ponca, Pawnee and Oto (later to include the Tonkawa), which was located at Ponca City, many miles from the Pawnee reservation. Only one or two days of the week could be spent with the Pawnee. The agency fell into disrepair, and procrastination ruled in the affairs of the Pawnee.

On the positive side there were the younger progressive spirits among the Pawnee themselves, who worked untiringly to persuade the people to adjust themselves to new conditions. They found opposition not only in their own ranks, but among white people in the Territory, who, sympathetic to Indian ideas, urged the Pawnee here and there to resist allotments.

The Skiri were the most progressive of the four bands. By 1887 a great many families were located on farms distributed all over the reservation, and a large proportion of these were Skiri. By 1890 most of the Skiri lived on their own farms, furnished their houses and dressed like white people, and spoke English in ordinary intercourse. The Tcawi ran them a close second. Of the other bands, while most were on allotted tracts, there were still many earth-lodges in evidence, and only those who were being educated in the schools were dressing and acting like white people. The Pitahawirat[a] proved most conservative and resisted change longest.

By the close of the decade the chiefs had accepted the inevitable. They blocked the agent in some minor measures, but for the most part expressed themselves eager to see the people educated and civilized. Officials were able to report that the tribe was anxious to have an allotting officer come to the reservation to register their individual tracts and issue certificates: the people were puzzled and uneasy about their legal rights as to leasing after allotment, and as to whether they would be subject to taxation, but it was felt they could easily be reassured.

The greatest discouragement and check upon programs of a progressive nature, from the years of removal on, was the physical unsoundness of the Pawnee tribe. In 1876, after the removal, the Pawnee numbered 2,026; in 1892 at the close of this period, the census listed 759. This tremendous decline, amounting to 62 per cent in a period of sixteen years, was the result of many interacting causes. Laboring under a blight of diseases and ill health, with the pride of their stock dying at an inexplicable rate, and all more or less weakened and ailing, a hopelessness came into Pawnee life from which there was no escape. This hopelessness and despair caused a deterioration of their home life, indicated by officials' reference to "filthy habits" and an "indifference to the condition of body or clothing." Their ancient medical lore was of no avail; their ancient gods had apparently deserted them. It is to be marvelled at that something of their old spirit and energy remained, and that they accomplished what they did in Indian Territory.

The white man's diseases had attacked them in the north. Pulmonary and venereal diseases in particular had vitiated their ancient stamina. But in the north the people were in a climate and a region to which the native constitution was adjusted from centuries of inhabitation. Until the white man came the people lived a free outdoor life. They were active. Sedentary as their way of life made them, the tribe roamed abroad on the hunt five months of the year; at home they were in the field and the open. The population of the region was not heavy; they had unpolluted streams and springs. They moved their villages at intervals of about eight years, avoiding pestilence.

The Nebraska country was relatively high, and the climate dry. In the removal the people came into a more fertile but humid country. Malarial fevers began to afflict them. In the winter of 1876, their first in Oklahoma, fevers, combined with other illnesses, if we are to believe the recorded figures, amounted to a plague. From 2,026 in 1876 the tribe declined in one year to 1,521![1] The manner of their removal involved long and continuous exposure, and the conditions of life upon their arrival were unhealthy and hazardous. Grinnell reports the condition in which their great friends, Major Frank North and his brother Luther, the organizers of the Pawnee Scouts, found them in 1876 in Indian Territory. The

---

[1] Further and continuous declines the succeeding years indicate that no part of the tribe was accidentally omitted in the 1877 census.

brothers North had come to enlist a company of one hundred scouts, "They were without food, without clothing, without arms and without horses. Their sole covering consisted of cotton sheets, which afforded no protection against cold and wet."[1] Every able-bodied man wanted to answer North's call. Every man who could wanted to get away from homes buried in suffering and disease, and to change the monotonous, restricted, and inactive life of the reservation for an active life in the army. Many who were not taken by North marched after his force on foot as far as Arkansas City, hoping to persuade him to enlist them.

Settled in camps of earth-lodges and tipis, with an inadequate food supply, insufficient clothing and no medical attention, inefficient and impotent officials remained satisfied for years to report the mortality and ascribe it to filthy habits of life, and the climate. Occasionally we hear that the people had poor protection from the weather, and that in addition to tuberculosis, pneumonia carried off a number.

A slight but temporary improvement in health took place in 1880 when for a season the food supply was adequate. The old men of the tribe said it was the first time in their lives that they had all the potatoes and vegetables they could eat. The people that fall looked well-nourished for the first time; the children fat and healthy.

The houses built for the Pawnee, and by the Pawnee under government instruction, made no sanitary provisions; as late as 1889 there were few if any outhouses, and luckily so, as the doctor commented, since the Pawnee without guidance were likely to construct them without vaults. As the people became settled in separate homes, the absence of suitable drinking water became a fertile source of disease. There were no wells; they used water from springs or creeks; they were not taught care in handling their water supply, and never cleaned out the springs. Even at the reservation school conditions for some years were bad.

In the reports, a doctor is first heard of in the tribe in 1881, but there are no indications of active medical aid until 1883. Then he began to teach them how to sink wells, and watch their water supply. He attributed fatalities in pneumonia cases to treatment by the native medicine men, and from this time forth there was a constant strife between the code of the medicine man and that of the agency physician. The diseases afflicting the tribe were ascribed to inherent taints, constitutional weakness, and inbreeding. It was not until 1897 that a Doctor Driesbach recognized that

[1] Grinnell, Pawnee Hero Stories and Folk Tales, p. 399.

Pawnee medicine men did effect relief and cures in many cases, and that the sure way to bring the tribe to faith in white man's medicine was to prove its superiority. We may judge from this the efficiency of much of the treatment afforded the Pawnee for years.

In 1890 Dr. Phillips ascribed some part of Pawnee ailments to the fact that at feasts many gorged themselves and then lay dormant for two or three days, tending to derange the proper functioning of the digestive system. The Pawnee habits of eating went back to a time when an active, roving life made heavy eating a necessity. Without the hunt, without warfare, the men were confined, inactive and indolent. Farming was not yet an adequate substitute. Without skinworking, and the activities of camp life and the march, the women were limited to housework and household duties. The change of daily routine was severe and called for a difficult constitutional adjustment.

The question of inbreeding deserves brief comment. Pawnee marriage customs did involve the mating of kin at a certain distance removed. In their old life, families who were the proud possessers of sacred and esoteric lore attempted to retain control of these things by regulating intermarriage. The bands had been for the most part endogamous, and intermarriage with other tribes was infrequent. On the average a band numbered no more than 2,500. The inbreeding, however, seems not to have had ill effects until inheritable weaknesses of a major sort were among the tribe.

As the years passed, the Pawnee came to look to the government physicians more and more for help when sick. Their medicine men were unable to cope with the illnesses which afflicted them. In a few outstanding cases, such as the use of quinine for malarial fevers, the white man's medicine had "power."

The educational program was neither more efficient nor more successful for many years than the development of farms and homes. The Pawnee Industrial Boarding School on the Pawnee reservation in Nebraska suspended operations at the time of removal. The funds saved were applied to the erection of a new brick school building on the Oklahoma reservation. This was not in operation until several years after the tribe located in Indian Territory. Its facilities were severely inadequate. Not more than one-fourth of the Pawnee children of school age could be accommodated. As a result, officials were not able to enforce treaty provisions; they could not compel continuous attendance even of those registered for schooling, since they could not provide facilities. There was a move to organize a day school, which would not only make provision for fifty additional pupils, but would obviate the objection and antagonisms of parents who did not want their children continually away from the family hearth. Sanitary conditions in the school buildings were not the best. Bathrooms and adequate dormitory facilities to avoid crowding were not available until the summer of 1889. Dr. Phillips in his report of that year stated that he expected these changes to reduce sickness at the school.

The aim of instruction in the reservation school was to give the children a background which would bring them closer to the conditions of life in white communities. The boys were taught manual arts and farming, the girls housekeeping and sewing; both groups learned to read. The instruction in industrial arts was for some time not very efficient, an agent commenting in 1881 that the school was only nominally "industrial." The schooling of the girls was impeded by the tribal practice of marrying them off young, at which time they would be withdrawn from school.

The general educational program of the Department of Indian Affairs began to be broadened in 1879 with the establishment of the Carlisle School at Carlisle, Pennsylvania. This was the first non-reservation school for Indians. Lieut. R. H. Pratt of the United States Army, when in charge of Indian prisoners of war exiled in Florida, conceived that education was a better method of handling them than imprisonment. At the same time, it would not do to return them to their reservations. As an experiment a number were sent to Hampton Normal and Agricultural Institute in Virginia, a school originally established for Negro education. The trial was so successful that Pratt was able to persuade the government to establish under his charge a school for Indians exclusively. The objective in organizing non-reservation schools was to divorce Indian children completely for a term of years from the ways of life of the parental generation; it was hoped that many could in this way be persuaded to take up life in white communities altogether, and that those who did return to the reservations would become leaders in the movement to civilize their peoples. The course at Carlisle ran from three to four years. It gave practical training in the manual arts, and common schooling as far as the high school grade. In addition, the "outing" system was adopted early, by which for one term of each school year a boy or girl boarded with and worked for a white family in the east. Many became self-supporting while at school, with small bank accounts of savings. Following the example of Carlisle, other non-reservation Indian schools were soon established, Chilocco and Haskell.

Thirteen Pawnee were enrolled at Carlisle the year it was opened; a few years later the number had increased to nineteen, including thirteen boys and six girls. Pawnee boys took work in carpentering, wagon-making, harness-making, tailoring, shoemaking, printing and farming. The girls learned sewing, laundry-work and house-work. In addition boys and girls had classes in regular school subjects. Thirteen Pawnee went to Chilocco when that institution opened in 1884; and later Pawnee were entered at Haskell. By 1889 between the non-reservation schools and the schools on the Pawnee reservation, most of the Pawnee of school age were in attendance at some government institution.

The schools were successful in teaching the Pawnee to read and use English, and Carlisle and Chilocco were particularly successful in teaching vocational trades and every-day manners. The outlet for a Pawnee to practice a trade was however, not apparent. Pratt, in charge of Carlisle, did all he could to induce Carlisle graduates to remain in the East and live and work among white people. A few Indians did so, including several Pawnee. The case of Mark Evarts is typical. Successfully trained as a harness-maker, and without close relatives at home, he worked some years at his trade in Harrisburg, Philadelphia and Newark. A man gifted in adjusting himself to alien ways, he lived successfully in the East. But in the end it was apparent to him that his life with white people was at best a makeshift, an apology for being an Indian. He returned home to his people, and the consciousness of his past and his fate overcame him. All the promises he had sincerely given to Pratt, a great friend of his, failed to stem the tide of fellow-feeling which surged over him back on the reservation. A Ghost Dance vision reconverted him, he immersed himself in Indian ways, recalled the teachings of his childhood, and became again a Pawnee. Those who returned to the reservation immediately upon graduation from Carlisle were even more rapidly drawn back into the mood of Indian life. Man does not live by bread alone, and the best that the government could claim it had given the Indian by education, was a means of making a living.

The government did not fail to apprehend that in the change of life from old Indian ways to the white man's civilization, the activities which of old had made the Indian men and women self-reliant and resolute were taken from them. The people no longer depended on the chiefs and leaders, and these on themselves; both looked to the agent for guidance and direction. The Indians neither made their own way of life, nor managed their own affairs. From cultural maturity as Pawnee they were reduced to cultural infancy as civilized men.

To counteract this tendency, however, there was only the weight of the government program to make the Pawnee self-maintaining farmers, to induce them to labor at manual pursuits, building their own houses, repairing their own implements, wagons and harness, and to give them the management of the freighting of their own supplies. In the later years a measure of self-government was introduced in the form of the Court of Indian Offenses.

Under the reservation system the only governmental authority was that of the Department of Indian Affairs, which, through the Department of the Interior, was part of the executive branch of the United States government. Laws and acts of Congress prescribed the manner in which the Department and its agencies were run, but for ordinary legal purposes on the reservation the agent in charge was sole arbiter. As soon as practicable a Court of Indian Offenses, by means of which the Indians adjudicated their own affairs, was instituted on an Indian reservation. Up to 1887 the tribes of the Pawnee Agency, including the Pawnee, Ponca, Oto and the Tonkawa, preferred to bring their troubles to the agent and accept his decision as final. In 1889 the Pawnee asked that a court of their own be established, and this was done December 1 of that year. The court was composed of three Pawnee judges, who sat the 3rd and 23rd of each month to hear cases on file. The proceedings were written down by a clerk. When the case had been heard each judge gave his decision, and the agreement of two carried. In the first year it functioned, the Pawnee Court of Indian Offenses tried twenty-four cases. These involved the settlement of Indian estates, the adjustment of debts, destruction of property, drunkenness and divorce. The Court continued to function until 1893 when the Pawnee, with the breaking up of their reservation became citizens of the United States and subject to Territorial Law. Along with the Court and its jurisdiction went the organization of the Indian Police. Earlier, in Nebraska, a force of Pawnee had at intervals policed the tribe. At first they were subject to the will of the chiefs, later they were directly responsible to the agent. In Oklahoma the force of eight policemen was responsible for the arrest and handling of those who came before the Court of Indian Offenses. Judges and policemen were paid small salaries by the government.

The disintegration of the old Pawnee culture which took place in the period from 1876 to 1892 was in part a correlative of the change in their economic and material life; in part however it was stimulated by direct government attack upon specific customs and ways.

Of their social and political life the power and control of the chiefs, priests and medicine men, and the customs of marriage and divorce, were directly opposed by officials. That the chiefs were finally losing power was not however a result either of the official opposition or altogether of the breaking up of the band villages; it flowed more directly from the gradual introduction of individualized property control. The traditional native view of a chief was that he was the "father" of his people, who must see to the well-being of every individual in the tribe. To do so the chief had to be able to control a larger quantity of property than the average individual in order to give and help wherever it was necessary. This he accomplished through his individual prowess on the war path and the hunt. But in addition, tribespeople who valued him as chief and leader contributed to his resources in order to aid him to maintain himself and succor his people. Individual ownership of homes and farms not only made individuals materially independent of the chief and tribe, but reduced the chief to a property equality with his tribespeople, making it impossible for him to continue the customs of paternal generosity which tradition commended to him. Without being able to give to and help the poor and distraught, the chief not only lost respect and self-respect, but he was unable to prove his supernatural right to leadership, or that fortune was with him, that the powers of the universe were on his side, and through him were guiding the people.

The agents did not understand this. They felt merely that the chief had power to command so long as the people lived clustered together around him. They expressed in their reports the hope that recognition of chiefs by the Department of Indian Affairs would become a memory.

The polygynous marriage customs of the Pawnee, based primarily on the sororate or marriage of younger sisters of the wife, were not interfered with up to 1881. Along with the way in which marriage was arranged by the parents without consulting the young people, and the ceremony itself, involving a transfer of horses and other property, Pawnee polygyny was, however, consistently considered reprehensible by officials. Polygyny as well as first marriages involved girls who were very young, often fourteen or fifteen. These were withdrawn from school at once, and as it was impossible to carry out an educational program which would send girls of such a tender age into the tribal life as civilizing influences, the practice of marrying them so young destroyed the efficiency of the school as an instrument of civilization. Divorce by mutual consent was a custom of the Pawnee, which involved a looseness of marital relations from the white standpoint.

Marriage customs were attacked in two ways: legally and ethically. Toward the close of this period the government program called for an attempt on the part of officials of the Indian service to insist upon civil marriage under the laws of the United States, to oppose wife-purchase and the marriage of the young girls, to register civilly the marriages of those living together in accordance with old customs, and to oppose easy separation and divorce. Since the individual men and women were becoming possessors of private property in the form of land, houses, stock and implements, by controlling the inheritance of estates in terms of the white man's law, and refusing to recognize "wives" not legally married, the program began to have an effect. After 1883 missionaries of the Home Missionary Society and the Methodist Episcopal Church worked in the tribe, and developed a small congregation of church members. The missionary influence was brought to bear against the Pawnee marriage usages from a moral angle. The agent cooperated with the missionaries in persuading the Pawnee to go through a Christian marriage ceremony as well as to secure a legal certificate. By 1890 officials claimed in their reports that the Pawnee were regularly seeking the missionary to perform the marriage ceremony for them; that by prompt action they had prevented all cases which came to their attention of "selling girls for ponies"; and that while polygyny had not been stamped out, there were no new cases of a wife being taken where the man already had a wife. A final claim was that divorces were unknown, or rare, which is to be doubted.

The dancing, gambling and feasting to which the tribe was addicted were marked out as dissipations contributing to indolence, and the agent by the most active measures at his command attempted to prevent social gatherings for such purposes as much as possible. In June 1891 the agent was surprised that the tribe assembled for a dance (probably a ceremony); he ordered it stopped at once and told the people to go to their homes and attend to their work. He could not however enforce his commands, and while some did go, most remained and carried out the dance. Such social affairs kept the people away from their farms for long periods, and the crops were neglected. In the old days the Pawnee methods of cultivation were adjusted to their calendric rituals, and by June, when the time for the hunt and summer ceremonies came, the crops were "laid by"; the tribe was not yet adjusted to intensive cultivation, involving constant care.

The conflict with the Pawnee medicine men was long and difficult. The government was determined to destroy their power over the people, and to persuade the Pawnee to depend on the agency physician. Unfortunately, except in a small part of the cases, the physician was notoriously unsuccessful in combating the diseases which were decimating the tribe; certainly he seemed no more successful than the native medicine man. The physician's services, paid for by government salary, were free to the people who sought his aid, while the native medicine man was paid in property by the patients he cured. Considering the medicine men charlatans and fakers, who deceived and befuddled the people, the officials regarded the customary compensation as extortion. But in spite of official antagonism the tribe was not drawn altogether away from their doctors: the Doctor Dances continued to be demonstrated, constituting practically the only major religious ceremonies which were demonstrated; and as late as 1888 an agent reported that the Pawnee "still have more confidence in their medicine men than the Queen of England has in McKenzie."

From a material standpoint, the close of this period found the Pawnee in a condition of partial adjustment to the new order, and relative prosperity. Most of the people were scattered on their farms, and doing well; they were accumulating stock around them. Between their government funds and their produce the tribe was practically self-sustaining.

In 1890 Grinnell described conditions upon the reservation: "As we came in sight of Black Bear Creek, I was surprised to see what looked like good farm houses dotting the distant bottom. ...Most well-to-do...Pawnees live in houses as good as those of many a New England land owner, and...better than those inhabited by new settlers in the farther West. Many...have considerable farms under fence, a barn, a garden in which vegetables are raised, and a peach orchard... By far the greater number wear civilized clothing, ride in wagons, and send their children to the agency school..."[1]

If their material life was at last approaching peace and security for the handful of Pawnee (759 in 1892) who had survived the long history of disasters, plagues and abuse, to what are we to attribute the revulsion against conditions which expressed itself in 1892 in the Ghost Dance? Before considering this aspect of the history of Pawnee acculturation, which will concern us in the next chapter, let us turn briefly to a recapitulation of the status of Pawnee culture in 1892.

---

[1] Grinnell, Pawnee Hero Stories and Folk Tales, pp. 400—401.

CULTURAL STATUS AT THE DAWN OF THE GHOST DANCE

By 1892 the aboriginal Pawnee culture of a century earlier had been profoundly altered. A tribe of villagers, accustomed to living in earth-lodges and tipis, and to maintaining themselves by digging-stick cultivation of corn, beans and squash, and by hunting the buffalo, had become a loose aggregate of people, living more or less in families on separate farm tracts, dependent for their maintenance in part on plow cultivation of the land, and in part on the philanthropy of their overlords, the United States government.

From a political and social standpoint the Pawnee had been transformed from an independent self-determining nation into a group of families subject to the will of representatives of an alien race. The Pawnee chiefs were chiefs only in name and ancient lineage; what power they had among the Pawnee flowed from a continuing respect for their origins and their conduct. But no directing leadership in the destiny of the tribe was open to the chiefs; they could decide what they wished in council; it must then be submitted to the approval and sanction of the Agent, a representative of another government which ruled them.

The hunt and the warpath were gone, and with them the activities of youth and early manhood, which, in terms of the tradition and beliefs of their race, gave value to the life of a man. The hazard and danger of life as they had lived it before made them energetic, active and self-reliant. He who did not depend upon himself was lost. Now there was always the annuity, the agent, and rations. For women the life had also been radically altered. Their former routine had been a difficult and laborious one, working in the fields, making tent covers and clothing, cooking, and tending the children. But it had been part of a life which had broad and deep meaning as a way of life, in which their function was basic and valuable.

The family relationships which had brought all the people close together in their villages were broken down with the substitution of frame houses on the farms for the old earth-lodge. In the earth-lodge a large, extended family lived together; the family line cohered around the women. On the farms the frame house was built for a man as head of a family, and was primarily for the small, limited family group as conceived by the white man.

From a material standpoint the arts and techniques which had been practised for centuries by the people, carried to practical perfection as their form of adjustment to the conditions of the world in which they lived, were broken down by the appearance of a new set of conditions in which they were no longer necessary or possible.

The extinction of the buffalo and the complete cessation of hunting meant the elimination of all the arts which had centered around the handling of skins. Tipis were no longer necessary; buffalo robes were not as good as blankets; the preparation of skin clothing was a thankless task when the agent issued the appurtenances of the white man for the asking. The technique of using wood for bowls and utensils, for mortar and pestle, for traps and bows and arrows, was passing into oblivion. The working of horn and bone, of which spoons and ladles had been made, was unnecessary in view of the ease with which the white man's pots and pans and utensils could be had. Pottery of clay had already become extinct for lack of use and function.

The beliefs and philosophies of men to be alive must be inherent in and consonant with the way by which men live. When the men no longer hunted the buffalo, when they no longer needed power and invulnerability on the warpath, when the women no longer had to contribute fertility to the fields they planted, the ancient cosmology of the Pawnee was without a reference. The ritual lore of the great sacred bundles of the tribe was handed on less and less; it died with priests who, increasingly subject to death as the mortality of the tribe increased year by year, had neither time nor inspiration to hand it on. The ceremonies, becoming functionless, became extinct.

Once the young men of the tribe joined in many brotherhoods. These societies of men concerned themselves with the activities of manhood in Pawnee life, hunting and war. Each had special powers and functions for aiding in the successful accomplishment of the ends of war and the hunt, powers derived from the greater bundles which came directly from the ruling forces of the world. These societies too became functionless, and as the membership died off, the brotherhoods no longer met to dance and sing.

The chiefs had constituted a brotherhood of their own. When youths became men, and took upon themselves the serious business of maintaining the welfare of the tribe, they could, by demonstrating in their daily behavior their growing wisdom and capacity for leadership, become eligible to sit in the society of the chiefs. The forms of the chief's society ritual was carried on down into the present; much that was of value in the old ethics of the tribe was still explained to the youths even a year ago by the few who had not forgotten. But here again, the paramount functions of the society were gone.

The medicine men of the tribe carried on. The Doctor Dances were given year after year; although after 1878 the great Doctor Performances through which the medicine men renewed their powers were no longer demonstrated. The function of the doctors did not disappear; health became a possession more difficult to secure as the years passed. But against the white man's diseases the folk medicine of the Pawnee doctors proved essentially futile; as did the white man's medicine itself.

With the passing of the greater part of the old ritualism and ceremony, the arts of ceremonial decoration, of making ritual costumes, bear-claw necklaces, otter-skin collars, of painting the body, went with them. The Doctor Dances kept something of the ritual decorative arts alive.

If we turn from this catalog of the decline of aboriginal Pawnee culture what can we see that had come to take its place ? Needing the Indian's land for the expansion of the white man, the government was compelled to give the Indian an economy which would be self-sustaining while it confined the tribe in narrower boundaries. It gave the Indian farming. This being seasonal, and subject to the vicissitudes of the elements, it did not mean independence. For a meat supply the Indian did not use his own resources; the government gave him meat. When his crops failed, the government rationed him.

What occupations took the place of the old ? The boys learned some manual arts. They could help to build their own houses, to repair their implements; the girls meanwhile learned some sewing, how to wash clothing, how to keep house. All these were essentially mechanical operations; their aesthetic returns are for the most part small. What creative satisfaction was to be had in manual arts, the boys did achieve in harness-making, carpentering, wagon-making, and the like, where they had opportunity to put into practise what they had learned.

The small measure of self-government which the Indians were offered through the Court of Indian Offenses was subject to the paternal control of the Agent and the government; it was concerned after all with the minor legal problems of their life. It helped to revive something of self-determination.

If we turn finally to the intellectual side of Pawnee life we find that practically nothing came to take the place of the old rituals and ceremonies, the old dances and social gatherings, the old traditions and songs. Missionaries had been among the Pawnee from 1835 to 1837, and again there were missionaries after 1883.

With what results ? In 1891 even the optimistic reports of the missionaries claimed only thirty-five church members, and twenty or more years later not over a seventh of the tribe even professed Christianity, according to official reports.

In 1892, after the best efforts of the Pawnee for over three generations to adjust themselves to living alongside the white man, the tribe had come to a cultural impasse, with nothing to look forward to and nothing to live by.

II
THE GHOST DANCE AMONG THE PAWNEE[1]

THE GHOST DANCE: ORIGIN AND SPREAD

The Ghost Dance religion of 1890 arose in the visions of Wovoka, the Paiute Messiah, about 1888, although its roots lie deeper in the past. Wovoka is said to have been a son of Ta'vibo the Paiute prophet of 1870, whose doctrines had been the stimulus of the Ghost Dance which swept through the tribes of northern California in the years from 1871 to 1874. The doctrines of the son do not seem to have differed materially from those of the father.

As a child Wovoka was brought up in a household where he could not fail to be influenced by the practices of the medicine man. He was known as a medicine man for some years before he developed the Ghost Dance doctrine. In January 1889, at the time of a total eclipse of the sun visible in Nevada, Wovoka was sick with a severe fever. He was then about 33 years of age. In the tribe the eclipse caused frantic excitement. "The air was filled with the noise of shouts and wailings and the firing of guns." The people were trying to drive away the monster who was devouring the sun.

Wovoka fell asleep, or "died," and "was taken up into the other world. Here he saw God with all the people who had long ago died engaged in their old time sports and occupations, all happy and forever young. It was a pleasant land and full of game... God told him he must go back and tell his people they must be good and love one another, have no quarreling and live in peace with the whites; that they must work, and not lie and steal; that they must put away the old practices that savored of war; that if they faithfully obeyed his instructions they would at last be reunited with their friends in the other world, where there would be no more death or sickness or old age. He was then given the dance which he was commanded to bring back to his people. By performing

---

[1] Informants: Mark Evarts, Ezra Tilden, Joseph Carrion and Mrs. Goodeagle, all of whom played roles in the Ghost Dance developments among the Pawnee. Published sources consulted: Murie, Societies; Mooney, Ghost Dance; Annual Reports of the Commissioner of Indian Affairs (see bibliography).

this dance at intervals, for five successive days each time, they would secure this happiness to themselves and hasten the event. Finally God gave him control over the elements so that he could make it rain or snow or be dry at will, and appointed him his deputy to take charge of affairs in the west... He then returned to earth, and he began to preach as he was directed, convincing the people by exercising the wonderful powers that he had given him."[1]

Wovoka had "five songs for making it rain, the first of which brings on a mist or cloud, the second a snowfall, the third a shower, and the fourth a hard rain or storm, while when he sings the fifth song, the weather again becomes clear."[2]

The first dancing among the Paiute involved no trances. But the people of the various Nevada reservations made their own interpretations of Wovoka's purpose and doctrine; they spread the word that Christ himself had come, and that people should dance. Wovoka never claimed to be the Son of God; he sincerely believed he was a prophet with a divine revelation to impart.

The doctrine initiated by Wovoka spread with startling rapidity. Conditions of communication among the Indian tribes were not what they had been aboriginally. A great many of the younger men who had been away to government schools returned with a knowledge of reading and writing, and having made firm friendships with boys of other tribes while at school, corresponded at intervals with them. By letter as well as by word of mouth the news spread that the Messiah had come.

The first spread of the Ghost Dance was from the Paiute of the Walker River reservation to their neighbors immediately around them: the scattered bands of Paiute in Nevada and Oregon, the Washo living alongside them, the Bannock, Ute and Gosiute, and the Shoshoni of the Fort Hall reservation in Idaho. From this central Rocky Mountain region the religion spread in three general directions: to some of the tribes north and south of the nucleus formed by the Paiute and their immediate neighbors; into the northern Plains; and into the southern Plains.

In 1889 the Ghost Dance was taken up almost simultaneously by the eastern neighbors of the Paiute: the Bannock, Shoshoni, Gosiute and Ute. To the north it reached the Pit River Indians in northern California in 1890. Mohave delegates came in 1890 to investigate reports which had reached them from the southern Paiute and through them the Ghost Dance penetrated southward to the Walapai, the Chemehuevi, and the Havasupai of Cataract

---

[1] Mooney, 771—772.

[2] Ibid., 772—773.

Canyon, reaching the Mission Indians in southern California in 1891.

In the spread of the Ghost Dance into the Plains, the Bannock and Shoshoni Indians of the Fort Hall Reservation in Idaho were instrumental. It was a Bannock Indian from Ft. Hall who early in 1889 visited the Shoshoni and northern Arapaho of the Wind River reservation in Wyoming bearing the news of the doctrine. That very summer these tribes sent delegates to find the Messiah in Mason Valley and learn the facts, and on the return of the delegation that fall the tribes of the Wind River reservation began the Ghost Dance.

The Arapaho and Shoshoni of Wind River now became in turn the transmitters of the Ghost Dance doctrine to the tribes of the northern Plains. A Gros Ventre from the Ft. Belknap agency was a visitor among the Arapaho, when in 1889 the delegates returned from their journey to see the Messiah. He heard the news and took it home with him to the Gros Ventre and Assiniboin on the Ft. Belknap reservation. In the fall of the same year northern Cheyenne from Montana, and Teton and Yankton Dakota[1] came to Wind River to verify among the Arapaho and Shoshoni the reports which had reached them of a Messiah and a resurrection. Some of the Cheyenne returned home at once with their report, but a number, accompanied by several Shoshoni and Arapaho continued westward with the Dakota. They left the Wind River reservation in November 1889, proceeding to the Fort Hall reservation in Idaho where they found the Bannock and Shoshoni dancing. Continuing their journey to visit the Messiah himself, all the Indians with whom they came in contact from the Fort Hall reservation until they reached Wovoka at Walker Lake were dancing the Ghost Dance. Several Shoshoni and Bannock from Fort Hall joined the party; they went by railroad to Pyramid Lake, Nevada, and thence by wagon to Mason Valley.

In the early spring of 1890 Porcupine and his northern Cheyenne companions had returned to the tribe on the Tongue River reservation in Montana, bringing the news.

Dakota Sioux had been along on the journey; the news had first reached the Oglala division of the Teton Dakota at Pine Ridge reservation in 1889. As a result of the pilgrimage the doctrine penetrated to the Sioux at the Ft. Peck reservation in Montana,

---

[1] Miss Ella Deloria tells me that Yankton Dakota did not take up the Ghost Dance. Mooney refers broadly to "Sioux of the Dakotas," failing to distinguish Yankton and Yanktonai participation in the movement and leaving open the implication that all took part.

and at the Standing Rock, Cheyenne River, Lower Brulé, Pine Ridge, and Rosebud reservations in North and South Dakota. It swept like wildfire through the Teton and Yankton Dakota; 20,000 of the Dakota became active in Ghost Dancing.

It was not long after the northern Arapaho and Shoshoni of the Wind River reservation had visited Wovoka in the summer of 1889 that the doctrine began to penetrate the tribes of the southern Plains. Letters from their kinsmen in the north told the southern Arapaho and Cheyenne in Oklahoma in the summer of 1889 what was going on. A delegate from the southern Arapaho was at Wind River agency when the pilgrims of the northern tribes had returned from Nevada to report. He joined the Ghost Dance there, and returned in April 1890 to the Arapaho and Cheyenne of Oklahoma. He inaugurated the dance among these tribes, becoming a leading prophet, Black Coyote. The Cheyenne of Oklahoma then sent their own delegates to visit their northern kinsmen; these returned with a favorable report, and the southern Cheyenne took up the dance the summer of 1890.

That fall saw the great development of the Ghost Dance in the southern Plains. Sitting-Bull, prophet of the Ghost Dance among the northern Arapaho, came to Oklahoma to instruct the tribes there in the doctrine and the forms of the dance. A great dance was held in September on the South Canadian River, near the Darlington Agency. There were present, besides the southern Cheyenne and Arapaho, the Caddo, the Wichita, Kiowa and Kiowa Apache. The second day of the dance, Sitting-Bull carried out his promise to show the people great things, by putting many dancers into hypnotic trances, the first time this was known in the Ghost Dance of the southern Plains. Sitting-Bull was at this time instrumental in persuading the southern Cheyenne and Arapaho to sign an agreement with the government by which they relinquished much of their reservation land for payment. He told them that they needed the money, and that the Messiah would soon restore the land to them. In spite of the failure by this time of a number of prophecies of the time when the resurrection and change would occur, the dance continued to spread.

After the great dance of September 1890 the Caddo, Delaware, Wichita, Kitsai, Kiowa, Kiowa Apache and Comanche took up the movement. Sitting-Bull visited the Caddo personally in December 1890, and, after instructing them by means of the sign language, "gave the feather" to the seven chosen as leaders of the Caddo Ghost Dance. At first the Caddo used Arapaho songs; then developed their own. The Delaware danced with them.

The Wichita and Kitsai first took over the dance from the Caddo. But in February, 1891, Sitting Bull was again in Oklahoma. He came to visit the Wichita and inducted the seven Wichita leaders ceremonially into office.

The same month a Kiowa who had been to visit Wovoka had returned, and as word spread that he had important news for all the tribes, a great council was held February 19, 1891 at Anadarko. Apiatan, the Kiowa, had a discouraging report to communicate. He faced the great multitude and told them that the reports of the great powers of the Messiah were false. The Messiah did not speak all languages, but only Paiute; he was not omniscient, for he had asked Apiatan who he was and why he had come; and he had no scars on his hands and feet, so he was not Christ. Wovoka had refused to call spirits of Apiatan's deceased relatives into their presence, saying he could not do so. By this time the Messiah was astounded at the forces he had set in motion. The Sioux Ghost Dance disasters of 1890 to 1891 were blamed on him. He told Apiatan that the Sioux had twisted everything up; he told him to go home to his people and tell them to stop dancing.

Sitting-Bull was present, and rose to answer. He told the people again what Wovoka had said to him the year before. Apiatan replied that it was not true; that Sitting-Bull was deceiving the people for mercenary gain. Sitting-Bull replied that the many horses he had received had not been asked for; and that those who had lost faith and wished them back could come and receive them.

This adverse report stopped the Kiowa from dancing for a time. They revived the Ghost Dance in 1894. But the other tribes who heard the report, including the Kiowa Apache, refused to believe it. They said Apiatan had been bought by the government to deceive the Indians in this way. They continued dancing. Apiatan received a medal from President Harrison.

In 1891 Frank White, a Pawnee Indian, was among the southern Oklahoma tribes who were Ghost Dancing; he participated in dances among the Comanche and Wichita, learned the doctrine, and observed the early forms in which the dancing was at that time organized according to the instruction of Sitting-Bull, the northern Arapaho. In the late summer of 1891 he returned north to the Pawnee.

The Cheyenne and Arapaho became the most inspired leaders of the movement in the south. They sent several delegations to visit Wovoka. One of these in the fall of 1891 brought back a message from Wovoka which had been written down by a delegate in broken English. I quote part of Mooney's version[1]:

[1] Mooney, p. 781.

"When you get home you must make a dance to continue five days. Dance four successive nights, and the last night keep up the dance until the morning of the fifth day, when all must bathe in the river and then disperse to their homes. You must all do in the same way...

"When your friends die you must not cry. You must not hurt anybody or do harm to anyone. You must not fight. Do right always. It will give you satisfaction in life...

"Do not tell the white people about this. Jesus is now upon earth. He appears like a cloud. The dead are all alive again. I do not know when they will be here; maybe this fall or in the spring. When the time comes there will be no more sickness and everyone will be young again.

"Do not refuse to work for the whites and do not make any trouble with them until you leave them. When the earth shakes do not be afraid. It will not hurt you.

"I want you to dance every six weeks. Make a feast at the dance and have food that everybody may eat. Then bathe in the water. That is all. You will receive good words again from me some time. Do not tell lies."

Up to the time of this direct communication the tribes in the southern plains had been holding one-day Ghost Dances at irregular intervals. The Cheyenne, Arapaho, Wichita and Caddo thereafter adopted the new rule, organizing five-day dances at intervals of six weeks, in accordance with the instructions of the Messiah.

Delegates from the Cheyenne and Arapaho of Oklahoma brought the Ghost Dance directly to the Ponca, the Oto and Missouri, the Iowa and Kansa.

The rapidity with which the Ghost Dance spread from the Paiute center through the plateau and into the plains was in part due to the increased rapidity and ease of communication. Such a speedy diffusion could not have happened under aboriginal conditions. But the full explanation lies deeper. Those tribes who accepted the doctrine at once were, like the Pawnee whom we are especially considering, at a cultural impasse. Those tribes who rejected the doctrine were either in an aboriginal state in which the values of their old life still to a certain extent functioned, or they were under the influence of specific religions brought to them by missionaries, or, as in the case of the Navaho and Osage, they were well off materially, and did not feel the need of the new doctrine. In 1870 a Ghost Dance movement, stemming from the doctrines of Wovoka's father, had spread with an almost equal rapidity through Californian tribes. The dance of 1890 did not affect those tribes. Conversely the movement of 1870 did not penetrate the Plains. Kroeber has suggested that in 1870 the Plains tribes had not been reduced to such a state of cultural decay as to make them susceptible to revivalistic doctrine, while the Californian tribes had been overrun some years before in the gold rush and by 1870 their old culture had been destroyed. Kroeber also considers that the experiences of the Californian peoples in 1870 to 1874 made them impassive to a second wave of similar doctrine.[1]

The doctrines of Wovoka as revealed in what he told Mooney of his vision experiences, and in the message he gave the Cheyenne and Arapaho, are clearly doctrines of peace. In only one region where the Ghost Dance was taken up was this aspect forgotten. The western Dakota, from of old militaristic in their antagonism to the whites and the changes taking place in their lives, accustomed to taking an active and resistant part, transformed the doctrine from one of peaceful faith and hope, into one of war. The rapport with the supernatural achieved in the dance was not only a guarantee of eventual participation in the new resurrected life, but it gave invulnerability in battle. The attitude of the Sioux culminated in blunders on the part of American army men, and brought on the conflicts of 1890 to 1891 and the Massacre at Wounded Knee. The Sioux troubles made government officials suspicious of Ghost Dancing wherever it occurred, and it was put down with all the force agents could muster, in order to prevent anticipated bloody revolt. Elsewhere, however, the doctrine remained one of peace, a simple hope that a change was coming which would give the Indians back their land, their buffalo and their old life. The message and vision of Wovoka emphasized that in the new life disease and death would be no more, an aspiration full of hope to a people like the Pawnee, who for generations had been undergoing the worst ravages of disease with their loved and venerated ones dying all about them.

DOCTRINE AND EARLY HISTORY OF THE PAWNEE GHOST DANCE

As early as 1890 rumors had reached the Pawnee of a Messiah who had appeared to an Indian somewhere in the mountains. He was supposed to have visited the dead people, and to have

[1] A. L. Kroeber, Handbook of the Indians of California, p. 869.

seen them dancing in a circle.[1] Nothing authentic and substantiated reached the tribe, however, until the fall of 1891[2] when Frank White came home to the Pawnee after his stay with the Wichita.

The Pawnee tell of White's learning the Ghost Dance among the southern tribes in the following way:

"One time Frank White went over to the Comanche, who were dancing the Ghost Dance. He went inside and sat down on the north side. He ate peyote, a great deal, until he was nearly overcome. He bent his head and covered his eyes. He was a goodlooking man who used to wear decorative red twine over his brow. The Comanche did not know him, and the next morning they asked him who he was, and he said he was a Pawnee. Then he left them and went to the Wichita. He ate peyote there, and watched them dance the Ghost Dance and learned it. Then he came home and brought it to the South Bands. He told them what he had learned."

The period during which Frank White studied the Ghost Dance among the Comanche and the Wichita was in the year following the great Ghost Dance of the fall of 1890, led by Sitting-Bull. The forms of leadership and organization he learned were those preached by Sitting-Bull, and initiated by him personally among the Caddo and Wichita.

Murie has spoken of White's experiences in the south. "Frank White... joined the dance. He went into a trance, saw the stream, the tree, the Messiah and then the village of people.[3] He also saw them dance, joined in, and learned some songs which were in Pawnee. The first song was as follows[4]:

we	*rįhi*	*írasï·ra*
now	place where	yonder you come

	wetįkuwatu	*rạwahe*
	now I long for	the $\begin{cases} \text{village} \\ \text{region} \end{cases}$

---

[1] Murie, Societies, pp. 630—632, recounts a long narrative of the story which was supposed to have reached the Pawnee in 1890.

[2] Murie, Societies, p. 633, says "in the fall of 1892." This is a misprint or a slip on Murie's part. In the account which follows Murie describes events of a winter and summer which intervene between White's return to the Pawnee and his arrest; White was arrested in 1892. Furthermore, we can date the time White left the Wichita by the fact that he left before the Arapaho delegation arrived in the fall of 1891 with the message from Wovoka, which, in spite of the objections of Sitting-Bull, necessitated a change in the form of the Ghost Dancing.

[3] Murie is doubtless referring here to the narrative of Wovoka's vision as known to the Pawnee which he gives, pp. 630—632.

[4] The form I quote here is a retranscription and retranslation of Murie's printed version, written by Dr. Gene Weltfish.

we   *rḷhi*   *irasĭ·ra*

a   *tsiksu*   *wétatŭ·ta*   *hi i*

and   { mind   now I do
      { spirit

The place whence you come,
Now I am longing for.

The place whence you come,
Now I am ever mindful of.

When he awoke from the trance he told the people what he had seen. Thus, he too became a prophet and possessed of the same power as Sitting-Bull."[1]

Frank White was a Kitkahaxki[x]. When he returned home to the Pawnee in the fall of 1891 he began to teach the doctrine and songs to friends of his in the South Bands. He told people, "The kingdom is coming soon now, so the people must prepare. This that I have is called ghost dancing. You must stop working because when the kingdom comes you won't take plows or things like that along. That's not ours."

When Frank White instituted regular dances, these were among the South Bands; the Skiri would come over and join in under his leadership. The first songs were Arapaho and Wichita songs and the few songs that White had already developed for himself. White taught songs to several singers who assisted him in leading the dancing. He organized the group of seven leaders who wore crow feathers. The dancing took place in the open, east of a tipi in which White and his co-leaders gathered. At first the crowds which gathered were small, but many of them shook as the spirits took possession of them and fell. White had great power over them, and when his voice grew louder dancers would fall under the spell. White would talk to the people and tell them his experiences and how when they fell they would see the Messiah and all the dead people, and how this was a promise of the coming change.

Those who first participated told others, and the excitement grew. Many were converted rapidly, and the crowds which came to dance under White's leadership grew larger. The arrangements gradually altered to take care of the crowds. White and his singers had their special tipi. Two of his leaders gathered paint among the people and took this into the sacred tipi. Here all the dancers who wished to have face paintings for the dance would go. Each one gave White presents in return for a face painting or a feather orna-

[1] Murie, Societies, p. 632—633.

ment. When all were dressed and painted for the dance, White and his singers came out onto the open space east of the sacred tipi, and formed the gathering into a circle. All joined hands, and with White and his singers leading in the songs, they danced round and round. Others rushed over to the dance ground to join in. Many shook and fell. White and his leaders put others into trances, and great excitement prevailed.

In the evening they stopped to eat, and then continued dancing until late at night. From time to time those who fell would get up and tell what they had seen. Each had a message from the other world, and had learned songs. These visions became sanctions not only for special developments of the Ghost Dance, and of the hand games, but also for important revivals of old aspects of Pawnee life, which before this had ceased to function.

One evening all the Pawnee were gathered together where the South Band people lived. White was conducting the ceremonies. It was a fine clear evening, near sunset, with clouds across the sky in the west. The clouds in the sky across the west were like people sitting in a row. White told the people, "Now if you all come out here in the open where there is no timber, you can plainly see the people in the west. Those are the dead people. They are all waiting there. Now you see them. Pretty soon now the high wind will come and all the white people on earth will be blown away. Those (here he referred to Behaile, Dorf Carian, Harry Coons, James Murie, Rice, Pepan—all half breeds), such as they are the wind will pick up too, even if they are half breeds, because they don't believe in this dance. These believe in the white man's church. The wind will throw them against the heavy trees and crush them. The people who believe will be saved, because when the wind blows the white people away, they will all be left standing here. Those who believe will be shaken and fall down, and after they arise and open their eyes there will be no white people here. The buffalo will be here; everything will be just as it was before the white people came, and all our deceased folk, our fathers, our mothers, our grandfathers and our grandmothers, will be here with us."

All the people stood and watched these clouds in the west. All the people believed it, except a few. When the clouds were gone they all went home.

One young man lay in a trance all night. White wanted all the people to hear his story, so in the evening of the next day, he ordered all the people onto a hill. There they stood in line facing west,[1] and the young man sat down facing them with the crier by his side. He said,

"When I joined in the dance I was filled with some kind of a spirit. I began to tremble and cry. I saw a strange being who wanted to catch me. I ran out of the ring and kept running away from the strange man. When he caught up with me I could see many wonderful things. He told me that if I stopped he would teach me the wonderful things I saw. I would not do this for I wanted to see some of my dead people. I ran until I was exhausted and could go no further and fell down as one dead. I was in a beautiful country where the grass was green. I saw a small pathway which I followed. I came to a clear stream of water and crossed it. Then I came to a cedar tree; on it were feathers of different birds and handkerchiefs of many colors. I took one of red silk and passed on. On a small hill I saw the Child of the Father in the Heavens dressed in purple. He held out his hands so I could see the cuts in them. He did not speak but I knew he wanted me to pass. I went by him and I saw at a distance the village of our dead people. As I neared the village four men came to meet me, each with a pipe in his hand. One of them said, 'My son, when you return to your people tell them you saw us and that we ask our people for a smoke. We are about to smoke to our people who are still living through the one who is leading us to your land. Go into the village and see your people.' I passed them and went on. Near the village I saw a woman. It was my mother. She embraced me and said, 'My child, I am glad to see you. We will go where our people are dancing.' So we went on and there in the center of the village our people were dancing the same dance we were dancing. I joined them and men came to me and blew their breaths upon me. I danced a while then one man asked me to tell you that I had seen the dance and that it was all true. He then told me to return, and when I turned round I awoke. I had been lying on the ground for some time. This is the end of what I saw."[2]

[1] This is the ceremonial arrangement followed later in smoking and opening the dance; see below.

[2] Murie, p. 634. This is the tradition of the way in which the smoke offering was introduced into Pawnee Ghost Dance arrangements.

In the vision two minor points are worth calling attention to. The dead blessed the young man in the Pawnee way when they blew their breath upon him. The closing statement, "this is the end," etc. follows the Pawnee literary form of myths and stories.

More significant is the suggestion of Christ as "leading the people," an identification of Christ with chieftainship, which concept determined important ritual aspects of the Pawnee Ghost Dance and Ghost Dance hand games.

This young man was blessed by the people, and they also took a blessing from him. But when they touched him many fell or trembled. "After this four men were selected to smoke to the dead people."[1]

Murie also tells the interesting story of an unbeliever.

"A woman entered the ring and began to act as if crazy. She slapped a man and struck a woman and continued to slap and strike people. Everyone sat down. This woman stood in the center and said, 'That young man, the prophet, is lying. He is not telling the truth.' Two men whom the chiefs had previously selected to act as police took her out of the ring and took her home as the prophet directed, for he said she was possessed of a bad spirit. The next day the prophet and his singers took this woman to the creek and cleansed her. Afterwards she joined the dance again and was all right."[2]

Dancing was sporadic during the winter of 1891, but gradually the dances followed each other in rapid succession. With few exceptions by 1892 the Pawnee were under White's influence and control. The situation forced itself upon official attention early in that year. "In February 1892 the Pawnee commenced what is known as a 'Ghost Dance', dancing in a circle, falling down in a trance, and after some hours they awake and profess to have seen their dead friends. About two-thirds of the tribe seemed at this time to be possessed of the idea of the second coming of Christ, to destroy all the whites and to bring back the buffalo and the wild game."[3]

On account of the coming end of the world, and the uselessness of continuing work in the face of the expected changes which would bring back old times and the deceased relatives of the living, all those who became convinced of the Ghost Dance doctrine stopped work. Many left their plows in the field standing just as they had been in the midst of their work cultivating their corn.

As soon as the agent in charge of the Pawnee received word at the agency in Ponca City that the Pawnee were Ghost-Dancing, he wrote to the clerk in charge at the Pawnee agency to put a stop to the dancing immediately. "But the Indians seemed defiant and aggressive and it seemed at this time that trouble might be anticipated. Knowing that all religious fanatics are persistent and determined, I at once went to Pawnee and visited the camp of the so-called prophet Frank White, and after talking with him

---

[1] Murie, op. cit.
[2] Murie, p. 635.
[3] Agent D. J. M. Wood, in Annual Report, 1891—1892.

and ascertaining his views, I told him he was an impostor and I wanted him at once to leave the reservation never to return. The next morning 200 Indians came to the agency and demanded a council. They were painted in high colors and seemed aggressive and defiant. After the arrival of an interpreter I opened the council in a two hours' talk on the coming of Christ and the true Messiah and the false Messiah as professed by them, and I plainly told them that the dance could not be tolerated and would not be; that this government would last and assert her power, and that they should be obedient to the law and be good Indians, return to their homes and cultivate their farms and raise something to eat. After they had spoken professing loyalty to the government and obedience to the law, they broke the council and returned to their homes."[1]

Although the effort to put a stop to Ghost Dancing continued, and officials would seek out meetings and try to break them up, the Pawnee were nevertheless gathering in secret to dance.

"At one camp about five miles east of the agency they decided one night to Ghost Dance. Word spread among the Indian folk and they gathered in numbers at the camp. There was one old man, George Esau, who had a great loud voice. The people were dancing in the moonlight. At night the echo goes a long way. When he cried out it could be heard clear over at the agency. One Indian who lived a mile north of town came on horseback to tell them. He said Esau's voice could be heard away over toward the west. 'The police may come; they can hear him.' Whenever they tried to quiet Esau he became worse, and his voice louder, and the people became afraid of him. Then they let him alone and stopped dancing, because they didn't want the agents to find out."[2]

It was in the midst of this year of excitement in the life of the Pawnee that the government had elected to carry out a further step in its program of civilizing the Pawnee and turning them into citizens. The plan was to complete the allotment of tracts in severalty among the Pawnee. Those who had already chosen plots and were living on them and cultivating the land were to be confirmed in their possession. All others must take them out. The Pawnee who had not as yet chosen to farm individual tracts were of course those who were most strongly opposed to the program. Furthermore the plan laid before the tribe involved the sale of their surplus lands after the Pawnee were provided with allotments per capita, and the opening of these lands to settlement by

---

[1] Agent D. J. M. Wood, in Annual Report, 1891—1892.
[2] Informant's narrative.

white people. This meant essentially the final break-up of reservation life.

The commissioners to draw up the agreement with the Pawnee for the allotment of lands in severalty and the sale of surplus acreage was due the agency. It was at this time that the agent was compelled to take further steps to stop the Ghost Dancing.

The agent reported on the episode as follows: "In about two weeks thereafter news again reached me of the renewal of the Ghost Dance. I procured the assistance of a deputy United States marshal and he went to Pawnee and arrested the supposed prophet Frank White, and took him to Guthrie, Oklahoma, before a United States Commissioner, and he was held over until district court for inciting Indians to an insurrection, and remanded to jail to await his trial before the district court. In about ten days I received a telegram that a writ of habeas corpus had been issued and the hearing was the next day. I at once went to Guthrie and was at the hearing when Judge Green, chief justice of Oklahoma, gave him a good strong talk, telling him of the danger of indulging in such things, and released him. He went back to the reservation, and there has not been a Ghost Dance since. All is prosperous and serene at Pawnee . . ."[1]

The Pawnee recall the arrest as taking place at the time of trouble over the question of allotments. Officials spread the word in the tribe that if they took out allotments they could dance all they wanted to, and no one would interfere with them. This of course was a reference to the fact that the program which the government wanted to carry out would break up the reservation, and make the Pawnee individual land holders subject to the laws of the United States and the Territory in which they lived, in which event the agent would no longer have executive power to control them. This argument for taking out allotments had weight with many, and contributed to their final acquiescence.

To keep the Pawnee quiet for a while, they say the agent had White arrested. A United States marshall and three Indian policemen, recalled as Harry Coons, John Morris and Jim Murie, arrested White, and it was understood by the Pawnee he was being taken to Red Rock. The Pawnee decided to fight to get the Prophet back. David Akapakis and some others took the lead and organized a party of men who got their guns and were going to fight. They gathered at the railroad station to take him away from the marshall. Said an informant, "The agent sent a telegram to a fort which was among the Cheyenne, and when the train came in a lot

---

[1] Annual Report, 1891—92.

of soldiers got off. There were too many soldiers so the Pawnee couldn't fight. The marshall took White away and the Indians went home."

It was while White was away under arrest that most of the Pawnee who had been opposed were persuaded to choose allotments. They wanted to continue the Ghost Dance, and having been told they could dance if they took allotments, they did so. It must be remembered that in dividing up their land, and selling a good part of it, the Pawnee were doing something which was opposed to the faith and doctrine of the Ghost Dance. On the other hand, for those who were strong in their faith, the act was meaningless, since the change which would destroy the white man would restore them their lands in their aboriginal state.

Frank White was held ten or twelve days, and brought back. According to Murie, after White's release, the Messiah himself did what he could to develop the Ghost Dance movement along less militant lines. "To do this he magnified the Christian elements."

In pursuance of the government land program, a special allotting agent, with clerical assistants, came to the Pawnee Agency in the summer of 1892. After the completion of their work, during which a total of 797 allotments in severalty were drawn up, the United States Commissioners came, empowered to treat with the Pawnee for the sale of their surplus lands. On November 23, 1892 they completed their agreement with the Pawnee. By it the allotments were confirmed; 840 acres were reserved for the school, agency, cemetery and religious purposes; and the residue of their reservation, 169,320 acres, was purchased to be thrown open to settlement. In compensation for their lands the government paid the Pawnee an advance of $80,000 to be distributed per capita upon the ratification of the agreement by act of Congress; and agreed to continue their perpetual annuity of $30,000 a year, thenceforth to be issued entirely in money.[1] The balance of the return from the sale of their Oklahoma lands was to be deposited in the United States Treasury as a trust fund to the credit of the Pawnee tribe, to draw interest at 5 per cent annually, which interest was to be distributed per capita.

The agreement was ratified March 3, 1893; and that year the lands ceded by the Pawnee were thrown open to white settlement. In selecting tracts for allotments the Pawnee had naturally been guided by the quality of the land. As a result the lands ceded and opened to white settlement were scattered all over what had been the Pawnee reservation, and before the year was out the tribe found

---

[1] Up to this time the annuity was half money, half goods and supplies.

white settlers in among them and on all sides of them. Almost at
once a town sprang up near the agency, the present Pawnee.

The Pawnee soon found that their legal status had changed; the
agent no longer had executive power to control their acts and
behavior. The people were now free citizens of the United States.
The white people who settled among them and were anxious to do
business with a tribe whose income, between their down payment,
annuity, and interests, was $ 177,000 in 1893, were quick to tell
them so. Then came the lease system for the Indian farm lands.
But that is another story. What concerns us here is the effect of
this change of status upon the Ghost Dance among the Pawnee.

At first, in 1893, the agent believed that by his prompt measures
with Frank White the year before, he had stamped out the Ghost
Dance. He wrote in his report, July 15, 1893: "This dance has
almost disappeared... There is some religious enthusiasm in
which they indulge and makes them more tractable and easy to
manage, as they say they must do right under all circumstances."
The agent felt that the tribe was well satisfied with their allotments,
and was prosperous and united.

We, however, can note that this religious enthusiasm was none
other than the Ghost Dance, in view of the ethical maxims quoted by
the agent, but that from the official standpoint the movement had
lost its militancy. By the following year, however, the agent himself
was aware that Ghost Dances were being held regularly; that the
Indians flouted his loss of authority, which they were now fully
cognizant of. From this time forth until the turn of the century, the
reports indicate that the agents were doing all in their power by
moral suasion to keep the Indians from Ghost Dancing; but the
religion continued none the less. At the turn of the century the
form in which it flourished was the four-day Ghost Dance hand
game ceremony, rather than the Ghost Dance proper.

FORMS OF WHITE'S SOUTH BAND GHOST DANCE

When White first brought the Ghost Dance to the Pawnee he
organized the dancing simply. He taught some of the songs to a
few singers, gathered the people together in a large conical tipi
for face-painting, and led the dancing outside this tipi, aided by
his singers.

Soon he had organized the dancing more ritually. He selected
seven singers, after the pattern initiated by Sitting-Bull among
the Caddo and Wichita, and these became a fixed organization for
South Band Ghost Dancing. There is some disagreement among

contemporary Pawnee informants as to who the original singers were. According to Joseph Carrion, they were, in the order of their selection and importance, Whitehorse (Pitahawirat[a]), Sam Cover (Skiri), Ezra Tilden (Skiri), Tom Yellowhorse (Skiri), Henry Shooter (Kitkahaxki[x]), Brigham Young (Tcawi), and Jim Keys (Skiri). In addition, however, Carrion corrects himself by agreeing with other informants that Joseph Long was the first of these "crows" selected. Mark Evarts believes that all the original singers belonged to the South Bands, and claims that the first four, after White himself, were Joseph Long, Rubin Wilson, Lester Pratt and White Elk, none of whom are Skiri. The presence of Skiri men in the group of main singers should however be anticipated because all the bands joined in the Ghost Dance under White's leadership. Also, when the Skiri later organized and led their own Ghost Dancing, the singers who were selected by the Skiri to take charge were men who knew the songs because of their earlier participation in the South Band Ghost Dancing, hence some Skiris must have belonged to the original group of singers. The men actually selected to form the organizations of the Seven Eagles and Seven Crows (see below) included several who are mentioned in this list of Carrion's. Those whom Knifechief and Mrs. Washington selected were chosen because they knew the songs.

In addition to face paintings, the early Ghost Dance forms included the use of feathers as hair ornaments. Two types were prominent, eagle feathers and crow feathers. These birds were used because of a definite symbolism which attached to them. Both birds were conceived to fly high and far, and to see and know many things. The Pawnee have always thought of the crow as a bird which finds what it seeks. Hence the crow can help people find what is lost—lost beliefs, lost ways of life.

In trance visions of the Ghost Dance, the visionary usually found himself associated either with the eagle or the crow, and thereafter wore the feather of one or the other. White wore eagle feathers, and when he constituted the seven men as the official singers, he gave them special crow feathers to wear. White did not himself lead the singing after this, but acted as general director, dancing in the center of the circle and putting subjects into trances.

A story is told of how White and Joseph Long were put to a test in early Ghost Dance days. There was a woman who went to Camp Creek. On the way she lost a strap with which she was going to bind up a load of wood. She wanted to find out if it was true that crows could find things, so she went to the tipi of the leaders and told them about her lost strap. Frank White said, "All right, sit down." Joseph Long had crow feathers. He put them on his head. Then he got up like a crow, and danced around the tipi. Imitating the crow, he danced his way outside and went along the path by which the woman had gone through the timber, and found the strap. He picked it up and brought it back into the tipi, and the woman took her strap.

The relation of this crow-concept to the Ghost Dancing is direct. The crow feather (as also the eagle) is one of the objects used by leaders, as they dance inside the circle, for hypnotizing subjects. It is moved back and forth directly before the eyes of the subject. It helps the dancer to fall into a trance, and this means that it helps the subject to see or find his lost relatives. In the trance-vision itself the bird may guide the visionary to his dear ones. In the same way the old Indian customs, the dances, the songs, the rituals, are found among the deceased people, or recovered in trance visions which are induced in part through the instrumentality of the birds.

In this early use of eagle and crow, those who learned about one or the other bird wore a feather of that bird. There was no organization or orientation of these except for White's seven crow singers. But there came to be felt an opposition between crow and eagle, analogous to the actions of the birds themselves, and this was carried over into the sides of the hand game arrangements. The opposition involved the question of which was abler or luckier in finding things.

For the Ghost Dance, White arranged to have a large cleared dancing ground. West of this was set up a special tipi. Herein White gathered the people, particularly the leaders. Those who gathered inside the tent were only men. The old men sat near the eastern entranceway on both sides, with the chiefs next to them to the west, and then the braves[1]; while other men present sat about anywhere. White himself would sit with his seven crow leaders at the west facing east. The only sacred objects kept on a covering at the western altar-place were the feathers and paints of the leaders, and several pipes (two or four). Two men were selected by White and the chiefs to act as tarutsius ("fire-tenders") and at the same time as policemen. They carried long sticks to whip the dogs with, driving them away from the dance ground while the dancing went on. They also controlled the dancers. After all the men had gathered, a smoke offering initiated the performance. White gave pipes to two or four chiefs and told them step by step what to do. The performance could begin either in the

---

[1] These are generic Pawnee patterns.

late afternoon or in the morning, and the smoke offering differed according to which time of day it was.

In the arrangement for the time near sundown, the two chiefs carrying the pipes lead the way out of the tipi and all the others follow. Outside, the chiefs stand at the east of the clearing, facing west. Behind them the men form a long flat arc facing west, with White and his seven leaders in the center. The announcer cries out to the people at large that the singing will commence as soon as the smoking is over.

(First Phase[1]) Each of the two chiefs holds the pipe slantwise toward the west, offering it, not by holding it aloft, but by holding it just in front of him. Both proceed simultaneously. After offering the pipe west, each walks clockwise around the clearing, carrying the pipe, and after reaching the same point at the east, stops there, offers a pinch of tobacco upward to heaven, and one westward, placing each on the ground. (Lighting the Pipe) Then each again makes a clockwise circuit, stopping at a point east of northeast, where squatting with the pipe in mouth and its bowl toward the east the pipe is lit by means of a brand which is brought forward by anyone for this purpose. (Second Phase; first mode) Each arises, puffing the pipe, and returns to the east, where facing west, he puffs four times upward to heaven and four times to the west, (Second Phase; third mode) then carries the pipe through a clockwise circuit and takes it to whoever is standing at the extreme northern end of the arc-like row of men. Standing in front of this man the smoker puts the pipe to the man's lips without releasing the bowl. Then the smoker proceeds in turn to allow each man to puff the pipe, moving from north to south down the arc of men. (Third Phase) After all in the line have puffed, the smoker takes the pipe and carries it through a clockwise circuit, coming to the east of the clearing in front of the line of men. Here he faces west, loosens the ashes in the pipe-bowl with a tamper, offering ashes once upward to heaven, then emptying some, and again to the west, emptying the rest of the bowl contents on the ground before him. (Fourth Phase) Holding the empty pipe in his left hand, the smoker touches the right hand to the ashes on the ground, then runs the right hand up the pipe from bowl to mouthpiece while the stem is directed heavenward. He repeats this motion with the left hand, and again with the right and the left, making four motions. Then the smoker makes four similar motions while he directs the pipe toward the west. (Self-Blessing) Holding the pipe,

---

[1] Parenthetical divisions into phases, etc. refer to the analysis of the smoke offering in Chapter 8, see especially pp. 186—207.

mouthpiece upward and bowl inward toward the body, he takes it in his left hand and runs his right hand up it from bowl to mouthpiece, opening the palm upward and outward toward heaven, then places the hand on the right side of his head and runs his palm down the head and side and leg to the instep which is pressed against the ground. This motion is then made with the left hand for the left side etc. while the right hand holds the pipe, and repeated once again with the right and once again with the left, making four motions. Then the smoker turns and returns the pipe to another chief in the line of men, who receives it with an *arm blessing*.[1] When the offerings have been completed, the pipes are taken inside the tipi and replaced on the altar-space at the west.

Now the arc-like line at the west closes around the clearing to form a circle of dancers, and women who have not up to this point participated join the circle. They may, however, sing two songs before forming a circle of dancers, and these are special Ghost Dance songs which are never danced to. Then the dancing begins from the east, facing west, circling clockwise.

Before describing the movements of the dancers, attention must be called to the form of the smoke offering which would be made if the dance were to begin in the morning.

If the dancing is to begin with a smoke-offering in the morning the orientations for the smoke would be reversed. That is, the arc-line of leaders and men would form around White on the west, facing east; the smoker would begin all his circuits from the west, and the motions with the pipe which he made slantwise to the west, while he stood at the east side of the clearing and faced west, would become motions slantwise to the east which he would make standing at the west of the clearing and facing east. Finally the pipes would be handed along the line of leaders and men from south to north, instead of from north to south.

This shift of direction also changes the position for starting the dance, which is now at the point directly west, facing east. Here White stands and leads, and the circle proceeds clockwise. This is the generic position for beginning Ghost Dancing and singing, and even if the evening orientations are followed, only the first song begins at the east facing west; it then ends at the west, facing east, and all subsequent songs begin at the west.

It will be seen at once that the whole smoking ritual involves two basic orientation concepts: upward and either slantwise to the west or slantwise to the east. The upward offering is to Tirawahat^n or the expanse of the heavens; the other is to the sun, according to

---

[1] See Chapter 8, p. 209.

his position in the morning or the evening, east or west. It follows, therefore, that the dancing begins facing the position of the sun. An adjustment is made so that up to about one o'clock by sun time, the orientation is slantwise to the east, and the dancing begins at the west; later in the afternoon, the evening orientation would be adopted.

The reference of the orientations is as follows: the offering to Tirawahat^n must be part of any and every Pawnee smoke offering; that to the sun concerns the land of the dead: this is conceived to be in the western sky (see above, White's speech to the people on one late afternoon). In the land of the western sky, the deceased relatives of the living are dancing and singing while the dance goes on upon the earth. Also the dead are smoking to begin their dance, and they point their pipes toward their deceased relations; it is thus a mutual smoke, emphasizing their desire for reunion. The sun is conceived as a brother of the Morning Star, who, since his marriage with the Moon[1] (as the Morning Star's with the Evening Star), has his home or lodge in the west.[2] To this he returns every night. As he passes across the sky he sees all that goes on upon earth, and reports when he reaches his home in the evening. Thus, while the pipe is offered to the dead, it is directed toward the position of the sun, because what the people desire is that it should be reported to the dead that they are smoking to them.

In the vision which is the traditional origin of the smoke offering for Pawnee Ghost Dances,[3] "the Child of the Father in Heaven" is spoken of. This is a definite reference to Christ, who is conceived by the Pawnee as in charge of the region of the west where the dead people are. A similar reference is made in Mrs. Cover's dream of later Ghost Dance times (see below).

A fundamental way in which the Christ legends were fitted into Pawnee ideology is of interest and importance. The human sacrifice to the Morning Star, carried out as a ritual of the Morning Star bundle of the Skiri Pawnee, involves the sacrifice of a captive maiden to a power conceived as deity as a propitiatory offering on behalf of all Pawnee. That is, the maiden dies for the people. In the details a scaffold is involved, to which the maiden is bound by thongs.

The crucifixion of Christ becomes in Ghost Dance conceptions

---

[1] See Dorsey, Traditions of the Skidi Pawnee, p. 6.
[2] Note the relation to matrilocal residence; the western region in old cosmology is dominated by female powers. See also, my Levirate and Fraternal Polyandry among the Pawnee, Man. 1930, no. 78, p. 99.
[3] Murie, Societies, p. 64. Quoted above in first section of this chapter.

identified with this background. The cross has always been used by the Pawnee as a star symbol. On the ancient star-map of the Pawnee, which was part of the Black Star bundle,[1] all the stars are indicated by small crosses, rather than by dots or five-pointed figures. Hence to a Pawnee it is natural to conceive the cross-scaffold as involving a star-reference. To this scaffold Christ as a holy untainted man who has been honored (the maiden must be virginal and while she lives among the Pawnee is honored) is nailed, with his arms outstretched, as a sacrifice (from the Pawnee view-point). With both Christ's crucifixion and the Morning Star Sacrifice Ceremony oriented from the west, there comes about a broadening of the western orientation to include not only the Evening Star ideas of earlier times, but as well the conception of Christ as the Father and Shepherd of the people in the other world, the Chief in the beyond.

The meaning of the final self-blessing is simple and direct. One had offered tobacco and smoke to specific powers, and one concludes by reaffirming one's desire and hope of continued and long contact with the earth, Mother Earth. Thus one presses the body to the ground firmly as a request for long life.

Murie has pointed out that the Pawnee Ghost Dance ceremony as first organized by White "seems to have been largely original with White and far from identical with the Ghost Dance as followed by neighboring tribes. It is clear, however, that White based his teachings upon the fundamental conceptions of the true Ghost Dance."[2] This reference is to the fact that in the vision pattern suggested by White there were seen by the visionary in order a stream, a tree (usually cedar), the Messiah or Christ himself, then a village of people, and upon approaching the village the people were seen to be dancing, playing games, etc. In addition White brought the undeveloped forms of the Wichita Ghost Dance; there were one day dances, or dances from early afternoon through to the next dawn. White had borrowed the concept of seven leaders for the dance from the Wichita organization as instituted by Sitting-Bull. Murie remarks further, "Some years after White's death some visiting Wichita brought in the regular ceremony. According to this there was no supreme leader, but all who had trances could teach and direct."[2]

The information I have is that Wichita were in part responsible for the changed conception of the dance, inasmuch as visitors from

---

[1] See Buckstaff, R. N., 279 ff., which includes a reproduction of the map. The original is in the Field Museum of Natural History.

[2] Murie, Societies, p. 636.

that tribe were present among the Pawnee when the Skiri Brotherhoods were conceived; the Wichita seem to have brought to the Pawnee the change to a Ghost Dance every six weeks for four nights, continuing the last night until the dawn of the fifth day. This they had adopted in accordance with the change among the Cheyenne, Arapaho, Caddo and Wichita, after the message from the Messiah was received. At the same time, a conflict of doctrine over the teachings of White, which culminated in a new conception of the significance of the Ghost Dance brought directly from the major Arapaho prophets by Pawnee delegations, seems to have contributed to the release of the Pawnee Ghost Dance from White's exclusive control. This doctrinal change occurred before Frank White's death in 1893.

In the early days after the dancing for the day was over, the people as a whole broke apart and went home, or went to their own tipis. But White, his seven co-leaders, and some of the chiefs would reenter the leading tipi. There they were served food. Before eating, a simple corn offering was made; corn was offered to Tirawahat^n and placed on the ground; then motions of blessing were made with the horn spoon over the altar objects.

After this feast, someone would begin to talk about his trance experiences. He would tell what he saw, and then sing songs which he had learned in his trance. In this way songs were added to the repertoire, and gradually the Wichita and Arapaho songs became only a minor phase (save for the closing song) of the Pawnee Ghost Dance songs.

CONFLICT OF DOCTRINE; REORGANIZATION OF CEREMONY

According to the conception of the Ghost Dance which Frank White brought among the Pawnee, Frank White himself was the sole authentic prophet of the dance and doctrine, and it was necessary for all sanctions to come through Frank White as intermediary. Those who had visions in trances reported the content and character to White, and in terms of his interpretation and permission made use of the vision. Feathers to wear in the hair, paints for the face, special symbolisms of dress, and the like, were possible only with White's approval. If a dancer wished to use a face painting, in accordance with his trance experiences, he had first to go to White and pay him for the privilege, or in any case, to offer him gifts. Individuals who had learned about the Ghost Dance in visions, and felt authorized to put on a dance, could do so only after conferring with White. He would teach the visionary what to do, and received compensation for his instruction. Ordinarily his instruction seems to have amounted to interpretation, to a suggestion that the visionary do as all had seen White himself do, with some explanation of the details. White would also counsel the visionary to tell the people in general what he had seen and learned. But even in such a case, according to reports, when a dance was put on by another, White's seven crow singers had to be invited to lead the singing and dancing, whether it was held among the Skiri or South Bands.

Gifts and money were lavished upon White: a small face painting often earned him five dollars; feathers and sanctions of various kinds brought him other money. Many people were jealous, or resented White's attitude, called him a liar and began to disbelieve him and say he was deceiving the people.

At the same time, White's conduct was not exemplary. It must be remembered that priests, chiefs, medicine men, and in fact all individuals who had claims to sacred office or inspiration in connection with old Pawnee ways of life, lived up to accepted Pawnee ethical standards of conduct.

As one informant describes White's behavior: "All this time White drank peyote, which made him wise. At the same time he used to drink whiskey. Whiskey and peyote do not mix, they cannot go together. That's what killed him.

"One time they were going to have a doctor dance north of town and when they were ready to begin, someone said, 'we can't start until the Messiah comes'—they considered White a great prophet, and called him Father and Messiah. Finally they saw him coming, hardly able to walk, supported on each side by a man holding his arm. Someone said, 'why, he's drunk,' but they whispered around, 'we can't say anything about it anyhow, because he's the Messiah.' They used to lavish gifts upon him, and finally they gave him the prettiest girl in the tribe to marry."

It was not long before revolt against White and his tactics took definite form. This reaction is in part to be explained by White's misbehavior, in part by jealousy of the way in which he was getting rich, and in part also by a sincere desire on the part of some to get more out of the dancing in a religious sense.

According to Joseph Carrion, White and he had been friends for a long time; in fact Frank White at one time married Joe's sister-in-law, which in terms of Pawnee kinship put them on strong grounds of familiarity. Joe Carrion danced along with Frank White for almost a year. In Joe's own words, "Frank White told me that I was going where I could find out something for myself about the dance." Carrion, along with John Moses, Jim Keys, Brigham Young and Henry Minthorn went to see Sitting-Bull the Arapaho. This was late in 1892, and they stayed there two months. Carrion told Sitting-Bull his story. Sitting-Bull got a permit from his agent to Ghost Dance for two days. The Arapaho painted the Pawnee visitors with a rainbow around the forehead, a crow on the right cheek (because, says Carrion, "a crow finds everything he looks for, and when one is under the crow influence one can almost read minds"), and an eagle on the left cheek (which also represents a bird that flies high above everything, sees all and finds things).

That night in the Ghost Dancing among the Arapaho Joe Carrion was overcome and fell unconscious on his back. "I saw a big circle of people above." He awoke about two o'clock at night after lying there for five hours. When he woke up, he found there was a drum beside his head; an old man came over and asked him what he had seen. "Nothing," he said; he didn't want to tell. The old man told him, "you must tell." "I got up and said, 'I don't believe it.' Then he hit a gourd against the ground, and I fell over again. I got up and still said, 'I don't believe it,' so he hit the gourd on the ground and again I fell over. The way he could do this to me convinced me, and when I got up I believed it all. Then I told him what I had seen. He said it was true. The next day the Arapaho were told they would have to stop the Ghost Dancing.

"Two days afterward a boy came with hand game sticks, bringing one round to each tent. He told everybody that there was to be a big hand game at a certain place. It was to last four days, with a Squaw dance afterwards."

The man in charge of the hand game told Carrion to get certain things for himself. He told him that he must fast four days and nights. Carrion wore only a g-string, and painted his body yellow. He neither ate nor drank.

During the playing of the game, he often got thirsty and would be about to take a drink, when someone would remind him that he must not. He was chosen to serve the food, but he was not supposed to partake of it. He also would pass the bucket of water around. The smell of the food helped him, seemed to satisfy his hunger a little. The first night he felt weak and wanted to cry. "They told me to go ahead and cry, that this was the same as going to church."

At sunrise he stood outside the tent and prayed.

"The fourth day I went onto a hill. Behind me there was someone sitting in the grass. I looked at the sun and saw things in it. I saw the sun whirling round, and I saw crows flying around the sun, and flying over me. I saw an eagle feather in the whirling sun. Then I saw a black sun streaked with white inside coming towards me, and as it came I fell over. I stood up and saw a buffalo bull stick his head out of the sun. Just before sundown I saw Jesus standing in the west in the sun with one hand extended toward me.

"Someone came and told me I was wanted in the tent. There Sitting-Bull's nephew[1] spoke to me and told me I had made good. He dropped water into my mouth four times with an eagle feather to cool my thick, dry tongue. Then he told me to take three swallows of water. He gave me sweet corn gruel to eat, and told me not to eat any more that night, but to eat a hearty breakfast in the morning."

At this time the old man questioned Carrion in detail about what he had seen, and Carrion told him about the circle of people, the birds and the man standing with his hand extended as if he were handing Carrion something. This, according to Carrion, the Arapaho interpreted as a gift of the hand game. The circle of people were the players, the man held in his hand the hand game sticks. The crow and eagle feathers belonged to the players, the clusters of feathers to the guessers.

Shortly after this the Pawnee came home. None of the others had visions among the Arapaho, says Carrion, because none of the others went through a four-day fast.

When Joe got home, crowds gathered around and wanted to know what he had found out, and if the Ghost Dance was true. Joe told the Pawnee that Frank White had taken something which did not belong to him and brought it over, and that White couldn't give them blessings and things to use, but that they had to get everything for themselves.

According to Carrion, this message which he brought home from the Arapaho introduced a different perspective into Pawnee Ghost Dancing. Before this people danced, but their experiences in the dancing did not give them sanction to carry out the dancing as leaders on their own account. White taught that only he could sanction them to do anything, and that they must pay him for the right. Now the people tried to find out things for themselves in trance-visions, and they did. It was after this that an extreme

---

[1] Sitting-Bull's nephew was the leader of this four day hand game among the Arapaho. Apparently he had derived it in trance visions experienced in the Arapaho Ghost Dancing under the leadership of Sitting-Bull, and his visions had been sanctioned by the interpretations of Sitting-Bull.

development of visions in which hand games and many similar sanctions were bestowed took place among the Pawnee. Carrion claims to have brought the inspiration for the hand game ceremonies from the Arapaho. With the liberation of the Pawnee Ghost Dance hand games began a rapid development (see Part Two).

While Carrion and others contend, as is usual in such cases among American Indian groups, that this difference of doctrine between White and the Arapaho indicated a conscious deception on the part of White, it is clear that no explanation of this kind need be invoked. Actually White's doctrine is much closer to generic Pawnee ideology, according to which the independent free vision of the individual is subordinated to a process of learning from one who knows a ritual, ceremony or performance. That is to say, in the older ancient Pawnee activities, the accepted method of obtaining participation was to receive the right or sanction to do so from those who were in charge of that activity, rather than directly from supernatural powers. In contrast to this, Carrion's doctrine looks a great deal like Plains patterns in general, which would be correct for Arapaho Ghost Dancing. It should be remembered in this connection, first, that White did not learn from Arapaho or other Plains tribes directly, but indirectly through the Wichita, whose ideas on these fundamental points are very close to Pawnee ideas, and second, that Carrion was not a Pawnee, although he lived most of his life among them and spoke a fluent Pawnee.

In a general way, also, the pattern of immediately telling the vision to the leaders and securing their interpretation is a non-Pawnee pattern. In older forms, among both Wichita and Pawnee, visions were kept a secret for long, and only in the course of one's life because of one's behavior did the general public of the tribe become aware that one had supernatural experience. In the Ghost Dance doctrine, the visions had to be told at once to show appreciation for receiving them, and one who didn't tell was not supposed to live long thereafter.

It is not possible to date accurately the time of the reorganization of the Pawnee Ghost Dance to accord with the regular four-day dance forms of the southern tribes. I believe Murie has dated it far too late. The organization of the Seven Brothers among the Skiri, which initiated the freeing of the Skiri Ghost Dancing from White's control, took place before White's death in 1893. The first forms of Skiri dancing followed White's forms. On his visit to the Arapaho Carrion had observed both Ghost Dances and hand games as four-day ceremonies. Whether this was responsible for a correction of Pawnee forms, or whether the Wichita taught the Pawnee directly, the four-day ceremony was the formal Ghost Dance among the Pawnee by 1895.

This regular Ghost Dance of the Pawnee was arranged to last four days. It began the evening of one day, or the late afternoon. Among the South Bands, all arose early in the morning, and faced the sun for a brief period (during which the smoke offering would be made if the dance was to begin that day); but they did not dance. Then in the afternoon the people danced from three to midnight. The Skiri say that in their band there was a brief period of dancing each morning, as well as a longer period of dancing through the afternoon and evening. Both bands continued the fourth night until the dawn of the fifth day, bathed and dispersed.

As each song was sung, the circle of dancers, holding hands, moved clockwise through one complete circuit, returning to the original starting point. This is determined by the main singer's position; he begins at the west and finishes at the west (except for the first afternoon song, as above). During the dancing period of the day, the dancers could carry out as many songs as they wished; there was no special number. The singing was initiated and led by the seven crow-feathered singers, and the others joined in. While the dancing went on, some "hypnotizers" would dance inside the circle directly in front of individuals they wished to throw into a trance, using feathers or other objects to focus and fix the eyesight of the subject, thus transfixing them. Usually the subject fell when he or she was touched with the object used. When individuals fell into a trance, they were laid down and the others continued to dance.

In these trances, the visionaries followed a general pattern. In one way or another the subject was guided to the other world, where all the deceased Pawnee were living together in the old way. There some special phase of the life would imprint itself upon the subject's mind, the playing of games, the hunting of buffalo, war societies and dances, and the like. When the subject awoke, such aspects of the trance vision, along with the bird or messenger who had guided the individual to the beyond, would become the subjects of songs, costuming, and paraphernalia.

The closing song was carried out in a special way. It is the special closing song of all Ghost Dances. As sung to conclude the occasion, it is repeated six times as follows:

1. The leader remains stationary at the west facing east, and leads the singing of the song once; all the dancers keep their places.

2. The leader dances from west to north, singing the song, and

stops at the north facing south; the rest of the circle dance through an equivalent part of the circuit.

3. The leader repeats the song, while the whole circle of dancers moves through another quadrant, the leader finishing at the east, facing west.

4. A third quadrant is similarly completed with the leader at the south facing north.

5. The fourth quadrant is completed when the leader is once more in his original position at the west facing east.

6. All now step back a few paces, widening the circle, and as they sing the circle closes in again. Throughout this singing the leader maintains his orientation at the west, and each dancer his or her relative position in the circle. Now, as the song finishes with the circle narrowed to its original dimensions, all break their handclasps, and shake off the blankets they wear, and the dance is over. The closing in of the circle during this last song signifies the coming together of the people, and the shaking out of the blankets expresses their desire to shake off them the bad ways, the new ways, the white man's ways.

The closing song is the Arapaho song as given by Mooney.[1]

FIRST FORMS OF THE SKIRI GHOST DANCE

As we have seen, Frank White brought the Ghost Dance to the South Bands primarily, being himself a Kitkahaxki[x]. When a Skiri wished to hold a dance among the Skiri proper, he was in the same position as any individual among the South Bands who felt he had the right to do so. The Skiri had to get sanction from White, and to invite White and his leaders to come over to initiate and lead the dancing.

After the visit of the five Pawnee to Sitting-Bull, the Arapaho, a change came over the Pawnee attitude toward the general Ghost Dance doctrine. The whole religious movement was liberated from the domination of White. An individual's own conscience and experience was the individual's guide to what he could and could not do, to what sanctions he had obtained supernaturally. It became unnecessary to pay White for rights, and the only checks upon the number of prophets who began to appear among the Pawnee with messages from the deceased were the natural ones: the force of character and the temperament of the claimant; the

---

[1] Mooney, pp. 1011—1012, no. 73. Note that this song was used as the closing song after the return of the delegation of Southern Arapaho and Cheyenne in the fall of 1891.

reputation and esteem in which he or she was held by the tribes-people, the abilities of the prophet as a leader, hypnotizer, organizer; and the experiences which were undergone by the layman under the leadership and influence of the prophet.

Those who are remembered as the chief visionaries of the period in which the Ghost Dance was taken up by the Skiri are Mrs. Washington, Goodeagle and Mrs. Goodeagle, and Mrs. Cover. There were others, of course. Chiefly, Mrs. Washington was responsible for the inauguration of independent Skiri Ghost Dances. She had many trance-visions, and often told very complex stories of the images and events which took place in them, so complex in fact that there were Pawnee who doubted her, partly because of their own vision experiences, which seemed to them different in kind (psychologically); partly because of jealousy of the constantly increasing part she was playing in the tribal developments.

Carrion speaks of Mrs. Washington as a fraud. He says that she made up a lot of stuff, and was a false prophet trying to win the people's worship. His reasons for the attitude are interesting. He claims that in a vision (as he has experienced such) you see merely one simple image or thing, not a complex array; and that if you add to what you see, that is wrong. He contends that Mrs. Washington had trance-vision after trance-vision, and kept on learning details of performances in her visions, like a serial story. This is impossible, he says, because going back to those who give you things in visions and asking for more, is imposing on them; and it is for such conduct that people lose their lives.

In truth, Carrion's attitude indicates a temperamental difference between him and Mrs. Washington, as well as difference in the quality of his imagination. Carrion was not subject to trances often, Mrs. Washington was; his mind did not experience much detail in the few cases in which he had visions, while Mrs. Washington did. Obviously, the quality of the individual's mind will appear in the content and character of his visions as well as in his waking life, which is well illustrated by the vision experience of Mark Evarts in relation to the Ghost Dance, given below; Mark Evarts is a man whose mind is rich in content. But the native concept of the vision is more or less fixed and absolute, not one which accepts the relativity of the vision to the subject; hence, in terms of one visionary's experiences, those of another may often seem fraudulent.

The early independent Ghost Dances of the Skiri were carried out in terms of the usual forms and patterns of White's South Band Ghost Dancing. There was the same form of the circle, the same orientation of the official or sacred tent, and the same pattern of the smoke offering. Those who had crow or eagle feathers from the Ghost Dance wore them, and usually a group of seven singers led the singing. These were men who knew the Ghost Dance songs. But at first there was no official organization of singers, policemen and the like. Each occasion was organized in the usual patterns, according to immediate needs. The first phase of the organization of Skiri Ghost Dances concerns the official constitution of a fixed group of singers, the Seven Eagle Brothers.

THE SEVEN EAGLE BROTHERS

As with many cultural formalizations, the Seven Eagle Brothers were not institutionalized by revolutionary act or decree, but by gradual changes. There were first of all a great many people who considered themselves "eagles" and a great many who considered themselves "crows." Among the Skiri there were in each of these classes men who were gifted as singers and leaders, whose knowledge of the ways of the Ghost Dance had grown through continuous and regular experience and participation. Seven singers were the number usually employed, following White's pattern, and by habitual practice there was general acceptance of certain men as naturally more proficient for the function. In other words the men who were chosen as the official Seven Eagle Brothers were probably seven main singers for the Skiri by custom and practice before the group was institutionalized as a brotherhood.

Knifechief is recalled as the man who first expressed the general attitude toward these seven men. At a hand game he selected them formally to be the main singers. Knifechief went to the place each one occupied in the hand game circle and told him to rise and follow him. Then he led the selected man around a circuit of the fireplace, and seated him in his new position in a row on the south side toward the west. The seven in their order were, according to Ezra Tilden[1]: Sam Cover, Emmett Pierson, Walter Keys (the senior), Tom Yellowhorse, Ezra Tilden, Leadingfox, and Harry Sergeant. These seven, when they were seated in a row on the south side, led the singing for the hand game.

Mrs. Washington was officially responsible for the organization of these seven as the Seven Eagle Brothers of the Skiri Ghost Dance. The first occasion on which Mrs. Washington managed a large Ghost Dance among the Skiri was one which occurred when many Wichita had come to visit the Pawnee; and it said by some

---

[1] Ezra Tilden and Tom Yellowhorse are the only ones of the seven still living.

that a suggestion of the Wichita was in part responsible for Mrs. Washington's determination to organize the Ghost Dancing with regular singers while the Wichita were present.

Frank White died in 1893, and he is known to have been alive at the time Mrs. Washington inaugurated these developments, which places the time of the first Seven Eagle Brothers as sometime in late 1892 or early 1893.

As one informant describes Mrs. Washington's activities: "When they used to dance among the South Bands, all would go there, and while the dancing went on, old Mrs. Washington fell in a trance. She found out something about the Seven Brothers, but not everything right away. Afterwards, every time she fell she would see something about the Seven Brothers.[1] The spirit told her to go ahead and put up the Seven Brothers. She used to have her own cattle. Once when they came home from the dancing, she was told that when she got home she should put up the Seven Brothers at a dance. So she killed her own beef, and put up the dance, and they told her how to go, everything, the smoke and all."

Mrs. Washington put up a special feast. She asked the chiefs and these seven men to be present, as well as others. Each of the seven sat on the south side with the eagle feather given him by Knifechief stuck into the ground before him. Along the north side were congregated the "crow" people, including those who played as "crows" in the hand games, as well as the men who later were organized into the Seven Crows; while along the south side the "eagle" people sat. As yet, however, there was no "crow" organization; the "crows" were merely an amorphous group who played the hand game together, and who had this affiliation because of Ghost Dance experiences.

Mrs. Washington stood at the doorway of the tipi. Up to this time she had been learning. Now she spoke, "Now, I want to tell you what I have in mind. We are going to have a Ghost Dance. A spirit told me to do it. I am going to do it today. These Seven Brothers are going to take the lead for us, and we're going to call them Fathers. Now I want you chiefs to decide when we should begin the dance."

Then the chiefs talked together and decided and one announced, "Let us move the camp and all come together on the third day."

This inaugural feast was not a ceremonial affair. After the decision of the chiefs was announced all those present partook of the feast provided by Mrs. Washington; this concluded the occasion

---

[1] This "serial story" form of learning in visions is the sort of thing about Mrs. Washington's claims that Carrion resented; see above.

for most. Some sat about a while longer, however, and sang Ghost Dance songs.

This introductory or inaugural feast at which a decision is made as to the time for a regular ceremony is a fundamental Pawnee pattern. Such feasts precede the actual performance of doctor dances and ceremonies, society gatherings and performances, and many other ritual activities. In all such cases the pattern is the same. An individual man or woman "puts up" the feast for the gathering, and obtains as a result certain definite rights of proprietorship over the actual ceremonial occasion which is to follow. [1] This "host" invites leading men such as chiefs to be present, and requests selected ones to come to a decision as to the time for the performance itself.

After this feast-gathering had broken up, the people got ready for the actual dance. Three days were allowed for moving into camp because the people lived scattered over a large area, and had to come in wagons and on horseback. They needed time to arrange things at home so they could be absent for more than a week, to pack, and to come. After all had gathered, at least three more days intervened before the dance proper began, so that the preparation of food, wood, and all other necessary things could be finished. Once it is begun, the dance must not be interrupted by such labors.

Mrs. Washington must be the first to move officially into camp. The chief who finally set the date for the gathering inquired if she was ready, and after she had said yes, and moved her tent, others would begin to follow her into the camping place.

For the dance the tipis and tents were set up in a half circle from south to north around the west. There was no special order of tipis. In the center a space thirty to forty feet in diameter was cleared of grass. Here the dancing began, but as more and more people joined in and the circle of dancers expanded, it would be pushed back beyond the edge of the cleared space onto the grass. The cleared space alone, however, was considered the sacred dancing ground.

One large tipi was set up west of the cleared ground at a distance of thirty feet, its doorway facing east. This was the tent used by the Seven Brothers, Mrs. Washington and other leaders.

---

[1] Neither vision nor vow is essential in all cases to give an individual the right to "put up" a ritual affair. It is sufficient in most cases among the Pawnee that an individual wants to do so, either because he or she wants to secure thereby whatever benefits in health, luck and prosperity accrue from the performance (and particularly to the one who has "put it up") or because he or she wants to see the ritual demonstrated and learn something about it, or both.

When each house-group had ready its quota of wood, meat and all else necessary, everything was in order and the dance could begin.

A sacred smoke offering opened the dance. If the people wished to begin dancing on an evening, the usual form was to hold the smoke ceremony, then dance a little, perhaps ten songs, and adjourn until morning. At the continuation of the dancing in the morning no smoke offering would be made; but if dancing were begun for the first time in the morning, a preliminary offering was necessary.

Inside the main tipi were the Seven Brothers seated on the south side. Four chiefs were selected to carry pipes and make a smoke offering. These came out of the tent leading the way, followed by the Seven Brothers, each wearing an eagle feather in his hair. They were directed by Knifechief. This was the first occasion on which the Skiri Ghost Dancers saw the Seven Eagle Brothers as an organization.

Outside, the arrangement in relation to the clearing followed the form already described for White's South Band Ghost Dancing. The Seven Brothers were in the center of an arc-like line of men which stood at the east of the clearing facing west (for an evening smoke-offering). In front of this line stood the four chiefs with pipes, also facing west. While the Seven Brothers were in the center of the line, Sam Cover, number 1 Eagle Brother, was not in the center of the seven, but at the south end of the seven; the others followed in the order given above, from south to north: this was the order of their selection. The significance of this arrangement is that now there was no main one who must be in the center—all were equal. In the row of men four chiefs took special places: two south of the Seven Brothers and two north.

Each of the four smokers had a special function. Their arrangement was from south to north as they faced west. Number 1 smoker at the south end of the row of four smoked to heaven; number 2 to the west (Christ); number 3 to the east (position of the rising sun); and number 4 at the north end of the row of four smokers, to the south, the noon sun.

The four smokers proceeded with their movements simultaneously. Number 1 took the filled pipe, (phase 1[1]) walked through a half circuit clockwise to the west where he faced east and offered a pinch of tobacco upward, placing it on the ground; (lighting the pipe) then he continued clockwise to the northeast, where he squatted toward the east, holding the pipe in his mouth. Here it was lit from a brand brought forward by another. (Phase 2; first

---

[1] See Chapter 8, pp. 186—207.

mode) He rose puffing the pipe and walked clockwise around the clearing stopping again at the west facing east, where he offered four puffs upward to heaven, and four downward to the earth. (Phase 2; third mode) Then he walked clockwise until he neared the row of men on the east of the clearing, when he went to the man who was at the extreme northern end of the row and offered him the pipe to smoke. This he did without releasing the pipe, holding the bowl in his right hand, the offered pipestem in his left. The man accepting the pipe to smoke merely puts his two hands around the mouthpiece of the pipe and holds it to his lips, drawing a puff. Then the smoke-offerer moved along southward to the second man in the row to whom he offered the pipe to puff, and so on down the row to the extreme south end of it. (Phase 3) The smoker then made a half-circuit clockwise to the west of the clearing, where he tamped the ashes loose (the pipe was now out) and offered ashes twice upward to heaven, emptying some each time on the ground, and again offered some ashes twice downward to the earth, finally depositing the last of the ashes from the bowl on the ground. (Phase 4) Now as he stood at the west, he held the empty pipe with the mouthpiece pointing upward, touched the ashes on the ground with his right hand, and ran his right hand up the pipe, from bowl to mouthpiece, opening his palm upward and outward toward heaven; he repeated this action with his left hand, holding the pipe in the same position with his right, then repeated it once more with his right hand and once more with his left, making four motions upward to heaven. Then he pointed the mouthpiece of the pipe slightly slantwise downward toward the earth, and made four similar motions toward the earth, each time touching the ashes on the ground before running his hand along the pipestem. He had now finished the smoke offering. (Self-Blessing; return of pipe) He walked with the pipe around the clearing clockwise until he reached a point just in front of the chief at the left (south) of Sam Cover, the number 1 Brother. He stood in front of this chief, and a little to the south, faced the chief, and made the motions of *self blessing*.[1]

Number 2 smoker (phase 1) meanwhile made a half-circuit clockwise until he reached the west, where he faced *west*, offered tobacco slantwise to the west, and downward to the ground, placing a pinch from the pipe-bowl each time on the ground, (lighting the pipe) came clockwise to the position at the northeast where the pipe is lit, (phase 2; first mode) continued clockwise until he again reached the west, where facing west he then smoked four puffs slantwise to the west and four downward to the ground. (Phase 2; second

---

[1] See Chapter 8, pp. 207—209.

mode) Then he walked clockwise until he came to the row of men east of the clearing; he offered the lit pipe to the man at the extreme northern end of the row, and to each man in the row southward until he reached the man at the extreme south end of the row. (Phase 3) Then he took the pipe, which was out, clockwise to the west of the clearing, where facing west he offered ashes twice slantwise to the west, and twice to the earth. (Phase 4) He then made four hand-motions to the west and four to the earth, (self-blessing and return of pipe) came clockwise around the clearing until he stood in front of the chief at the right (north) of Harry Sergeant, number 7 of the Seven Brothers; here he made the motions of self-blessing, and then returned the empty pipe to this chief, who received it with a blessing.

Number 3 smoker followed an analogous procedure. The unique character of his smoke appears in the following: the position at which he stopped to make offerings of tobacco (phase 1), offerings of smoke (phase 2; first mode), offerings of ashes (phase 3), and motions of blessing (phase 4), was at the *east* of the clearing, facing *east;* he there held the pipe slantwise to the east, and slant-wise downward to the ground, and made offerings to the position of the rising sun and to the earth; he offered his pipe down the row of men from north to south as the others had done. He made the motions of self-blessing in front of the chief to the left (south) of the chief to whom the number 1 smoker returned the number 1 pipe (that is, the second man to the left or south of Sam Cover, the number 1 Brother) and returned the pipe to this chief.

Number 4 smoker proceeded analogously. The place of his offerings of tobacco, smoke, ashes and motions was at the *south* of the clearing, facing *south*. He returned the pipe to the chief right (north) of the chief to whom the number 2 smoker returned the number 2 pipe (the second man to the right or north of Harry Sergeant, the number 7 Brother).

In carrying out these simultaneous offerings there was no collision of the smokers: similar actions, such as offering the pipes to the row of men, were done in the order of the smokers. Before the number 1 smoker returned to make his self-blessing and give the pipe back to the chief, the number 4 smoker had completed his offering of the pipe to the men in the line.

After the smokers had all finished, they returned to their places in front of the row of men. Each pipe was now returned to the man who had made a smoke offering with it, and as Sam Cover began to sing a Ghost Dance song, these smokers took the pipes back into the tipi. Inside this main tipi or sacred tent, a covering had been spread at the sacred altar place at the west, and on this the pipes were laid, mouthpiece to the east. There was nothing else on the altar place. There was an alternative to replacing the pipes on the altar inside the tipi. The four men who smoked could stand at the east of the clearing holding pipes with their arms folded, while the singing and Ghost Dancing went on. These four men did not participate in the dancing.

If the smoke was in the morning, the row of men would be at the west facing east, all the smokers would start their circuits from the west, and would offer the pipe down the line from south to north, but the orientation of positions at which each smoker made his offerings of tobacco, smoke, ashes, and motions would be identical with what has been described.

The differences between this four-fold smoke offering and that described for the South Bands above are differences of complexity. These were based on Mrs. Washington's visions; it was her smoke-offering. The essential concepts, however, remain the same: upward for heaven, downward for the earth, westward for sunset and Christ, and two positions for the sun: eastward for the rising sun, south for noon sun. Of these heaven and earth orientations are generic for all Pawnee smoke-offerings, and the strict theory of Pawnee theologians is that they must be included in any smoke offering.[1] The offerings to Christ and the sun are two aspects of the same intention, since the sun is a messenger who carries the news of what goes on among the people on earth to those in the western land of the dead. The sun at noon is supposed to be in position to see clearly what is happening below, and to hear what is said to him.

The additional complexity of the smoke offering is particularly interesting because it is symptomatic of a tendency of Skiri religion in general as opposed to South Band religion. In other aspects of Pawnee ritualism and ceremony, while certain basic concepts of the religion are the same for Skiri and the South Bands, an enormous multiplication of specific interrelations has added great complexity to the Skiri forms. The great number of Skiri Pawnee bundles is probably a result of this tendency. Continuous differentiation of function has resulted in a subdivision of bundle powers, and the development of a specific bundle for a specific power. Among the

[1] So fundamental is this minimum of smoke offerings, upward to heaven and downward to earth, that Mark Evarts today begins to smoke a cigarette by making one puff upward and one downward, and finishes his smoke by flicking a bit of ash off as he makes a motion upward, and then another bit of ash off as he makes a motion downward before he puts the cigarette out.

South Bands there are ancient bundles which each possess a group of functions that among the Skiri are differentiated and associated with separate bundles.

After the smoke offering, Sam Cover led the Seven Brothers in singing one or two Ghost Dance songs, without any dancing. Then the line closed around the clearing to form a circle of dancers, women came to join in, and the regular dancing began. Usually on a first evening of Ghost Dancing, only ten or twenty songs were sung. After the closing song, the general public would break up, each group of people returning to the family tipi. The Seven Brothers, the four chiefs who smoked, other chiefs, Mrs. Goodeagle, Mrs. Cover, Mrs. Washington, and some individuals who were special leaders, gathered in the main tipi of the dance. Here two old men acted as tarutsius, fire-tenders and servers. Food was brought in and set out in buckets at the east of the tipi near the door. Sam Cover then made an offering with corn before the group ate. It was a simple offering. He took some of the corn in his hands, stood behind the collected food and made inclusive arm motions (to indicate that this food was offered on behalf of all the food being partaken of), then came clockwise to the west of the fireplace where he raised the corn aloft to heaven and then placed it on the ground before him. He pressed it into the ground, rubbed his hands together and made four motions upward to heaven with both hands, touching his fingers to the corn on the ground before each motion. Then he made four similar motions towards the earth; blessed himself, walked through a circuit to his own place on the south, and sat down. All present said "Nawa" and then the food was served. The tarutsius must serve the food in a special order: first the chiefs at the west (the four smokers), then the seven brothers on the south, then old men who are seated on both sides of the entrance-way at the east, then all others present, serving them from west to east down both sides of the tipi.[1]

At this gathering the order and time of the events of the next morning were announced.

The next morning dancing began before sunrise. Two or three of the Seven Brothers went out onto the dance grounds, stood at the west facing east, and sang several Ghost Dance songs. As the people awoke and heard these they came out hurriedly to join in. As soon as four or five came, including women, all began to dance around clockwise. Gradually as the people gathered, the circle expanded. An old man walked around crying out to the people

---

[1] There is for every Pawnee ceremony an *order* in which those present are served; see Chapter 8, pp. 220—229.

to come and join the dancing. Some chiefs walked around the circle of dancers carrying pipes in their folded arms, but no smoke offering was made. Should the singers pause for a rest, pipes (but not these sacred pipes) were often smoked non-ceremonially.

After ten or twenty songs, the people ended the dancing with the finishing song, and returned to their tipis for breakfast. When they stopped the old man crier went through the camp calling out to the people to be ready to dance about one o'clock.

At one o'clock the dancers reassembled. The Seven Brothers took their places at the west side of the clearing, in order, each with special face-painting and wearing his eagle feather. Sam Cover led the singing, and the dancing began at the west, circling clockwise. Sam Cover and Emmet Pierson, the number 2 Brother, carried leather rattles which they shook in time to the dancing.

The dancing continued until about five in the afternoon, or just before sundown. The evening meal was prepared by women while the dancing went on, so that everything was ready when the finishing song concluded the dancing for the day.

After the dancing, the people gathered in the space between the cleared dance ground and the sacred tipi to the west of it. The Seven Brothers sat down on the east side of this space, facing west (this would of course be west of the cleared ground), while the chiefs sat on the west side facing east. In this way the chiefs and the seven brothers faced each other across this cleared space. The people gathered around the sides forming more or less a circle. One chief was selected to talk. He said:

"We have all come together today to worship God. Now you must try to think what you are here for. Now the ground is open, there is nothing in the way (i. e.,it is outdoors), God can look straight down upon us. Here's the sunlight over us, he's the one who knows all about it, and he knows also what you think about; you can't ever hide it. Now we are going to eat."

The main tarutsius now came forward. This chief gave the tarutsius a horn spoon which he had been holding while he spoke. In the center of the space around which the people had gathered, the food had been set out in buckets. The tarutsius received the spoon. (Filling the spoon[1]) He walked clockwise around, passing behind the food and around it, then with the spoon took some corn from the buckets, made a clockwise circuit and passed outside of the circle of people between the Seventh Brother (who is at the north end of the seated row of Seven Brothers) and the people at his right. (First phase[1]) Outside the circle the tarutsius walked clock-

---

[1] See Chapter 8; the Food Offering and Service, pp. 220—228.

wise around the sacred dance ground (not the space around which
the people are gathered) which was now vacant, and came to the
west of it where he stopped facing east. At this point his back was
to the back of the seven seated Brothers. Here he offered corn
upward to heaven, then bent down and pushed some off the spoon
onto the ground, then turned to the west to which he offered the
spoon of corn slantwise, then pushed some more off onto the ground,
and finally placed the rest on the ground as an offering to the earth.
(Second phase; first mode[1]) He then put the spoon on the ground
beside him, and touching and pressing the corn into the earth,
made three sets of motions with his hands and arms: four upward
to heaven, four westward, and four to the earth. (Self-blessing;
return of spoon[1]) Then he picked up the spoon and went through
the motions of the final self-blessing with it, pressing his feet firmly
to the ground. With the spoon he turned and reentered the circle
of people between the First Brother (who is at the south end of the
row of seven seated Brothers) and those at his left, walked through
a half circuit clockwise until he faced the chiefs sitting at the
west, and returned the spoon to the chief who had given it to him.
All the people say "Nawa."

The food was then served. A number of men were selected to do
the serving, some serving the chiefs, others the Seven Brothers,
and still others the people in general. The chiefs must be served
first, and then the Seven Brothers, and then the public at large.

After all had eaten, the dishes were put away. The people might
come back and dance on the dance-ground until the sun had fully
set. They stopped finally at full sundown. Many of the people
did not camp on the grounds and had to go home for the night.
Others had to look out for their horses.

In this way the people danced at the encampment for four days,
and the last day they continued dancing all night. As individuals
had trance visions, they would begin to wear different feathers and
paints according to what they saw, and at later Ghost Dances
would bring out these Ghost Dance things and use them.

After the entire dance was over, the people generally slept a full
day. Later they might decide to hold a hand game. In these early
Ghost Dance times among the Skiri, a hand game could only be
held after a full Ghost Dance had been carried out. Later hand
games were interspersed in the Ghost Dancing.

Such were the ceremonial forms of the first Ghost Dancing
among the Skiri proper.

Although Mrs. Washington was in this way responsible for the
first organization of the Seven Brothers, Mrs. Goodeagle came to

be known as the Mother of the Seven Brothers. This was because she clothed them according to directions which she received in a Ghost Dance vision.

Mrs. Goodeagle saw two eagles in her vision, a white one and a black one. The black eagle did not speak to her. The white eagle told her to put up a feast and dress the Seven Brothers. She did so. She gave each of the seven a special shirt, and a white sheet to wear. At the back of the head on the sheet two black ribbons were stitched, so that they hung down for about two feet in the back. All the seven were dressed alike.

Then later someone else fell into a trance and told afterward that Mrs. Goodeagle was the Mother of the Seven Brothers, and that the people must call her that. So all the Skiri considered her the Mother of the Seven Brothers.

PERSONAL EXPERIENCES OF MARK EVARTS

In 1897 or 1898, Mark Evarts came home.[1] He had been away a number of years, first at the Carlisle school, and then working as a harness maker in Harrisburg, Philadelphia and Newark. When he got to Oklahoma, the Ghost Dancing had been flourishing both among the South Bands and among the Skiri. The organization of the Seven Brothers among the Skiri was already existent. Mark was not unacquainted with the Ghost Dance. He had heard about it at the time it began to spread among the tribes. He had made a brief visit home at the height of the excitement. But the rest of his story after his arrival in Oklahoma is best told in Mark's own words:

"I told them I did not believe it. I said, 'You can't make me believe it.' Because I was educated and because the white man taught me that the Indians were superstitious. But the white man didn't look at himself and see how superstitious he was.

"One day the Pawnee were all going up to the Oto. After a lot of them had gone, a fellow named Sam Thomson said to me, 'Mark, let's go up to where the Oto are camped now.' We went north to a place about seven miles south of Red Rock. We got there in the evening. We looked into the timber, and there on the other side of the creek we saw the smoke from the encampment. We didn't know where to eat and spend the night, but we found two old ladies in one tipi and we went in there. We asked them if we could sleep there, and stay around during the camping. While I was there I heard someone say, 'this tipi is a special hand

---

[1] Mark had been home on a visit in 1893.

game tipi.' Of course at that time I didn't care about that, but they talked about it.

"One morning I took my horse out and tied him where there was good grass. I looked about me, and looked up at the sky, and all at once felt as if I had swallowed something. I felt sorry for myself. I said, 'Here I am. I have no father, no mother, no home,' and then all at once something struck me. I thought that there was nothing good in this world. I let the horse go and didn't bother with him. On the north side there was a big hill. I climbed it and facing west I began to cry. I was sorry for myself. I was alone. Sorrow came all over me. All day I stayed there, until sundown, with nothing to eat or drink. About at nightfall I fell asleep there.

"The next morning I started to cry again, fasting there. I stayed there about three days and nights with nothing to eat and drink, but at the same time I never felt hungry. On the fourth day, in the morning, I felt like sleeping. Everyone in the camp knew I was up there. I went to lie down with my head on my hands.

"Just after I went to sleep I heard someone call me. He said, 'Now look at the south,' and not very far off I saw a badger. He said, 'Now if you want to do that, take the citizen's clothes off. You have to have different clothes.' While I looked at him, it was as if I took my clothes off and put them in a hole in the ground. And someone said, 'now put your Indian clothes on and then you do that.' Just as I heard that I awoke, and again I began to cry. About noon I felt as if I must sleep again. I could hardly stand up. I went to lie down on my back, with my head towards the east. All at once I fell asleep. I saw someone standing way up above me in the sky, and I was with him. He faced the north, and I stood at his left side. He said, 'now look way down there. Here you are, and there you are lying, down there.' I looked down and saw myself lying there with my mouth open. Near my head there was some bird. The bird walked around close to my head, bobbing its tail up and down. It had a white feather at each side of its tail. Finally I saw it go right into my mouth. I lay there like a log. I could see it go down inside, and could tell when it got down to the stomach. This one told me, 'go down and kick your feet.' I kicked my feet, and I woke up. Then I began to cry again. As the sun went down, I found my eyes were very tired. When the sun was pretty near down I was looking west. I could see the sun whirl around and around,[1] and once in a while white spots came off it as it whirled, and then green. Then it seemed to be coming toward me, then it seemed to be going away again. At half sunset, over the grass you

---

[1] Mark's gesture at this point indicated a clockwise motion.

could see the shadows coming. Some one said to me, 'now right there, you see the sun there. Right there, that's what's going to hurt you, the shadow of the grass.' The shadows began to twist over like fishhooks, and were sharp. 'That's the people's talk. They'll use bad words on you, and tell you you're crazy and call you names. Let them talk all they want to, don't mind them. It isn't yours, it's mine. When they curse you, they curse me.'

"Just before it got dark, as I was standing and crying, I looked east, and right there in the bottom I saw an owl fly up along the grass, with white on each side of the tail. He flew around and around as it got dark, and finally into a hollow a short distance off. As he disappeared into the darkness of the hollow, I heard three doctors singing. Each one had a gourd rattle. They were coming up toward me. There was no one there I could see, but still I heard them coming toward me as it grew darker. I was looking in the other direction, but my mind was behind me: I knew they were coming. When they were about halfway, they changed the song into a humming, saying, 'I'll kill you. H-hm, h-hm, h-hm, I'll kill you.' They had something to hit the ground with. I made up my mind that I didn't care if they killed me. Let them. I wasn't afraid. I was a man.

"I used to think I was a brave man at that time, but I wasn't either. I found out that time. All at once it came into my mind that it was the scalped man coming. I looked out of the corner of my eye and could see him coming close. I looked around and could see he had a club he was raising over my head to strike me and kill me. I thought, 'let him go ahead.' I was looking upward, and it felt as if something was taken out of my mouth, and another thing put in. The brave one was taken out, and the coward put in. Then I ran off.

"That night these men were after me all night. They chased me around. They chased me pretty near to Ponca City. I couldn't get back to the camp, because they would turn and bar my way. Just about at the time the moon came up, they changed into the night crow. It came close to me calling 'ka, ka, ka,' and I had to run again. When I came to one place, there were seven horses, all white. He said, 'When you chase them round, the last one, if you get it, it's yours.' But I was tired. It was near morning, and I was very tired. I wanted to sleep. Just as I would be about to fall asleep, these horses would come up. It was the seven of the dipper that go around the North Star. Then morning came. I woke, and there was nothing wrong with me. I came home. When I went back to the place on the hill where I had been standing, my aunt was there, waiting to take me home.

"After that I had to join the Ghost Dance. I used to paint my face with yellow and two blue streaks across each cheek.

"The reason this made me feel the Ghost Dance was true, was because it all began with my father and my mother, and they were both dead. That's why—because they were ghosts—that we call it the Ghost Dance, and that I had to go and join it. After this I believed it was all true."

After his vision, Mark Evarts was sick for some time, and did not begin to dance with the Ghost Dancers at once. He lived some time alone at Osage City.

Once he was on his way back to Pawnee when he met the Pawnee camped at Skeedee. Mark Rudder and others were there. They told him it was a good thing he had come, because they were going to make feathers for the Crows.

Mark Rudder organized and led a brief hand game that night. People from the town heard about the game and came out, swelling the crowd. Rudder avoided the ceremonial complications of the game; it was played for enjoyment, and people who joined in sat as they pleased.

It was a full moonlit night. The game was played in a tent, and after each game they went outside to dance. The moon was in the southeast. "Louis Behaile was touched, he got shaky, all at once he cried. He stood crying with his hands up toward the moon. After we came back inside the tent, he told it. 'I felt something in my mind, when we went out. It seemed I was going to see something. It's coming. We went out. When we were dancing around, all at once I looked up at the moon, and the moon looked down and saw me and laughed at me. That's why I cried.'"

At the hand game Rudder told all the men to come the next morning. "We've got something to do here. We've got the crow feathers and the cedar. We're going to make feathers for the Crows, for each one of you. And those who are outsiders, if you want me to make them for you, you come and I can do it. We're going to take a whole week to camp here. We're going to make these feathers."

The place at which they were meeting belonged to Jonathan Eustace. Jonathan told Mark Evarts to stay right at the camp, and unsaddle his horse. So Mark stayed there. At that time Mark Evarts had nothing to do, and usually lived at Rush Roberts' farm.

The next morning, the men came about ten o'clock to Rudder's tent. His tent faced east. Inside, Rudder sat at the west, with a wooden cross set up behind him, and a small pile of crow feathers in front of him on a spread. Rudder set one man to work preparing cedar sticks, another to work preparing the horn ends of the feathers so they could be attached to the sticks with sinew. Still another was called and told to get sinew ready for use as thong. While the work proceeded the other men present told stories. One man said that he heard the crows calling "ka-ka-ka," and understood what they meant, so he came to the camp and there sure enough he found them all working on the crow feathers. The others laughed. The men preparing the things took their time. They were working at it all day. When dinner came in the evening, Mark Rudder had all the things wrapped up and put aside. The work was finished the next day.

Only wing and tail feathers of the crow were used. Four feathers, either from the wing or tail, were attached to the stick. Each man present was asked which kind of feathers he wanted put on his. The sinew was soaked in a bowl of water to soften it for use. The head end of the cedar stick was spread or thickened so that when the feathers were tied on they spread outward. Across the top of the sticks indentations were made in the form of a cross and when these crow sticks are used ceremonially and set in the ground, the ends of this cross must point in the cardinal directions. Red paint was put in the grooves of the cross. The feathers were bound onto the sticks while the sinew was wet, after which the sticks with the feathers attached were hung out in the wind to dry. The sinew tightened in drying. Each man who wanted a crow stick came forward and took one.

THE SEVEN CROWS AND AFTER

Mark Rudder was thus instrumental in developing the decoration and recognition of Crows. As yet, however, there was no official organization among the Crows, similar to the Seven Brothers of the Eagles.

Once when they were Ghost Dancing near the north round house, a young woman "got the shakes" and fell. When she recovered, she sat there crying. The old man crier went to her and blessed her. Then he asked her if she had something to say. She said, "Yes. When I fell, I went down a road leading west and saw a big hill across my way, and the road went up the hill. I went up that hill. When I got on top of the hill I looked down below on the other side. There was a big camp there. As I went down the hill I saw a man coming out of that camp. He met me before I got to the camp, and told me to stop, not to come any further. I stopped. He stood right there in the road. He said, 'Now my girl, I came to meet you here. I'm the one who told you to come. We are dancing over here. We know you folks are dancing over there and I want you to tell them to have Seven Brothers of the Crows just as well as the Eagles. Now when you go back you can tell them. Sometimes when the Seven Eagles are tired singing, you have to turn over the singing to the Crows to help out. That's why I say you should have Seven Crows. One more thing: When you have the Seven Eagles sing, you must put one woman between each two Eagle brothers, because when they sing the women must sing too. And you must do the same way with the Seven Crows.' I wanted to turn my head to look around, and as I did that, I woke up, and got up."

In accordance with this vision, Mark Rudder as the main Crow selected six to join with him as the Seven Crows. Five of the Skiri selected were: John Moses, Jonathan Eustace, George Beaver, Yellowcalf, White Fox. Mark Evarts himself became one of the Seven Crows later, succeeding one man who died.[1]

After that when they held the Ghost Dancing, the Seven Eagles were put on one side (the south), the Seven Crows on the other side (the north). Still later, someone had a trance vision and saw that it should be done the same way in the hand games.

After the organization of the Seven Crows, Mrs. Cover was made the Mother of the Seven Crows by analogy with the Mother of the Seven Brothers organization. Mark Rudder selected her. She was not chosen as the result of a vision, or because she clothed the Crows.[2]

Thus the ground plan arrangements finally became among the Skiri: A central clearing for the dancing; a special Ghost Dance tipi due west of it; a sacred tipi south of the cleared ground for the Seven Eagle Brothers; and a sacred tipi north of the clearing for the Seven Crow Brothers. Certain alignments of the games were later determined by these orientations (see for example, Boy Chief's game).

---

[1] John Moses and Mark Evarts are the only ones still living.

[2] A dream of Mrs. Cover's of this general period illustrates certain concepts of the Pawnee Ghost Dance:

"She dreamed she saw Christ standing at the west, facing east. Before him were many little children. At the extreme south was Emmet Pierson and other chiefs, at the extreme north were Mark Evarts, Eaglechief and others. A voice spoke, saying, 'As you see these standing, these are the ones to take care of Christ's children, his people.'"

The Pawnee speak of a chief as a "father" to all his tribespeople, and here this idea has been interwoven with Christian beliefs.

The smoke offering of the Skiri Ghost-Dance was not altered by this new organization. Only the Seven Eagle Brothers participated directly. The Seven Crows organization was an alternative one, to assist in the singing. After a day of Ghost Dancing, Sam Cover, the leader of the Seven Eagles, might officially turn over to the Seven Crows the singing and leadership of the dancing for the following day. With the Crows leading, the formal positions for beginning and ending the songs and dancing remained the same.

Every day after the dancing, the people gathered outside for the formal food offering and blessing before eating (see above). The chiefs talked. The arrangement outside was the same as that previously described, except that now instead of the Seven Eagle Brothers on the east facing west, the two organizations were seated together, the Seven Eagles south of the mid-point, the Seven Crows just north of it, making a row of fourteen seated side by side.

After the organization of the Seven Crows, the form of Skiri Ghost Dancing passed through only minor alterations; so far as memory of informants goes, it remained constant—constant at least while the Ghost Dancing was a serious belief and practise of the Pawnee.

With the alternative organizations of Seven Brothers and Seven Crows for the Ghost Dance singing, in the event that both groups of singers were tired at the end of a day of dancing, and neither was anxious to take over the leadership the next morning, a custom of playing a hand game to decide who would carry the burden the next day tended to develop. In the central leading tent in the evening, the Ghost Dance leaders and the two organizations ate together, with the Seven Crows on the north side, the Seven Eagles on the south. Here in the talk which accompanied the meal, the members of the two brotherhoods might challenge each other to play a hand game that night. The losers would get up early and begin the dancing; the winners could sleep late.

Each formal occasion of four-days' Ghost Dancing was in general charge of one man, and was "put up" in the main by one woman. After a woman had offered to put the dance up, the chiefs gathered and selected one man to be in charge. This man's job was to handle all matters which came up during the entire period of dancing, a hard task and a great risk, because whatever happened while the dance was in progress was credited to the one in charge for blame or praise. If there was good luck, people spoke well of him; and if there was bad luck, people agreed it was his fault.[1]

---

[1] Such responsibility of the leader is true for all Pawnee ceremonial venture. The method of having someone, usually a woman "put up" the

Mark Evarts led several times, and says that whenever he had the lead he had good luck. One time a baby was born while the dance was in progress—that was good luck. Tobacco was being ceremonially prepared to be handed to Mark for making a smoke offering. While they were praying that good luck might go with the tobacco, a grandchild of Linford Smith's was born. So all present thanked God, and hoped it would be that way throughout the dancing.

While these developments were taking place among the Skiri, the Ghost Dancing of the South Bands continued to follow the formal arrangements which had been instituted by Frank White. As members of the organization of seven singers which had been developed by White died, new members were selected to take their places. The smoke offering was not altered.

Murie, in discussing Pawnee ceremonial Ghost Dance, forms, states[1]:

"In 1904 three Pawnee went to Walker Lake, Nevada, to take instructions of Jack Wilson, still the recognized leader. Here they learned what is now regarded as the correct ritual for the ceremonies. According to this formula, a special painted tipi is set up near the center of the camp as the temple... The modern Ghost Dance camp is pitched in a circle and the ceremonial tipi set off center toward the north or south side according to the place of the host..."

The arrangement of which Murie speaks, in terms of which the leading tent was on the north or south according to the place of the host, refers to Ghost Dance hand games, rather than Ghost Dances proper; for in the hand games, as will be described below, one side (either north or south, viz., either Crow or Eagle) is "host" and in charge.

GHOST DANCE SONGS[2]

The songs "dreamed" or secured in visions in the Ghost Dance ranged over all the subjects that could naturally come to mind. Some emphasized aspects of the Ghost Dance doctrine, viz., that in the other world all was as in former days, that the Christ was

---

affair, viz., supply the bulk of the meat and other food necessary, as well as the method of selecting one man to be in charge, are general Pawnee patterns.

[1] Murie, p. 636.

[2] The song texts of this section have been retranscribed and retranslated from the Densmore versions by Dr. Gene Weltfish.

coming, that there would be a reunion with the departed, that a great change was coming. Others embodied the memory of societies of former days, the gift of paraphernalia, or of hand games. No attempt has been made to transcribe songs for this study; a few representative songs are available from Densmore and Murie.

Frank White's first Ghost Dance song has already been given. The free rendering:

> "The place whence you come
> Now I am longing for.
>
> "The place whence you come
> Now I am ever-mindful of."

refers to the land of the departed from which a messenger came in White's vision.

A song of Roaming Chief recorded by Densmore from the version of Effie Blane, reports a Ghost Dance trance vision of Roaming Chief.[1] The reference is to the coming of Christ, and the feeling among the people that all was to be well.

> *ra a*   *(hi i i a)*   *he i ra a*   *(hi i i a)*
> he comes   yonder he comes!
>
> *he ra*   *(i hi i a)*   *he ra*   *(a e ee)*
> he comes!   he comes!
>
> *heru*   *(u u)*   *kitu*   *tixwakiἀ·hu*
> then   all   they are saying
>
> *rịhi*   *weturahe*
> here   now it is good!
>
> *ra a*   *(hi i)*   *i ra a*   *(hi i i a)*
> he comes   yonder he comes
>
> *hera*   *(i)*   *hera*   *hera*
> he comes!   he comes!   he comes!

He is coming, yonder he is coming
He is coming! He is coming!
And so all the people say
All is well here now.
He is coming, yonder he is coming
He is coming! He is coming! He is coming!

_____

[1] Densmore, Pawnee Music, song no. 66, p. 92. "A Ghost Dance was sometimes held especially for Roaming Chief and he 'cried as he sang this

A song recorded by Effie Blane[1] reports a vision of a boy crying for his mother, and asking from the depths of his sorrow, if his mother is really to return to him:

piraski	*rawakakawitiku*		
boy	crying sits down		
piraski	*rawakakawitiku*		
atira	*kawe ráà·hu*[2]	*atira kawe ráà·hu*	
mother	is she coming now,	mother is she coming now ?	

      tiratpári   *tiratpári*
    here I roam here I roam.

> A little boy is sitting crying,
> A little boy is sitting crying,
> "Is mother coming now ?
> Is mother coming now ?
> Here I wander about, here I wander about."

Two songs recorded by Effie Blane[3] refer to the Crow as the messenger from the beyond. One, without Pawnee text, is given in free translation by Densmore as:

"The crow, we see his likeness moving inside the circle of dancers."

The other song is given in full:

ka·ka	*tíwa·ku*	*ka·ka*	*tíwa·ku*
Crow	he says	crow	he says,
wétatù·ta	*(tu)*	*tátù·ta*	
now I do		I do	
atira	*ɩrira·a*	*atira*	*ɩrira·a*
Mother	whence she comes	Mother	whence she comes
(Moon)		(Moon)	

> The crow is calling, the crow is calling,
> "Now I am active, I am active
> In the place whence Mother Moon comes, in the
> place whence Mother Moon comes."

---

song.' It was also customary to sing this song at a hand game." (p. 91). The song would not be sung to hand game play, but in the Ghost Dance intervals.

[1] Densmore, p. 76, no. 47. The explanation which precedes this song in Densmore's account is misconceived, and may refer to another song; a *piraski* is a boy up to the age of puberty.

[2] This is not the interrogative used in ordinary speech or in text material. I am thus unable to control the form of the question grammatically, but since the substance of the song calls for an interrogative I leave it as it stands and have translated it in that way. The complex *we ráà·hu* would be the declarative form, "now she is coming." G. Weltfish.

[3] Densmore, nos. 50, 51; pp. 79—80.

The song embodies the relationship of the crow to the Moon from which the bird's power comes, and indicates also that the Moon is the night overseer of things on earth, reporting them in the beyond. The crow is telling the people on earth of the activities in the land of the departed.

The song was based on a Ghost Dance vision of Effie Blane herself. Used at a hand game it was probably not sung to the play of the game.

Several songs reflect the vision of old societies, and their subsequent revival (see Chapter III—Revivals of Societies).

A song recorded by Wichita Blane[1] reports a vision in which Christ gave the Young Dog Dance society pipe (probably) to the visionary:

> *we ra a   (i ya)*
> now he comes
>
> *ha   i ra a   ha   i ra a   (hi a)*
> See! yonder he comes See! yonder he comes
>
> *ha i ra a   ha i ra a   (ho hi a)*
>
> *he   tiwerihaktsa*
> (Emphasis)   here now it stick lies!
>
> *atias·   pirau   kura   (u)*
> father   child   his
>
> *kuraha·ku^x*   *tikuha·ku'*
> his own stick   he to me stick gives
>
> *i ra a*
> Yonder he comes.

> Now he is coming
> Lo, yonder he is coming, yonder he is coming
> Lo, yonder he is coming, yonder he is coming.
> This stick that is lying here,
> The son of the father
> His own stick he gave to me.
> Yonder he is coming.

A song recorded by Effie Blane belonged to Running Scout and referred (probably) to the revival of the Wolf Society. Of this song, Densmore writes: Running Scout "was very religious and remained in a Ghost Dance trance for several days. His friends

---

[1] Densmore, no. 59, p. 86.

thought him unbalanced but when he awoke he told them that
he had been to the Messiah who told him to 'go to the village.'
Following this instruction, he saw many men dancing. Some had
fox skins around their heads while others used fox skins in hypnotizing their fellow dancers. For this reason Running Scout always
wore a fox skin in the Ghost Dance. The skin was not made into
a cap but the head and tail were fastened together and hung at the
back of his neck in such a manner that the tail rested on his shoulder.
He also gave the call of the fox while he was dancing."[1]

1 — *ɿrihe   we ɿsɑrɪt*
      so here now stop!
1 —   "
1 —   "

2 — *kiwaku   rirɑraxra*
      fox (es)   they have them

1 — *ɿrihe   we ɿsɑrat*
      so here   now stop!
1 —   "

Here now you must stop!
Here now you must stop!
Here now you must stop!
They are holding fox skins
Here now you must stop!
Here non you must stop!

Densmore in one case records a free translation of a song without
text[2]:

"The yellow star has noticed me,
Furthermore it gave me a standing yellow feather,
That yellow star."

The reference is apparently to one of the old star powers and
reflects the gift of an ornament of "power" in a Ghost Dance
vision.
    A song without texts used at victory dances was "'in the style
of the Lance dance songs'... The words mean, 'They are coming
yonder, the men who belong to the Lance Society (Tirupa)[3].'" The
reference here is to the resurrection of the membership of the old
Fighting Lance Society (tirupahe), and to the revival which took
place in the Ghost Dance years.[4]

---

[1] Densmore, pp. 84—85, no. 58.   [2] Densmore, p. 84, no. 57.
[3] Densmore, p. 68.   [4] See Chapter III, Revivals of Societies, pp. 112—115.

III
CULTURAL SIGNIFICANCE
OF THE GHOST DANCE

In 1892, as we saw in Chapter I, the United States government program of assimilation had reduced the Pawnee to a cultural impasse. Their old life was gone, and nothing adequate had been given them in its place. The Ghost Dance doctrine which reached the tribe in 1892 brought hope into Pawnee life. It promised the coming of a new and restored Indian earth, on which the white man would be no more, on which the buffalo would roam again, and the Indian peoples live in peace and plenty. According to the prophecy of the doctrine the change was destined, and did not depend on the voluntary intervention of the Indian. Faith in the doctrine and message of the new religion was, however, an essential condition to participation in the benefits of the new order. The activities of the Ghost Dance were modes of converting the unbeliever, and of reinforcing the conviction of the faithful. The first tenet was to dance. The feet of the dancers pounding the earth was symptomatic of the rumblings of the earth which presaged the change. In the beyond, the message declared, they too were dancing, and to dance here in the same way was an augury of the coming reunion. A second tenet prescribed the casting aside of the white man's ways as an expression of faith. To put aside white clothing, white labor, and white customs, was in still another way to participate with the people dancing in the beyond, and to demonstrate concretely one's conviction that these things of the white man's were of the passing present, soon to be swept away. A third tenet concerned the visions and the seeking of them. These visions were moments of intercommunication between those here on earth and their deceased kinsmen in the beyond. To secure them was to prove one's strength of faith. In attaining them one saw the people in the other world alive and well and happy; one saw and foresaw the new earth that was to be. These visions reinforced the tenet which prescribed a casting aside of the white man's ways, for in the land of the departed the old ways of life went on still as they had in former years on earth. To do as one's kinsmen were doing in the beyond meant not alone to put aside the alien customs of European culture, but actively to take up again the native ways of the Indian. The Pawnee turned back to the past for values and satisfactions lacking in the present.

The revival of Pawnee culture which began to materialize in the years of the Ghost Dance went back for its material primarily to three sources in the old culture: the bundles and bundle rituals, the societies, and the games. The general attempt to resuscitate the aboriginal forms, supplemented and fortified by the inspirations and mandates of the visions, resulted in three types of cultural rebirth. The activities of old ceremony, performance and play were fostered; the paraphernalia were put in order, renewed, and recreated; and concepts from the old context were enshrined in symbols and facsimiles which were carried in the dance and integrated in new cultural forms.

BUNDLES AND BUNDLE RITUALS

The principal bundles of the Pawnee in aboriginal times were the sacred bundles,[1] often spoken of as village or band bundles, and the medicine men's bundles. The former were predominantly concerned with cosmological powers and references; the latter with the animate forms of the earth, the waters and the air (animals and trees, fish and water-creatures, birds). By 1892 sacred bundle ritual demonstrations had practically ceased; of the medicine men's ceremonies, the great doctor performances of the fall had ceased in 1878, but the Doctor Dances of the spring and summer continued at irregular intervals, and such medicine men's ceremonies as the Buffalo Dance were also carried out on occasion, while the Bear Dance had died out. Resuscitation of the old bundle rituals was the most difficult problem of revival and could not be fully met; a good part of the sacred rituals and paraphernalia had been buried in the grave with their final priests. There were two modes or types of occasion on which bundles were opened in aboriginal times: to demonstrate the ritual, and to renew or repair the bundle parts and contents. There is little evidence that the Pawnee succeeded in actively rehabilitating the ceremonies of the sacred bundles, but they did succeed in reconstructing the medicine men's

---

[1] I avoid any attempt to here catalog or describe the many bundles of the four Pawnee bands, which would of necessity be lengthy and for the most part irrelevant. The interested reader may consult Murie, Societies, pp. 549—556.

Bear Dance, and a number of sacred bundles were opened and an attempt made to put them in physical order.

The bundles and bundle rituals were esoteric possessions and knowledge, controlled by individuals. As such their inheritance and transmission followed traditional modes, and according to the orthodox old Pawnee doctrine no revival of extinct forms was possible. The sanction of the Ghost Dance doctrines and visions was in definite conflict with old customs of transmission, and came to predominate.

In the traditional view, the knowledge and learning of an individual had to be handed down by actual instruction of the young. This was somewhat different for the two kinds of bundles, typified by the sacred bundles (with which the society bundles can be associated, as essentially derivative), and the medicine men's bundles. For the sacred bundle type the offices of ownership and priesthood were independent: a chief owned the bundle physically, and his wife took care of it. He did not necessarily know the ritual lore of the bundle. A priest controlled the ritual, demonstrated it on the proper occasions, and advised the owner of his bundle obligations. The physical bundle was ordinarily inherited directly in the male line. The ritual knowledge, however, was transmitted by the priest to his successor by means of instruction over many years. The priest usually taught a close relative (not necessarily in the male line exclusively) because of the desire to hand on his learning in his own family line. But lacking close kin of suitable temperament, the priest taught whom he pleased. For the medicine men's type of bundle, ownership and priesthood centered in the same individual. The doctor himself was owner of the physical bundle, and of its associated teachings, and officiated as his own demonstrating "priest" on ritual occasions. In the course of his life he taught a man to be his successor, and gradually turned over the ritual functions to him. The successor was usually a close relative, such as a "son" or "nephew," etc., but here too the medicine man was at liberty to instruct whom he would, and on occasion chose more distant relatives when near relations proved unwilling to attend seriously to the learning of the traditional material.

Ordinarily a man taught his successor largely by demonstration. That is, the apprentice took part in the actual demonstrations of the ritual (and the curing of the doctor) watching what went on. In the course of the procedure the master explained the detail. As the teacher found his pupil mastering phases of the activity, he turned over to the pupil such parts as were understood. In this way, as a rule, a man learned another's teachings in the course of many years and came to control *all* of it only if the teacher lived to be an old man. In fact the Pawnee conception was that as a man taught what he knew he gave up part of his life, and that when he had given over all his teachings, he would die. Hence the old and learned always held back something until they were ready to die. If a priest or medicine man died, what he had not taught his successor was lost. Usually when an old man knew he was on his deathbed he called his apprentice in and in dying whispers told him the essentials of what he had not as yet communicated. When upon death a medicine man's bundle was inherited only that part of the contents whose use and function were fully understood by the heir were retained; the rest was buried with the deceased medicine man. Because of the independence of owner and priest, a sacred bundle persisted in spite of the loss of part of its significance; the physical bundle survived, though it might be less and less understood with the passing generations.

Religion and ceremonialism in a primitive culture are maintained as oral tradition alone. There is always a gradual loss through cultural forgetting, and a somewhat compensatory gain through the development of new ramifications. The conditions of life of the Pawnee in the Nineteenth Century contributed to a rapid increase of the rate of cultural forgetting. This acceleration was in part due to the loss of function of the ceremonies and rituals, which made demonstrations more infrequent, and hence instruction rarer. At the same time, with loss of functional meaning there was lacking the incentive for the old men to teach and the young men to learn. But in addition, we must not overlook the increase of the death rate among the Pawnee. The learned died before their time; and those destined to carry on their teachings died at an early age. Death interfered abnormally with the traditional mode of handing on the knowledge of the ancients.

The traditional pattern of transmission involved the concept of private or personal ownership of ritual knowledge. What was lost through death was therefore lost beyond recovery. There was no sanction for carrying out any ritual, other than that the one who attempted it had learned about it from ritual predecessors.

The Ghost Dance doctrine supplemented by the Ghost Dance visions altered the general view. In a vision the subject would "see" some old way of life. He would "remember" it. His vision then became a command upon himself and others around him to carry out the old form. The non-esoteric phases of the aboriginal life could be readily revived, which in part explains the great renaissance of games and dances, and the special developments of the Ghost Dance hand games. But the esoteric activities were more difficult to bring back to life. When there were men alive who knew the way, the vision was a specific mandate upon them (often expressed in the vision) to renew the activity. Often, however, a ritual or ceremony was no longer officially in existence; those who had known and controlled it were long dead. Then many men who knew something of it would combine their resources, pooling their memories to revive the ceremony.

The vision mandate in these cases substituted for the old official transference of knowledge. In the Ghost Dance vision the subject "saw" the deceased ritual controller (the "ghost"). The deceased spoke to the visionary, and (in theory) told him to revive the old cultural form, and told him how to go about it. Such visions brought a new sanction into Pawnee life and thought. Where formerly it would have been sacrilege to have carried out a dance or ceremony to which one had not the right through learning and purchase, the trance vision now constituted a supernatural command that the performance be revived.

It was in this way that the Bear Dance, one of the major medicine men's ceremonies was reconstructed and revived. When the Bear Dance was studied by James Murie in the early years of this century, it was the revived form which was studied and recorded. The following account is quoted from Murie[1]:

"At the death of Bear Chief of the Pitahawirat[a], the main bearskin and other things belonging to the Bear Society were buried with him. He had not taught the secret ceremony to any one; so it was supposed that the Bear Society was lost. At a meeting of the medicine society when the ceremony had ended, a woman arose, her name Woman Yellow Corn, and said, "I had

---

[1] Murie, Ceremonies of the Pawnee. In press, Bureau of Ethnology. Murie was unaware of the nature of this whole procedure as a revival, which gives the naive form in which the revival methods are described considerable weight as substantiation of the interpretation of the writer, which is based on work with present-day informants.

The account is presented by Murie as the Skiri Bear Dance, but I have found on internal evidence, such as the affiliation of the owners of the revived ceremony, the choice of individuals for leaderships, the story of teaching associated with the ceremony, and the fact that the bears are "yellow bears," etc., that the form must be considered that of the Pitahawirat[a] band. Murie's confusion about the band affiliation was in part the result of the pooling of knowledge, which overrode band lines. Of interest is the fact that in Murie's account of the felling of the cedar tree, the tree is made to fall westward, a Ghost Dance orientation: in earlier times the tree would have to fall eastward.

a vision. I saw Bear Chief wearing the bear robe over his shoulders and the bear claw neckpiece around his neck. He was painted with yellow earthen clay, and had black streaks from each eye down the face. He said, 'My sister, Father (bear) and Mother (cedar-tree) have not had any smoke for many years. We (dead people) are watching for our people to have the ceremony. The people think the ceremony is lost. It is not, for one of the Bear men who knows the ceremony is still with you. I ask that you tell the people so that they can have the ceremony, for it is time.' I woke up and the last few days have been crying to think that I should be the one to tell you. I have a cow which you can have so you can have the ceremony."[1]

"The leaders of the Bear ceremony each in their turn arose, went to the woman and blessed her... They said, 'My sister, this is very hard. None of us know the ceremony, but Father (bear) and Mother (cedar-tree) will plan a way themselves so we can have the ceremony...

"Some days later the members of the Bear society met and compared their knowledge of the ceremony. When all had spoken a man named Big Star... questioned the others as to their knowledge of the ceremony. He found that none in the meeting knew the ceremony. So he said, 'Brothers, this is hard. You see I am paralyzed, and I could not sit and carry the ceremony out. If you will all agree I will try it. Before we do anything we must select men to be the leaders. You and I know that there are some men here who are descendants of deceased men who were leaders in the Bear Society...' So he selected... Little Warchief... Little Sun..., Good Buffalo..., and Roaming Chief..."

(These men were then ceremonially inducted into office. Big Star then seated himself with these leaders at the altar, and made arrangements to collect among the people the ceremonial utensils, etc. for a set of things needed to carry out the ceremony).

"When all the others had gone out, Big Star told the four men to watch as he carried on the ceremony, that he would carry on the ceremony for them. He also told that Tirawahat[n] had planned through the woman for them to have the ceremony, so he was willing to carry the ceremony on for them without pay; that in olden times men paid to learn the secrets of the Bear ceremony, especially in going after Mother Cedar-tree; that he himself did not purchase the right to carry the ceremony on, but that Bear Chief who was the last man to know the ceremony had given him the

[1] Indicating that the one whose vision caused the revival felt obligated at the same time to put up the ceremony.

right to sit near him and watch; that Bear Chief took pity on him and taught him the ceremony and songs without pay. He then told them to go to their homes, that on the morrow when they entered the lodge each one was to take his seat. They were then dismissed with the exception of Little Warchief.

"When they were alone Big Star questioned Little Warchief about the songs and asked if he knew them. Little Warchief said, 'Yes, I know the songs.' Big Star was glad of this for although he could carry on the ceremony, he was afraid that he would not be able to sing the cedar-tree songs."

(Later at the preliminary feast to set the date of the ceremony), "when all were in, Big Star said, 'You, who are sitting at the altar and those of you at the stations, old men and chiefs. Today we sit in this lodge as men of the Bear Society. We are gathered together here, through Woman Yellow Corn, who had a vision of one of our departed relatives, who asked that we have this ceremony, that Father and Mother might receive our smoke...'"

The medicine men's activities which had not ceased, such as the Doctor Dances and the Buffalo Dance, took a new lease on life as a result of the Ghost Dance impetus. The people attended and participated enthusiastically, and young men began again to learn the doctors' ways.

It is probable that reconstructions of sacred bundle ceremonies were attempted, but we have unfortunately no record. The main effort of revival, as regards the sacred bundles, was directed toward bringing to the attention of the people the bundles still in the possession of the Pawnee, (viz., neither buried nor sold), and to open these in order to renew the contents. I do not know with how many bundles this was attempted. The procedure of renewal was also ritually and physically difficult. In the old days the main priests took charge, and the necessary materials were made available in advance. In Oklahoma neither priests nor materials were available. Mark Evarts described for me the events which took place in 1903 when an attempt was made to renew the tuhutsaku or Left-handed bundle. I quote a few passages:

Frank Leader was the main priest, assisted by Running Scout, Goodeagle, Knifechief (the elder), and John Box. When the bundle was lying open on the altar, Leader spoke:

"Now what you see here, it's a long time since we opened it. Now this here sweet grass," (picking it up), "it's been here a long time. That's what they used to light pipes many years ago. Now these things before me that I have, God put them before us. What

---
[1] Referring to the Ghost Dance prophecy of a coming change.

you see here our old grandfathers had their hands on, but this old woman," — referring to Gillingham's mother —, "when no one's around she ought to untie it; bugs are spoiling some of these things. It isn't like it used to be a while back. We could untie the bundles every year, sometimes twice a year; now everything has kind of rotted. Now today we've untied it all. God himself looks down on this here. It is his will that things are changing on earth.[1] I don't know. I only have what I see here, but there used to be an old man, a priest, who sat here, and when he opened the bundle he would cry over it. I can't do anything. I have nothing to change these things. Now this bird where the head is coming off, I can't sew it with sinew; it will tear. It must be sewn with thread. The only way I have to do is to grease the things and make smoke. I can't go through it as they used to a long time ago."

Although the reconstruction of extinct ceremony, and the renewal of partially disintegrated bundles, proved extremely difficult, the attempt was made. At the same time the cosmological references and type paraphernalia of old bundles were recalled to serve as source material for conceptions and objects integrated in other cultural forms. Thus we find ideas from the old forms of ceremonialism, from the Evening Star bundle, the human sacrifice of the Morning Star bundle, and the Calumet ritual, interwoven with Ghost Dance thought in such developments as the Ghost Dance ceremonial forms and the Ghost Dance hand games; and replicas of old sacred objects appeared at hand game altars, symbolising the references of visions to the old bundles and ceremonies. (See Chapters II, VIII, IX, X, XI.)

REVIVALS OF SOCIETIES

The old societies were a major type of revivals during the Ghost Dance period. There is evidence for a revival in one form or another of the raris arusa (Horse Society), hatuxka ("Those coming behind"... Crow Lance Society), raris skirixki (Wolf Society), tirupahe (Fighting Lances), asitsakahuru (Crazy Dog Dancers), raris kaka (Crow Society), pakspahukasas (Roached Heads), asakipiriru (Young Dog Dancers), raris arika (Horn Society or Horn Dance), and pitararis iruska (the old War Dance).[1]

---

[1] I have limited myself in this discussion to the facts of revival; the society forms, ceremonial smoking, performances, etc., will be discussed elsewhere. For some description of the old form of these societies, see Murie, Pawnee Indian Societies, pp. 561, 570, 577, 576, 579, 581, 582, 616, 608. (Page references follow the order of the societies as listed above.)

These old societies were concerned primarily with war and hunting, and, becoming functionless, had practically ceased their activities by 1892. Each society was controlled by a bundle, from which the powers necessary to the activities of the members were derived, and which in turn derived its powers from greater sources in the major sacred bundles. A full and complete revival of a society would have meant a recreation of the structure of membership, in some cases involving hereditary seating plans, the renewal of the society paraphernalia, the carrying out of the society performances preliminary to regular seasonal activities of its members, and the war path and hunt itself. Some of these societies were entrusted with the policing of the organized hunt. Hence a complete revival could not be accomplished. But a number of societies were reconstructed to a point just short of completion. These were the Horse Society, the Young Dog Dance, the Horn Dance, the Crazy Dog Dance, the Roached Heads, the hatuxka, and possibly the old War Dance. No reconstruction of the membership arrangements was attempted, but led by men who had been connected with a society in former times, leaderships were instituted, singers were taught the old songs, and the dance performances of the society were carried out more or less exactly. Where old paraphernalia was available a renewal ceremony for its physical repair was attempted, while in some cases replicas of the old sacred objects of a society were made. My informants had witnessed regular participations of revival forms of the Horn Dance, Roached Heads, Crazy Dog Dance, Young Dog Dance,[1] Horse Society and old War Dance in the great gathering of bundles for Emmet Pierson's hand game. (See Chapter X.) At this game the altars of these societies were arranged generically: each had one or more pipes and drums, and lances and other sacred objects were set out before the altar. The dancing to society songs in the game intervals required that the drum of the society be moved to the regular drum position, the hand game drum being moved aside.

My informants recalled witnessing in the Ghost Dance period, four or five performances of the Crazy Dog Dance, performances of the Horse Society, the Wolf Society, the Roached Heads and the Young Dog Dancers. In Nebraska days, since these societies were for men only, and for masculine functions, such performances could only be participated in by men and by men who were members. The Oklahoma revivals, in terms of the Ghost Dance, were on behalf of all the people, and all who wished joined in dancing to

[1] A song recorded by Densmore reports a Ghost Dance vision in which the Young Dog Dance pipe was given. See Chapter II, Ghost Dance Songs.

the songs, whether specially costumed or not. I am told that on occasion even women were known to join the dancing.

The Crazy Dog Dancers was revived before 1895 by Skiri Tom, one of the survivors of the old organization. The original membership had been practically annihilated in Nebraska days while on the warpath against the Sioux; the misfortune was so great that a few members who survived hesitated to reorganize. Skiri Tom made Charley Box his main singer, with George Beaver to assist him; White Fox was also a singer. Skiri Tom reconstructed objects closely like the old paraphernalia, a crow-feathered dogwood lance, a pipe, drums and rattles. In the revival dance performances, the dancers were not naked, as in former times, although Skiri Tom himself is said to have worn only a loose jock which exposed the genitals from the rear and caused laughter among the women. Nudity in the old days was a sign of recklessness; those who courted death in war could be bold and foolhardy in the dance. Skiri Tom died about 1906 or 1907; his paraphernalia were buried with him, and the performance of the Crazy Dog Dancers ceased with his death. The songs, however, are still used.

The Roached Heads, originally a Skiri society, was revived on behalf of the tribe under the leadership of George Washington; a performance witnessed was held inside Washington's lodge; the north side was in control.

A performance of the Skiri Wolf Society,[1] witnessed by men and women about 1900, was a departure from its original forms. In aboriginal times this society never danced in the villages either before or after the hunt; on the war path itself, the war party leader organized the performance. As a result, and contrary to the forms of the other societies, no women participated as singers at Wolf Society performances, while in 1900 women singers were employed.

Murie has described the revival of the Horn Dance (raris arika).[2] The society was revived in a modernized form in 1893. "It took its form from the dreams of a woman..." In consecutive dreams she was told how to get an eagle skin, to make the crook crow-feathered lance, and the drum. "The whole ceremony was finally given. At the west side of the lodge upon a robe was the eagle and the pipe, in front of it the crooked stick. A smoke ceremony was made. The woman had a buffalo lariat, or rope, with eagle

---

[1] The revival may have been led by Running Scout. A song recorded by Densmore, Pawnee Music, p. 85, reports a vision of Running Scout which probably refers to the Wolf Society. See also Chapter II, Ghost Dance Songs.

[2] Murie, Societies, pp. 623, 638.

feathers strung upon it so she could wear it over her shoulder. Her face was painted yellow. She selected a bearer of the crooked staff who was a descendant of the staff bearer in the old one Horn Dance. In part of the dance, dancers imitate various animals. The ceremonies are weird and exciting. A food offering of meat and corn is made. The dance is still given and led by this woman" (1914).

The Horse Society (raris arusa) was revived early, probably by Frank Leader. Murie describes at length a ceremony for renewing the society lances held May 23, 1902.[1] The paraphernalia included two lances, four rattles, four hand drums, and a red pipestone bowl with tubular dogwood stem, the stem incised with black bands to resemble trachea markings.[2]

Of certain societies we cannot be sure that the revival was extensive. All the societies mentioned were used as sources for the content of Ghost Dance visions, and the visionaries made facsimiles of old society objects which they carried in the dance. When the visions were as well bestowals of special rituals, such as hand games, the society objects became part of the bundle and altar. The Crow Lance Society (hatuxka) was revived in this way by Mark Rudder; a lance was placed at the altar, and a brief dance led by Rudder opened the game occasion (see Chapter X). The Society of Crows (raris kaka), a derivative of the hatuxka of aboriginal times, was independently revived by George Beaver, and it is probable that paraphernalia made by him were integrated with his game set.[3] Fancy Eagle is credited with the making of a hand drum which was associated with the old Fighting Lances (tirupahe[4]) and used in hand games.

In addition to the use of paraphernalia, songs of these revived societies were used in the intervals of the hand game ceremonies. It is also probable that the use of drums in the hand game ceremonies was based on old society forms.

---

[1] Murie, Societies, pp. 561 ff.

[2] Ibid., p. 567, p. 566 fig. 5. Two hand drums in the Field Museum (F M 79368—1,2) are probably those of Leader; the face bears in red a representation of the raris arusa sheathed lance with its sets of fringed feathers.

[3] F M 73962 is the revival lance; it is not encased in buckskin. F M 79364 and 79365 are hand drums decorated with Ghost Dance symbols, which are said to have been used for the raris kaka by Beaver.

[4] F M 71934. Reference is made by Densmore, Pawnee Music, p. 68, to a song which apparently concerns the revival of this society. See also Chapter II, Ghost Dance Songs.

The games[1] most important in the old social life of the Pawnee were for men the large hoop and pole game, the hand game,[2] and the moccasin game[3]; for the women, the stick dice game, the plum seed dice game, shinny and double-ball. Boys played at the hand game of the men among themselves,[2] and played a boys' form of the hoop and pole game; girls played the womens' games.

All three revival phases took place with the games, paralleling the ritual revivals. The activities were renewed, viz., the games were again played, and played with renewed enthusiasm; the paraphernalia were renewed and reconstructed in that game sets began to be made again in the old way: such were essential for the hoop and pole games, the plum seed and stick dice games, shinny and doubleball; and lastly the games becoming vision sources, sets of paraphernalia were ceremonialized. On the one hand such developments as the ritual hand games took place, and on the other game objects like shinny balls, hoops, etc. were used as vision embodiments and symbols, carried in the dance and employed to induce visions in others. (See Chapter II.)

In these revivals of old forms, we see that those forms were stressed which were most overt and apparent in the old culture: games basically, the non-esoteric activities of the societies (songs and performances) next, and the bundle activities least of all. This weighting follows the probabilities, in terms of the degree to which the old activities were shared by all the people in aboriginal life; those which were common and familiar possessions of the people were readily remembered and revived, while those calling for special traditional learning were difficult to recapture.

When individuals in Ghost Dance trances were transported to the other world they came there upon villages of Pawnee living as they had of old. The whole concept of the doctrine being an awakening or renewal, the type of life most often visualized in the trances was the tribal life of the early spring and early summer. In aboriginal days the spring was a season of reawakening. With the first thunder came the opening of the great bundles and the chanting of the creation ritual. This ushered in the spring activities of the people. With the passing of winter, and the renewal

---

[1] For descriptions of these games consult Culin, Games, pp. 274, 409, 463, 625, 657.

[2] See Chapters V, VI.

[3] The moccasin game was played by the Pawnee, instead of the hand game, with Central Algonquian tribes.

of life in the waters and upon earth, the villages were plunged into a round of activities. The young men got ready to go on the warpath, and all their moccasins, garments and weapons had to be put in order. The women made the moccasins, and helped them in other ways to prepare. Meanwhile the games had begun among children and adults. As the time neared for the departure of the war parties, the great war society dances and performances were held. A visitor to the villages at this season would have been directly impressed with three phases of the outdoor scene: the work of individuals, in view here and there; the games; and the spectacular and colorful dances of the warriors before their departure. These aspects of Pawnee life, being old and familiar, dominated the imagery of the Ghost Dance visions.

NEW CULTURAL FORMS

The Ghost Dance proved not only a force for cultural revival, but with a return to the past as an inspirational source and guide, and vision sanctions as immediate drives, the doctrine was an impetus to cultural development. Several noteworthy forms are on record. The Ghost Dance ceremonial forms themselves have already been described. The rapid development of the many Ghost Dance hand game ceremonies were the most striking development and reintegration of the old and new; these form the subject of the entire second part of this study and need not concern us here. In addition the development of the modern iruska, or new war dance, among all four bands, a form of social gathering for feasting and gift-giving; and the spread of the peyote ritual, began at this period.[1]

---

[1] An anecdote told by Murie (Ceremonies of the Pawnee, in press, Bureau of Ethnology) indicates in a lighter vein, the freedom to make ritual changes which came with the Ghost Dance doctrine, and the occasional results. "It is said that in 1893, the husband of the Skull Bundle keeper, a rather young man, took a notion he would shell the corn for the people and distribute it in a new way. He gathered some men, shelled the ear of corn from the bundle, and distributed it himself. The people remonstrated, but he told them he had had a vision and was going to do just as he was told. In June he started to Wichita Mountains. When he got about 35 miles south of Pawnee (it was very hot and dry; the dust was about five inches thick) his wagon broke down and he had to stay there several days, but at last got his wheels repaired and started out again. Travelling was very hard. The old woman who was keeper of the Skull Bundle, struck him on the back and said, 'You will shell corn, will you. See what you have done.' That year the crops burned up, it was so hot."

According to Murie's[1] account the modern Skiri iruska was taken over from the Oglala Sioux, but went back to a form of the Omaha grass dance. It began to appear among the Pawnee in 1897, and was fully organized by Eagle Chief in 1911. An independent development of the iruska took place among the Kitkahaxki[x]. "About 1894 while the Ghost Dance was still intense a man named Sitting-Bear began to have dreams of songs and the forms of the iruska. Later, he organized the ceremony and led it until his death in 1903. Interest in it then declined, but the drum came into the hands of Little-Sun, one of the leading singers. According to this ritual, the drum was sacred and its keeper was the keeper of the ritual as in the case of the bundles. In 1912 Little-Sun revived the ceremony with the assistance of Eagle-Fly-High, also a pupil of Sitting-Bear." An independent development of the modern iruska took place among the Tcawi under the leadership of Roaming-Chief,[2] and thence spread to the Pitahawirat[a].[3]

Murie has described how the peyote ritual reaching the Pawnee in 1890 was stimulated by the Ghost Dance excitement, and how some forms of the peyote worship were like Ghost Dance forms.[4] Frank White, the great Pawnee Ghost Dance prophet, was also a peyote devotee. (See Chapter II.) Murie adds, "It may be well to note that the founder of this Pawnee cult began to have his revelations during the Ghost Dance excitement. One of his individual doctrines is that while under the influence of peyote one may acquire knowledge or understanding of things previously unknown to himself. In this way, he is said to have learned rituals belonging to bundles and societies and also to have amassed considerable astronomical lore."[5] This indicates the extent to which the effort to bring back cultural aspects buried and forgotten was a definite part of the Ghost Dance doctrine.

---

[1] Murie, Societies, pp. 624—625, 628. Cf. for a description of the forms of these rituals, pp. 624—630.

[2] Several shields in the Field Museum, depicting warriors' visions of Ghost Dance times, are associated with the development of the modern iruska. F M 71844, and F M 59527 (two shields). One of the latter was identified as probably belonging to Roaming-Chief.

[3] The story of gradual changes in the form of Pawnee visiting party arrangements, associated with the modern iruska development, is a complex tale on its own account, and is reserved for treatment elsewhere.

[4] Murie, Societies, pp. 636—637.

[5] Ibid., p. 638.

THE PAWNEE AT THE TURN OF THE CENTURY

I have gathered the detailed evidence on the cultural revivals and developments from 1892 on in this summary form, in order to emphasize the reality of the Ghost Dance period as a time of Pawnee renaissance. Like greater cultural movements of this kind, it was a turning backward to the past, an attempt to resurrect, preserve and copy the ancient records. From them a new and revitalized cultural movement flowed. Unfortunately, from the standpoint of Pawnee destiny, several conditions combined to destroy this movement, and as the faith was overthrown, the revivals disappeared and activity based on the new forms in part waned. As a result, we cannot today fully reconstruct the movement of changes or prove the full extent to which the old culture began to revive. I believe the evidence presented is indicative, but only a part of what contemporary recording would have offered.

A cultural renaissance to be effective must be in the hands of a free people, and the directions of its flow must be relatively unimpeded. It was impossible in Oklahoma after 1892 to bring back the old material conditions of life of the Indian; his vision that the buffalo, the old habitations and old landscape would reappear was a mirage. This alone would perhaps have only checked the movement, and turned it in other directions. But the Pawnee were not a people with an independent destiny. Until 1893, they were so many cultural children fathered by the paternal solicitude of the agent and the government; after 1893 the Pawnee were so many unassimilated citizens of the United States.

In 1893, with the allotment of their lands in severalty, the surplus lands of the Pawnee were thrown open to settlement by the white man. The town of Pawnee sprang up almost at once in their very midst. The choice of allotments had not been controlled so as to maintain the reservation lines, and when the unallotted surplus lands became the homes of white men, the Pawnee found themselves side by side with white men for the first time in their history. The allotment in severalty made the Pawnee individual land owners; they were transformed from full wards of the government into citizens subject to the laws of the United States and the Territory in which they lived. As such the Agent no longer had absolute control over them; he could persuade and he could withhold annuity money to help reinforce his suggestions, but he could neither command nor enforce his orders.

The Pawnee found their new freedom much to their liking. For one thing, there was no authority which could compel them to stop the Ghost Dance. For another, they found themselves well off financially, with the white settlers among them eager to deal with them. In the town of Pawnee some were able in spite of preventive measures to get drunk at will, at which times as the agent observed, they would proclaim aloud their rights as citizens of the United States.

The allotment of lands had been made per capita. 797 allotments were recorded. A fair estimate would place the 797 as including about 160 families, and 160 to 200 would probably total the number of able-bodied men available for farming. As each family of five members controlled 800 acres of allotted land, it was impossible for the government to expect that the full acreage would be cultivated by the Pawnee men. At the same time the new status of the people left the government with no financial obligations toward the tribe except the permanent annuity, and the payment of interest on trust funds. The Pawnee had to become self-supporting, and if they could not win their sustenance from their own lands, the lands must be put to work for them. As landowners they were allowed to lease large parts of their allotted lands to white farmers and cattlemen; in theory every able-bodied man was to retain a plot of forty acres worked by himself.

The lease system grew by leaps and bounds. At first the lands rented by the year at twenty-five cents an acre for grazing land to one dollar for farming land. The Pawnee land was one fourth rich bottom land, one fourth hilly and rough land, and about one half level upland. The Pawnee reserve was suited to corn and fruit, and in 1897 a trial of cotton was begun. The farm lands continued to rise in rental value. The leases provided for improvements on the land as well as the money rental, and as unplowed land was broken it became more valuable. Rental values rose by 1905 to $ 4.50 an acre for the best farm land. The leasing began in 1894; in 1895 there were 97 leases of Pawnee allotment land and the number increased year by year. At first the payment of lease money was made directly to the Indian, or was paid by the lessee to the agent and by the latter turned over to the Pawnee lessor at once; later as the government found the Indians squandering their money as fast as they received it, the money was kept on deposit for the Pawnee by the agent and drawn on as needed.

There were two reasons for the rapid increase of the lease system. The white man wanted to lease the land from the Indian, because it was profitable land, and at a low rental. The Indian wanted to lease the land to the white man because it brought him money without a kind of labor which was disagreeable to him, especially at the time of the Ghost Dance faith. As time went by Indians and white farmers resorted to various subterfuges to get around the ruling that certain lands they held could not be leased. The Indian would claim that he was employing a white man and intended to pay him, but when harvest time came, instead of the Indian paying the white farmer money, the white farmer gave the Indian a part of the crop.

The immediate results of the lease system were two-fold: on the one hand, for the first time in their lives the Pawnee had plenty of money; on the other hand, they had to make no effort at all to support themselves. In 1897 the Pawnee leases brought an income of $ 12,114.95. In 1900 the income of the tribe from their annuity ($ 30,000), interest on their two trust funds (from the sale of the Nebraska reservation and from the sale of the surplus Oklahoma lands), and leases was over $ 75,000. In that year the population had dwindled to 650, so that the per capita income was about $ 116 or the income of the average family of five close to $ 600 annually, a substantial and adequate income in 1900 on the Oklahoma frontier.

Year by year the Pawnee labored less and less on their own lands; in 1904 their self-maintenance was 42 per cent from their annuity and interests, 43 per cent from leases, and 15 per cent from "labor in civilized pursuits." By 1899 the agents had fully realized the extent of the blunder which had been made; they were aware that the Pawnee could not be made to labor when he had all he needed without it, and pointed out in their reports that white men would have acted in the same way.

Along with the disappearance of all demands upon them to be self-reliant and self-maintaining, the Pawnee were stripped of their last outlets for self management. Leases were made not by the Indian but by the agent; lease money was paid not to the Indian but to the agent. All that the Indian had to do was to draw his income. At the same time with the change of status to citizens, the function of the Court of Indian Offenses vanished, and the court was abolished April 21, 1894; the Indian police were disbanded in October of the same year.

Temporarily with their increased income, the living conditions of the Pawnee improved; they ate better, they dressed better, and they lived better. But the idleness which had come to them was in keeping with their desire during these years to congregate in encampments for Ghost Dances and other performances, so that they leased their houses with their lands and made shift to live here or there as the occasion demanded. During these years there was a constant fall of the population. From 797 at the time of the allotments in severalty the Pawnee were reduced to 633 in 1904. The decrease was steady. The diseases which had persisted in the tribe continued to take their toll during these years. Doctors ascribed failure to control them to their inheritability, to the conditions of continual exposure incident to camp life and continual dancing, and to the pernicious influence and control of the Pawnee medicine men who as a result of the Ghost Dance revival had regained their status with the people.

The Pawnee not only did not have to work to live, but were in a position to pay white men to do their necessary work for them. They paid high prices, and their money went as fast as it came. Their funds were augmented from time to time by the sale of inherited allotment lands.

The conditions of idleness only served to reinforce the revival of the old cultural forms. The Pawnee disliked isolation most of all, and gladly leased their scattered allotments, coming together for a continual round of Ghost Dances, performances, games, and hand game ceremonies. Stripped of their last vestige of responsibility, with no activities that were meaningful or satisfying save these old and new forms of Indian life, they turned to these with a kind of desperation. The experiences of these years, even while the Ghost Dance brought some hope into their lives, caused a number of young men to commit suicide. Eight suicides were recorded in the period from 1892 to 1898. They were reported as occasioned by slight causes, and were traced to the "pernicious influence of the Ghost Dance."

The indolence of the Pawnee became such that in the early years of the century the officials and missionaries began to plead for a change of program. They held that the only solution possible was to throw the Indians on their own resources entirely. Some agents developed the suggestion that at least those Pawnee men who could manage their own affairs should be allowed to lease their own lands and receive the payments themselves. This movement to take away entirely the guidance and control of the agency resulted later (after 1916) in issuing many titles in fee simple to Indians, often without their consent.

Under these conditions, at the turn of the century, the cultural revival of the Pawnee was doomed. It could not take roots in any soil; it was based on no firm way of life. It gradually passed, leaving the Indians still with an empty life, living off the funds which came from the government, and the payments of white farmers who leased their land. But those forms of life which had arisen in answer to their need for social gatherings remained. The modern iruska, with its large scale intertribal visiting parties, the peyote ritual, and the hand games. Later still the modern pow-wow was to arise to draw the Indians of the entire state into a continual round of visiting. To the continuing hand game ceremonies, the major intellectual product of the Ghost Dance years, we can now turn to see in what way they were formed, and what needs they filled.

Part Two

IV
THE HAND GAME:
DISTRIBUTION AND CHARACTER

In this part I have traced the changes in the Pawnee hand game which were functions of the Ghost Dance revival and the renaissance of culture. As a preliminary, this chapter sketches the place of the hand game in the aboriginal culture of North America. It was part of a wide distribution of guessing games, and the principles of chance play involved in the hand games may well have been basic to the principles of chance involved in other forms of guessing games. The consideration herein is not exhaustive; while a new treatment and re-classification of American Indian games seems called for by modern study, such a discussion, amplifying and correcting Culin,[1] must be intensive, and is necessarily irrelevant to the present theme.

The hand game is one of the guessing games of the North American Indians. These games, along with dice games, were, according to Culin, the only games of chance played by the American Indians. The guessing games present considerable variety: differences in objectives of play, paraphernalia used, forms of play, methods of concealment, methods of scoring, type and form of accompanying music, and ritualisation, are widespread. This variability in the guessing games is if anything increased by the errors and misunderstandings of early travelers on whose accounts Culin had to depend for information from some regions. In some cases modern information has superseded the early accounts; in others the cultures are extinct, and confusions must remain.

The guessing games of North American Indians have a contiguous and continuous distribution throughout certain regions of the continent. Guessing games are absent throughout the cultures of the arctic and sub-arctic regions: the Eskimo, the Athapascan peoples of Alaska and northwestern Canada, and the Algonquian peoples of northeastern Canada, the Hudson Bay region and Maine.

---
[1] Culin, Games.

These games are also absent throughout the southeastern United States. Conversely, in one or another form, guessing games are present throughout the Northwest Coast, California, the Plateau, the Great Basin, the Southwest, the Plains, and in the Eastern Woodlands from the Great Lakes and St. Lawrence southward to the edges of southeastern culture. This contiguous distribution of the presence and absence of guessing games implies historical relations of one or another sort. Such a major development of guessing games is unknown from other primitive regions of the world, so that the American Indian guessing games must be considered an indigenous development.

This does not mean that the guessing games must have had a unit origin in time and space and then diffused over the continent. Any guessing game is a complex combination of themes which have no necessary or inherent relation to one another; for example, a method of scoring points won, and the associated guessing objective by which points are won; the objects used in play, as sticks, discs, bones, and the associated method of scoring; the fact and form of musical accompaniment, and the associated type of play. The exact historical understanding of the development of the guessing games must be based upon a consideration of these independent themes, in their special distributions, and the elaboration and integration which they have undergone in special complexes. I shall not attempt this here.

Culin has considered the guessing games under four heads: stick games, hand games, the four-stick game, and the hidden-ball game. This classification is not thorough. While it is true that the four-stick game is undoubtedly a unit form which has developed out of the background of guessing games, the hidden-ball game, as Spier has argued,[1] has two typical forms which we have no reason to identify. The stick games appear in several variant forms, which could be considered as different from one another as the two types of hidden-ball game, or the hand game and the hidden-ball game.

The four-stick game has a limited and localized distribution. It occurs among contiguous tribes of northeastern California, western Nevada, and Oregon. In this game four sticks consisting of two pairs of like sticks are arranged in a serial order under a basket tray or blanket, and the opposition must guess the arrangement. There are six possible arrangements, of which four are identical with the four possible arrangements of the hiding counters in a four-hand hand game. Among the Klamath Dorsey reports

---

[1] Spier, Havasupai Ethnography, p. 351.

that the two additional positions are ruled out of the scoring.[1] These are the positions in which the similars lie paired. This indicates that these positions are actually additional and not fully integrated in the game.

Of the hidden-ball game, the northern type is the moccasin game. This is played by Algonquian tribes of the Eastern Woodlands and Great Lakes, by the Iroquois, and by several Plains Siouan tribes. An object is concealed under one of four moccasins, the opposition having to locate or avoid it. Scoring methods are variable. The essential chance is a one-out-of-four, which is identical with the chance of full success in a four-hand hand game, or the four-stick game of the Klamath.

The southern type of hidden-ball game is the canute or reed game of the Pueblo region. Eliminating special variations, the type is played by all the pueblo tribes, the southern Athapascans, the Yuman tribes of Arizona, the Pima, the Papago and the Ute. A small round object is hidden in one of four receptacles or places — these being other than moccasins — and the opposition attempts either to locate or avoid the hidden object, or to locate it on a particular guess. Among most pueblo tribes four reed tubes are used as places of concealment; the Hopi variation is a tubular shaped cup instead of a reed. At Zuni and among several of the Rio Grande pueblos the reeds are further concealed in mounds; while the Hano, Pima and Papago fill their tubes or cups with sand. The Yumans bury the object in one of four heaps of sand. An anomalous form is used by the Navaho, who conceal the object in one of four moccasins and then bury the moccasins in sand; suggesting, as remarked by Spier,[2] a combination of the southern and northern types of hidden-ball game. In general, locating the concealed object on the first guess is associated with the use of mounds of sand, while the reed game proper employs the principle of locating the hidden object on the third guess, with which is associated a complicated manner of scoring.

The two most widely distributed guessing games are the stick games and the hand games. The stick games are absent in the entire southern region of guessing games, that is, among Caddoans and Kiowans of the Plains, all groups of the Southwest, all Shoshoneans (including the entire region of the Great Basin), and southern California. This confines the stick games to the Northwest Coast, northern and central California, the Plateau, and a sporadic belt of occurrences through the Plains and the Eastern Woodlands to the Algonquians of the New England Coast.

---

[1] Culin, Games, p. 329.   [2] Op. cit.

The most typical developments of the stick games occur on the Northwest Coast, in northern California, and in the Plateau region. Two types are distinguishable here on the basis of the paraphernalia of play; while the principle of play is the same. On the Northwest Coast, among the Interior Salish, the Athapascans of California, the Klamath, and sporadically in northern California (as well as among the Teton Dakota of the Plains), a varying number of sticks among which is included an ace is divided into two parts, and the opponent guesses to locate or avoid the ace. Centering among the Coast Salish, but occurring also among the Klickitat, Chinook and Makah, is a variant in which the sets consist of ten wooden discs, one of which is an ace. The pack is divided while concealed under shredded cedar bark, and the guesser tries to choose the ace.

Variants of the stick games which occur in California, the Plains and the Eastern Woodlands, include one very general form in which an odd number of sticks is divided into two packs, and the opposition guesses for the odd number, the even number, or optionally even or odd. Other variants involve the guessing of the exact number of sticks in a bunch, or special manners of guessing chance distributions.

The basic principle of play of the typical stick games, the western stick and disc games, and the odd or even game, is a choice between two alternatives, some form of hiding or concealment (large numbers of sticks in the odd or even form being a method of concealment) being a preliminary.

The hand games proper are those which employ the hands as places in which an object to be guessed for is concealed. Such games are absent east of the Mississippi, among the pueblo and Athapascan peoples of the Southwest, and among most of the Algonquian tribes who play either the moccasin or stick game. Hand games occur in the Plains, throughout the Great Basin, California, the Plateau and the Northwest Coast. Hand games to the exclusion of other guessing games are played by all Shoshonean peoples save the Paiute of Pyramid Lake (who share with their Washo neighbors the four-stick game), and the Hopi (who like other pueblo groups play the reed game); by Caddoans; by Kiowans; by several Algonquian and Siouan tribes of the Plains; by the Kutenai; and by all Shahaptians except the Klickitat. Except for the development of the Ghost Dance ceremonial hand games, whose distribution is considered in Chapter XII, the hand game, wherever played, is a gambling game.

Reported information on the hand game, particularly the early material used by Culin, is especially weak in failing to distinguish two types of play. When an individual plays a hand game, he hides a counter in one hand, or he hides two different counters one in each hand, and his opponent guesses for the hidden counter, or a given one of the two differing counters. As soon as more than two individual opponents play the game becomes more complicated. Typically, two players of one side each hide one counter or two differing counters, and opposing players guess the distribution. Probably both forms of play occur side by side in many more tribes than we have on record, the former for individual play, the latter for team play.

Some variants should be mentioned. Among some Californian tribes play is side against side, four players composing each side, but the guessing is individual player against opposing individual, as they sit; this form is consistent with the patterns for betting, which elsewhere even with team play, is individual against individual. Occasionally, as among one Pomo group, two players hide counters but the opposing guesser may optionally try to locate the whole distribution or the separate arrangement of either opponent's hands; this optional manner seems intermediate between two-hand and four-hand forms. The Achomawi, Haida and some others use one counter, and the opposition guesses in which hand (usually of four) it is located. Among some tribes one counter is passed along the players of a side (number not clearly stated) and opponents must locate the counter as to player, or hand. Among Yuman peoples, each member of a side conceals a counter, and the guesser tries for the whole distribution at once (apparently the sides usually consist of four members), and the guessing continues only for those unlocated. These variants, based on Culin, are local developments, and probably specializations of the hand game theme.

The type forms are the two-hand and four-hand manners of play already mentioned. In the two-hand form whether one counter or two is concealed the principle is the same; and in the four-hand form whether two counters or four are concealed the principle is the same. In the first case, the chance is one out of two, in the second one out of four (for a perfect guess). It is probable that the Plains method of play for the four-hand form, in which, if the guesser locates the counter of one opponent only, his side loses one tally and he continues to guess only for the counter not found, would prove more widespread if better information were available.

The early data used by Culin emphasizes predominantly the two-hand form. Later information on hand games of the Plains, Basin, California and the Plateau, of Kroeber, Lowie, Wissler, Spier, Gunther, Dorsey and others, as well as Powers' early material on California, in most cases reverses the emphasis, describing primarily the four-hand form. This form, being more complicated, undoubtedly confused the casual observer of earlier days. As a result we cannot be sure of independent distributions of the two forms, or the distribution of their coexistence. What Gunther states for the Klallam, "... they play with two bones, guessing for the marked one. Occasionally in a big game four bones are put into play, being held by two people,"[1] is likely to be an option much more widespread in the Plains, California, the Basin and the Plateau than our records show. Culin's data indicates a definite emphasis upon the two-hand form among tribes of the North Pacific Coast, and Boas has confirmed this.[2] The material sets of bones to hide catalogued by Culin, are for the most part of four bones, two pairs of similars, suggesting the four-hand form as the mode; nor does the occurrence of sets of two bones rule out the four-hand form, in view of the manner of giving each player one bone.

Before discussing the problem offered by the principles of play of the hand games and guessing games, some important characteristics of the distributions should be noted. No American Indian tribe plays all four types of guessing game. Four tribes play three games: The Klamath, Achomawi and Washo, play the local four-stick game as well as the stick and hand games; and the Plains Cree play the stick game, the hand game and the moccasin game. With such rare exceptions, the American Indian tribes who play guessing games play at most two variants. The overlapping in the Eastern Woodlands is between the moccasin and stick games; in the Plains either between the moccasin and stick games or the stick and hand games, not between the hand and moccasin games[3]; while the main overlapping occurs in the Northwest Coast area, the Plateau and California, where stick and hand games occur side by side.

The stick games involve typically the chance principle of one out of two; the moccasin game, the reed game, and the four-stick game,[4] involve a one-out-of-four chance for a perfect guess. Hand games may involve either: two-hand hand games offer the one-of-two chance principle, four-hand hand games the one-of-four chance principle. The overlappings of the game distributions, except for the Northwest Coast and sporadic cases elsewhere, are

---

[1] Gunther, Klallam, p. 274.

[2] In conversation.

[3] In some cases, tribes of the Plains whose native game was the hand game played the moccasin game when opposed to tribes more accustomed to the moccasin game (Pawnee).

[4] I assume here that the limitation of positions of the Paiute four-stick game (Culin, 334) or of tallying for only four positions by the Klamath (Culin, 329) are typical of the four-stick game.

primarily between a two-alternative game and a four-alternative game. This suggests that as regards the chance principles involved the stick games may be related to the two-hand hand game, and the moccasin, reed and four-stick games to the four-hand hand game. An individual hand game must be a two-alternative game. As soon as a four-chance principle game is required four hands are necessary. To utilize the same principle for individual play, the objects must be objectified (four-stick game) or the receptacles objectified (moccasin and reed games).

In terms then of the principles of chance involved, the guessing games of the American Indians are probably differing developments of associations of other themes to the two-chance themes which appear in the hand games. These two-chance themes, the two alternative and four alternative manners, might be considered in terms of limited possibilities to be accidentally re-invented principles if our distribution showed a reasonably chance occurrence of the one-out-of-three or one-out-of-five principles. Two cases are on record suggesting a one-out-of-three chance: Meeker and Prescott report that the Oglala and Santee Dakota used three moccasins in the moccasin game; Meeker makes optional the use of two, three or four moccasins by the Oglala; Prescott describes three as the Santee norm. Prescott's statement is disputed by the reports of Neill and Riggs, who both state that four moccasins are the number used.[1] In addition to these statements, Catlin describes the Iowa as using three or four moccasins.[2] These are the only cases in which a one-out-of-three chance is mentioned, and it seems at best an option. Five alternatives do not occur. These facts support the theory that the two-alternative and four-alternative chance themes have usurped the development of Indian guessing games because of the two-hand and four-hand forms of the hand game.

This theory concerns only the principles of chance involved in the play of the games. Such associated themes as paraphernalia, forms of scoring, musical accompaniment, etc., must be considered separately before statements relative to the total game complexes as such can be made. Furthermore, some specialized developments call for special explanation; the third-guess manner of the Pueblo reed game, associated with elaborate scoring devices, may have to be considered in relation to sources quite different from those of the general North American guessing game development. Such detailed problems require a more relevant place for discussion.

The Pawnee hand game, described in the next chapter, is primarily of the four-hand form, and belongs to the central area of distribution of the hand games, the Plains and the Basin.

---

[1] Culin, pp. 364—365.   [2] Ibid., 366.

V
PLAY OF THE
PAWNEE HAND GAME

To understand the changes which make up the history of the Pawnee hand game, as considered in this study, it is essential that the skeleton of the game play itself be clearly understood. Only in this way can the ritualization which occurred in ghost dance times be visualized against the old game background. The game itself is interesting on its own account. In actual play it has its own excitements and exhilarations, and the pleasure of winning and annoyance of losing can be readily shared by an outsider who participates for a short time.

The Game Sets: Culin catalogs hand game sets in various museums.[1] The Pawnee and Wichita sets pictured and described by him are all Ghost Dance hand game sets, not sets used for the early gambling game. Pawnee sets always consist of eight sticks used as *tally sticks* with which to keep score, and two special bones or die, used as *counters* in hiding.

Sides and Officials: In the playing of the game, two sides oppose each other; any number of players may be joined to either side, even numbers being immaterial. They are definitely immaterial in the Ghost Dance hand games where the affiliation of the individual in the Ghost Dance determines on which side that individual plays. In the old men's gambling game even numbers as regards the players were also immaterial, the visitors or guests always being considerably outnumbered by their hosts; but since in placing wagers individuals bet with individuals, the numbers of those who wagered was the same for both sides. When the boys played and chose sides, the sides were usually more or less even in numbers. The two sides form two halves of a circle, the head end being either at the west or at the north. In all Ghost Dance hand games but one it is at the west; in that one it is at the north. In the old hand game the orientation of the sides was determined by the direction from which the guests or visitors came, with the head end always either west or north. At this head end sit two tallyers, who are the leaders of their respective sides, usually with two

---
[1] Culin, pp. 276 ff.

assistants. These leaders are called *rɪxkɪtᵃ*. Leadership is important in both the old games and the Ghost Dance games. In the old game the main leader of the visiting side is the man who comes bringing the pipe. In Ghost Dance games there are always four individuals behind the altar, following the generic ceremonial pattern of the Pawnee. The two inner ones — next the east-west line, or the north-south line in the one case — are the main leaders, the two outer men being their assistants. These tallyers keep the score with the tally sticks. The leader of each side selects one player to do the guessing for that side.

Putting the counters in play: There are preliminaries to the actual playing of the game proper: in the old games, the smoking of the pipe brought by the leader of the visiting party, the betting, and often a special dance by the visitors; in the ghost dance hand games, the smoke offering, the selection of the guessers, and usually an old dance song sung by the drummers of the host side. The leader of each side selects a guesser for that side by arising, going to one player and giving him a counter.

When the game proper is ready to begin the two guessers arise and face each other across the head end of the arena, each on his side of the midline. Each has one counter. The guesser of the host side puts his hands behind his back while he conceals the counter in one hand, then brings both clenched hands forward and moves them in rhythm while his opponent guesses. Then whatever the outcome, the opponent hides his counter and the first guesses. Calling the guesser of the host side A, and that of the guest side B, there are now four possibilities:

1) A found B's counter and B failed to find A's. In this case they are won by A who puts them in play on his side.

2) A failed to find B's counter and B found A's. In this case they are won by B, who puts them in play on his side.

3) A found B's counter and B found A's counter. In this case the procedure is repeated, until possibility 1) or 2) as above is realized, with the exception noted below.

4) A failed to find B's counter and B failed to find A's counter. In this case the procedure is repeated, until possibility 1) or 2) as above is realized, with the exception noted below.

If either possibility 3) or possibility 4), as above, occurs four times in succession, it is customary for the guessers to yield their office to two others, who try all over again.[1]

---

[1] In one Skiri Ghost Dance hand game, that of George Beaver, it is said that no change was made after four misguesses, but the procedure continued until one guesser had won both counters.

When in this way, the guesser of one side has won both counters, he takes them to two players —usually two seated side by side —of his side and gives one to each. These two players conceal the counters, and the opposing guesser comes across the arena to locate them.

The Play: The two counters when won by the guesser of one side are given to two players of that side, one to each. Each player conceals the counter given to him in one hand so that there is no evidence from his closed fists in which hand it is held. Usually the counter is concealed while the hands are held behind the back, or for a woman, under the skirt. The players who have the counters then bring their fists forward and shake their clenched hands back and forth before the guesser of the opposing side, who stands at a little distance, watching their movements and trying to add to mere chance some significant slip or move which may reveal to him which hand to choose.

In making a choice, with two counters concealed each one in either of two hands, there are four possible combinations: the two outer hands, the two inner hands, the two right hands of the hiders, and the two left hands of the hiders. There are special motions used by the guessers to indicate which of these possibilities is chosen.

To indicate the two outer hands, the guesser spreads his arms slightly outward to the sides, *or* raises both hands with erect thumbs and points the thumbs outward from his body, *or* raises the right hand with the thumb and index finger spread. To indicate the inner hands the guesser extends the right arm as if slicing between the players with the open right hand. To indicate the two right hands of the players, the guesser motions with his own right hand leftwards, *or* raises his right hand with index finger erect. To guess the two left hands of the players, the guesser motions with his own right hand to the right, *or* raises his right hand with index and third finger erect.

As soon as the guesser's choice has been indicated in one of the above ways, the players who hold the counters open the indicated hands so that all may see whether or not the guess has been successful. The player may if he wishes, when the guess has been unsuccessful, also open the hand containing the counter.

There are three possible results of the guess:

1) The guesser is fully successful if with his single guess he has chosen the two hands in which the two counters are concealed. In this case he wins the counters for his own side. Neither side scores points. The guesser who has won the counters takes them

across the arena to two players of his side, and the opposing guesser must now come across to try to find them.

2) The guesser is completely unsuccessful if his guess has indicated the two empty hands. In this case the players holding the counters score two points for their side, which are recorded by the keeper of the tally sticks for that side. Usually the guesser of the side in possession of the counters stands near the play, and, otherwise inactive, he indicates to the tallyer at the head end whether one or two points have been scored by holding up his right hand with index finger erect, or with index and third finger erect. In the excitement of play, other players of the side scoring points who are close to the play usually also indicate to the tallyer what has happened, and many shout "asku," one, or "pitku," two, as well. If the side holding the counters scores two points, the same two players conceal the counters again, and the guesser of the opposing side must try his luck again.

3) The third possibility is that the guesser locates one counter, and misses the other. In this case the side holding the counters scores one point (for the one not found). Then the successful player whose counter was not indicated hides again, while the unsuccessful player awaits the outcome. The guesser now has only to indicate which hand the one counter is concealed in, and has a one-out-of-two chance. If he finds this one counter, he has now won both for his own side, and takes them across the arena to two players of his side. No further points are scored. If, on the other hand, the guesser fails to find this single counter in play, the side holding the counters scores another single point. Now both players (the same two) hide again, including the one who lost the first time, and the other who has twice scored single points. With both hiding again the guesser must try his luck once more with all the possibilities open.

The Musical Accompaniment: Besides the special songs which are sung before the game proper begins, and the songs sung in the intervals between the games, hand game songs are sung to the actual play of the game. The side holding and hiding the counters sings continuously while the counters remain in their possession. As soon as the guesser has won both, the song ceases abruptly, while the opposing side begins as abruptly to sing. In the old Pawnee hand game the clapping of hands was the only instrumental accompaniment. In the Ghost Dance hand games, drums are used. The songs in the intervals are sung by the side which has just won the game.

Scoring: As will be seen from the account of the game *in play* points are scored by the side in possession of the counters when the guesser of the opposing side fails to find the counters. Success in guessing does not score points but wins possession of the counters.

The record of the scoring is kept with the eight tally sticks which lie at the head end (altar end) before the two leaders. In the old hand games these eight sticks are in one heap between the tallyers or leaders; in the Ghost Dance hand games, four are bunched in front of the leader of each side. When his side scores a point, the tallyer takes one of the sticks and places it before him in a separate group, until the eight sticks have all been put in scoring play by having been won by one side or the other. Thus in the old hand game the tallyer would take sticks from the bunch of eight lying between the leaders; while in the Ghost Dance hand game he would take sticks first from the bunch of four not in play lying before his opponent, and then from the bunch of four not in play lying before himself. After the sticks are all in scoring play, a point is recorded for one side by taking one of the sticks already won or scored by the other side and adding it to the "score" bunch of the first side.

A hypothetical illustration of scoring will make the method clearer:

1)   / / / / / / /
          A   B
2)   / / / /   / / / /
          A   B

1) represents the arrangement of tally sticks before scoring occurs in the old handgames. 2) represents the same in the Ghost Dance hand games.

If A's side scores two points the respective arrangements are:

1)   / / / / / / / /
         A   B
2)   / / / / / /   / /
         A   B

If B then scores two points:

1)   / / / / / / / /
         A   B
2)   / / / /   / / / /
         A   B

are the respective arrangements. Then should B again score let us say one point:

1)   / /   / / /   / / /
          A   B

2)   / /   /   / /   / / /
          A   B

illustrate the way the tally sticks would lie.

Now suppose that A scores three points. The resultant arrangements:

1)   / / / / /   / / /
          A   B

2) / / / / /   / / /
          A   B

show that the original groups of sticks in both cases are now all in play. From this point on the scoring consists merely of moving the number of sticks won from one side to the other until as a result of the run of play all the eight sticks cluster on one side or the other. Thus at the point represented above, if one side or the other were lucky enough to run out the game in one turn, A's side would need three points in a row to do so, B's side five.

The only difficulty in following the method of scoring is that it must be remembered that all the tally sticks must have been put in scoring play by having been once won by either side, before accumulating all the sticks wins the game. This is obvious in the case of arrangement 1) of the old hand game where the sticks lie in one bunch between the tallyers. Here if both sides have already scored points the side which is running out first scores by winning the sticks not as yet in play, and then the sticks already won by the opponent. In the Ghost Dance games where each leader has four sticks before him, these belong only ceremonially, as it were, to his side, and have no reference to the scoring of the game. They must be put in scoring play in the same way that the eight bunched sticks are in the old game. Thus when one side wins four sticks in its first turn, all eight are in front of the tallyer of that side, but only four have been put in scoring play. These lie in a separate bunch, and the side must win in addition the four sticks which lie in front of their own leader, but which are not yet in scoring play, before the game has been won. If in these Ghost Dance games each side has already scored, a side running out tallies sticks in the following order: first, those before the opponent not yet in scoring play, then those before the side's own leader not in scoring play, then those which the opponent has scored.

After winning a game: A hand game occasion, whether in the old form or the Ghost Dance form, is never ended by merely winning a game. To use an analogy, one of these games is like a "rubber" in bridge. In the old game, such "rubber" games are played until the possessions that one side can bet are exhausted, or until, because it is late, all agree to stop. In the Ghost Dance games, special arrangements of the number of "rubber" games to be played are made beforehand. Some of the Ghost Dance hand games have a fixed number of games to be played, usually seven, and regardless of the final outcome, viz., whether one side has won four, the other three, or one side has won all seven, the usual custom is to cease playing when the seven games have been finished. Other Ghost Dance hand games have variant methods which are optional, such as to play "even up" a certain number, which means that one side must win so many *more* games than the other.

When one game has been won, there is an interval during which dancing and singing takes place, led by the winning side.

After this a second game begins. For this second game, the guesser of the winning side retains his office, while the guesser of the losing side, by giving another player of his side the counter, inducts him into office as guesser for the side. So that in *putting the counters in play* for a second or later game, there will always be one guesser who participated in the previous game—the guesser of the side which has won—and one new guesser for the other side.

After the counters have been put in play in a second game or later, the players to whom they are first given by the guesser who wins both, are, in the Ghost Dance hand games, those whose turn it is to play.

Taking Turns to Play: In the old games there is essentially no formal method of taking turns. As will be detailed below, the main object being to win actual stakes which are valuable, the counters are given to hide to players who are thought to be lucky or especially able in deceiving the guesser. These will be any two chosen by the guesser, regardless of what positions they are seated in. That is, the individuals may be next each other, or widely separated in the row of players. But, after such individuals have had a turn, and have lost the counters, the custom would be for the guesser, when he had rewon the counters from players of the opposing side, to give them to hide to two other players of his side.

In the Ghost Dance hand games the whole routine is formalized. For each hand game there is an order in which the players seated around the arena take turns. This order may or may not differ from one game to another. The most general form is for the players to take turns as they are seated from the head end to the doorway, thus usually from west to east. The counters are always given, in such a case, to two players sitting alongside each other.

Each player who is given a counter to hide has a continuous turn until he and his partner have finally lost the counters. Then when they are rewon by the guesser of that side, they are given to the next two players in order. This method of allowing continuous turns overrides the interval between games. Thus not only is the guesser of the winning side retained, but the first time in the second game that he gives the counters to two players of his side, he gives them to the two players who "ran out" the previous game, and whose turn was not over, but was interrupted by the winning of the game. On the other hand, on the side which has just lost the game, the first two players to hide are the next two to those who last played.

VI
THE OLD PAWNEE HAND GAME[1]

When the Pawnee lived in Nebraska, and for some time after they removed to Oklahoma, the hand game kept its traditional place in Pawnee life as a gambling game. It was a game for men only, and primarily an adults' game; the women did not participate and were not supposed to come near where the men were playing. The game was conceived as a warpath, and so dramatized: and warpaths for the Pawnee were activities excluding the participation of women. The men's game was usually a contest between two Pawnee bands, in which one would visit the other for the express purpose of playing a hand game and gambling on the result. Small boys, in imitation of their elders, would play hand games and gamble. And in the same way that one Pawnee band visited another to challenge them to play the hand game, men of one Pawnee band would visit a tribe with whom they were on friendly terms for a hand-game contest. For the most part, it was a game for the younger men; maturer men, like chiefs and braves, usually did not gamble.

The three old types of play will be more lucid from short narratives[2]:

THE BOYS' HAND GAME

When small boys played a hand game, it came about as part of their play around the village. Some group of boys would decide to play the way their elders did, and as many or as few as there were,

---

[1] The old Pawnee gambling hand game has not heretofore been described. Culin, in his monographic treatment of Games of the North American Indians, quotes, p. 276, on Pawnee a passage from G. B. Grinnell, Story of the Indian, p. 27. The description of the method of play in the passage differs fundamentally from that herein reported. Examination shows that the quoted passage is a generalized description by Grinnell of the hand game among Indian tribes of the Plains. No reference suggests that he intended it as a description of play among the Pawnee. Culin was no doubt misled by the fact that, following the passage quoted, Grinnell tells the story of a game between Pawnee and Cheyenne scouts in the army, in which a Cheyenne was caught cheating; but in recounting this episode Grinnell does not describe the form of play. Grinnell was familiar with the game among more than eight tribes, and was probably not overconcerned in a popular treatment with the local tribal variations in play.

[2] As told by Mark Evarts; somewhat edited.

they would go off somewhat from the village and choose sides. Someone of them would find sticks and break up eight sticks to make a tally set, and would make two little rings of willow to use as the counters to hide. Some of the boys would steal wood from the woodpiles in the lodges or around the tipis, and build a fire where the boys had decided to play.

When they had the place ready and the fire going, each boy would make up his own mind which side he would be on, so long as the division came out evenly; and each side selected its own leader. To the boys it made no difference what the orientation of their arrangements were; if the sides were north of the fire and south of the fire, or east of the fire and west of it, made little difference to them. Usually they had the scorekeepers at the west, in imitation of their elders. The boys would bet anything they had, such as things they wore, betting on the outcome of the individual games, and would go on playing games as long as a losing side had anything they could put up against the winnings of their opponents. They picked their guessers and decided for themselves which side should guess first. In the play of the game, they followed out the game as given above, playing it and scoring it the usual way. They kept no order in giving the willow rings to players to hide, giving them as much as possible to boys who were known to be good hiders and quick and adept at deception. Their principal object was to win the game, on the outcome of which they had wagered shirts, rings and other things that could not well be spared.

The boys sang songs to the play of the game, and accompanied the singing with hand-clapping. The side which held the willow-rings did the singing and hand-clapping, using it to confuse the guesser. The songs were boys' songs essentially, that they had made up at one time or another, or that they had learned from other boys, although when possible they learned and used adult songs. They were often coarse and always more or less funny. Such refrains as the following are typical:

"My grandmother's out of joint," etc. (referring to her knee).

"My grandmother fell—she raised a cloud of dust," etc.

"Hurry up grandma and come, come quick we want to win."

"The balls swing round, swing round," etc. (referring to the testicles).

The songs indicate the license in speech and action between boys and their grandmothers, which accurately reflects the family conditions.

The boys who held the willow-rings to hide would motion with their hands back and forth; they made efforts to deceive as well as confuse, and it seems likely, that, as in the adults' game, the hidden rings were shifted back and forth from hand to hand as adeptly as possible. Often the boys would fight over the play of the game. The guesser particularly had to be bold and fearless, because even when he won the willow-rings, those who held them would often refuse to give them up. Then he had to fight for them.

THE INTER-BAND GAME

The men's game as played by Pawnee bands against each other is illustrated by the following narrative of a game played in Oklahoma in early days by the Kitkahaxki[x] against the Skiri.

A Kitkahaxki[x] man who wanted to go to play the Skiri, asked a friend to join him as assistant leader, and got together a party of Kitkahaxki[x] youths. Mark Evarts, a Skiri, was then a boy at school, and a friend of the Kitkahaxki[x] organizer. This man asked Mark to join the party so Mark started off with the Kitkahaxki[x]. As he passed under the windows of the girls' dormitory building, a girl leaned out and called, "Where are you going, Mark?" He answered, "We're going to play a hand game, give me something to take along," whereat she threw down a shawl of hers for him to take along to bet with. Each member of the party carried a supply of articles to wager. The leader carried a pipe.

The leader spoke of their going saying, "Well, we're going on the warpath to play the Skiri a hand game."

When they got to the Skiri village, the village crier came out and asked, "What is it?" The Kithahaxki[x] leader, carrying the pipe, replied, "We've come on the warpath for the hand game." At that the old crier ran back and began calling out through the encampment,"There's a party from the west have come to our Skiri camp on the warpath for the hand game. Now boys get the wood and pile it up right here." Boys began to haul wood and heap it up in one place outdoors. A crowd of Skiri gathered around the visiting party. Knifechief, as the Skiri leader, took the Kitkahaxki[x] leader and two or three others home to supper. Other members of the party were taken into other lodges to eat. While they were eating, a large fire was started outside on the game ground. Soon the announcer could be heard outside calling, "Come on everybody."

They form two halves of a circle. The Kitkahaxki[x] sit in a semi-circle on the west side of the fire, from north to south, the Skiri on the east side from north to south. The two leaders of their sides sit at the north with the eight tally sticks in one bunch between them. All the Skiri players are seated (Fig. 1). They are the home players. They outnumber the visiting challengers. Skiri chiefs, warriors and braves stand around to watch the game; they do not play. An important Skiri chief may come to look on, may sit at a distance and smoke calmly. By his presence he expresses his interest in the welfare and doings of his people. Some Skiri players, perhaps the leader, leave the circle to sit beside him and smoke with him, to show their appreciation of his presence.

The Kitkahaxki^x leader has the pipe in his hand. All who are going to play have found their places. Women come and stand at a little distance to look on. They must not sit down or join the circle. They never play the hand game.

The fire forms a long narrow line between the sides, fifteen feet long from north to south, only two to three feet wide (see Fig. 1). At the south ends of the lines are two men who function as tarutsius, "fire tenders."

Now the players place their bets. Blankets, shirts, vests, horses are waged on the outcome. Each bets against a friendly enemy of the other side, individual against individual. The two articles are tied together, making one bundle. The bundles are thrown down in one heap before the leaders. The winning side will carry off the whole pile of plunder, and each winning player takes from it his individual stake and his winning.

The leader of the Kitkahaxki^x party begins to speak.

"Brother, I thought of coming to see you for the hand game. Well, my brother, we are here. I've brought this pipe for you. I want you to accept it to smoke."

He rises. He takes the filled pipe to the fire and lights it with a brand. He draws a few puffs himself, then, standing before Knifechief, the Skiri leader in the game, gives him the pipe to smoke without releasing it, then takes it to his left and lets the assistant leader on the Kitkahaxki^x side take a few puffs. Then he carries it back to Knifechief, gives it to him, and sits down in his own place.

Knifechief smokes and then passes the pipe to the Skiri at his left, and from him it is passed on down the Skiri side from north to south. Each one smokes and passes it on. By the time it reaches the tarutsius of the Skiri side it is likely to be smoked out. This smoke is a gift of the Kitkahaxki^x to the Skiri. Except for the two Kitkahaxki^x leaders, no Kitkahaxki^x smoke, only the Skiri.

When the pipe has reached the Skiri tarutsius, the Kitkahaxki^x leader arises, walks around the east side of the fire and receives the pipe back from him. He carries it with him around west of the fire, and stops north of the fire where facing south, he loosens the ashes with a pipe tamper, and twice raises the pipe bowl upward,

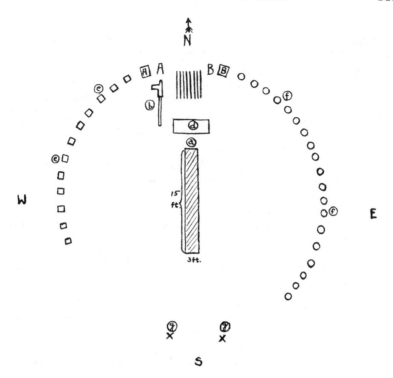

Figure 1. Plan of Game between Kitkahaxki[x] and Skiri

A - Kitkahaxki[x] leader, [A] - Kitka-
    haxki[x] assistant
B - Skiri leader [B] - Skiri assistant
a - long fire
b - Kitkahaxki[x] pipe in position af-
    ter smoking

c - tally sticks
d - position of stakes
[e] - Kitkahaxki[x] men (guests)
[f] - Skiri men (hosts)
g x - tarutsius (fire-tenders)

an offering to heaven, each time emptying some of the ashes on the
ground before the fire; then he loosens the ashes a third time and
deposits all that remains on the ground, an offering to the earth.
Without further motions or gestures he takes the pipe with him
to his place and sits down. He now places the pipe on the ground
before him, mouthpiece pointing south, bowl turned to the west
(see **Fig.** 1). He can put the pipe on the ground because now it
is empty. Up to the time he began the smoking he had to carry the
pipe and hold it in his arms.

    The set used by the Skiri consists of eight dogwood sticks and two
white bones; these are not decorated in any special way. The Skiri
leader Knifechief now announces:

"All right now, let's go ahead." Knifechief gets up and gives one bone to a Skiri man; the Kitkahaxki[x] leader rises and gives one to a Kitkahaxki[x] man. In this way the two are selected as guessers for their respective sides.

Now all the players begin to sing and yell. The two guessers are on their feet facing each other. The Skiri hides the bone first, the Kitkahaxki[x] must guess first. The one who wins them gives them out to hide to any two players on his side regardless of where they sit. He picks them because they are clever at hiding the bones, at deceiving the guessers, at confusing them by shifting the bone almost invisibly from one hand to another. The guesser watches closely. He notes the gestures with the hands and arms, the body movements; he watches eyes for a hint.

As soon as one guesser has won the two bones he takes them to his side of the fire to two players. His opponent crosses into enemy territory to follow the trail and find them. His side is quiet now, while the players of the side hiding the bones are all singing and clapping hands. Some are yelling to frighten the guesser. Others make gestures to confuse him. The hiders imitate some animal in their body movements and the positions of their clenched hands.

He wins them back. At once his side begins to yell with their hands over their mouths, he-e-e-e- in a high loud voice. Then they begin to sing. Old hand game songs, songs caricaturing things and people, funny songs, coarse songs.

To follow the trail of the bones when they are won and carried across to the other side is to trail the enemy. The guesser searches for tracks. A player on the hiding side goes to the fire for handfuls of cold ashes from the fire's edge. He sprinkles it like falling snow. He calls aloud, "The snow covers up the tracks now, you cannot see them."

Thus after an enemy raid in late fall when men started after the retreating warparty to regain captured horses the falling snow obliterated the trail. To the Pawnee the little dramatic act has similar power to obliterate the unseen trail of the bones from hand to hand, to blind the guesser. The guesser shields his eyes with his hand and peers through the falling ashes to see the tracks.

In time to the clapping of hands and the rhythm of singing, the hiders and all the players of that side move their arms and bodies back and forth, back and forth. When they hide some imitate crows, some deer, some buffalo, some turkeys.

The Skiri win the first game. Their side carries off the stakes.

Now the Skiri begin to sing Crazy Dog Dance songs, songs of reckless bravery, self-abandonment on the warpath. Men careless of death sang such songs before they set out for the country of the enemy, sang such songs before they went into battle, before they broke into the enemy camp. Knifechief gets up to dance. He dances the steps of the Crazy Dog Dance. It is his place to dance first, he is a brave man and the leader. Others join him from the Skiri side. They do not dance out in the circle, but standing at their places. Knifechief carries a stick in his hand.

As the dancing ends, all the Skiri yell, he-he-he-he-e-e-e-, hitting their hands on their mouths. Knifechief speaks,

"I can remember when I was in the army and we chased the Cheyenne. We chased them out of their camp. They ran and left their blankets behind. I took the blankets away from them."

Knifechief sits down.

"Well, bet some more."

The Skiri who have won stakes bring back their winnings. The Kitkahaxki[x] have to bet other things against what they have lost. The Kitkahaxki[x] leader bets his blanket, a squaw cloth with one side red and the other black. All the Kitkahaxki[x] bet again. They have come to play the hand game and have a lot of stuff with them to bet. The bets pile up again. The betting is even, man against man, and the pile comes out even.

The guesser who won for the Skiri plays again. The Kitkahaxki[x] choose a new man to try his luck against the victor.

Again the Skiri win and carry off the stakes.

The Skiri sing Crazy Dog Dance songs. Knifechief dances. He calls, "We charged again and chased out the Cheyenne, and they left everything behind, tents and horses, and we carried them away. And a pair of leggings I took away from them."

He is recalling victory in battle and the garnering of the spoils. He is gloating over the victory in the game. The game is a battle; the Skiri have carried off the plunder.

Knifechief sits down.

The bets are laid for a third game. The Kitkahaxki[x] leader says, "I'm going to bet a beef." He puts up a beef against the squaw cloth Knifechief has just won from him. All bet again.

The game begins. Again the Skiri are winning.

All this while Mark has been standing on the Skiri side. They have given him no place to sit and play.

The guesser for the Kitkahaxki[x] in the third game is a friend of his. He calls out to Mark, "Come over here." He asks him to sit on the Kitkahaxki[x] side next to him. Mark walks around through the north outside the circle of players and sits down.

The Kitkahaxki[x] are losing again. The Skiri have won six

points; only two sticks are left in the center. The Kitkahaxki^x guesser calls out to the leader of his side, "I want him to guess now." He shows them Mark. He says, "You're a good boy; everything you do is lucky. Go ahead."

The Skiri begin to yell. The Kitkahaxki^x pat Mark on the back and wish him luck.

Mark arises. He goes to the fire and leans forward over it. He touches the ashes and rubs his hands together. He touches fire to his eyes to warm them and make him see clearly. He watches the guessers. He chooses quickly. He finds the bones.

Now the Skiri are trying to confuse him. They yell. They want him to put up the shawl he has with him. He tells them he doesn't have to now. He goes on guessing against the Skiri man who has won two games. The Kitkahaxki^x players begin to come to life. They win the game.

Now the Kitkahaxki^x sing the Crazy Dog Dance songs. The Skiri are silent. The Kitkahaxki^x leader gets up to dance. He tells how he went on a warpath and captured many horses. This time the Kitkahaxki^x have carried off the spoils.

There is a fourth game. The bets are laid again. The Skiri choose a new guesser. Mark is against him now and wins again.

The games are even. The Kitkahaxki^x have won back their losings. They decide to stop now. It is late. The Kitkahaxki^x go home.

Later the Skiri set upon Mark because he played with the Kitkahaxki^x and won for them. For a long time he couldn't go near the Skiri camp. They would get hold of him and scold him angrily. Mark says he joined the Kitkahaxki^x side because the man who asked him was a friend of his, and because the Skiri did not give him a place and ask him to join in.

CHARACTERISTICS OF THE OLD GAME

Competitions like the above between the bands of the Pawnee were played in this way in the old days. Women never played. The games were always outdoors. The songs sung were old type hand game songs. They were coarse but not about women. One ran:

> "They're bathing in the water now...
> They're bathing in the water now..."

All would laugh because of the reference to washing, bringing up a picture of one scrubbing himself all over and around the loins.

Those who hid, many of them, imitated animals. Some of these imitations:

Crow: Each hand clasped with index finger erect. The arms are bent so that the hands are held out about shoulder high like wings. The player calls ka-ka-ka like the crow while he motions with his hands back and forth like flapping wings.

Turkey: Right hand clasped, index finger extended, is brought to forehead to imitate the beak; left hand with index finger out is placed behind like tail. The player calls tut-tut-tut like a turkey.

Deer: The hands clasped palm side down, held bent at wrists about waist high, imitating the forefeet; the index fingers are curled down; the arms are moved alternately, gracefully and slowly, forward and back. No sound.

Buffalo calf: Two hands tight shut in fists with thumbs erect; the bottoms of the fists are set to the sides of the head above the ears, the head bent forward, the thumbs moved like little horns, slight motions. The calf makes no noise unless caught, then "br-r-r-rrr."

Buffalo: The two hands clenched at the sides of the head as for calf, but the index fingers erect for larger horns; the head is moved slowly around to one side and another as the animal peers this way and that.

These animal imitations are by some wholly in fun. But those who use a certain imitation usually retain it throughout the play of hand games, and are known as such and such an animal player. And there are some among the players who have the right to characterizations because of their knowledge and power. In the hand game above described, one man who imitated the deer was a deer performer in the Doctor Dance.

The structure of the old hand game comes out clearly in the above narration. The play of the game has been detailed heretofore. Points of significance:

The games were always played outdoors.

Women never participated.

The long fire outdoors with each side in a semi-circle.

The leaders as tallyers at the head end.

The tally sticks in one heap between them.

The betting.

The selection of hiders in any orders.

The attempts to trick and deceive.

The singing of old hand game songs for the play accompanied only by handclapping, without instruments.

The Crazy Dog Dance between the games, danced by the winning side, the winning leader counting a coup.

The animal imitations.

The host side starting the play, the guest side initiating the guessing.

The visitors bringing a pipe smoked only by the hosts.

As to the alignment of the sides:

There is no such thing in these games as hereditary or traditional sides.[1] The Kitkahaxki[x] came from the west and occupied the west half of the circle, the head end being at the north. Original geographical band arrangements in Oklahoma may be indicated as follows:

N

Skiri

E

W Tcawi

Kitkahaxki[x]

Pitahawirat[a]

S

These geographical positions would determine the arrangement of the hand game play. A division into east and west sides meant the head end was the north; a division into north and south sides meant the head end was the west. Pitahawirat[a] against Kitkahaxki[x] would put the Kitkahaxki[x] on the north, the Pitahawirat[a] on the south, with the leaders and tally sticks at the west. The other bands would have divisions into east and west sides with the leaders and sticks at the north.

In Nebraska the arrangement also follows geographical locations, but these were different:

N

W Skiri   Kitkahaxki[x]   Tcawi   Pitahawirat[a]   E

S

In Nebraska all games would have an east-west division of sides with the head end at the north. A game played in Nebraska between the same two bands as above, the Kitkahaxki[x] visiting the Skiri would put the Skiri on the west, the Kitkahaxki[x] on the east (the exact opposite of what was played in Oklahoma) with the tally sticks and leaders at the north.

Such were the arrangements and characteristics of games played by one Pawnee band against another.

THE INTER-TRIBAL HAND GAME

In earlier days, before the Pawnee were removed to Oklahoma, and for some time thereafter, the hand game was a contest, not only between the bands of the Pawnee, but a contest played by any

---

[1] Murie, Societies, p. 636.

Pawnee group against another tribe with whom they were friends traditionally, or with whom they had recently established friendly relations. Among those with whom the hand game was played by the Skiri Pawnee in relatively recent times, one informant remembers participating in games with the Osage, Ponca and Omaha, Oto, Kiowa, and Arapaho. Friendly gaming relations are remembered with the Sac and Fox, but with them the moccasin game was played, not the hand game. The following narrative of a game between the Skiri Pawnee and the Kiowa, played in Oklahoma many years ago, probably before 1880, will make the procedure clear:

The story is told by Mark Evarts.

One time a large party of Skiri Pawnee were on a buffalo hunt. They were led by Bowchief. While they were out hunting, they came near to the place where the Kiowa were encamped, and went over to visit them. It was not an anticipated visit, so that the traditional forms of visiting were not involved.[1] The chief of the Kiowa was Bigbow.[2] Bowchief of the Skiri Pawnee and Bigbow of the Kiowa were friends.[3]

At the Kiowa encampment, the Skiri Pawnee danced their Crazy Dog Dance, led by Bowchief on horseback. He was the only mounted Skiri in the dance.[4] After the performance, the Kiowa gave the Pawnee buffalo meat and buffalo hides.[5] Then the Pawnee left with these gifts and came home.

Two days later, in the afternoon, the Pawnee saw a party of Kiowa coming to visit them. They were received in friendly fashion, and they danced the Kiowa Crazy Dog Dance for the Pawnee. This time Bigbow led the dance, mounted. He was the only Kiowa on horseback. Bigbow, in the dance, called aloud his exploits on old warpaths. After the dance the Pawnee gave the Kiowa calico and corn.[5] Then the Kiowa went home. The Pawnee hunters who had visited the Kiowa were all men. The Kiowa who returned the visit were mostly men; a few had wives with them.

---

[1] The traditional forms would have required sending a gift of tobacco in advance, and other formalities.

[2] Otakáyot in Evarts' rendition of his Kiowa name.

[3] Inter-tribal friendship was a definite formalized relationship in former times. It was of paramount importance, as through interlocking friendships tribes traditionally hostile to each other were drawn into peaceful relations.

[4] It is said that in the old form of the Crazy Dog Dance, a man mounted indicated thereby that he had captured horses on a warpath.

[5] This giving away after the dancing is similar to the old forms of intertribal visiting of friends, at which lavish giving away was done. In the above case the formal arrangements preceding the visits seem to have been omitted because it was a chance meeting.

While the Kiowa were visiting the Pawnee, some Skiri youths thought of visiting the Kiowa to play a hand game against them. They decided to go over to challenge the Kiowa the day after the Kiowa went home. Mark was with them and became excited about the anticipated hand game. His father was sick, but he paid very little attention because his head was full of the hand game and he wanted to go.

The Kiowa were then camping about two miles from the Pawnee. Late in the afternoon, the day after the Kiowa had gone, Mark saw men gathering at the edge of camp. They were ready to go; they had bundles of things with them to bet. When Mark stepped out of the lodge, these youths motioned to him to come on. So he forgot all about how sick his father was inside, and went. He persuaded himself that his father wasn't very sick anyhow.

The whole party went on foot, carrying their stakes. There were twenty-five or thirty in the group. They took no horses to ride because all who were going wanted to play, which would leave no one to take care of the horses. Some mean fellows among the Kiowa might steal some. And if they had horses with them they might be tempted to wager them and lose the horses.[1]

After dark they reached the Kiowa camp. They were directed to the chief's tent. Knifechief, leading the Skiri party, carried a pipe, already filled with tobacco. Knifechief and a few others went into the chief's tipi. From outside Mark heard a Kiowa in the tipi call, "hαkahí" —"all right, that's good."

This was in December. It was very cold, and outside the men waiting wanted to get into tents to warm up. David Gillingham, Mark's chum, went with Mark into one tent. A Kiowa man sitting at the west called out a welcome, hαkahí. From the south side, where she had been sitting, his wife rose and spread a blanket for the two visitors on the north side of the tipi close up to the west where the Kiowa was sitting. She put two pillows on it. David and Mark sat down there. The Kiowa filled a black pipe and gave it to David to smoke. Mark nudged David and whispered to him that he should not make any gestures with the pipe. Both knew that the Kiowa had special ways and motions in using their pipes; Mark was afraid David would try them and make a mistake. He knew David was a great show-off. The Kiowa pipe-smoking was very complicated. David nudged Mark back and told him to keep quiet. David wanted to show off, so he made some motions with the pipe, imitating Kiowa motions he had seen somewhere.

---

[1] Incidentally, the Pawnee warparty always travelled on foot, with the object of returning riding captured horses.

The Kiowa watched him with astonishment. Then David handed the pipe to Mark, who took it and smoked it quietly and without ceremony. When it was handed back to the Kiowa he made several gestures with it before he put it down. Then his wife picked up a bowl of pounded meat which was on the south side, brought it over and placed it before them. Mark tried to make David talk to their Kiowa host in sign language to keep David's hands busy. Meanwhile Mark ate as fast as he could. Then the woman took a kettle, put dried meat and fat in it, and hung it over the fire suspended from a horizontal bar across two forked uprights.

When the meat was cooked the boys were given meat and fat to eat, and soup to drink. David told Mark not to eat so fast. While they were eating and drinking, outside a Kiowa was heard shouting. When he heard the announcement, their Kiowa host grunted. He

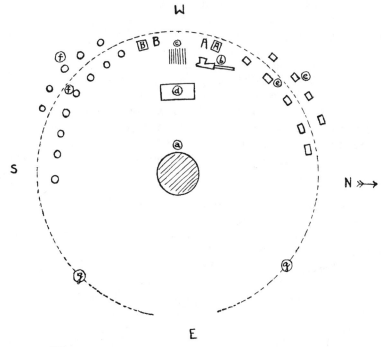

Figure 2. Plan of Game between Skiri and Kiowa

A - Skiri leader and assistant
B - Kiowa leader and assistant
a - round fire
b - Skiri pipe in position after smoking

c - tally sticks
d - position of stakes
e - Skiri men (guests)
f - Kiowa men (hosts)
g - outlines of tipi

told the boys in sign language that the man outside, the crier, had announced that the Pawnee were here and had come on the warpath for the hand game; that they had come bringing a pipe. The crier had said too that as it was getting late, the people had better come at once, women and all, for the hand game. It was to be played inside the big tent of the Kiowa chief.

When they had eaten enough, the Kiowa told the boys to take with them the meat that was left. By signs he said that if they felt hungry later, they would have it to eat. He gave them a pointed stick, and showed them how to stick it into the meat and so carry it. He said, "I'm in a hurry now, I want to get a place there to sit." All three went over to the chief's tipi. The tent was big, but the crowd was so large that there was not room enough inside for all, so the bottom of the tent cover was rolled up all around, and those who couldn't get in settled themselves around outside. Many had to sit outside this way in the cold. If such a large crowd had been anticipated, the hand game would have been played in the open around a huge fire, but it was too late to gather enough wood to build such a big fire.

The Pawnee were sitting around the north side of the tipi, inside and out, Knifechief, as the leader, sitting at the west. The Kiowa sat around the south side, with the Kiowa chief at the west next to Knifechief. In the middle was a large round fire. The Skiri Pawnee were on the north because the tribe was camped north of the Kiowa and had come south to play.

The game began at once. There was no pipe smoking. The Kiowa chief had received the pipe when Knifechief had entered his tent upon arriving.

Between the leaders at the west are the tally sticks. Alongside them lies the Pawnee pipe, now empty, pointing to the north.

The betting begins, of vests, shirts, blankets, anything of value. Each man bets against one of the other side; the two things are tied together; the bundles are heaped at the west before the leaders. In the excitement of the game, the cold is forgotten, even by those who must squat outside. The first guessers are chosen and play begins.

When they hide the bones, the Kiowa sing old hand game songs, accompanied by the beating of one hand drum. When the Pawnee have the bones, they sing their old hand game songs. They clap their hands; they do not beat a drum.

The Pawnee won the first game and took the stakes. Then they sang one Crazy Dog Dance song. Two Pawnee danced. One told of a war exploit, "Once when I was in the army,[1] we charged the

_____
[1] Referring to an episode while a Pawnee scout with the U. S. army.

Cheyenne camp early in the morning, and they fled. When I got into the Cheyenne camp I took blankets and other things away from them." The Pawnee sing and dance only one song, because it is late and cold, and the Pawnee have a long way to go to return home after the game. They want to hurry, and play quickly. Should the Kiowa win a game, they would dance their Crazy Dog Dance to the songs of their society and their leader would rise to recite an exploit, holding the Pawnee pipe. But the Pawnee when they dance, do not carry the pipe they have brought.[1] On this occasion, the Kiowa did not win, and had no chance to dance carrying the pipe.

Wagers were made for a second game, the Kiowa betting against their losings. Again the Pawnee won. Again they sang a Crazy Dog Dance song, and another Pawnee recited a war exploit.

In the third game Knifechief rose and sprinkled ashes to hide the tracks, and the Kiowa guesser searched for the trail.

The Pawnee won three straight games, and that was all they played. There was no fighting over the bones in these games; that was only the way that small boys played.

Knifechief rose. He said, "Now my brother, I beat you. That's all. We're going home." All the Skiri took up their winnings and started for home.

While the game had been going on, Mark and David had found time to eat up the meat they had received so that no one could ask for some. They managed to finish it by the time the game was over.

On the way home, one of the Skiri who was a friend of Mark's gave him a pair of leggings he had just won. Mark says that because of the good fortune of the Pawnee that night he believed the Pawnee would always have good luck in hand games, but subsequently he found out he had been mistaken. In later games they often lost.

---

[1] Carrying the pipe while counting coup was correct only if the reciter had carried a pipe at the time of the exploit. This meant essentially that he had been the leader of a war party. If the exploit had occurred when no pipe was carried, he could count coup, but without holding the pipe. In the above narrative the special significance of the distinction drawn between the right of the Kiowa leader to carry the pipe, and the Pawnee lack of that right, is that it represents dramatically the fact that for generations past, as a result of their treaties, which the Pawnee held sacred, few if any war parties had been sent out ceremonially by the Pawnee. War exploits during the Nineteenth Century were limited essentially to defensive tactics, or to fighting as members of the United States army (see Chapter I).

The essentials of this game follow those of the inter-band Pawnee hand games. Interesting is the fact of the arrangements on sides according to geographical locations. In playing Osage, Arapaho, Ponca and Omaha, as well as Kiowa, the games were usually held in tipis, though they could be held outdoors if the crowd was large. They were played around a round fire. Instruments were not used by the Pawnee for game-singing, but tribes opposing them followed their own custom. When the Skiri played the Osage, the Skiri were on the south, the Osage on the north; when the Skiri played the Arapaho, the Skiri were on the north, the Arapaho on the south; when the Skiri played the Ponca, the Skiri were on the north, the Ponca on the south. The Osage in the game in question came from the north to the Skiri. The Skiri went to the Arapaho going north—the Skiri camp was south of the Arapaho camp, hence my informant feels the alignment was in error, and that there must have been a special reason for it. Once the Skiri, on their way north to Arkansas City, met the Ponca for a hand game. They had stopped to camp south of Ponca City. The Ponca were all around them, but the particular party which came to play gathered to the southwest of the Pawnee camp, and came from that direction; hence they were placed on the south side.

VII
THE GHOST DANCE HAND GAME

The old gambling hand game of the Pawnee, along with other games, dances and social affairs, had gone the way of the rest of Pawnee aboriginal culture by 1892. Occasionally games were played, but the old life which began with early spring and included one round of work and play that ended with the winter, was no more. The Ghost Dance, with its doctrine of a return of the old Indian life, and its mandate to stimulate that return by actively reviving whatever could be recalled, amounted to a partial renaissance of Pawnee culture. We can judge what was lacking most in Pawnee life before the Ghost Dance by considering some of the revivals. Memories of the societies and brotherhoods with their dances and songs were recaptured in reconstructions of the old paraphernalia, and the singing again of the old songs. But games were preeminent, as they were also among the Arapaho. The joy of play had gone from Pawnee life before this. All was somber and hopeless, full of death, disease and constant frustration. Of these game revivals the most notable was the hand game.

The game was revived first as a game. This is apparently the significance of the constant iteration by informants that Tom Morgan's game was not a ceremonial one originally, was the first of them all, and did not come in response to a vision. The Arapaho suggestion of a ceremonialized game combining Ghost Dance ideas of the deceased playing in the beyond, with the game play, reached the Pawnee.

Once the games were begun, whether it was by Morgan or by Carrion, by direct inspiration or through borrowing from the Arapaho, the idea of learning Ghost Dance hand games in visions spread like wildfire and the games sprang up like mushrooms. This radical development by individuals only came after the movement to dethrone Frank White as the sole prophet of the Pawnee Ghost Dance. As late as 1930 I was able to list twenty-two individual game developments of the Pawnee. No doubt, if all the facts were known, there were many more. For a game to persist after it was once created, the owner had to be well thought of by his people, so that someone would "put it up"; and the public had to believe

155

in the supernatural sanction of the game. Many games were probably demonstrated briefly and then forgotten.

The Pawnee developed an interesting check upon the validity of these Ghost Dance hand game revelations. They knew that any one could make up the game with sticks, altar arrangements, smoke offerings, and special complexities. For this reason the people were especially interested in watching the play of a game the *second* time it was demonstrated by the owner. Their contention was that if the game was just made up the owner would not be able to repeat his own arrangements accurately, while if the vision was a true one he would always remember his ways, could in fact never forget them.

The game visions were supposed to give full directions to the visionary as to the details of the game. This included the essentials of the ritual aspects, as offerings, and ceremonial arrangements, the character of the hand game set, the way to play the game. Each composite of these things constituted a set of teachings similar to the ritual lore of a bundle owner in former times, and the paraphernalia used in demonstrating the game constituted a bundle.

The Ghost Dance hand game was a ceremony, not a gambling game, and as such the elements of gambling of the earlier game were eliminated. But the concept of luck involved in the play of the game was carried along with a changed meaning; it may have been in fact the use of luck as an omen which stimulated the rapid growth and widespread playing of these games.

Gambling for the Pawnee, as doubtless for most primitive peoples, is associated with feeling of the existence of luck as a definite quality of the world. To win in a gambling game is to win not only the stakes: to win is to get a vote of confidence, a promise that the gods are on your side. The immediate benefit of the victory is of course the spoils. But beyond these immediate stakes there are greater stakes which have been won. You cannot know, you cannot guess what ultimate benefits of fortune will accrue. But you have assurance that *luck* is on your side. You must await the outcome of events and see what happens. Something good, something lucky and fortunate, is bound to happen to you. When it does, that is because you won when you gambled. The need for luck is everpresent because of the precariousness of life. This need was acutely felt in Ghost Dance times. It was because luck was against the Indian that the white man was conquering. The Ghost Dance doctrine was a promise that fortune was to be on the other side. Now in addition one needed luck to be with the winning side. To be assured of the ultimate change of the Ghost Dance one needed the luck of visions; and to be assured that one would be saved when the great destruction came, one had to be in touch with the controlling influences of the spirit world, which could be had only through visions.

In the early games, as we saw, the men who played imitated various birds and animals as they played. The belief is that birds and animals play hand games too, even as men. In the Ghost Dance two birds were preeminently the choice of the dancers, the eagle and the crow, because of the known characteristic traits of these birds—their wide, far-flung flights, on which they saw the world below them and everything that went on in it. When you were influenced to fall into a trance because of either of these birds, or when in your trance either of these birds was your guide and helper to find lost relatives and lost ways of life, you became associated with that bird. When in the hand game you played as a "crow" or an "eagle," you played to find out which was luckier, which held promise of the greater good fortune. In the early Ghost Dance hand game days it is said by all that the losers cried desolately and the winners were jubilant. As there never were material stakes for a Ghost Dance hand game, clearly it was nothing won. Bad luck or good luck had been discovered as one's portion. To lose was an ill omen.

An incident by Mark Evarts illustrates the foregoing:

Once at a Ghost Dance game played by Mrs. Washington, Mark held the counter in his left hand. The guesser indicated that hand as his choice, when, as quickly as it was guessed, it seemed to pass to his right hand, and there it was. This, according to Mark, was a sign of good fortune. A while later Mark was given Ridingin's daughter to marry. Goodeagle, the girl's grandfather, told the people at the time Mark was married to the girl, that he had had Mark in mind for a long time. Mark feels that this was what his hand game luck forbode. He considers this connection of the events reinforced by an experience which had occurred to him some time before he played in this hand game of Mrs. Washington's. One time when he was near a creek with a large clump of cottonwoods, an eagle came circling, looked at Mark and went off again. "Now Goodeagle and Mrs. Goodeagle represent two eagles," says Mark, "and that may have been the time they thought about me and considered me." Thus the experience with the eagle is reinterpreted in the light of hand game luck and the good fortune which followed it.

An interesting aspect of the above experience is that Mark considered the fact that the counter changed hands miraculous. Not from Mark did I ever learn that in the old game changing the counter from hand to hand in this way was a regular form of deception and part of the game. Other informants told me about this old method of play after I had recorded Mark's experience, and only then did I become aware that in terms of Ghost Dance hand game ethics Mark had cheated, unconsciously falling into the habits of play he had been used to in his boyhood.

The concept of luck associated with hand game play was broadened conceptually in the Ghost Dance. Winning was a sign of greater faith, and since the coming change could be attained through faith alone, losing was a bitter dose indeed. It marked one as a disbeliever, a sinner, an unfortunate who could not be saved.

In the chapters which follow I have considered the Ghost Dance hand games in two ways. In the first discussion the material facts of the games have been used to define the generic aspects of game rituals and ceremonies, and to bring out the significance of the various parts in order to consider in a later discussion the contrast with the old game and the meaning of the changes. In other chapters the details of the individual games are presented so far as known, in a form which makes them at once comparable with the analysis which precedes. In this way repetitions have been reduced to a minimum.

The order in which the games are presented, especially those of the Skiri, is an attempt at something of a chronology.

The exact order is of course impossible to determine at this date. Many were developed well-nigh simultaneously. If the owners of old games are interviewed each is likely to contend for the priority of his or her own game. But certain games are known to be very old, certain others to be very recent. In addition special traits of the individual games place them in one or another of relative periods of time, before which they could not have used certain forms, and after which they must have. In short, on the basis of internal evidence as well as tradition a fairly sure chronology of the games *as groups* had been obtained. The question of priority within the groups is problematical.

There are first of all the games of the South Bands. Of these I have heard of only five: Joseph Carrion's, Tom Morgan's, White Elk's, Charley Brown's (this and White Elk's are collaborative), and Annie Eustace's. Tom Morgan's game as we saw was probably a nonceremonial one, which he altered to suit the new fashion, while Carrion's was the game he learned among the Arapaho. These two are then definitely older than the White Elk-Brown game, and that of Annie Eustace, for both of the latter were developed *as* Ghost Dance hand games.

Of the seventeen Skiri games known to me at least by name, nine fall into an early period. These are the games belonging to Mrs. Washington, Mrs. Goodeagle, Goodeagle, George Beaver, Mark Rudder, John Moses (old form), Skidi Jake, Boychief's mother, and Pierson. Of these I know nothing of the proper place for Beaver's, Skiri Jake's and Goodeagle's games. Mrs. Goodeagle gave the order of the other six as: her own, Mrs. Washington, Rudder, Moses, Boychief's mother and Pierson. Her statement is probably correct as regards the subsequence of Rudder,[1] Moses and Boychief's mother, but as regards the priority of Mrs. Goodeagle's game over that of Mrs. Washington, there can be much question, in view of the part Mrs. Washington played in the Ghost Dance itself, and the general feeling among the Pawnee that there was considerable jealousy between the two women.

Subsequent to this early period, in a general middle period, after Pierson's game, come games of Emmet Pierson and Lonechief (collaborative), Barclay White (from Mrs. Washington), Boychief (from his mother), and Tom Yellowhorse. The Pierson-Lonechief games are definitely placed as just after the earliest developments. White's and Boychief's games follow Pierson's in time, inasmuch as these games were inherited, and their former owners were alive and or active at the time when Emmet Pierson derived his game; while that of Yellowhorse, perhaps the most played game today among the Pawnee, is said to have followed after Pierson's.

Finally we can be reasonably certain that four other games fall in a late to recent period: a second one of Pierson's, a new or changed game of John Moses, a game of Charley Allen's and one of Irene Goodeagle (made for her by her grandmother). The last was made up in the last few years. The Moses and Allen games followed their conversion to the Baptist Church of recent years, and Pierson's second game just preceded that time; it was a simplification of his older game.

While the exact order of these games is not of paramount importance, some conception of their relative order is, because there were gradual changes introduced in the Ghost Dance hand games throughout the period of their creation, and these changes tell an interesting story.

---

[1] Tom Yellowhorse considers Mark Rudder's game earliest of the Skiri Ghost Dance hand games.

VIII
ANALYSIS OF
THE GHOST DANCE HAND GAME

The Order of Events
Ownership and Affiliation
Paraphernalia
Altar Arrangements
Official Arrangements
The Smoke Offering
    Introductory
    The Ceremonial Circuit
    Preparation of the Pipe
    Designation of the Smoke-Offerer
    Receiving the Pipe
    Smoke Offering Proper
        First Phase: Offering of Tobacco
    Lighting the Pipe
        Second Phase: Offering of Smoke
        Third Phase: Disposal of Ashes
        Fourth Phase: Blessings
    Self-Blessing
    Returning the Pipe
Putting the Counters in Play
Play of the Game
Activities of the Game Intervals
Food Offering and Service
Comparison of Food Offering and Smoke Offering
Speeches at Hand Games
Hand Game Songs
Ghost Dance Practices at Hand Games

THE ORDER OF EVENTS

Method in the presentation of ceremony requires that the conceptual essentials of order, arrangement and symmetry be brought clearly to mind, and that the generic be distinguished from the accidental or optional. In the analysis, phase by phase, of the hand game rituals, I have attempted to carry out such a method. It remains, however, to offer a summation of essential ritual sequence itself, to portray clearly and in an integrated manner what happens at a hand game ceremony. I have chosen to preface this outline to the analysis of the parts, so that as each phase is considered on its own account, its place in the whole ceremony may be visualized.

The announcement that the hand game belonging to a particular individual is to be demonstrated at a definite time follows the decision of some individual to put it up, or of the owner to put it up himself. The preparations before the game consist essentially of gathering the food for the feast, and beginning whatever cooking will take longer than the time of play may allow. The game bundle is taken out, and it is made sure that its contents are in order.

Before the people assemble, the game owner takes the bundle to the place at which the game is to be played. The place has been swept clear (in indoor games) and mats spread for seats. The bundle is opened and the altar arranged. Some of the altar arrangements may be made while the people are gathering. For some games there are secret ways in which the game owner and his chosen rixkita perform special thurification rituals with the bundle contents before anyone else is permitted to enter. Painting and costuming of special officials where it is carried out at all, takes place before the ceremony officially opens, but from this the gathering public is not barred.

The official opening of the ceremony is the designation of the smoke offerer, the preparation of the pipe, and its reception by the offerer.

After the smoke offering, special insignia for rixkita, guessers, watchers, the game owner, etc. are given out, not before. These objects must be on or at the altar during the ritual smoke offering, so that they are included. The drums may in earlier times have been kept one on each side of the altar until after the smoke offering; in the games I witnessed they were in their positions for use before the offering, and the offerer proceeded to those positions to smoke them. The insignia are often handled in ritual and ceremonial ways before being given out; this is done by the game owner.

In giving out the insignia, it should be noted that the watchers have been designated by the owner, while the guessers have been indicated by the rixkita. In general, guessers receive insignia first, then watchers.

Then the two main rixkita arise and give the counters for hiding to the guessers of the respective sides. For games which do not possess insignia for guessers this is the first indication of who the guessers are to be.

Now the drummers of the host side lead the singing of one or two old songs. Then the guessers arise, face each other and put the counters in play.

Now follows the play of the game, according to the prescribed forms, the drummers of each side drumming and singing while the counters are in possession of their side.

When the game is over, the guesser or watcher of the winning side returns the counters to the rixkita of that side. The insignia are not returned.

The main singers of the winning side arise and lead the ghost dancing. If a rattle is to be used the main singer gets this from the rixkita of his side at the altar. Simultaneously the rixkita of the winning side arises with the pipe and game set and holds it symbolically aloft.

After the Ghost Dancing all return to their places.

The two main rixkita arise and again give the counters to the two guessers, the same two who have already functioned. The singers of the winning side sing one or two old society songs. Old men here and there arise and dance in their places.

After the songs there is a pause. Here individuals who are prominent and wish to speak to the assemblage come forward and talk.

Then the guesser of the side which lost rises and gives the insignia and the counter to another player of his side, who is thus constituted the guesser for the next game.

After the final rubber game, ten Ghost Dance songs should in theory be sung. Before they are sung the drum of the losing side is returned to a position before the altar. The winning side Ghost Dances as in any other interval. Then the singers of the winning side sing one or two old society songs, after which the drum of that side is also returned to a position in front of the altar.

The food is then brought in, received by the game owner, and set in its place.

The rixkita of the winning side chooses the offerer for the food offering. The rixkita may at this time make a speech. The offerer comes forward, receives the spoon, fills it, and makes the offering.

The servers are then selected by the rixkita. These begin the ritual order of service.

After the feast the winning leader may talk for a while. Then the occasion is at an end. The people leave.

The bundle contents are put together. The bundle is returned to the house of its owner. The drums which may have been borrowed are returned.

OWNERSHIP AND AFFILIATION

Every ghost dance hand game when played is the demonstration of the ritual of an individual ghost dance hand game bundle, which is individually owned.[1] The games are said to be affiliated with the side (Crow or Eagle) to which the owner belongs, and in a more general way with the band of the owner. These affiliations of the games may be summarized as follows:

Owner	Game Side	Band
South Band Games:		
Joe Carrion	Crow	kitkahaxki[x]
Tom Morgan	Eagle	pitahawirat[a]
White Elk (-Brown?)	Crow	kitkahaxki[x]
Annie Eustace	Crow	kitkahaxki[x]
Skiri Games:		
Mrs. Goodeagle	Eagle	
Goodeagle	Eagle	
Mrs. Washington	Eagle	
Skidi Jake	?	
George Beaver	Crow	
Mark Rudder	Crow	
John Moses, I, II	Crow	
Boychief and his mother	Crow	
Emmett Pierson, I, II	Eagle	
Lonechief	? Crow ?	
Barclay White	Eagle	
Yellowhorse	Eagle	
Charley Allen	Crow	
Irene Goodeagle	Eagle.	

Each ghost dance hand game bundle contains the objects to be used in that game: the game set of sticks and counters, feather ornaments, a pipe, etc. The bundle with its associated ritual of play, smoke offering, etc. was in each case derived in a ghost dance vision by its owner or by the individual from whom the named owner inherited the game. The visions of any individual in the ghost dance associate that individual with either the Crow or Eagle, hence the affiliation of the game owner, and, in addition, the vision determining the game is itself a Crow or Eagle vision, hence the affiliation of the game and game bundle.

Of the games on record, fourteen are based directly on the original visions: These are Carrion, Eustace and White Elk of

---

[1] With the exception of collaborative game demonstrations.

the South Band games, and Mrs. Goodeagle, Goodeagle, Mrs. Washington, Skidi Jake, Beaver, Rudder, Moses I, Boychief's mother, Pierson, Lonechief, and Yellowhorse. In these cases the game sets and paraphernalia were made by the original visionaries and the owners as named in response to their vision teachings. Of the games not generally associated with vision experiences, several are derived from one or another of the above fourteen. Thus Emmett Pierson is said to have made his second game as a simpler arrangement for more secular play, basing it on his major game; John Moses revised his game into a new form to accord with his conversion to the Baptist faith; Boychief's game was inherited from his mother, and is supposed to have been the game essentially as she played it; Barclay White took over the game of his mother, Mrs. Washington, but in his case it is said to have been changed by him to accord with vision experiences of his own; and Irene Goodeagle's game was made for her by Mrs. Goodeagle, her grandmother, as a play set simpler in routine than the original. Tom Morgan's game, an early one, was not based upon a vision, but at first merely a play set like the old games, was later changed to agree with the newer fashions in hand game play as these developed. Allen's game was a late one, based on his affiliation to the Baptist Church.

All the ghost dance hand games, in theory, could be played in the afternoon or evening, outdoors or in, depending on the season of the year. I know of only one absolute exception, that of Pierson, which should be played only in the spring. In recent times, with the disappearance of Pawnee earth lodges and tipis, the bands have erected for tribal use two large frame structures, similar in general plan to earth lodges. One called the South Round House by the Pawnee is used by the three South Bands. It is located centrally to these groups to allow them to gather there with a minimum of travel. The other, the North Round House, is similarly located for the Skiri, and used by them. This latter is the lodge to which Densmore refers,[1] and in which she states that the hand game and victory dance observed by her were held. This should not, however, arouse a false notion that it is a sacred ceremonial lodge. In old Pawnee religious practice there were no band or tribal ceremonial lodges. Each ritual was held in the lodge of the owner or controller of that ritual, including sacred bundle ceremonies, Doctor Dances and performances, Bear Dances, Buffalo Dances, Deer Dances, Society Dances and all others of which we have any record. In building the lodges of a village, the owner of a

_____
[1] Densmore, Pawnee Music, p. 69 and plate 7 e.

ritual requiring a large arena generally made allowance for it when erecting his lodge, so that several lodges, notably the two for doctor performances, were generally larger than others in the village, and had a large open arena in front of them. These were known because of the performances held in them as the medicine-men's lodges. But these were not used for other ceremonial or religious functions. Similarly the lodge in which the most important sacred bundle kept in a village was housed might be known as the main ceremonial lodge of the village, but was not the ceremonial lodge par excellence and exclusively. In a few cases (for special reasons) bundles could be moved into other lodges for ceremonial uses. The contemporary Round Houses of the Pawnee are an adjustment to the need of a gathering place for council meetings, games, dances etc., the need becoming more acute as all the old earth lodges disintegrated and no new structures of the kind were built. Many of the games which have been played in recent times have been played in these Round Houses, but not all. All could however be played outdoors as well. A few require special outdoor structures which are set up by the owner for the game occasion.

What few earth lodges were inhabited by hand game owners in the last decade of the Nineteenth Century were used by them when their games were played indoors, unless the ritual required a special tipi-like structure. In such cases it was the earth lodge of the game-bundle owner which was used, in accordance with the old custom.

Boychief's game was always held in the afternoon in a tent, which is a persistence of the way in which it was first played. Allen's recent game has always been played outdoors under a shade or arbor-like tent. The South Band games, when played at the Round House, are held preferably in the afternoon. This preference goes back to a time when the people could gather only on horseback or in wagons. The South Bands were more scattered than the Skiri, so the games were held early enough in the day to allow the people to return home the same night.

The functional patterns of the ghost dance hand game bundles are in harmony with those of the old sacred and medicine men's bundles. The owner of the bundle is also the individual who alone fully understands the ritual procedure. This aligns the ghost dance hand game bundle with the pattern of medicine men's bundles, and opposes it to that of sacred bundles for which ownership and priesthood are divorced. On the other hand, in hand game ceremonies the owner never occupies the seat of a priest or demonstrator. In the old rituals, whether sacred, or medicine men's, or society, the four main seats behind the altar (usually at west) were filled by those who knew the whole ritual, along with assistants. In the case of the sacred bundle rituals these were the priests proper; in the case of other rituals the bundle owner himself, who is his own functioning "priest." The owners of sacred bundles, who have called in priests to demonstrate the ritual, never sat behind the altar; usually they took a place on the north side just east of the priests. The hand game arrangement follows in one sense the sacred bundle pattern in that the owner does not sit behind the altar. Behind the altar are specially appointed leaders, or rixkita, who take active charge of the proceedings. They confer constantly with the owner and follow the owner's orders. The position the owner takes is on the side to which he or she is affiliated; the particular place is at the owner's own choice. Wherever the owner's place, he or she is prominent throughout the game, overseeing everything, walking about when necessary to direct smokers or control arrangements.

Ghost Dance hand game bundles are owned by men and by women. This is a departure from all earlier forms of bundle control. No pre-Ghost Dance bundle of the Pawnee was ever owned by a woman. In the case of the sacred bundles, the owner was always a chief, a man, whose wife "took care of" the bundle while a priest guarded the ritual; for other bundles the owner and priest were the same, and his wife took care of the bundle physically. As a result of this caretaking, in the accidents of inheritance it often happened that a bundle came to be for life in the possession of a good woman who was faithful to the ritual requirements of her office. This happened for example when a man died, and his wife refused to yield the caretaking to the wife of her son, who with matrilocal residence would be of another lodge and household. She would claim that the young woman was not serious enough for the office, did not know what to do, etc., and community feeling usually supported the contentions of the older woman. In this case bundle and owner were housed apart from each other, contrary to theory. Nevertheless, native thought did not recognize the woman as the owner of the bundle. It was hers only as something she was caring for. But Ghost Dance hand game bundles were owned outright by women who derived them in visions. Women in some cases also took care of a husband's bundle, and, as happened to Mrs. Goodeagle, were left in possession of it upon the husband's death.

The presence of women in the hand games at all was a Ghost Dance change. In the old gambling game with its war-party tactics, women never participated, and were at most tolerated as spectators. The participation of women must be traced to the elimination of war ideology, and the free type of individual religious participation permitted in the Ghost Dance wherever the religion spread. In hand game leadership, however, women were barred. When owners appointed rixkita to sit behind the altar, women owners as well as men chose men exclusively. In this the old restriction was still active, although the fact that the leaders should be chiefs (who were never women) may be the explanation. In one game, that of Pierson, in which some game owners (not however those controlling the occasion) sit behind their own altars, the women's games were always presided over by men. In the seating arrangement most often followed, the men cluster toward the altar end on both sides, the women toward the east; an avoidance of women close to the altar which recalls still further the old restrictions.

Ghost Dance hand game bundles are handed down after death in the same manner as other bundles. They follow the form of inheritance of doctors' bundles, because of the identity of owner and "priest." If the teachings of the bundles are known to the heir, the bundle survives and its ritual continues to be demonstrated. This was the case with the game Boychief had from his mother, and that of Goodeagle, which his wife retained. If, however, the ritual had not been taught to an heir, the bundle was buried with the deceased owner; this happened to the game of Skidi Jake. The bundle and its teachings could also be turned over to a successor before death. This was what happened to Mrs. Washington's game bundle. She "retired" and left her bundle to her son to carry on.

Of interest is the fact that while in the active Ghost Dance times the doctrine overrode the old patterns and caused a revival or renewal of forms that had been buried in the grave, and which, prior to the Ghost Dance no one would have had the right to demonstrate, as the years passed and Ghost Dance faith ebbed, the old mode reasserted itself. Many of the old hand game bundles have now disappeared in the same way that earlier the ancient ceremonies passed away. They have been buried with the deceased. This happened as recently as 1930 with Pierson's game.

In handing down a bundle the heir was of the same affiliation (Crow or Eagle) as the bundle game inherited. Thus several members of the same family were associated with the same side. This came about in several ways. Crow and eagle ornaments and objects, when used hypnotically to cause a trance, dominated the vision, or were supposed to. Since leaders aided the members of their own families to trances, similar affiliations would result. In addition, the visions of the head of a family, as father or mother, themselves determined in their content that the other members of the family take the same affiliation. In this way Goodeagle and Mrs. Goodeagle were both associated with the Eagle; their visions were complements of each other's. Crow and eagle affiliations were among the possible animal affiliations of earlier times and could associate family members together from that fact alone. Hence we find some clustering of relatives in the Ghost Dance. Many who did not have their own visions were later taken to one side or another by close relatives, and would thereafter maintain such affiliation. In the later period after the excitement of the Ghost Dance had passed, hypnotic trances were no longer induced, and children would normally affiliate with the father's or mother's side.

These facts adequately explain the cases of associated family affiliation which occurred; they were not extensive. There was no rule requiring kinship affiliation. Any number of cases in game affiliations today illustrate the divergent affiliation of members of a family. Murie asserted that the Crow and Eagle membership was hereditary, implying almost that ceremonial moieties existed.[1] That the sides were not hereditary groupings can be asserted categorically. They were arrangements founded on affiliations discovered in the Ghost Dance.

In still another way Ghost Dance hand game bundles follow old bundle patterns. The demonstration of a bundle ritual requires that a definite supply of food be available for a large gathering. For old ceremonies this was buffalo meat and corn principally. For a few orthodox hand games, as that of Pierson, special foods are required, but for most games only corn is essential; other foods may be bread, coffee, cake, apples, etc. A number of individuals cooperate in pooling the money needed for the supplies, or in bringing together the foods. But one individual always initiates the occasion by offering to "put it up." For a sacred ceremony this individual supplies the first buffalo, in more recent times the first beef, and as much more as he can. Others then come forward to help. The one who puts up a ceremony may be either the owner of the bundle (aided in such cases by the family) or a layman. For the fixed calendric ceremonies of the old sacred and medicine men's bundles, it is usually the duty of the bundle owner to put up the demonstration. A layman puts up a ceremony for two reasons: either he wants to receive the special blessing which accrues from the demonstration and is visited especially upon the generous giver who feasts the supernatural powers, or he wants to

---

[1] Murie, Societies, p. 636.

be in a favorable position to see the ceremony and learn it. Both desires together usually motivate the man or woman who puts up a ceremony. For many old rituals a vision or dream was the immediate stimulus which led a man or woman to announce that he or she would be responsible for the ceremony. But this was not essential. The putter-up had the right to ask about anything done in the ceremony, and the priests were obligated to answer. This was the chief method by which a layman learned esoteric things. George Dorsey followed the procedure on many occasions thirty years ago when he worked with James Murie among the Pawnee. Some ceremonies such as doctor dances and chiefs' rituals were not only held at stated seasons, but could also be carried out at certain other times in response to laymen's offers to put them up. For such rituals it was by putting up the ceremony at such an optional time that a layman received instruction. But for most fixed bundle rituals the procedure was also possible.

Hand games are always put up either by the owner or for him by a friend. The one who puts it up determines what alternative of play shall be followed. If a game can be played "straight" or "even up," or all men against all women, etc., it is the putter-up who generally decides the form. Usually he also decides how many games ("rubber games") shall constitute the occasion. He has a voice in choosing the leaders of the sides, and the other functionaries. In all these ways the functional relation of the putter-up to the ceremony is of the same kind as that established by the procedure in earlier days.

In the games one side is always the host side, the other the visiting or guest side. The side with which the putter-up is affiliated becomes the host side, since this side is actually furnishing the feast. For obvious reasons the individual who puts up a hand game ceremony is of the same affiliation as the game. A Crow rarely puts up an Eagle game, and vice versa. In many cases, also, it is the owner himself who puts up the game, and who thus combines the functions of owner and putter-up. As a result of these two factors superficial confusions occur in that it appears that the owner as owner has decided the details of play, chosen all officials, and the like, and in that the preliminary songs and first hiding seem to be initiated always by the side with which the game bundle is affiliated. Actually, however, the individual who has put up the ceremony is functioning in these cases, though his function may be concealed by a convergence of offices.

I have grouped all the post-Ghost Dance hand games as Ghost Dance hand games. But two games, the second of John Moses, and that of Allen, are in respect to doctrinal concepts church games rather than Ghost Dance games. In form they are, however, determined by the essential structure of the Ghost Dance hand game.

Collaborative Games: Two pairs of games were in former times played with dual control. These were the Pierson-Lonechief games, and the White Elk-Brown. In such a form two bundles are opened, one for each side, and the play is bundle against bundle; half the game set of each bundle is used. In other aspects the arrangements are the same as for the usual form in which only one bundle is opened.

The great spring game of Pierson is a further development of the form of dual opposing control. In this game all the game bundles and revived societies participate. On each side is ranged a series of game bundles, and a series of societies.

These methods of dual control at the altar are reminiscent of the form of arrangement in Doctor Dances, although even in these, while the main two doctor-priests, N 1 and S 1, share the leadership in the demonstration, the bundle of only one of these is opened and present.

PARAPHERNALIA

The paraphernalia used in the Ghost Dance hand game include: the game set proper; ritual or ceremonial objects essential for generic ceremonial reasons; and symbolic and ritual objects related to the particular game bundle.

The game set in all cases consists of a set of sticks or other objects used for tallying, and two objects used as counters for hiding. Some bundle sets are double, that is, there are either two sets of tally sticks or two sets of counters, or both. For a particular game only one set was chosen and used, the other remaining bundled up. The optional use of one of the two sets was usually associated with special restrictions. One set often involved greater risk, and if in use, should the counters be dropped while in play the game would have to stop at once; otherwise great misfortune would ensue. The alternative set would involve no such risk. Such a difference between optional sets was associated with the vision derivations and indicated by the symbolic markings on the pieces.

Tally sticks numbered eight for all games with three exceptions: Allen's recent game employs twelve sticks. Carrion, when he first played, used twelve, after the manner of the Arapaho. Goodeagle had an optional set of twelve tally sticks, in addition to one of eight.

If of wood, the sticks were dogwood or cedar, two trees considered sacred by the Pawnee from ancient times. Those which were not wood were usually long eagle tail-feathers, of the bald or black eagle, or both. The sets of eight tally sticks were divided into two groups of four, one of which was associated with each side. In accordance with their associations, the sticks were usually distinguished by coloring, by the addition of feathers, etc., or by both. Colors associated with the north for this purpose and for other aspects of Ghost Dance hand game paraphernalia, were blue, green and black; for the south white, yellow and red. In the case of sticks, drums, face paintings, etc., these colors were applied. In the case of feathers used as tally sticks or ornaments, while the stem might be painted, a distinction was made in the choice of feathers. Bald eagle feathers, with some white in them, are usually called white eagle feathers, and associated with the south; while feathers of the black eagle were associated with the north. For ornaments the crow feathers were used for the north, smaller white eagle feathers for the south.

This color symbolism is consonant with the old color symbolism of Pawnee ceremony. In particular, in the Ghost Dance it referred primarily to the two horizons, the northern and the southern, divided by an east-west midline. The dark colors are referred to the dark horizon, the north, the bright colors to the bright horizon, the south dominated in Pawnee latitudes by the passage of the sun across the sky.

Each hand game bundle included a pipe which was used for the ceremonial smoke offering of the demonstration. These pipes were of the old Pawnee type, a long stem of dogwood inserted in a pipe-stone bowl. There were four types of old pipes: ceremonial bundle pipes which had stems carved with trachea-markings; medicine men's pipes, with smooth dark stems; chiefs' pipes, large and decorated; and pipes for ordinary use, usually with smaller bowls and shorter stems. The hand game bundle pipes were usually plain-stemmed and smooth, more like those of medicine men than any others. But they could be decorated at the desire of the visionary who originated the bundle. One or two hand game sets had two pipes. Pipe tampers accompany the pipes.

The demonstration of a hand game ritual involves a ceremonial food offering, and for this there is usually a horn spoon in the bundle.

Associated with each bundle there was in earlier times at least one drum. This was of the same affiliation as the game and the bundle. When the form of hand game demonstrations had developed to the point where two drums were required, one for each side, the bundle drum was used for the demonstrating side, and a drum belonging to one of the game sets affiliated with the other side borrowed for use at the demonstration. These drums were usually double-faced, with thong attachments by which they could either be held in the hand or suspended from forked sticks. Dogwood drumsticks accompanied the drums. Both faces of the drum were usually decorated with Ghost Dance symbols, whose reference was to the visions of the owner.

Some games had ceremonial objects in the bundles which were used as altar spreads (such as an eagle skin, a wildcat skin etc., not placed on the ground, but upon another spread, usually of cloth, which was on the ground); as hair ornaments by the owner, the leaders, the guessers, and the watchers; and as symbolic objects forming an essential part of the altar arrangements.

Ornaments were generally feathers, crow or eagle, occasionally hawk or owl. Altar objects were of various kinds. Some referred to recalled aspects of old ceremonies, such as the Morning Star sacrifice. Others involved revivals of societies, dances, and ceremonies like the pipe dance. Still others recalled medicine men's ways. If these were part of the altar at a hand game it indicated that the owner had experienced Ghost Dance visions of such a nature, and had participated in reviving these old forms either conceptually through Ghost Dance and hand game or actually and overtly.

Some game sets included bunches of eagle and crow feathers to be worn by players of the opposing sides.

Where a game had originated in special Ghost Dance circumstances, as that of Beaver, and was played in a special tent, the tent itself was decorated in Ghost Dance symbolism.

Some bundles had rattles, either gourd or leather. These rattles were used at such game demonstrations to accompany the Ghost Dance singing and dancing in the intervals. If there were no rattles, the singing and dancing was without instrumental accompaniment.

Special altar objects might have special vision reference, rather than formal reference to old cultural aspects. Such were the five corn tassels of the White altar, referring to a family of five members.

An occasional demonstrator had special ways of costuming. Rudder used to wear a shirt whose left side was black, and right side yellow.

ALTAR ARRANGEMENTS

The basic plan of the altar arrangements is the same as that of all old bundle altars of the Pawnee. At the head end, usually the west, a spread is laid out, upon which sacred and ceremonial objects are laid, and before which the sacred symbolic objects are placed. The spread for most of the hand games is merely a piece of cloth of some sort. If there is a special spread in the bundle, like a bird or animal skin, this is put upon the cloth spread. On the spread are placed the pipe and tampers, the game set of tally sticks and counters, the horn spoon, rattles if there are any, paints and miscellaneous symbolic ornaments.

The arrangement of these objects is a simple symmetric one, in relation to the associations of the objects with the two sides. In the center lies the pipe, usually with the mouthpiece pointing eastward, the bowl end westward, the bowl opening toward the side (north or south) with which the game is associated. In exceptional cases the pipe points in the direction with which the game is associated. Of the tally sticks and counters: the four tally sticks associated with each side lie on that side of the pipe, oriented east-west, viz. they lie parallel to the pipe in most cases. The counter for each side lies with the tally sticks of that side. Special hair ornaments used by players are grouped according to the side with which they are associated. Thus for several games there are twelve eagle feathers and twelve crow feathers used by the players of the two sides. The twelve eagle feathers are bunched and lie on the south side of the pipe and tally sticks, the twelve crow feathers similarly on the north. Rattles which may belong to a bundle are placed alongside the pipe, parallel to it, with the gourd or rattle end (head end) toward the east. The horn spoon is concealed under a fold in front of the ceremonial official in charge, usually the rixkita in charge for the side which owns the bundle.

In most games certain sacred objects are placed in ritual positions in front of this basic altar. Thus some have seven eagle feathers set in a row, which are either left in that position throughout the ritual demonstration or are given the seven Eagle Brothers to wear. Some games have special crosses referring both to Christian ideology and to the Morning Star Sacrifice. For another there is a small cedar tree; for still another game, with Pipe Dance connotation, two calumets, one for each side, leaning upon a forked stick. In addition, if there are ornaments worn by the official guessers and watchers, these are set in the ground in front of the altar until after the smoke offering, when they are given out to the selected individuals.

Before the game proper begins, and during the intervals of Ghost Dancing, the drums are placed before the altar, each on its associated side, in a vertical position, with the drum sticks lying upon the drum. Before the smoke offering the drums are usually moved to their official places at the approximate semi-cardinal directions.

The essential form of official positions behind the altar is represented by the following diagram:

West

Eagle: Crow:
South 2   South 1   North 1   North 2

Altar

The main leader of each side is in the position indicated 1, the assistent leader in that marked 2. The main leaders are the two men who keep tally. The leader of the side owning the game is the main leader for that demonstration. This can be either N 1 or S 1. Accordingly the ceremonial order of precedence is for a Crow game N 1, S 1, N 2, S 2, for an Eagle game S 1, N 1, S 2, N 2. This is the order which is generally followed in offering the pipe to smoke to the leaders (see Smoke Offering, Phase 2, Mode 3); in some cases, however, the form followed is to give both leaders of one side the pipe, then both of the other, the first two in this case being the leaders of the side demonstrating the ritual.

For a few games, such for example as those of Goodeagle and Boychief, an ancient ceremonial variation is introduced, in that a fifth man is seated at the altar between the two main leaders. This is an ancient holy position. In the sacred rituals dominated by the Evening Star Bundle and its priesthood, five priests officiate, the four priests of the Leading Bundles in the positions as indicated above, while the priest of the Evening Star bundle has the sacred central position. In the doctor performances the wife of the main doctor sits in such a position (a little to the rear) holding a sacred pipe which is not used in that ceremony. In the games a man in this position has also a sacred esoteric function. He does not play the game, although the leaders do.

The special and unique details of game altars are indicated in the figures illustrating the altars of the individual games.

OFFICIAL ARRANGEMENTS

Several aspects of the official arrangements have already been described under previous headings.

The game owner does not sit behind the altar, but moves about freely as his or her presence is required to take charge. When sitting, the game owner chooses a position on the side of affiliation.

Behind the altar are four game leaders, called rixkita, as already defined (see Altar Arrangements). These keep tally, but also participate in the play. In some games a fifth man who does not play is seated centrally to the four. He is a ceremonial overseer, sits with arms folded, and watches the progress of the game. He represents the powers of the west looking down upon the people on earth playing the hand game.

The men chosen as rixkita were in theory chiefs for orthodox games. They should be affiliated with the side they lead.[1] The participation of chiefs in the hand game is an innovation of the Ghost Dance hand game. In the old hand game, dominated by gambling, the chiefs did not join. At best they sat at a distance and looked on. Here they are the leaders of the two sides.

Significant also is the fact that these positions behind the altar are the positions of priests, or ritual demonstrators, in older patterns, and such were never filled by chiefs. Occasionally of course a doctor or priest was also a chief, but the men who sat behind the altar in the Pawnee bundle ceremonies were never there ex officio because they were chiefs, but because of their specific office as priests or doctors. The owners of the sacred bundles were chiefs, but they never demonstrated the rituals. Here they are in charge of the demonstration, directed by the game bundle owners.

This change of concept must be correlated with the changed significance of the western orientation, which comes in with the Ghost Dance. The west is the abode of the deceased, whose chief in some views is Christ or the Father, and the prayers and dances of the Ghost Dance are directed toward bringing about a reunion of the living and the dead. On earth it is the chief who is father of his people and who is responsible for their welfare. Hence here it is the chief who leads them and brings them into closer harmony with their deceased relatives led by their deceased chiefs. We see then that while the west is still the direction of powers of especial sanctity, it is so with an altered significance, which is reflected in

---

[1] Selecting only chiefs of the same affiliation as the game, and of the same band affiliation, the tendency was for a game owner to develop a custom of asking certain specific chiefs to take charge of his game demonstrations. But for all the games the rixkita could be and were often different at different demonstrations. As an informant remarked, "Can't wait for one if he's late, but have to start off, so may select another." This comment indicates that the usual rixkita were known in advance of the game, but changes could be made in selection up to the last minute.

the officials who represent the western powers and guide the ceremonial undertaking. In the older forms the four represent the four old men priests of the Evening Star who preside over her eternal garden of ever green corn in the western heavens, and the fifth or central position is usually conceived as that of the Evening Star herself, and is often represented as such by being filled by a woman, as at Doctor Performances.

In the usual game arrangement, the men and women players are separated, the men being clustered between the head end or altar position (usually west), and the western semi-cardinal directions (northwest and southwest). The women are ranged from these points eastward to the door, or if out of doors, to the symbolic eastern door position. Other arrangements of play such as men against women, and the like, require special seating plans.

Games use either one drum or two. In the old pre-Ghost Dance hand games of the Pawnee, drums were not used, the singing being accompanied by hand-clapping only. The earliest games of Ghost Dance times, such as those of Morgan and Carrion, did not use drums at first. When drums were first introduced, only one was used. This was placed centrally at the west between altar and fireplace. The singers gathered around it, those associated with each side being grouped on that side of an imaginary east-west line which divided the drum into two halves.[1] Drumming and singing was done only by those associated with the side in possession of the counters.

With the development of a formal organization of sides and two sets of singers, and the specific association of paraphernalia with one side or the other, came the use of two drums, one for each side.

The drums are placed at about northwest and southwest respectively. Here the singers of that side encircle the drum. The main singer sits with his back toward his own side and faces the opposing side across the drum. Until the development of the two organizations of Seven Brothers and Seven Crows among the Skiri, the singers were merely those who were able singers, who knew old game songs and Ghost Dance songs. This continued to be the case for the South Band hand games, where no formal organizations developed. When these organizations had come into being among the Skiri, the singers for all orthodox Skiri hand games had to be the Seven

---

[1] One drum is still used by the Wichita in playing the Ghost Dance hand game. It is placed between west and northwest. The singers seat themselves according to their affiliation in the same manner that the Pawnee followed in the early days.

Brothers for the Eagle side and the Seven Crows for the Crow side. This was the case with the following games at least: Goodeagle and Mrs. Goodeagle, Mrs. Washington, Beaver, Skidi Jake, Rudder, Boychief and his mother, Pierson and Lonechief, White, Yellowhorse, and John Moses in his early game. It is not possible to say with exactness at what point this form of organization supplanted the more amorphous older pattern.

After the Seven Brothers were organized, games utilized these singers for the Eagle side, employing for the north side merely able Crow singers. When the Seven Crows were organized the use of both organizations supplanted earlier forms. With each step of formal organization in the Skiri Ghost Dance, the form was taken over thereafter by all the Skiri hand games, obliterating older ways.

In such games as the church games of Moses and Allen, one drum is again resorted to, placed centrally, and the singers for both sides cluster round it. In former times the drums used in orthodox games were double-faced and were suspended from forked sticks. The church games employ single-faced drums placed on the ground, and latterly some owners of Ghost Dance hand games have become indifferent to the distinction and use any drum available, as Tom Yellowhorse.

The orthodox hand games require a central round fireplace. This is already there if the game is played in a lodge or Round House, but if played outdoors it must be indicated. For some games a fire in the fireplace was required. The recent church games have neither fire nor fireplace.

There were differences as to the required presence of official tarutsius, waiters. In only a few cases were they essential to the formal pattern of the particular game, but they were optional for most. The institution of the tarutsius is an ancient one, and an essential part of old ceremonies. Usually there are two, one of whom is the main tarutsius of the occasion. One tarutsius is stationed on each side of the doorway at the east. It is the function of these men to take charge of the fire, the lighting of the pipes, the service of food, etc., in fact of all the menial ceremonial tasks associated with the performance which are not specifically delegated to some one else. In doctor dances the tarutsius on that side of the east-west midline on which (at the altar) the bundle in control was placed was the main tarutsius. For the office they hold, while it has its disadvantages, the tarutsius gains definite advantages. He is considered a sacred or holy man, although not one of social or political prominence. A man ambitious to be prominent and "noticed" would never become a tarutsius. It was an office sought by a humbler personality. The man shared the blessings of the ceremonial occasions. He participated in the entire ritual activity, from its very inception, and hence learned it. Usually a tarutsius knew more about the ritual of a given bundle than any one but its main demonstrator. The owner of the ritual could not withhold from the tarutsius anything that the latter wanted to know. Partly because of his humility and poverty and partly because of the actual work performed, a tarutsius usually received special consideration in the distribution of gifts which accrued to the demonstrator of a ritual.

For the hand games the servers were not officials in the sense of the tarutsius, but usually individuals chosen for that service for the particular game. The institution of watcher, present in some games, bears a special resemblance to the old office of tarutsius. These watchers were two special individuals (usually men), chosen one for a side by the game owner, and permanent for that game occasion. They wore special hair ornaments. The watcher accompanied the guesser around the arena, helped in guessing and signalled the score (see Play of the Game). In several functions they are like tarutsius: They light the pipes, during the intervals they are supposed to sit next the doorway, and they are usually food servers to the ceremonial officials. The watchers were chosen because they were particularly lucky, and controlled the playing of aftermaths for tie scores. For guessers there were often also special insignia.

In addition to the tarutsius positions at the doorway most bundle ceremonies have special arrangements of old men, chiefs and braves near the eastern doorway. In a few hand games some of these arrangements are revived. Thus Annie Eustace is said to have placed a tarutsius on each side of the doorway, an old man on each side next to the tarutsius (west of him), and on the south side, west of the old man, several chiefs, on the north side, west of the old man several doctors. These were her particular arrangements. Goodeagle placed an old man with a chief beside him on each side of the door. Boychief, with his game oriented from a northern altar, placed old men on the east side of the south doorway. On the other hand, we are occasionally told specifically that a game did not have any such arrangements. Thus in White Elk's game no old men, chiefs or doctors are said to have been given special seats near the doorway. These variations of pattern are themselves indications of the nature of such seating arrangements. In old ceremonies, detailed elaborations of form are peculiar to the

concepts of the particular bundle, and vary accordingly from
ceremony to ceremony.

THE SMOKE OFFERING

Introductory
The Ceremonial Circuit
Preparation of the Pipe
Designation of the Smoke-Offerer
Receiving the Pipe
The Smoke Offering Proper
    First Phase: Offering of Tobacco.
Lighting the Pipe
    Second Phase: Offering of Smoke
        First Mode: To Powers
        Second Mode: To Ceremonial Objects
        Third Mode: To Men
    Third Phase: Disposal of Ashes
    Fourth Phase: Blessings
        First Mode: Motions for Powers
        Second Mode: Motions for Objects
Self-Blessing
Returning the Pipe: Arm-Blessing

Introductory

The smoke offering rituals of the Pawnee Ghost Dance hand
games are ritually of the same pattern and intention of reference
as similar offerings of the ancient Pawnee rituals. This makes
them worth careful consideration on their own account for what
they reveal of Pawnee ceremonial ideology. They involve in most
cases a simpler series of references, and so strip the ritual forms
to their bare essentials, revealing the basic anatomy of the
smoke offering. It has been my experience that the smoking
rituals of older ceremonies, such as the doctor dances, at first
almost defy analysis and controlled structuralization because of
the varied detail of the offerings and motions involved and the
rapidity with which they are carried out. After analysis of these
simpler hand game ritual smoke offerings, however, the essentials
became clear, and with these controlled it was possible to master
every detail of the complicated ritual smoke offerings, with the
associated meanings.

These smoke offerings at the games are then valuable for analytical and comparative study in revealing the basic forms of
smoke offerings. But there is a more specific and fundamental
reference. In these game bundle rituals as in all Pawnee rituals,

the smoke offering of the ceremony is *the* authoritative summary of the important ideology connected with the ritual. The powers offered smoke, the objects venerated and singled out for special emphasis in the smoke offering are the significant references of the ritual demonstration. Among the Pawnee, in olden as in recent times, when a novice or apprentice begins to learn from a ritual teacher, it is the smoke offering which he must set himself first of all to master. For any ritual, when the general public is witness that an individual can go through a smoke offering ritual competently and unfalteringly it is assumed by all that he knows that ritual and the teachings associated with the bundle to which the ritual belongs. It is thus imperative upon the recorder that the smoke offering of a ritual be controlled in detail wherever possible. In terms of it other aspects of a ceremony which are apparently forgotten may be reconstructed, or at least visualized; while related ceremonies and rituals reveal their kinship in their smoke-offering patterns. But unless one is fortunate the exact detail of the smoke offering, and its correct meaning, is the esoteric aspect most difficult to elicit from informants. Those whose ritual it is never tell it, but only demonstrate it, and to do so without the correct order of the entire ceremony is an act that an orthodox Pawnee attempts with fear and trembling.

All the Ghost Dance hand games save the church games of Moses and Allen, and the derived game of Irene Goodeagle, require formal smoke offerings at their demonstrations.

In the following account discussion of ritual aspects associated with the smoke offerings are considered under special heads, while the smoke offering proper has been treated as a distinct unit, divided into its structural phases.

As far as possible, the direct account of the smoke offering proper is kept in the form of a running description of the actual sequential order of ritual events, while the detailed motions employed are subordinated so that they do not obscure the continuity and essential references.

The Ceremonial Circuit

The basic ceremonial circuit of all Pawnee ritualism, except the rituals of the chiefs, is clockwise, from west through north, east and south back to west. Fundamentally, this circuit determines the order in which stations, or places at which ceremonial offerings or movements are to be made, are attended to. A number of subordinate determinants of order and sequence modify the serial arrangement in particular cases.

In terms of the ceremonial circuit, procedure which is determined by the circuit alone, is from left to right. In the hand game rituals the movements at the altar are not determined by the concept of the circuit alone. Certain of the altar objects—for the games, the entire game set, and the upright sacred objects before the altar— are divided between the two sides, half being primarily associated with the north Crow side, half with the south Eagle side. In attending ritually to these phases of the altar, that half which is associated with the side to which the game bundle belongs is emphasized by being treated first.

Similarly, in offering the pipe to the rixkita[1] behind the altar, the side to which the game belongs is emphasized, and these rixkita attended to first (unless the game ritual prescribes the opposite—which occurs in one case).

Therefore in a Crow game, for these aspects at the altar a right-left order will appear, instead of a generic left-right order. In addition there are cases in which ritual prescribes offerings to individuals in one order, while these individuals are seated according to other conceptual references. Thus at the doorways, if there are a tarutsius and an old man on a side, the tarutsius must be next the doorway, the old man next to the tarutsius. In giving such men the pipe to smoke, ceremonial order would generically require on the north side that the old man receive the pipe before tarutsius, but this is never done. In giving tarutsius the pipe first, and then the old man, the procedure is right-left.

For all such right-left procedures, and any others that can occur, there is a ceremonial adjustment which synchronizes the right-left procedure with a generic left-right or clockwise movement. In essence, this is to interpose a complete clockwise circuit of the fireplace. Practically, however, this could not be done without lengthening and complicating the movements beyond all reasonable limits. Two ritual alternatives are possible. In the first, the offerer holding the pipe turns completely around clockwise, before proceeding to offer at the right; in the second, he turns the pipe around clockwise, as he holds it. Of the former, my informant remarked, "A body turn is just as good as going around the fire — because you turn." The simple turn of the pipe may be used in moving from right to left sides of altar, and the like, and is especially seen in use when men smoking ceremonially are seated, and the pipe has to be offered to one seated at the smoker's right.

---

[1] Correct phonetic rendition: *rixkit*ᵃ.

Here the pipe is turned through a circuit before it is offered, while in offering it to one on the left, it is moved directly leftward.

The alternative of the body turn may in some cases be used in order to shorten a ritual procedure. Such occurs for example when a smoke-offerer, after attending to the north drum, makes a body turn and crosses between altar and fireplace to the south drum, instead of walking clockwise around the fireplace.

The concept of the ceremonial circuit is associated in Pawnee cosmological thought with the movements of the stars around the North Star, and it is felt that everything on earth must move synchronously and in harmony with the celestial movement. While this is the basic conceptual determinant of the ritual movements, in all rituals other more specific concepts make for special variations and arrangements which are adjusted into the broader pattern. Thus for the sacred bundle rituals, and some doctor dances, the cosmological beliefs respecting the relationship of the female western powers dominated by the Evening Star and the male eastern powers dominated by the Morning Star, defines the earth between the fireplace and the western altar place as a sacred path, which cannot be crossed in ritual movements around the arena. As a result in some rituals movement is alternately clockwise and counter-clockwise, with the sacred pathway uncrossed, although in the ceremonial activity if the ritual offerer is before the altar he moves about freely within the sacred precincts and in leaving them moves clockwise toward the north.

In the rituals of the hand games, the affiliation of the hand game bundle is the chief reference which complicates and affects the ceremonial order.

As already noted, the order of offerings at the altar and to the rixkita are determined not by the ceremonial circuit, but by the emphasis of the game bundle, producing right-left sequences which call for ritual adjustment. The generic clockwise circuit, however, determines the order in which the drums are attended to, and in which the drummers, the old men at the doorway, and the general assemblage of men are offered the pipe. Thus for all games, the north or Crow drum is first offered smoke, where it stands at the northwest, then after a circuit through north, east and south to southwest (or a body turn), the Eagle drum. Again, in offering the pipe to drummers, the Crow main drummers receive it first, the smoker continuing around to the southwest to give the pipe to the Eagle drummers. The old man at the north side of the doorway receives the pipe before his colleague on the south side. Finally, if after the main ceremonial stations have been smoked, and the pipe is not out, it is offered to all the assembled men, the procedure is always to begin on the north side with the man just to the north of the leaders behind the altar, and proceed down the north side from west to east, then continue up the south side from east to west, finishing with the man who is seated to the south of the leaders behind the altar.

In calling attention to the way in which the ceremonial circuit determines the order of procedure with drums, drummers, old men, tarutsius, laymen, etc., it should however be understood that the reference is to the order in which the sides are attended to. Left-right procedure for all these means that the north is attended to before the south. It does not mean that the order of attending to drummers in relation to old men, tarutsius, etc., is so determined. This order is prescribed by other considerations, primarily the functional ceremonial importance of the stations and the individuals representing them.

These aspects determined by game emphasis can be summarized as follows:

The leaders are given the pipe ceremonially, in the order N 1, N 2, (with a body turn) S 1, S 2, *or* N 1, (with a body turn) S 1, N 2, (with a body turn) S 2 for a Crow game; but in the order of S 1, (with a body turn) S 2, N 1, N 2, *or* S 1, N 1, (with a body turn) S 2, N 2 for an Eagle game. Similarly the altar objects are smoked first north, then south for a Crow game, first south then north for an Eagle game (this appears in the form of first leftward, then rightward for a Crow game, first rightward then leftward for an Eagle game). If there are ceremonial feather ornaments, etc. standing in front of the altar, when they are an odd number (which they usually are), the smoke offering is first to the central one, always, and then, for an Eagle game, first on the left of the central, then on the right, etc., for a Crow game, first on right of the central, then on the left, and so forth.

Preparation of the Pipe

The pipe used for a ritual smoke offering at a hand game is always the pipe which is contained in that hand game bundle. It is administered by the individual who is in ceremonial charge of the occasion. Such an individual is the main rixkita of the side to which the bundle belongs: N 1 for a Crow game, S 1 for an eagle game—of those game rituals in which four rixkita are seated behind the altar. In those games in which the owner places five men behind the altar, the fifth being a presiding ceremonial official who does not participate in the play of the game, thus constituting him an impartial overseer, it is this fifth or central leader who is the ceremonial administrator.

The man behind the altar who is ceremonially in charge prepares the pipe by taking it up from the altar spread on which it lies and filling it. It is filled with kinnikinnik, a mixture of sumac and store tobacco. Orthodox Pawnee would place on top of this mixture a bit of Indian grown tobacco, if that is obtainable. When the pipe has been filled, this same leader selects the man who is to make the ceremonial smoke offering. Thus, in connection with the offering, the ceremonial administrator has a triple office: he fills the pipe, he selects the smoker, and he hands the pipe to the smoker.

The Designation of the Smoke-Offerer

While the leader in ceremonial charge selects the man to make the smoke-offering, in most cases his choice is made with the approval of the game-bundle owner. The smoker in many cases is known to those in charge before the game assembly. It is preferable to select a man who is more or less familiar with the pattern of the particular smoke offering. But this is not at all essential. The smoker is usually coached on the ritual in advance. The essential aspects are, however, illustrated by what actually takes place at the ceremony. The bundle owner, who alone is fully cognizant of the smoke pattern and its implications, is present, and guides the smoker through the ritual. He or she either walks alongside the smoker and tells him step by step, "Now do this, now do that," *or*, standing to one side, waits for the smoker to make inquiry whenever he is in doubt about any step; *or* allows the smoker to proceed alone, merely stopping him for a correction when it is apparent he is about to make an error. I have seen all these things happen. The implication clearly is that the delegated smoker is not supposed to know all the details of the ritual. He acts for the ritual-owner according to instructions, and is unaware of the meaning of those detailed acts that are unique to the particular smoke-pattern.

On the other hand, a man selected to make a smoke offering must be a man who is familiar and at home with pipe handling. All smoke offerings involve many detailed acts and motions that are generic to Pawnee pipe handling, and for these no instructions are offered by the game owner. The game owner tells him the direction of his offerings, the orientation of his motions, the order of ceremonial precedence in giving the pipe to officials, and the order in which ceremonial objects at the altar should receive offerings of smoke, but it is left for the smoker to make the proper motions and handle the pipe in traditional ways *with respect to* the specific references and objects indicated by the game owner. Thus the game owner will merely indicate "east" and the smoker will offer smoke to the east, handling the pipe traditionally, and using generic pipe-handling motions. The game owner will indicate that feathers standing before the altar are to receive smoke before the game set on the altar spread, and also in what order the feathers are to be smoked, and the smoker proceeds to do what is customary and ritually essential without further notice. A novice in pipe-handling and smoking cannot be the offerer at a ceremony; he can participate in the smoke-offerings of some ceremonies in which the laymen or general public follow the main smokers, and imitate their actions, and in this way he gradually picks up pipe-lore; or, he can learn by studying directly with a man learned in ritual. Actually a man learns ceremonial pipe-lore as part of his teachings, whatever particular bundle-priest, doctor, or ritual owner he apprentices himself to and studies under. He learns to know two things: the particular ways to handle the pipe of the ceremony he is mastering, and something of the generic pipe-handling; and the latter knowledge he fills out by observation at ritual demonstrations.

In many cases the individual selected by the main rixkita or ceremonial administrator is one of the other three rixkita at the altar. I do not remember seeing the official in charge smoke; this would I think be ceremonially impossible because the preparation of the pipe and the offering of smoke are functions that for hand game rituals should be performed by distinct individuals. This is not however the case at Doctor Dances, where the pipe is prepared by the man who owns it and smokes it, but is handed to him by someone else seated behind the altar. It is not however essential at hand game ceremonies that the smoker be one of the rixkita; I have seen drummers or singers selected, and it is probable that men not officials in the particular ceremony, who are learned pipe-handlers, can be chosen. Finally there is no connection between the affiliation of the smoker and the affiliation of the game: a Crow can be selected to make an offering for an Eagle game, and vice versa.

Receiving the Pipe

The designated smoker rises at his place, and comes forward to a position in front of the altar. The ceremonial official is

holding the filled pipe, and hands it to him. For all the ritual
hand games with which we are here concerned, the position in
which the pipe is handed is with mouthpiece up, bowl down, and
bowl opening toward the receiver. The one behind the altar
holds the pipe in his right hand, the hand covering the joint of
bowl and stem so that, should the parts unexpectedly be loose,
they will not separate. The smoker receives the pipe by taking
hold of the pipe stem with his right hand, adding his left, and then
as the other man releases the pipe, he takes a firm grasp of the
pipe and stem at the joint with his right hand. The hands of the
two men must not touch each other in this interchange; touching
hands in passing or handing pipes has special significance, and
usually indicates a participation in the blessing of the smoke, which
is impossible before the smoke offering.

The smoker walks away from the altar carrying the pipe mouthpiece upward, bent slightly away from the body, with the bowl
opening toward himself.

The Smoke Offering Proper

The smoke offering proper may be said to begin with the carrying of the pipe away from the altar by the smoker. He now proceeds to go through the formal ritual of the bundle smoke. This
consists, first, of offerings of tobacco, after which the pipe is lit;
second, of offerings of smoke from the burning pipeful in three
modes: to orientations of powers, to sacred and symbolic objects,
and to sacred and official individuals and others; third, of emptying the pipe of its ashes when out, with which is associated the
symbolic offering of the ashes of the burnt out pipeful as the
ashes are emptied; and finally, a series of motions of sanctification
or blessing with the ashes and empty pipe, and with the empty
pipe alone. Thereafter follow the self-blessing and the return of
the pipe.

Of these four phases of the smoke offering proper, the second
phase, the offerings of smoke, and the fourth phase, the motions
of blessing, are the longest and most detailed. If we consider the
reference of each of the four parts comparatively, it is seen that
they are of three kinds.

First, generic aspects which are carried out in each of the four
phases — for example, an offering to heaven and to earth is generally considered essential by Pawnee theologians for practically
all smoke offerings, thus including of course all the orthodox hand
game rituals. Hence to heaven and to earth would be offered:

tobacco before the pipe is lit, smoke from the burning pipe, ashes or the ash-filled pipe, and blessings over the empty pipe.

Second, there are general aspects of the smoke offerings which in theory can be carried out in all four phases, but which in practice at hand game ceremonies are usually carried out only with the second, third and fourth phases. Such is, for example, an offering to the western orientation which becomes so important in Ghost Dance doctrine. To the west, in some games no tobacco is offered, but usually smoke, ashes, and blessings. In general it can be said that the aspects which are carried out in all four phases, or which can be so carried out, are the mode of offerings to orientations of powers, while all other offerings are limited to the last type.

Third and last, are those offerings to sacred and ceremonial objects, and to individuals present. These in their fullest exhibition are limited to the second phase of the smoke-offering, the offering of smoke itself, but all save the activities associated with the offering of the pipe to men present, can and do reappear in the final phase of motions of blessing, unless this is abbreviated or ceremonially telescoped.

A smoker, from the time he leaves the altar with the filled pipe, proceeds in his movements from place to place to make offerings, at a pace between a slow run and a walk. He is supposed to move rapidly to establish the moving continuity of the smoke offering, and also, particularly after the pipe is lit, to succeed in making the necessary offerings while the pipe is still burning. The ritual rapidity expected is of course a sign of sureness of ritual knowledge, since one unlearned in smoking-lore is inclined to be careful and cautious, moving slowly in order to give himself time to think out the necessary offerings and motions. Only in bundle rituals where offerings are made by priests, and doctor rituals where the medicine man himself makes the offering is the smoker absolutely sure of himself. Hence in other ceremonies the movements are much slower, deteriorating in some hand game rituals to movements with many pauses and breaks for instruction in what next to do, and even ceremonial disruptions of the smoke as the smoker goes out of the circuit altogether to be told what to do. This actually happened at Mrs. Goodeagle's hand game. In these cases, however, the older Pawnee feel that the smoke is being handled incorrectly, and that ill fortune will follow.

In order to present the detailed facts on the smoke-offering proper, it is convenient to consider each of the four phases as a separate unit. In each phase the pipe handling calls for distinct motions and types of motion, and the description of these has been subordinated to the summary statement of the activities and their references in order to bring out clearly the course of ritual events. The lighting of the pipe, a generic aspect of Pawnee smoke-offerings, intrudes between the first and second phase of the smoke-offering proper.

1. *First Phase:* Offering of Tobacco. The smoker leaving the altar with the filled pipe begins a clockwise circuit. In some of the game smokes, as he reaches the eastern doorway he goes somewhat toward the door, and facing east while he pauses momentarily, he offers tobacco eastward to the Morning Star. (This ancient cosmological reference is retained in only a few of the orthodox hand games.)

> *Motion:* The pipe is held in the left hand, while with the thumb and index finger of the right hand a pinch of tobacco is taken from the bowlful and offered toward the east with the fingers. The pipe is held slanting obliquely eastward, between an upright and a horizontal position, and the hand is similarly directed. Then the pinch of tobacco is either placed on the ground at the smoker's feet, or cast toward the east; the choice depends upon the custom of the particular bundle ritual. It should also be noted that bundle rituals vary in exact position between the fireplace and the doorway at which the tobacco is offered. In some it is close to the fireplace, in others between the door posts, and these differences are intended to imply actual differences of ceremonial meaning.

The smoker now continues his clockwise circuit until he returns to the west. In those game rituals which involve no offering of tobacco at the east eastward, the smoker makes a continuous circuit, beginning at the west and ending at the west, without a pause. At the west the smoker stops in front of the fireplace, facing east. Here variations in the offerings of tobacco occur. For most rituals he offers a pinch of tobacco upward to Tirawahat^n or Heaven, and one downward to Mother Earth.

> *Motions:* In offering upward to Heaven, the pipe is held in the left hand, with the mouthpiece pointing vertically upward, while the pinch of tobacco is taken as before with fingers of the right hand, the hand held aloft momentarily. Then the smoker stoops slightly to place the pinch of tobacco on the ground before him (it is never cast on the ground). (See Plate I a, b.) This spot on the east-west midline, just west of the everted outline or wall of the fireplace is the place of many offerings. It is the eastern end of the sacred pathway from fireplace to altar.
>
> In offering downward to the earth, the pipe held in the left hand is allowed to point slightly slantwise toward the ground, while the pinch

Plate I

a - Taking tobacco from pipe bowl for
offering

b - Offering pinch of tobacco to
heaven

c - Offering pipe to heaven

d - Offering pipe to earth

Smoke Offering, First and Second Phases.
Demonstrations by Mark Evarts.

of tobacco is merely placed on the ground. The pipe is never held for this offering pointed vertically downward—a direction with the special connotation of offering to the animal powers.

At this point it may be noted for clarity that in such a game ritual as that of Boychief, which is oriented from a northern altar, these offerings are made just north of the fireplace, facing south.

Additional offerings of tobacco which may be made at this position include offerings to the west, the place of the departed dear ones, an offering actually included in many of the game rituals.

> *Motion:* For an offering to the west, the smoker turns his body right about face without altering the position of his feet, which still are set eastward, momentarily points the pipe with his left hand slantwise westward, while with the right he offers a pinch of tobacco on the ground before him in the same place as the other offerings.
>
> This is the usual form. In some cases, it seems to be optional to turn the *feet and body* so that the west is faced, offer the tobacco by holding the pinch aloft slantwise westward with the right hand while the pipe is directed similarly with the left, then turn left about face back to the position at the fireplace facing east and stooping, deposit the tobacco on the ground. The choice might rest either with the ritual owner or the smoker, but the former's instructions and wishes would be carried out if they were expressed on this point. The variation is part of generic pipe-lore, without specific ritual significance. The first is the shorter, quicker method, the second the completer.

The usual order of these three offerings is Heaven, Earth, West, but some rituals follow the order Heaven, West, Earth. The former sequence emphasizes the primary or elementary significance of Tirawahat^n and Mother Earth, implying that they are basic to all other powers and motions and should be offered first of all. The latter sequence reflects the idea that while offerings must begin with Tirawahat^n, the offering to Mother Earth from which all life on earth flows shall conclude the offering sequence, making it complete. It should also be noted that in some rituals the offering of a pinch of tobacco upward and then placing it on the ground is considered a combined offering for Heaven and Earth at the same time, and only the one motion is made.[1]

This general plan of the order of offerings up to this point finds exception in the tobacco offering form followed by the ritual offerer at a demonstration of the game ritual of Yellowhorse. Here the offerer came directly from the altar to a position west of the

---

[1] In explanation the thought is offered that, in any case, "Mother Earth receives everything."

fireplace, facing east, where offerings for Heaven, Earth and the West were made, then proceeded counter-clockwise through the south until, passing the east, a pause facing east was made while a pinch of tobacco was offered slantwise east and cast on the ground; after which the smoker continued counter-clockwise to the position at which the pipe was lit. Thereafter he proceeded clockwise.

While this form may have specific significance, I incline to believe that it is a version of the offerings in a briefer form; it involves less circuiting in the movements, and so speeds up the ritual.

The smoke offerings of the Beaver and Goodeagle hand games, rituals with medicine man connotations, include offerings of tobacco by the smoker as he stands at the west facing east to orientations in the following order: upward, slantwise east, slantwise south, slantwise north, slantwise west and slantwise down. The motion upward is for heaven, that downward for the earth. The slantwise east offering is for the Morning Star, as a result of which, in this ritual no pause is made in the first circuit for this tobacco offering, which is here included in the offerings made at the west of the fireplace rim. The south and north offerings are to the South and North Stars respectively, ancient cosmological references, particularly important in the theology of Skiri medicine men, of which Beaver and Goodeagle were noted exemplars. The slantwise west offering has its usual Ghost Dance significance, although for the most part this meaning is combined with a reference to the Evening Star and her domain, at least for some ritualists.

Motions: For the offerings already described, the motions in this ritual are the same.

For the south and north offerings, the motion is similar to that for the west. The body is turned a quadrant rightward and leftward respectively for these offerings, the pinch of tobacco offered slantwise in these directions while the pipe is held in the left hand so pointed, and after the body is turned back to normal position, the tobacco is deposited on the ground. The feet all the while are kept on the ground in one place, directed eastward.

These south and north offerings, similarly to that for the west described above, may be carried out by turning body and feet so that the offerer faces in the direction in which the offering is made, turning back to position facing east for the deposit of the tobacco.

With the completion of the tobacco offerings, the smoker proceeds clockwise through the north to the position east of northeast in which he squats for the pipe to be lit.

Lighting the Pipe

In all Pawnee rituals, and in all the hand games, the position in which the pipe is lit is ceremonially and conceptually the same. The smoker, whatever his movements in making offerings of tobacco, arrives at a point just east of northeast, where he squats down (without sitting) and holds the pipe before him, mouthpiece between lips, and bowl pointing obliquely downward and directed diagonally toward the east. Here the pipe is lit for him, either by a special official functionary, such as the tarutsius, or watcher, for such games as have these officials, or by someone asked to do so by the game owner or official leader. The pipe is always lit with a brand. If a fire is burning in the fireplace this is a brand from the fire; if not, it is a firebrand brought in for this purpose. All the sacred bundles contained braided sweetgrass with which the bundle pipe was lit in making a smoke offering. In doing this, the sweetgrass was first set afire with a brand from the fire, and then the sweetgrass torch used to light the pipe. A few games, such as Mrs. Goodeagle's and others of the older orthodox games had such sweetgrass pipe-lighters in the game bundles. Games without sweetgrass lighters employ an ordinary stick firebrand.

Exceptions to the complete uniformity of all rituals as regards the position in which the pipe is lit, may be noted as follows: For Boychief's game, with its orientation from a northern altar, the position is south of southeast, which maintains the analogous position with a shift or turn of the whole pattern of orientation clockwise through a quadrant. In Goodeagle's game where two simultaneous smoke offerings are made, the pattern is worked out symmetrically so that one smoker has the pipe lit east of northeast, and one east of southeast.

Inference from the careful comparison of the connotation and reference of all Pawnee bundle rituals and Pawnee mythology indicates that the east of northeast position for pipe lighting symbolizes a reference to the Northeast or Black Star, which controls the region of darkness. Before the marriage of the Morning Star and Evening Star, which brought light and fertility into actuality, all was darkness, and the Black Star ruled. The lighting of the pipe while it is pointed eastward symbolizes dramatically the coming of the powers of light and life.

2. *Second Phase:* Offering of Smoke, or of Pipe to Smoke.

a. First Mode: Offering to Orientations of Powers.

As the smoker rises with the lit pipe he puffs it a few times to make sure it is burning properly, using the tamper with his right hand to loosen the tobacco and stimulate the flame, while he holds the pipe with his left hand.

The smoker now begins a clockwise circuit. In old bundle rituals, where an offering of tobacco had been made to the east (the Morning Star) at the east facing eastward, the smoker would also pause at the east for an offering of smoke, but according to the information available this was not done in hand game smoke rituals. Such an offering is however ceremonially correct, and possible for all smoke rituals in which an offering of tobacco has been made eastward from a point east of the fireplace. Such an offering would be of either four puffs of smoke or two; four is conceived as ceremonial completeness, two as abbreviation.

> *Motion:* Facing east, the smoker draws in smoke, and as he puffs it upward and outward toward the east, the pipe is taken from the mouth, turned, and its mouthpiece directed slantwise toward the east. It is held with both hands, the left upon the pipestone bowl, the right on the joint of bowl and stem and reaching somewhat above the joint. The right hand is used to steady the stem and direct it properly. The position in which the pipe is held is identical with that in which it is held and put to the lips of individuals who are offered a pipe ceremonially by a ritual smoker. In other words, the power of the orientation to which the pipe is directed is offered the pipe to smoke, not symbolically, but actually, while the smoker exhales the smoke for him.
>
> In returning the pipe to the mouth for another puff it is brought directly back, without special ritual turns. The puffing is repeated identically the requisite number of times.

If an offering of smoke is made to the eastern Morning Star powers, the smoker continues to move clockwise after the offering; if it is not he has moved clockwise continuously from the position east of northeast at which the pipe was lit. He continues until he reaches the west, where he stops just west of the fireplace facing east, the same point and position in which the major offerings of tobacco were made.

At this point, west of the rim of the fireplace, the smoker proceeds to make offerings of smoke, or offerings of the pipe to smoke, to the same powers and orientations to which tobacco was offered. The correct ritual forms require without exception that these offerings be made in the same order as those of tobacco. Thus if at the west of the fireplace the smoker offered tobacco to Heaven, to Earth and then to West, he now smokes Heaven, Earth and

West in that order, while if he followed the sequence Heaven, West and Earth, he now maintains that ritual order. I have remarked above that occasionally a smoke ritual includes one deposit of tobacco at the west of the fireplace for Heaven and Earth combined. This cannot be done with the smoke offering, where separate offerings must be made upward to Heaven and downward to Earth. The identity of sequence of offerings of tobacco and offerings of smoke is well illustrated in that of Beaver, who repeats with smoke the order of his offerings: upward, slantwise east, slantwise south, slantwise north, slantwise west, and downward. A complete ritual here requires four puffs of smoke for each power or direction; but, the owner of a particular ritual may have conceptual reasons for subordinating certain references to others, in which case the subordinated offerings consist of two puffs of smoke, the emphasized offerings of four.

> *Motions: Upward:* The pipe is held as if put to the lips of the power, as described above, and pointed directly upward. The bowl opening in this position is toward the smoker, the bowl directed downward, the mouthpiece upward. (See Plate I, c.)
>
> *Downward:* The pipe is directed slantwise downward, away from the smoker toward the west. (An offering to earth; a direct vertically downward position would be to animal powers). Similarly each puff of smoke is blown downward as the head is inclined downward. (See Plate I, d.)
>
> *Westward, Northward, Southward:* For these offerings the body positions and turns are similar to those for the offerings of tobacco directed to these powers. The smoker remains fixed in his position, not moving his feet from the ground, but turning his body through a right turn until his face looks westward, through a quadrant leftward, and through a quadrant rightward, respectively: *or* he turns *feet and body* so that he faces the direction offered. The pipe in each case is moved so that it is offered slantwise in the direction smoked.
>
> *Eastward:* If, as occurs in the Beaver and Goodeagle smoke offerings, the gift of smoke to the eastern powers is made here west of the fireplace instead of east of the fireplace, the smoker performs it by facing east, directing the pipe at a high slant upward eastward, while he offers the puffs of smoke.

Occasionally in a hand game ritual smoke, additional conceptual offerings of smoke are included in the offerings made at the position west of the rim of the fireplace. Such are, for example in Pierson's ritual, offerings of two puffs of smoke to the southern horizon, from west to east, one of which is for the Sun, the other for the Moon. The horizon included is intended to indicate the usual pathway of the sun and moon.

> *Motions:* The smoker faces east, draws in smoke, then, without directing his pipe in any special way, begins to puff out smoke with

pursed lips toward a point on the horizon just south of due east. He continues to puff out as he turns his head clockwise toward his right until his head reaches a position where it faces about west of southwest over his right shoulder. The identical motion is repeated for the Moon.

In Pierson's ritual, an offer of smoke northward to the North Star is made following the offerings to the Sun and Moon, by merely turning the head, without directing the pipe, and making one puff northward.

These offerings of smoke conclude the first mode. From his position west of the fireplace, the smoker now comes to the western altar, where the second mode begins. There are two correct manners of approaching the altar from the position at the west of the fireplace rim, a short one, and a long one. In the first, or short manner, the smoker turns right about face and walks directly down the sacred pathway to the altar. In the second, the smoker leaves his position at the west of the fireplace and proceeds clockwise through a complete circuit of north, east, south and back to west, where he comes straight to the altar from south of it. These two manners seem to be definitely optional, not only for hand game smokes, but for most ritual smoke offerings. A ritual smoker seeking to telescope a long and complex ritual, would use the short form at this point, along with the short optional forms of other modes and phases.

b. Second Mode: Offerings to Ceremonial Objects.

When the smoker arrives before the altar he begins there the first part of this mode of the smoke offering. This consists of offering the pipe or puffs of smoke to all the ceremonial objects at the altar, after which the smoker will proceed to the drums, which for most games have already been set in the positions in which they will be used during the game proper. All objects at the altar are smoked while the smoker moves about before them, facing west.

The smoking at the altar takes into account first of all the ceremonial objects which are set in the ground in front (eastward) of the altar spread. These objects may include: feathers, feathered sticks, lances, leaning calumets, cedar tree, bows and arrows, crosses, miniature scaffold, and Christ's picture. In general the order in which objects in front of the altar spread are smoked is the order in which they are arranged from front to back, that is from east to west. This order is the same as that of their ceremonial or conceptual importance. Whatever is of primary or paramount importance is set foremost before the altar with subordinated objects behind it, between the major sacramental object or objects and the altar spread.

In general the main object set out before the altar spread is either single, or a row of similar objects in a north-south line. If it is a single object, such as a lance, an erect feather, or a feathered stick, this is first smoked.

Motion: The smoker blows out a puff of smoke down upon the standing object so that it suffuses the head or top end. For a single main ceremonial object, he may smoke it at top, middle and bottom, or he may offer it two puffs of smoke.

In dealing with a row of objects, we have such as six, seven or eight feathers or feathered sticks, three feathers, two lances, five corn tassels, etc. In such cases, an odd number are so set that the middle one is on the east-west midline, and half the remainder to each side, while an even number are set half to each side of the east-west midline. In smoking the full or complete unhurried way, smoke is puffed to each one of the objects. The order has already been indicated above. For an odd number, the central one is smoked first, then the one immediately to the right (north) or left (south) of the central one, and so on, alternating until the end ones are reached. The side emphasized is the side, usually, to which the ritual belongs, unless as in Mrs. Goodeagle's game ritual, there are special conceptual reasons for altering that generic pattern. Thus for example for a Crow altar led by seven feathered sticks, the smoker puffs to 1. the central one, 2. the one just north of central, 3. the one just south of central, 4. the second north of central, 5. the second south of central, 6. the extreme north, 7. the extreme south.

For an even number of sticks, six, eight, etc. the emphasis on the north or south side must begin at once. If it is a north emphasis the first one smoked is that just north of the midline, then that south of midline, then second north of midline, second south, etc. until all have been offered individual puffs of smoke.

Motion: The motion is essentially the same as that described above for a single object: a direct puff at the top of the object, sometimes allowing the smoke to drift downward over it, by declining the head further as the smoke is puffed out.

There are two ways of abbreviating these offerings. For a large odd number (seven) or a large even number (eight), the central and extreme ends can be smoked. This would be four for the even number, instead of the more complete eight individual puffs, and three for the odd number, instead of seven. A still more abrupt form is merely to smoke from center northward or rightward over the objects, then from center southward or leftward over them—for a north emphasis, reverse for a south.

Motion: In such an inclusive puff, the pursed mouth would begin to direct smoke at the central one, and then continue to puff out smoke over others as the head moved above the objects toward the right (or left). It is one continuous puff of smoke distributed over all those on one side.

Unusual objects before hand game altar spreads include the two leaning calumets of Goodeagle's, Christ's picture and a cedar tree in Boychief's game, a cedar cross in Rudder's game, and crosses and a miniature scaffold in Moses' old game.

In offering smoke to the calumets, Goodeagle's game belonging to the Eagle or south side, the south white calumet is first offered one or two puffs, then the north or green calumet. There is nothing unusual in the motions.

Christ's picture receives two puffs, directly at it, while the associated tree, smoked immediately after the picture, is offered a puff at the top, one at the middle, and one at the base.

The cedar cross, which is the main ceremonial object before Rudder's altar, is smoked so that what the Pawnee call a "five pointed star" is made. Five puffs are offered, first to the top of the vertical, then to the joint or crossing, then at the north end of the horizontal, then the south end of the horizontal, and finally at the base of the vertical. The end of the horizontal of a cross which is first smoked is an indication of the side to which the ritual is affiliated.

In Moses' altar, each cross can be fully smoked as above, or, as they are smaller ceremonial objects, one puff for each cross is sufficient. For the scaffold, the cross-bar, then each of the upright forked verticals is offered a puff.

These types of objects include all the objects before the altar spreads save the bows and arrows. They may be arranged so as to subordinate one to another. Thus as shown in the figures Rudder sets the cedar cross out in front, a row of three crow feathered cedar sticks just behind it; Goodeagle sets the leaning calumets out in front, with a row of eight black eagle feathers just west of them; and so on. Games which have bows and arrows (sometimes carried by the guessers during game play) generally have these placed on the ground between the upright ceremonial objects before the altar, and the altar spread. These bows and arrows would be offered smoke after the upright objects. In general the head of the bow and the head of the arrow are pointed in the direction with which they are associated. This means that in some sets with them they are both pointed in the same direction, while in other sets (regardless of the affiliation of the set itself) there are two bows and arrows, of which one is in color, feathering, etc. affiliated with the Crows and used by the Crow guesser, the other similarly associated with the Eagles. In this case the Crow bow and arrow point north, the Eagle bow and arrow south. In offering puffs of smoke to these, each is offered one puff at the head end and the tail end, the bow and arrow set first smoked being the one which agrees in affiliation with the game set, and points in the emphasized direction.

An altar set which merely had a row of upright objects in front, and bows and arrows lying behind, and for which the most abrupt abbreviated method is used, merely requires that the smoker make one leftward and one rightward puff over the uprights, and to make similarly one leftward and one rightward puff over the bows and arrows.

After these offerings the smoker moves forward to just in front of the altar spread to continue with offerings to the objects on the altar.

The objects on the altar spread include the game set of tally sticks and counters, the concealed horn spoon, and hair ornaments for guessers, watchers, and players. Rattles belonging to sets are usually placed on the altar spread parallel to the pipe. In some games there are special animal or bird spreads, which lie upon the cloth spread, and upon which the other objects are placed. These include the whole eagle skin of Pierson's game, and the wildcat hide of White's game.

Such sacred objects as the eagle skin and the wildcat are the most important objects on the altar proper. These are the first objects smoked. In ancient bundle rituals such skins would be smoked to nose, and along the body, but in the hand game ritual smokes, the briefer form of offering one puff to the nose is generally followed.

> *Motion:* In offering a puff of smoke to the eagle or wildcat nose, the pipe mouthpiece is offered directly to the mouth and nose of the animal while the smoker bends forward and puffs right at the nose.

For all the other objects, hand game smoke rituals practically always follow a simple brief form. The smoker standing before the altar spread blows one puff of smoke leftward or southward from center altar out, and one rightward or northward from center altar out. These offerings are intended to include all objects on the altar proper.

Motion: The smoker does not move the pipe, merely puffing out smoke as he moves his head to the one side or the other over the altar.

The side which is first smoked is determined by the affiliation of the game.

It is possible to smoke a number of objects on the altar individually, such as the rattles, when there are such, and the bunched feather hair ornaments. The rattles lie head or rattle end toward the west, and in smoking them a puff is directed at the head end, and drawn eastward along the length of the rattle. For bunched feathers a puff is merely directed at the cluster. The pipes are not pointed for such offerings. The two puff motions over the altar spread are included in all game smokes, and are intended basically to be offerings to the game sets, although in the shorter form, as above, they are conceived to include all objects on the altar.

When the smoker makes his offering to objects on the altar proper, as he makes each individual offering, the rixkita behind the altar say "Nawa."

From the altar the smoker proceeds next to the north or Crow drum. The drums are usually two-faced for the hand games. If these are still before the altar (they generally are not), they are set vertically so that one face is directed southward, one northward. To smoke them in this position the smoker blows one puff against each face, first the north, then the south. If the drums are in game position, the smoker reaches the north or Crow drum at about northwest, where it is suspended from forked sticks with the Crow drummers seated around it. Here he blows two puffs at the face which is uppermost. At each puff the drummers say "Nawa." He then proceeds clockwise around the fireplace to the South or Eagle drum, where he offers two puffs to the upper face, at each of which the South drumers say "Nawa." In proceeding to the Eagle drum, the circuit of the fireplace is optional; if he makes a complete turn of his body clockwise, he can proceed directly across between fireplace and altar to the Eagle drum.

This concludes the second mode of this second phase of the smoke offering. He will now proceed to offer the pipe to certain individuals present, unless this third mode is to be omitted.

c. Third Mode: Offerings to Men.

According to Pawnee theory the phase of the smoke offering in which smoke from the burning pipe is offered is not ritually complete without offering the pipe to at least the major ceremonial officials of the occasion, who are usually supposed to represent definite conceptions which are part of the ideology of the ritual. Also in theory the pipe should be kept in circulation in this phase of the offering until it goes out. It is considered definitely unfortunate if it goes out before the first two modes of this phase of the offering have been completed, and in part it is a fear that the pipe may go out, with attendant unknown misfortunes, that impels the smoker to abbreviate the ritual and hurry through it. It is best that the pipe be still burning properly at the conclusion of the offerings at altar and drums, so that it can be offered for actual puffs to ceremonial officials. I have seen this whole third mode omitted, but criticism was expressed of the smoke in various quarters because of the omission. There is a point at which, if the pipe goes out while it is being offered to ceremonial officials, this mode should end (see below); but if it continues beyond that point the pipe must go through the rest of the offerings whether it is out or not, in which case it is handled as if it were alight.

In one case witnessed the pipe went out while the first mode was being carried out, the offerings to the powers. This was a very bad sign indeed. The smoker stopped and waited for the pipe to be relit (where he stood). But several old men were dubious, and thought that the smoke should have stopped at once. It was a very unlucky sign.

After the smoker has offered two puffs to the south drum he continues clockwise to the altar. Here he begins a series of offerings of the pipe to men present. In offering the pipe to these he never releases it. He holds it basically in his left hand, with his right hand further forward on the stem supporting the pipe stem and directing it to the lips of the receivers. Between the offerings he may as necessary puff the pipe himself and use the tamper to make sure it is burning well. The men who take the pipe to their lips to smoke place both palms on the stem near the mouthpiece covering and almost concealing the tip, draw the pipe to their lips for a puff and then release it. The hands of the offerer and those accepting the pipe to puff must not touch.

In going counter clockwise to offer the pipe, as explained above under the *ceremonial circuit*, either the pipe must be turned clockwise, or the offerer himself turns round clockwise, usually in this mode of the smoke, for brevity, the former. The fullest form, in which the smoker, after offering the pipe to one individual, proceeds through a complete circuit before offering the pipe to the next man to the former's right, I have never seen at a hand game. It is avoided for the sake of brevity. I have seen it carried out in smoke offerings of Doctor Dances.

Summarizing the essentials of all the hand game smoking rituals for this mode, the following individuals may receive the pipe. The movements from place to place are indicated between the numbered stations.

1. The rixkita behind the altar. Order:
   a. For an arrangement with 4 rixkita:

   Crow game: N 1, (pipe turn) S 1, N 2, (pipe turn) S 2; *or* N 1, N 2, (pipe turn) S 1, (pipe turn) S 2.

   Eagle game: S 1, N 1, (pipe turn) S 2, N 2; *or:* S 1, (pipe turn) S 2, N 1, N 2.

Note: If one of the rixkita is making the ritual offering, someone else has been shifted into his place and receives the pipe for his station and seat.

   b. For an arrangement with 4 rixkita and a fifth central official:

   Crow game: The central official, N 1, (pipe turn) S. 1.

   Eagle game: The central official, (pipe turn) S 1, N 1.

From these stations at the altar the offerer proceeds clockwise to the North drummers at the Northwest.

2. The main two Crow drummers.

From here the offerer proceeds clockwise through the north, east and south to the South drummers at the Southwest. Or he may turn his body completely round clockwise and cross between altar and fireplace. The former is preferred.

3. The main two Eagle drummers.

4. (Possible) The Game Owner, wherever his place, (proceeding clockwise).

Now the offerer continues clockwise to the north side of the eastern doorway.

5. Old man north of doorway.

6. (With pipe turns) Doctors or (and) chiefs and braves west of the above or north old man.

From here the offerer moves clockwise past the doorway to the south side.

7. Old man south of doorway.

8. Chiefs and braves west of this south old man.

At this point if the pipe has gone out, the offerings definitely end, and the smoker proceeds to the third phase of the offering, the emptying of the ashes. If the pipe is still burning, the smoker may at his discretion continue with the following individuals. Since to participate in the smoking of the sacred pipe of the ritual is to share the blessings of the ritual event, it is better ceremonial manners for the smoker to continue further, but as this makes for a very lengthy procedure it is often omitted. In that case, the smoker puffs the pipe a few times more himself until it is out. If he begins to offer the pipe on the north side, as below, he must continue with it up the south side until all the men present have participated, even though the pipe is out, and they merely touch the pipe to their lips. .

9. The men present on the north side from west to east (beginning with the man just north of the rixkita).

As at most hand games the men are seated only between west and about northwest, when all on this side have smoked, the smoker carries the pipe, puffing it meanwhile himself to keep it going through a clockwise partial circuit from northwest through north, east and south to the point at about southwest where the men on the south side are clustered.

10. The men present on the south side from east to west (that is beginning with the most eastern at southwest, and continuing until the man immediately on the south (right) of the rixkita has received the pipe to smoke).

The essentials of all hand game smoke offerings for this mode include the first three stations: the rixkita and the two main drummers for each side. The official stations on both sides of the doorway are recognized in the ritual of only those games which officially designate individuals for those places.

After the completion of this mode of the second phase, proceeding clockwise, the smoker returns with the pipe, now out, to the position west of the fireplace rim, facing east, in which the major offerings of tobacco, and of smoke to orientations of powers, were carried out. Here he takes up the next phase, the disposal of the ashes.

3. *Third Phase:* Disposal or Offering of the Ashes.

The smoker arrives at the west of the rim of the fireplace with the pipe, which is now out. This is the position in which the major offerings of tobacco and of smoke to the powers were made.

The theory of the disposal of the ashes here is that as they are loosened and dumped from the pipe bowl, the burnt out pipe is shown to those powers who were offered tobacco in this position. These are, basically, Heaven, Earth and the West. A ritual requires that whatever of these three orientations has been offered tobacco should now be shown the pipe as it is emptied of ashes in the same sequence. For those rituals which include a longer sequence of tobacco offerings at the west of the fireplace, such as Beaver's and Goodeagle's, only Heaven and Earth, or Heaven, West and

Earth, receive the pipe as the ashes are emptied. The reason for this is that this third phase and the following fourth phase in which blessings are made with ashes and empty pipe are considered one continuity of blessings after the smoke, and all powers not directly shown the pipe with the ashes in it, are included in the ritual sequence of the phase which immediately follows.

Making sure that the pipe is out, the smoker holds it in his left hand, while with his right he tamps some of the ashes loose. He now offers the pipe to Heaven, and then dumps some ashes on the ground at his feet.

> *Motion:* After tamping ashes loose, the tamper is placed alongside the pipe stem, then the right hand supports the left as the pipe is offered upward.[1] The position of the pipe is bowl opening upward, the whole pipe more or less horizontal, with the mouthpiece leftward, the bowl rightward. Here the intention of the position is that the bowl of ashes is directed toward or shown to the powers, and it is the bowl which is directed with the right hand. The pipe is elevated until it is at arm's length above the head. Now the smoker stoops holding the pipe in the same way, lowering it, and as it reaches a point just above the ground, (the sacred place for offerings), he turns the pipe bowl away from him so that the ashes loosened are emptied outward upon the ground. (See Plate II a, b, c, d, e, in order.)

The offering to Heaven is usually followed by one to the Earth.

> *Motion:* Smoker merely loosens ashes with tamper, and deposits on ground, as above. In this way, when he does not elevate the pipe, but nevertheless holds it about horizontal the offering is for the Earth.

In offering to west, whether this is before the offering to Earth or after, the motion is the same.

> *Motion:* Loosening some ashes, the smoker takes hold of the pipe as above, then *either* merely turns the body so that he can elevate the pipe horizontally directing the bowl with his right hand slantwise west, *or* turns right about face fully so that he faces west while he elevates the pipe. In either case he turns back to face east as he stoops and dumps ashes on the ground before him.

The offerings of ashes are in their longest form two each for Heaven, Earth and West. Usually one for Heaven and one for Earth, (with two for west where that is included), is sufficient. The offerer controls the loosening of ashes so that the final ritual dumping completely empties the pipe. If, however, he is not quite successful in this, after the ritual offerings he merely tamps and empties ashes

---

[1] Plate IIc shows pipe held in right hand alone; this is correct, but holding it when aloft in both hands (as these are placed in IId) is also done.

Plate II

a - Loosening ashes with tamping stick

d - Lowering the pipe

b - Grasping pipe to raise it. Note
position of tamper along stem

c - Holding pipe aloft — offering ashes
to the heavens

e - Turning pipe bowl to spill ashes on
ground

Smoke Offering, Third Phase, Disposal of Ashes.
Demonstrations by Mark Evarts.

Plate III

a - Passing hand upward along pipestem, motion of blessing to heaven (profile)

b - Same as a (full face)

c - Motion of blessing to earth

Smoke Offering, Fourth Phase.
Demonstrations by Mark Evarts.

on the ground, until by blowing through the pipe he is sure it is clear. He now places the tamper on the ground beside his left foot, and takes the pipe in both hands, ready for the fourth and last phase, the motions of blessing.

4. *Fourth Phase:* Blessings with the empty pipe.

The theory of this last phase of the smoke offering is that individual sacramental motions with the pipe should be made for each power and object which received puffs of smoke in the second phase but not the stations or men. Correct pipe manners really require that if the second phase has not been telescoped or abbreviated, this last phase should not be. A smoker who wishes to abbreviate the ritual sequence should anticipate by correctly telescoping the second phase in order to permit telescoping of this last. Nevertheless I have seen this last phase carried out in somewhat more curtailed form than the offering of smoke.

Thus in the fullest demonstration of the last phase it is composed of two modes which reproduce with motions of blessing the first and second modes of the second phase.

a. First Mode: Blessings for the Powers.

The blessings begin with Tirawahat^n in all cases.

Motion: Smoker holds the pipe first in the left hand, while as he stoops slightly, he rubs his right palm over the ashes on the ground. Then returning to an erect position, he rubs the right palm upward along the pipe from the extremity of the bowl projection, over the right side of the bowl and up the stem, past the mouthpiece. As his hand leaves the mouthpiece, he opens the palm upward and outward. The pipe meanwhile has been held with the left hand at the joint of bowl and stem, the mouthpiece directed vertically upward, the bowl downward, the bowl opening toward the body of the smoker. (See Plate III a, b; two views of the same.)

The smoker next takes the pipe analogously in his right hand, stoops and touches the ashes with his left, and repeats the motion as above with the left hand.

Four motions are ritually necessary for this offering, as follows: alternating right, left, right, left. I do not think that an abbreviation to two motions would for the blessings toward Heaven be accepted as adequate.

From this point the blessings follow the order of offerings of the

---

[1] The gesture of the motion of blessing toward Earth is shown in Plate IIIc.

particular ritual, as heretofore explained.[1] In each case the motion is to touch the ashes with the free hand, which is then run along the pipe from bowl to stem and opened outward in the direction of the power offered the pipe, while with the other hand the pipe is directed toward that orientation or power in the identical manner in which it was held with the two hands while the puffs of smoke were offered to that power. The same optional variations of body turns in offering northward, southward and westward are true for these blessings. In general the smoker makes the same number of motions of blessing for each direction that he has made puffs of smoke. Usually Heaven, Earth and West receive four, North and South two or one. The blessings for the pathway of Sun or Moon are analogous to the smoke offerings:

Motion: After touching the right hand to the ashes on the ground, the smoker rubs the right hand over the pipe from bowl to stem while the pipe is directed toward about east of southeast. As his hand leaves the mouthpiece and is opened outward, he sweeps it slowly around from east of southeast to about west of southwest, turning his body the while, so that the pipe follows.

One motion is all that is made, with the right hand. For a similar motion for the Moon, the identical action is repeated, with the right hand. Left hand motions for this are impossible both physically and conceptually. The physical fact is obvious. Conceptually, it is the right hand horizon that the motion is made for and to, and symmetry requires use of the right hand.

These motions at the west of the fireplace facing east complete this mode of the last phase. The smoker now retrieves the tamper which has been lying on the ground next to his left foot during this time, and places it along the pipe stem. He should not, in correct pipe manners, leave it behind. Taking pipe and tamper, he now proceeds to the altar for the second mode, the motions over the sacred objects. In going to the altar he may either proceed through a complete clockwise circuit, or directly down the sacred pathway.

b. Second Mode: Blessings over Sacred Objects.

If the smoker is detailed and complete in his motions of blessing over the sacred objects he will follow the exact order in which he gave puffs of smoke to the erect objects before the altar, those lying on the ground between the former and the altar spread, and those on the altar spread, making the same number of motions for each individually as he made puffs of smoke. In each case also the motion is made in a manner which reproduces the manner of smoking, and with the right or left hand according to which side is blessed. There are thus three types of motion which occur in

---

[1] See page 203.

hand game rituals for this mode: a direct motion to anything, a motion over things, and a motion along things.

Motion 1: To an object: The hand, left or right, is run along the pipe from bowl to mouthpiece, while the pipe is held in the other hand and more or less directed at the object, and as the hand rubbed along the pipe passes the mouthpiece it is touched to the object lightly.

This motion would be used for upright feathers or sticks, for lances, cedar tree, Christ's picture, the five points of the cross, the ends of the bows and arrows, the nose of the eagle and wildcat etc. The right hand would be used for anything north or right of the midline, the left for anything south, to which should be added that symmetrical arrangements would be carried out. Thus for example, for the cross, the right hand would touch the top of the vertical, the left, the joint; the right, the right extremity of the horizontal; the left, the left extremity of the cross bar; and the right, the base of the vertical. Important ceremonial objects which received more than one puff of smoke, and therefore now receive more than one motion, require that the hands be used alternately. Thus for the cedar tree, which is smoked at top middle and base, the right hand would touch the top, the left the middle, the right the base. For the nose of wildcat and eagle, the right and left hands would touch them alternately, and similarly for Christ's picture. It should also be noted that right then left is the required order unless the order of offering emphasizes the south side first, as for example with eight feathers in a row before the altar of an Eagle game, in which case the feather just south of the midline is first touched with a motion of the left hand while the right holds the pipe, then that just north of midline with the right hand and so on.

Motion 2: Over objects: The hand is run over the pipe, then palm down moved from center outward over the objects, following the manner in which the smoke has been diffused.

This motion would be used in all abbreviated forms over objects before the altar spread, and in all forms for the objects of the game set on the altar spread. Whether it is first right over the north side, then left over south side is of course determined by the ritual emphasis of that game set.

The third type of motion over altar objects could be used with the eagle and wildcat skin, in which cases the motions would be from head to foot along the body—the skins lying head eastward, tail westward; or it could be used for rattles of the various kinds, and pipes. For rattles and pipes, the motion is from west to east, or from away from the body of the officiator toward the body, as the smoker faces west. This is because the rattles lie rattle or gourd end west, handle east, and the pipes similarly bowl westward, mouthpiece east; the symbolic motions are made *over them* as actual hand motions would be made *on them*.

The motions over the length of the animal skins would not occur unless smoke were offered down the animal's back; if the offering were only to the nose, only a direct motion of the first type above would be employed.

The motions for the rattles occur for a number of games which possess rattles. As for pipes, the identity of the motion over pipes lying on the altar with the motion for rattles is worth recording here, although for most of the hand game bundles, there is only one official pipe, and since that is in use for the ritual offering, the place lies vacant on the altar, hence no motion for it is made. But for many rituals, as some of the revived society dances associated with Pierson's game, there is more than one pipe. In such a case, with the pipe in use motions are made over the other pipes on the altar. The motion for the pipe also enters the ritual food offering (see below).

> *Motion:* Along objects. The hand is rubbed down over the pipe, and then without contact back along one side of the animal skin; repeat for other side with other hand. The hand position is thumb straight forward, four fingers of palm together diagonally outward. For the rattles, the hand after being rubbed down the length of the pipe is reached out so that it is over the farther head end of the rattles, then brought quickly along over the rattles toward the body. It should be noted that for animal skins and the like the smoker leans down so that the hands almost touch the animal, while for the rattles (and pipes) the motions are made in a more erect position, the motions being three feet or more above the objects. For the rattles, the fingers of the palms are directed diagonally inward while the motions are made.

Before considering the latter part of this mode, the motions over the drums, it is well to point out that in the most customary telescoped form, the smoker would make merely two motions over the erect objects before the altar, a right hand rightward over the northern and a left leftward over the southern, (two over the objects between the erected symbols and the altar spread—if there are any such—similar to the above), and two over the objects on the altar cloth, for the game set as well as all other objects there, similar to the above. For both of these sets of two motions, the order of north and south is determined by the game bundle affiliation.

As the smoker makes motions of blessing over objects on the altar proper, the rixkita sitting behind the altar say "nawa."

The smoker now proceeds clockwise to the north drum, where he makes two motions upon the upper drum face; the Crow drummers say "Nawa" for each motion.

> *Motions:* First right hand, always, then left. The right hand is rubbed down the pipe which is held in the left, then touched to the drum face at a point near the circumference opposite to where the smoker stands. Thus usually the smoker stands just south of the north drum and faces about north, so that his right hand will first barely touch the drumskin at about due north or just west of due north. The hand is then moved circularly over the drum face from this point clockwise to just west of south. Then the hands are changed and with the left hand an analogous motion is made from just east of north counterclockwise to just east of south.

The smoker then proceeds clockwise through north, east and south to the south drum at about southwest, where he makes motions of blessing over the drum face analogous to those made for the north drum. The Eagle drummers say "Nawa" for each motion.

> *Motions:* He faces about south, and the motions begin at about south on the drum face; the right hand motion first is for the western half, the left for the eastern half.

The smoker has now completed this mode of the offering, and proceeds clockwise to a position in front of the altar.

Self-Blessing, after Smoke Offering

After completing the smoke offering proper, the smoker comes before the altar with the empty pipe. Here he takes a position slightly to the north or south of the sacred pathway, according to whether he belongs to the Crow or Eagle side. He stands on his side of the midline. Very often the smoker is an assistant *rixkita*, in which case his position for the *self-blessing*[1] is in line with his own seat behind the altar.

Standing before the altar, the smoker faces obliquely the ceremonial official who gave him the pipe for the offering. In a ritual return of the pipe where no altar is present, as at smoke offerings outdoors in the Ghost Dance itself, an analogous position is taken: The smoker stands before the official who gave him the pipe, and a little to the side with which his own position associates him.

The pipe has been smoked out, the ashes cleaned out; it is empty and all ritual motions and offerings have been completed. The pipe is held first in the left hand, the tamper lying along the pipe stem, the mouthpiece directed upward, or upward with a slight slant forward from the handler. In most cases this is adequate, or

---

[1] I have used this expression elsewhere in this study as a term; its reference is in all cases to the performance described at this point.

the pipe may be held in a directly vertical position—in either case the intention is to direct it skyward toward the heavenly powers during the blessing. The pipe-bowl opening is toward the body of the handler. The right hand is placed on the right side of the extremity of the bowl and rubbed up along the pipe over bowl and stem. This motion is similar to all the rubbing motions in making offerings with the empty pipe in the final phase of the smoke offering. In the motion the hand is not closed in a tight clasp around the pipe, but is none the less curled about it so that it encompasses and touches as much of the surface as would normally be touched in grasping it at each point. As the hand passes the tip of the mouthpiece it is opened outward and upward, then at once placed on the right side of the head, drawn downward over the ear and cheek, across the collar bone, inside the right shoulder and down to the right side above the hip—this avoidance of the shoulder is of course merely an adjustment to the physical fact that the right hand cannot be rubbed over the shoulder and biceps of the right side, which is what is conceptually intended, as becomes clear when an individual blesses another—down the right side over the hip bone, down the thigh, over the knee-cap, down the shank, over the top of the ankle, along the foot to the toes, where the foot is then firmly pressed to the ground. Returning to an erect posture, the handler shifts the pipe and tamper to the right hand, holding it analogously as before, and performs an analogous motion with the left hand over the pipe upward and down the left side pressing the left foot firmly to the ground. A full self-blessing requires four motions, in the order, right, left, right, left. Rarely if ever is the self-blessing seen abbreviated to two motions.

In a smoke offering performed at Mrs. Goodeagle's hand game Knifechief, in making the motions of self-blessing, each time he had run his hand up the pipe, held it aloft a moment before rubbing it down his body. This was the only time I witnessed such a gesture as usually the hand is in continuous motion. My informant on this occasion said that this pause by Knifechief was not correct— that it was like giving oneself away.

The pressure of the feet to the earth at the conclusion of the motion is an eloquent and dramatic gesture by a Pawnee. He reaffirms his contact with his Mother Earth, and by so doing asks continued firm pressure and contact of his body and feet with the earth, long life and an active strong body during life.

Returning the Pipe

After the smoker has performed self-blessing, he returns the pipe to the official who prepared it for the offering and from whom he received it. This individual in receiving it, takes it with an *arm blessing*.[1]

The smoker takes pipe and tamper together in his right hand, the mouthpiece still directed upward, the bowl downward and the bowl opening toward his own body, and coming to the altar, offers it to the receiver. The one who accepts the pipe places his left hand over the offerer's right hand, which is holding the offered pipe, and places his right hand upon the inner side of the offerer's right elbow joint. He draws his open right hand downward along the offerer's arm from elbow to wrist, where his hand comes in contact with the pipe, then over the pipe. As his two hands oppose each other around the pipe and the offerer's hand, the offerer releases the hold of his right hand on the pipe, and the receiver draws the pipe away between his two hands. He then grasps it at joint of stem and bowl with his right hand and replaces it in position on the altar. In Ghost Dance smoke offerings, where it cannot be immediately replaced upon the altar, he holds it or carries it as the formalities of the occasion require.

With the replacement of the pipe on the altar, all present say "Nawa," and the smoke offering ritual is complete.

PUTTING THE COUNTERS IN PLAY

The essential mode of putting the counters in play for Ghost Dance hand games is that described in Chapter V. The guessers face each other across the arena, and hide and guess alternately until one guesser has won both counters.

The rixkita in charge of each side select the guesser for that side. If insignia are not given out to them, the first indication of the guessers chosen is that after the smoke offering the rixkita of a side rises and goes to the individual to hand him the counter.

The singing while the counters are being put in play is begun by the host side, and the guesser of that side hides first, his opponent guesses first. There is one important exception to this rule. The game of Boychief, oriented from the north, causes a fundamental change. The singing for this game, although the game is associated with the Crow side, must be begun by the Eagles, and the Eagle guesser is the first to hide. This change occurs because with the north orientation the west is completely dominated by the Eagle

---
[1] Used as a term elsewhere in this study.

side; the west is the region of the powers in control, and beginning the game is determined by them. In the ordinary altar arrangement the western region is divided between the two sides.

There is usually one old society song sung by the host side before the counters are put in play. Or a game owner may have a special opening song of his own, which is the first song sung.

As soon as both counters are won by one guesser, they are taken over to two players of that side, and as the serial order of turns begins, the singers of the side in possession begin old hand game songs or Ghost Dance hand game play songs.

PLAY OF THE GAME

There are a number of special variations in the manner in which the different hand games of the Pawnee may be or have to be played. These play variations are considered part of the teachings of the original game vision experience. According to the vision certain variations are optional for that game, or a definite and fixed manner of play is prescribed, without alternative. When there are optional modes of play the choice of the mode used at a particular demonstration is made by the individual who puts up the ceremony. He or she knows the possible alternatives of play in advance, either from past experience or from conference with the game owner prior to the game, and makes a choice.

There are first the game variations of the order in which the players take their turns. For any game the sequence for turns is fixed; no alternative is possible. Variations of the serial order of turns are comparative, from game to game. It is intended that at every game every individual present[1] shall take a turn to play at least once if the game continues long enough.

The usual form for taking turns is to give out the counters for hiding from west to east down both sides. The rixkita N 1 and N 2 are first to hide on the Crow side, S 1 and S 2 on the Eagle side. Then, two by two, the players of the sides receive the counters to hide, down the north side from west to east and down the south side similarly. When the position of the drummers is reached at about the western semi-cardinal directions, the counters are given two by two to the drummers before continuing eastward down the side. In this way, in the usual seating arrangement, men players

---

[1] Except the fifth central rixkita, who merely presides. A guesser who is fortunate enough to keep winning will also thereby lose his turn to play. The fact that all present must participate and take turns explains the invitation of white men and women present to play.

of a side will all have taken turns before the counters reach the women.

The game of Boychief, oriented from the north, is not a fundamental variant. Consonant with the shift of the whole orientation through a clockwise quadrant, the players take turns from north to south on both sides, beginning with the rixkita at the north. The shift of orientation does involve a change for putting the counters in play (see above).

In Mrs. Goodeagle's game the turns of the players are in the order: On the north side from the west (beginning with rixkita N 1 and N 2) eastward; on the south side from the east (beginning with the two women seated nearest the doorway) westward. The drummers take their turns as the drum position is reached.

In the Yellowhorse game turns on the Crow side begin with rixkita N 1, N 2 at the west; the next two to play are the two women at the extreme eastern end of the north side; the third pair are the two men immediately to the east or left of rixkita N 2; the fourth pair the two women immediately right or west of the second pair (women at extreme east); and so on, alternating the two ends of the sides, coming eastward from the west and westward from the east until those taking turns are the players at the center of the side at about due north, after which the entire order is repeated. On the Eagle side, the first two to play are the two women at the extreme eastern end of the south side (nearest the doorway); the second pair are rixkita S 1 and S 2; the third pair the two women west of the first pair; the fourth pair the two men right or east of rixkita S 2; and so on, until the middle is reached, after which the order is repeated.

Another variation which occurred was to begin with the two players at the middle of each side, at about due north and south, and proceed alternately eastward and westward from these for the north side, westward and eastward from these for the south side.

Some games involved special orders for taking turns which unfortunately I have not been able to record. The variations of order are said to have special conceptual references in connection with the vision teachings of the bundle. In the old gambling hand-game there was no order or sequence for taking turns; and it was not essential that all present should play. In the Ghost Dance hand game the order is fixed and serial, and all present should participate.

The west-east order emphasizes the western stress of the Ghost Dance so that for the south side the clockwise ceremonial circuit is overridden. Other variations, however, recall the clockwise circuit, in terms of special starting points. Mrs. Goodeagle's order is simply the ceremonial circuit, beginning on each side at such a point that the movement of turns is clockwise.[1] Yellowhorse's arrangement is a combination of the western emphasis, clockwise motion, and some special idea of the significance of the central points at north and south; while the other variant reverses the mode.

The required participation of all present is an integral part of the conceptual significance of winning or losing. The whole side is playing against the other side to determine ritual and religious luck—which have greater faith as opposed to which are greater sinners, which are to share the blessings of the coming resurrection, which have greater power to recall and revive the old life. Winning is a sign of greater "medicine" or "power" of the group.

While the usual seating arrangement was based on the Ghost Dance affiliations of the players, with the men of a side clustered toward the west, the women toward the east, two other plans were followed optionally by some games.

In one of these all the women were pitted against all the men. Here the men would be on the north side, the women on the south, regardless of the Crow and Eagle affiliations. It is said this variation could be used for many of the games; it is particularly recalled as employed often in the early days by Tom Morgan. The sexes are placed along the horizon with which in ancient cosmological ideas they are associated. Winning in this case indicated which sex had greater power and luck.

In another mode, which occurred rarely and only in the first days of the hand games, all the individuals who had experienced visions in the Ghost Dance played on one side against all the innocents. This is almost a facetious gamble on whether it is better to be naive or sophisticated in matters of faith. According to my informant, it was practically the equivalent of pitting the old against the young.

Stakes for which Ghost Dance hand games could be played, in addition to the conceptual significance of winning or losing, included: the determination of which side should have to rise first the next morning to start the Ghost Dancing; and which side should supply the food and do the cooking the following day. The former refers to starting the Ghost Dancing proper, the latter to both four-day Ghost Dances and four-day Ghost Dance hand game ceremonies. The gamble on the food supply is said to have

---

[1] Incidentally, guessers and watchers as they move from side to side giving and taking counters, proceed clockwise around the fireplace each time, not straight across the arena.

been possible only with Tom Morgan's game. Such stakes as these recall the actual gambling stakes of the old hand game.

As a game occasion involved the playing of a number of "rubber" games, the actual number to be played and the way these had to be scored, were matters to be specifically determined.

There were three modes in which games could be scored: straight, even-up, and the setting of a fixed goal of won games. In playing straight a definite number of rubber games are decided on before play begins. This is usually five or seven; when five is decided on, an addition of two is optional if after the five have been played there is still time and a desire to continue. In playing straight it is of no consequence how the final score stands. The succeeding arrangements are the same whether it be 7—0, 6—1, 4—3, etc. The side which wins the last game leads in the last interval, chooses the food offerer, etc. Play should end for a game played straight when at most seven games have been played. At a game I attended the Crows were unlucky enough to lose seven straight games in quick order, and were so disgruntled, like the proverbial gamblers, that they insisted on continuing. Two additional games played were won by the Crows. The old people considered the whole thing irregular. The run of bad luck was blamed on the broken way in which the smoke offering had been carried out by the offerer, who was a Crow.

Some games could only be played straight. This was true of the four South Band games and the church games of Moses and Allen. It may also have applied to the games of White and Boychief.

In playing even-up, rubber games are scored so that those lost by the leading side are deducted from their winnings, and the objective is to win a certain number of games *more* than the opponents. Thus any tie score reduces the standing score to zero. 3—1 means that the side which has won three games is 2-up, 3—3 that neither side has scored any games up. The number of games-up set as the goal is a choice which rests with the putter-up, within the practices allowed by a bundle ritual. The most usual number played even-up was four; but five or seven were allowed with some bundles. Beaver's game when first played was played twelve games even-up, because the man who put the game up chose that number. It was never played thereafter for that number because it is said that it took all night and most of the next day for one side to become twelve games up. Games besides Beaver's recalled as having been played even-up were those of Mrs. Goodeagle, Rudder and Yellowhorse. Mrs. Goodeagle is said to have preferred to play even-up in former years, but to have dropped the practice some time ago. Those games known to have been played even-up could also be played straight.

A third manner mentioned as optional for the games of Mrs. Goodeagle and Pierson is the way in which Mrs. Goodeagle has usually played in recent years. In this an objective is decided upon, a certain number of games. For Mrs. Goodeagle's game it was usually five rubber games, for Pierson's seven. This number of games must be won by one side or the other in order to win. In this manner the minimum number of games played is that set as the goal while the maximum is one less than twice that number. In Mrs. Goodeagle's game a special aftermath method of play is used when a score reaches a tie at 4—4. It is probable that this form of play was used earlier with other games besides those mentioned.

The method of playing off a tie is similar to special types of aftermath or final play used particularly by White Elk and occasionally by Annie Eustace. I have discussed it below together with these.

All games are played similarly as regards the choice and activities of guessers. These are first chosen for each side by the rixkita in charge of that side. The guesser who loses a game chooses another player of the same side to take his place. Some games have in addition functioning "watchers." These are permanent for the game occasion. They are chosen by the game owner and wear special insignia such as feather hair ornaments. Individuals considered especially lucky are selected as watchers. These not only light the pipe for the smoker, but are constant assistants to the guessers in the play of the game. The watcher is the one who takes the counters from two players of the opposing side who lose them, and who gives them to two players of his own side. He is the one who signals the scoring to the rixkita of his side who is keeping tally. He confers with the guesser when the latter is puzzled or in a run of hard luck. He may either suggest to the guesser which combination of hands to indicate, or at the guesser's invitation he may come forward himself and do the guessing.

In Mrs. Goodeagle's game if the score is tied at 4—4 the crucial and deciding game is played by specially selected players or hiders (chosen by rixkita), and by the two watchers functioning as guessers, the regular guessers being dispensed with.[1] The two players for each side are a man and a woman. These are seated between the fireplace and the altar, on the respective sides of the sacred pathway,

---

[1] In Mrs. Goodeagle's game a compromise was adopted in which turns to play were taken as usual. See Chapter X.

the man to the west and the woman to the east. In White Elk's aftermath the players face each other across the fireplace, recalling more directly the old gambling hand game. White Elk's aftermath is optional. After five games have been played straight, two additional games can be played straight or instead two out of three games can be played by special hiders and special guessers. The guessers in this form of White Elk's aftermath are the same for the full two-out-of-three games; but the hiders who lose a game are replaced by others. In Mrs. Goodeagle's game the winners of the aftermath have scored the game which breaks the tie and completes the score; in White Elk's the side which wins two-out-of-three in the final is considered to have triumphed that day regardless of the outcome of the preceding five straight games.

The significance which attaches to these aftermaths of play lies partially in the fact that the old gambling game forms are reproduced. Instead of any player hiding the counters according to turns the two who are selected to hide for all are chosen because they are adept and lucky. Similarly the watchers in Mrs. Goodeagle's game, the special guessers in White Elk's, are chosen because of their luck and cleverness at guessing.

The positions of the men and women who are special hiders, the men to the west and the women to the east, is opposed to the ancient cosmological orientations, in which the western powers are male, the eastern powers female. It is determined instead by the seating arrangements of the men and women at the hand game.

In the games which were played with dual control (collaborative games), the methods of play are similar to the above. But during game play half the set of tally sticks of each bundle, and one counter from each bundle, are used. In Pierson's major game play proceeds normally, but since a whole series of games and societies are pitted against another series, for each "rubber game" the set used belongs half to one bundle of each side; and when a game is lost, not only is the guesser of the losing side changed, but the half-set of the losing side is retired, and that of another bundle of that side (the "next" in serial order, west to east) used for the following "rubber game." When a game is won the special society singing by the winners involves the use of paraphernalia of one of the society bundles which has been stationed on that side.

ACTIVITIES OF THE GAME INTERVALS

When a "rubber game" has been finished the drumming and singing stops. The guesser of the losing side returns at once to his place. The two players of the winning side who have just run out the winning points give the counters back to the guesser for their side (or to the watcher, where such an official functions). The guesser or watcher returns the two counters to the rixkita in charge of the side which has won, and then takes his own seat. In most games the watcher should sit during the intervals at the tarutsius position near the eastern doorway on his own side; the guesser takes his customary seat among the players.

Now the leading drummer of the winning side rises and takes a position at the west of the fireplace (or analogously with respect to an "indicated" fireplace outdoors) facing east. If the game set includes a rattle or rattles, this main singer first proceeds to the altar, receives the instruments from the rixkita of his side, and then goes to the position at the west. Other singers (two or three) of the winning side join the main singer, taking positions on his right (south). As the main singer leads off, starting a Ghost Dance song, men and women from both sides assemble in a circle around the fireplace, joining hands. There is no restriction on who may join in; both winners and losers dance. The Ghost Dancing was for the benefit of all, but led by the singers of the winning side, because these had established their greater luck and power. This is the usual manner for Ghost Dancing. The circle forms as large as necessary to accommodate those who wish to participate.

Usually two or three Ghost Dance songs are sung and danced to in each interval. Three is preferred ritually, and four is considered better yet, but at hand games of recent years I never saw four Ghost Dance songs used in a game interval.

Each song is sung through once, led by the main singer and his associates of the winning side, while all stand in their places, holding hands. As the singer begins a repetition of the song he begins dancing clockwise, that is, leftward from his position west of the fireplace. The step is the usual sidewise shuffle of the Ghost Dance. The whole circle of dancers moves clockwise through an entire circuit until the main singer is back at his position west of the fireplace facing east. The singers who have rattles shake them in the right hand in time to the song; if there are no rattles, no instruments at all are used. Drums are never used for the Ghost Dancing.

For the Boychief game, oriented from the north, the song-leader of the winning side starts the Ghost Dance songs and dances from north of the fireplace facing south. In this way he faces the doorway. Said my informant, "This is to permit the voice to go out; one cannot sing into the wall," a remark which reveals the reason for the orientation of many another ritual action.

While the main singer of the winning side leads the dancing, a performance is simultaneously carried out by the rixkita of that side. After the counters are returned to him he takes these, the tally sticks of the game set, and the ceremonial pipe of the bundle, and rises from his place behind the altar. He holds the counters concealed in his right hand, and with the same hand holds the pipe and tally stick (or feathers) clasped in one bunch. The mouthpiece of the pipe and the head ends (feathered ends) of the tally sticks are upward, the bowl and the tail end of the tally sticks downward, the bowl opening of the pipe inward toward his body. Clasping set and pipe in right hand, the rixkita proceeds slowly to a position at the west, between the circle of dancers and the altar, where facing east he raises the set aloft toward heaven and holds it there silently a few moments. He then proceeds clockwise through the north until he reaches a position at the east between the dancers and the doorway, where facing west he again holds the objects aloft a few moments. Then he comes clockwise back to the west where he repeats his first offering motion. There is no correlation of his movements with those of the dancers. He is guided by his own ideas of how long he should hold the objects aloft, and how many times he should offer at west and east. Usually after he has made the motion once at the east and twice at the west he waits quietly, holding the set in an upright position before him, without raising it aloft, until the dancing ends. Then he returns to the altar, gives the things to the rixkita of the other side (who has retained his place behind the altar) and this other replaces the objects upon the altar. The winning rixkita meanwhile takes his own seat.

While I neglected to make sure that this offering by the rixkita was in all cases prescribed, I believe it was for those games derived in visions. It was carried out in these in essentially the same way. The intention is to show the powers who have given the game that the people are thankful and are dancing.

When the Ghost Dancing is finished, the rixkita takes his place behind the altar, the dancers return to their places, and the singers to their seats around the drum. The main singer returns the rattle to the rixkita who replaces it on the altar. Then the main singer takes his place at the drum.

The leader of the winning side returns one counter to the opposing rixkita. Both rixkita rise. Each goes to the individual who functioned as guesser for his side and again gives him the one counter.[1]

---

[1] The return of the counters to guessers may also follow the singing of the old song.

Now the main singer of the winning side, or if he yields his leadership, another of the singers of that side, leads in singing one of the songs of the old societies, Young Dog Dance, Crazy Dog Dance, Horn Dance, etc. The choice is made by the singer who starts the song. In early Ghost Dance days the singer usually revived the song of a society with which he had formerly had some affiliation, hence at games of a particular band the songs used were generally songs of a society associated especially with that band. The other singers of the side join in singing and drumming. Here and there among the men players of either side one will arise and dance in his place in time to the song. This again diverges from the plan of the old interband and intertribe hand game where only the winners danced and counted coup: the society song is now being revived by the winners, who have luck and power, but on behalf of all the people. Those who rose to dance in earlier times were generally men formerly associated with the society. No effort is made to dance the old step, which for most of the dance societies would require that the dancer come out into the center of the arena.

After this singing the guesser of the side which has just lost rises and walks to another player of his side and gives him the counter, thus designating his successor. If a hair ornament is worn by the guesser, he also gives the feather to the guesser of his choice. Then the two guessers, he who previously won, and he who has just been chosen, arise and face each other across the arena, and put the counters in play for the second game.

After the final rubber game of the occasion, the main drummer of the losing side returns his drum to its position in front of the altar and then resumes his place with the drummers of his side at the drum position. The drummers of the winning side keep their drum before them; after the final interval of Ghost Dancing they sing one or two old society songs to drum accompaniment.

In theory the final interval of Ghost Dancing, led by the winning singers (in "straight" play those of the side winning the last game rather than the side which wins in total score) should consist of ten Ghost Dance songs instead of three or four. The tenth song should be the closing Ghost Dance song, and should be sung six times, once at west, once through each quadrant, and finally once at west, opening and closing the circle, after which the blankets are symbolically shaken out.

At hand games in recent years I have not seen the final interval of Ghost Dancing go this length; usually two or three songs, as for the intervals, is considered enough. The theoretical ten-song close seems to have fallen into disuse since the hand game ceased to be a four-day ceremony. For the final dancing the game set is held aloft as in other intervals.

After the Ghost Dancing the drummers of the winning side sing one or two old society songs. Then their drum is returned to a position before the altar on its respective side, and all is ready for the feast.

In the church games of Moses and Allen the intervals are not given over to the Ghost Dance. Occasionally songs of a Ghost Dance type are used, but these are considered profane songs.

In these two games, after a rubber game, the drummers rise with the drum (there is only one drum for these games[1]) and take it outside the arbor or tent-like structure toward the east. Here the drummers form a circle standing around the drum. They hold it with the left hand, while the drumsticks are used with the right. Usually they sing "Forty-Nine" dances, Soldier dances, or Victory dance songs, and the younger boys and girls (about twenty-five years of age and younger) gather about them gleefully and dance. The dancers do not hold hands. The dances are recent diffusions among Oklahoma Indians, and here as well as among the Wichita are considered profane and irreligious. They are said to have sexual associations. I have been told stories about these, usually in the form of what happened at such and such a dance among some other tribe than that of the informant telling me, but I have not been able to find any definite concept of sexual license associated with the dance, nor have I observed any especially loose conduct at these dances. Nevertheless the young people regard these as social dances designed for them. They are always excited and eager to participate, while the religious hand games do not arouse them in the same way.

The older orthodox and conservative people react oppositely. Many will not attend such games at all, and if they do, will never participate in the dancing. They look askance at the whole procedure, as older people among ourselves would at some new dance that seemed to symbolize moral change and breakdown. It is considered especially bad by the older people that songs like Ghost Dance songs are occasionally used at these games.

The view taken by the older Pawnee of these two games indicates how strong a feeling of sanctity was associated with the old Ghost Dance hand game ceremony. In the days when it was a four-day ceremony sexual continence was prescribed for participants as it was for the Ghost Dance ceremony proper.

---

[1] The drums of these games are single-faced, and in use for the game are placed on the ground.

After the interval of dancing the drum is brought back inside and the next rubber game begins. There is no offering of the set aloft in these two games. The drum accompaniment for the dancing of the intervals occurs in no other hand games.

THE FOOD OFFERING AND SERVICE

After the play and the final Ghost Dance and Society songs, all is made ready for the feast.

Today the fireplace of the hand game ground is generally not used for cooking, whether the game is held indoors or out. Instead, the food is usually prepared by his family at the house of the man who has put up the game. Other delegated women assist. For games at the Round Houses, any convenient house or outdoor fire may be used. In former times, when the games were played in lodges of the bundle owners, the cooking was more generally done in the game lodge, while the assemblage waited. Cooking over the fireplace in the same lodge in which the ceremony takes place is the older ritual form, followed still today for the Doctor Dances, the only major ancient rituals still demonstrated. The tarutsius do the cooking while the people wait quietly, talking softly among themselves until all is ready.

The food served at hand games must include corn, besides which there is usually dried meat, fried bread, hot coffee and various other foods, even fresh fruits, cake, etc. When it is time for the feast, the food is brought in by those who have prepared it. Others may assist. The owner officially "receives" it and tells those bringing the food how and where to place it. It is set out at the east of the arena, between the fireplace and the doorway. The corn in buckets is set nearest the fireplace, all the other foods merely being assembled east of the buckets of corn. Usually the buckets of corn are set in an arc, concave side westward, symmetrically as regards the orientations. For one game the buckets number nine and are set in a "five-pointed star" arrangement, that is, a central one, and two forming an arm extending in each cardinal direction.[1] For most games the number of buckets of corn was immaterial; it was determined by how much corn had been "put up" and the number of the participants. Usually there were seven buckets or more. I have seen the number run as high as twenty.

---

[1] The central one, representing the zenith, is conceived as a fifth point.

Designation of the Offerer: When the food is in place, the offerer is selected. For practically all the games, the offerer must be a man who is a member of the side which has won at the game occasion. The preferred choice is one of the main drummers or one of the rixkita. The main rixkita of the winning side selects the offerer. At a game presided over by a fifth or central non-playing rixkita it was this man who chose the food-offerer. Sometimes the game owner made a speech of prayer and thanksgiving before the offerer was selected.

Receiving the Horn Spoon: The rixkita who chooses the offerer gives him the horn spoon of the bundle. He may make a short address before he does so.

The offerer comes to the altar and takes the spoon from the rixkita with an *arm blessing*. This is the mode of receiving the spoon for a food offering for all the hand games.[1]

As for a smoke offering, the game owner may accompany the offerer in his procedure, instructing him. In any case it is the owner who is responsible for the correct ritual.

Filling the Horn Spoon: The offerer with the horn spoon held in his right hand proceeds clockwise as he leaves the altar, until he reaches the buckets of corn east of the fireplace. Here he fills the spoon. To do so, for an arrangement of the buckets of corn in an arc, he comes inside the arc, that is, between the food and the fireplace. There are then two alternatives: a complete ritual method, and an abbreviated form. In the former, he dips the spoon into each bucket individually, from left to right down the row (or, from north to south), until with the dip into the bucket at the extreme south of the row, he has about filled the spoon. In the shorter form he takes corn from the bucket in the middle of the row, and from the one at each end. The order is middle bucket, extreme right or south bucket, and (turning completely around before proceeding, in order to maintain the clockwise ceremonial circuit) the extreme left or north bucket. The body turn for ceremonial purposes is here equivalent to a circuit around the fireplace.

In the arrangement of nine buckets in a cross, or "five-pointed star," the offerer first stands north of the buckets, and leaning over dips some from the central one, then moves to the east of the buckets and dips from the extreme eastern bucket —the one at the outer point of the cross-bar directed eastward; then moves to the south and dips from the extreme south bucket; then to the west, between buckets and fireplace, where facing east he dips from the

---

[1] Note in contrast that a pipe received by a smoke offerer is taken without touching hands.

extreme western bucket; and finally to the north where he dips corn from the extreme northern bucket. He has thus made a complete circuit, and dipped corn from five of the nine buckets, the central one, and the four outer ones. In a complete ritual form, he would now repeat his circuit, taking dips of corn from each of the four inner buckets.

After the spoon has been filled with corn, the offerer comes around to a position behind all the food. There are several ways in which he reaches this position. If he has followed the briefer form of filling the spoon, he finishes standing at the north end of the row of buckets, facing east; with the cross arrangement of the buckets he finishes at the north facing south. In both these cases, he may either come clockwise around the food to the east behind it and stop, or proceed through this position and then through a complete circuit of the fireplace clockwise until he again reaches east of the food facing west. On the other hand, if the complete form has been followed in filling the spoon from the row of buckets, the offerer finishes at the extreme south of the row. From here he must proceed with the spoonful through a clockwise circuit of the fireplace, coming back outside or east of the assembled food to a position between food and east where he faces west.

In this position, the offerer makes two motions. The first is with the right hand, while the left holds the spoonful; the second, after changing the spoon to the right hand, with the left.

Motion: The free hand is extended out to the side; the right hand out to the right or north as the offerer faces west, at about normal shoulder height, the left analogously. At the constant height with the palm open and directed downward the hand is then swept inward around over the food until just past a position straight forward. The hands are changed and an analogous movement made with the other.

In the words of an informant, speaking of these motions, "this brings everything together," and implies that the offering is of all the assembled food. By contrast, he pointed out that the reversed type of two motions, as used over the altar objects, a right from center rightward and a left from center leftward, "means everything on this side and everything on that side," an interesting commentary on the exact and specific meanings of gestures to the informed native.

After these motions the offerer with the filled spoon proceeds with the phases of the ritual corn offering proper.

At the hand game of Boychief, in which the orientations are from the north altar, the entire procedure over the food takes place at the south, where the food is gathered between fireplace and southern doorway. The orientations are shifted to agree with the shifted altar and doorway, and are analogous throughout.

The Corn Offering Proper. There are two general methods of carrying out the offering with the corn, a full or complete ritual, and an abbreviated form. Either of these must follow the ritual form of offerings of the particular bundle.

A. The complete ritual form:

1. First Phase: Disposal of the Corn.

The offerer leaves the point east of the food carrying the filled spoon, and proceeding clockwise. He comes to the west of the fireplace rim, where he stops facing east. This is the same sacred place at the eastern end of the "sacred pathway" at which the tobacco and smoke offerings to the powers were made. Here he offers corn to Heaven, Earth, and Westward, depositing some on the ground after each offering, so that the spoon is emptied at the last. In the order of these offerings, and the matter of whether the offering for heaven and earth are made with one motion, and the matter of whether the western orientation is included, the offerer follows the pattern which was carried out for the offering of tobacco and the disposal of ashes in the smoke offering earlier in the ceremony.

> *Motions:* The positions of the body are the same as they would be for a similarly directed offering with the pipe. The spoon of corn is held upward, or slantwise westward, with both hands. The share of the corn that is pushed from the spoon after each offering is pushed off with the right hand while the left holds the spoon. As the corn is held aloft or westward, it is said that the offerer makes a silent prayer that the food may be eaten in good health by all, etc. For the offering to earth, the spoon is merely held downward and some corn pushed off; if it is the final offering of this phase, all the corn left on the spoon is pushed off with one motion.

These offerings are intended to be actual gifts to the powers of a portion of the food. Physically, all three parts are deposited on the same spot on the earth, the same place where the tobacco and ashes were put. As one informant remarked, "That's why we say, 'Mother Earth received everything.'"

After the corn has been disposed of, the offerer places the empty spoon on the ground beside his left foot, and proceeds with the second phase.

2. Second Phase: Sacramental Motions.

a. First Mode: To the Powers.

This mode of the corn offering in its extended form must for any ritual follow the exact order of the first mode of the second phase of the smoke offering, the offering of smoke to the powers. This will be to Heaven, Earth and West, or the longer series of the Beaver, Goodeagle, or Pierson games. For each offering of a puff of smoke, there will be one sacramental motion over the corn.

Motions: Upward: The offerer stoops and presses the corn into the ground with both hands, returns to an erect posture, and rubs his hands firmly together several times, then raises his hands aloft, and opens them outward and upward. Four motions, each time complete as above.

Westward: Either two or four motions. In this case, the hands press the corn into the ground only once, then the offerer turns to the west, and either two or four times rubs his hands together and opens them slantwise toward the west.

Downward: Stooping slightly, four complete motions, pressing the corn into the earth with both hands, rubbing the palms together, and opening the hands over the earth.

Other directions are strictly analogous to the western. For such horizon orientations as the offerings to the sun and moon, both hands are moved through the half-horizon circuit from east to west across the south, the palms facing southward, the left hand below the right.

b. Second Mode: To Ceremonial Objects.

This mode in form follows the manner of handling the pipe in the smoke offering, after the ashes have been disposed of; that is, it is equivalent to the full ritual form carried out in the second mode of the fourth phase of the smoke offering. I state this equivalence because the empty spoon is now handled and rubbed as the empty pipe was handled. In conceptual equation the ritual sequence here is identical not only with the second mode of the fourth phase of the smoke offering, but also with the second mode of the second phase, the offering of smoke to ceremonial objects. The same number of motions are made, as puffs of smoke were given, and in the same order.

Motions: The motions are strictly analogous to those in the second mode of the fourth phase of the smoke offering. The empty spoon is held in one hand, while the other is rubbed over it toward the object, and touched to the object, along the object or over the object, according to the different types of motion called for (see above).

As the motions are made over altar objects those behind the altar say "Nawa"; while the drummers say "Nawa" when the drums are blessed.

In carrying out this mode, the same formal abbreviations are possible with the spoon, as we have seen carried out with the pipe. In the shortest form, two motions would be made over the objects before the altar, two over the game set on the altar, and then two at each drum. The emphasis for the altar objects is that of the game, while for the drums it is always north, then south, in terms of the ceremonial circuit.

After the motions over the drums, the offerer makes the self-blessing and returns the spoon.

B. The shorter ritual form:

In the shorter ritual form the order of modes is reversed in the process of telescoping, and the motions are made over the altar and ceremonial objects before the corn is deposited at the west of the fireplace. Summarizing the procedure of the offerer:

He leaves the east with the filled spoon and proceeds clock-wise through the south and directly to the altar. Moving the spoonful of corn from one hand to the other as necessary, he makes two motions over the objects before the altar (a right and a left, both from center outward), then similarly two over the objects on the altar, then two to the north drum, and turning around two to the south drum. Then he goes straight down the sacred pathway to the position west of the fireplace facing east, where he disposes of the corn exactly as he would in the extended ritual form. He then places the empty spoon on the ground beside him, and carries out the sequence of motions of the first mode of the second phase, as above, exactly as he would in the extended form. Following this, he picks the spoon up, makes a complete clockwise circuit of the fireplace and comes in front of the altar where he makes a self-blessing and returns the spoon.

The essential point of this telescoped form is that when the offerer goes to the altar with the spoon full of corn he must use the most abbreviated series of motions at the altar, while in the extended form ritual manners require him, strictly speaking, to go through the entire series of motions which were carried out with the pipe in the smoke offering ritual.

The corn offering carried out at Boychief's game in the early Ghost Dance days, according to my information, was a ritual exception to the generic forms. Here the essential offering of the corn was to the picture of Christ, accompanied by a prayer, and apparently the other orientations were skipped. Similarly the spoon was returned without a self-blessing. See below the details of Boychief's game.

The Self-Blessing. After the completion of the sacramental motions, the offerer makes a circuit of the fireplace, and coming back to the west, stands facing the altar and the rixkita behind it diagonally, from a position a little to the left or right of the sacred pathway, according to the side with which he is associated. The motions of self-blessing are as they would be with a pipe.

Returning the Spoon. After the self-blessing the offerer returns the horn spoon to the rixkita who gave it to him. It is taken from him with an *arm-blessing.* The rixkita who takes it then puts it back in its place under a fold of the altar spread. All present say, "Nawa." Now follows the service of the food.

Special Offerings. In reference to a few of the games, informants recalled that on some occasions the game owners themselves made the ritual corn offering, and that in doing so they had special personal modes to follow. These are detailed in the notes on the individual games.

Food Service. After the ritual corn offering, dishes, cups, etc. are distributed. When the games were orthodox ceremonies the ceremonial officials were usually given ceremonial utensils, as in the older rituals. Latterly they as well as the populace present use their own utensils. These are brought for each family by the women of the household, and at this point there is much scuffling about as the women bring forward the bundles of utensils from behind them, or hurry out to get the bundle left in the wagon or parked car. After the utensils are untied, they bring those for the men to them.

For the distribution of the food, the leaders of each side appoint four men to serve the side. Watchers were often "ex officio" two main servers of the corn; in this function their office was again consonant with the traditional office of tarutsius.

The corn is always served first, then the meat, coffee and other foods. There is a definite order in which those present are served and while this order is more or less the same for the games, it is not so sui generis. The order for any game is part of the ritual form of that ceremony. Essentially it follows the order and sequence of the third mode of the second phase of the smoke offering, the offering of the pipe to ceremonial officials and men present. However, it adds to that order the subsequent service of all the women present. This does not materially destroy the ritual identity, for it must be remembered that among the Pawnee, women never smoke the pipe ceremonially (or otherwise), nor handle it ceremonially, and in the older ceremonies, such as the doctor dances, while they never shared the smoke offering, they did share in eating corn from the sacred bowls of corn which were ritually distributed, and their participation was subordinated to that of the men.

The general form of the food service is to serve the rixkita, then the main drummers, then others. When there are servers for each side, the rixkita of one side are not served before those of the other, but the leaders of both sides served simultaneously, and similarly with the main drummers. When the servers are officially few the emphasis upon the altar and rixkita is preserved, and those of one side are served before those of the other; for the drummers, as usual this means serving the north or Crow drummers before the south Eagle drummers. For an altar seating plan with five rixkita there is usually a central corn bucket (the central one, for example in the cross arrangement of buckets) from which the main central rixkita and N 1 and S 1 are served. In this case the assistant rixkita (N 2 and S 2) are not served at that time. With only four rixkita, the two main ones for each side are served together. Then the two main drummers of each side are served. Following this, since most games have no further important officials, as shown by the formal smoke offering, the service proceeds to the people. In the few games with official old men, chiefs, doctors, braves, etc. near the doorways, these men are served after the drummers and before the general populace, in the same order as the pipe was given to smoke. Watchers or tarutsius are generally served plentifully, but last. In serving the people several formal orders are followed: the general one is west to east down the north side, and east to west on the south side, the order in which the pipe is offered to laymen present. Some games have special plans of service to the people, in some cases following the order in which turns to play are taken in the game play proper. These plans include, having on each side two servers serve from west to east, and two from east to west; in one game on each side one server serves from west to east, one from east to west, while two begin at the middle (about north and south) and proceed westward and eastward respectively.

In serving the important ceremonial officials, such as the rixkita and drummers, these must be served their portions of everything before others are served at all.

At some point in the service, either before anyone is served, or immediately after the officials are served, the owner or rixkita in charge calls the servers' attention to the fact that a substantial portion of the foods should be put aside for such and such a person or persons who are sick and have not been able to be present. This must be delivered by a specially delegated individual (at old bundle ceremonies it would be one of the tarutsius) to the home of the sick one, so that he or she will eat at the same time as the assembled people. This is an ancient ceremonial manner of aiding the recovery of the sick by having them share in the food which has been blessed and which is being partaken of by the powers along with the people. It is not carried out as rigidly at recent hand game play as it was formerly, but it should be remembered that certain of the orthodox games, such as that of Yellowhorse, are gradually coming to be less and less sacred ceremonies, and more and more mere social affairs.

After all present have partaken of the food served, the occasion is at an end. Usually no one leaves until the rixkita in charge makes a short address, and formally announces, "Now we have eaten, now we have finished, now we go out," etc., a type of announcement ritually necessary to all Pawnee ceremonial occasions.

COMPARISON OF FOOD OFFERING AND SMOKE OFFERING

As may be seen by a comparison of the food offering and service with the smoke offering, there is for each ritual a fundamental pattern of offerings, which dominates throughout. The orientations and references are those determined by the teachings or concepts associated with the bundle in use and its origin. The harmony of all the offerings at any ceremony may be seen more clearly perhaps at the older ceremonies, in which there is consonance not only of the smoke and food offerings, but of these with meat offerings, blessings with sacred gifts to the powers, etc. It is this fundamental agreement of the ritual offering pattern which discloses the reason for the Pawnee conception that he who knows the smoke offering of a ritual knows the ritual. For such an individual, by simply applying the ritual lore associated with the handling of corn, meat, gifts, etc. to the form he understands for the smoke offering, can at any time substantially construct or reconstruct the other offering; and in addition, in terms of the formal pattern, he knows without qualification the important stations or ceremonial officials who must be selected, and how they must be placed, and in terms of the blessings he knows the essential altar arrangements and what sacred objects are indispensable.

A comparative chart, affiliating the parts of the hand game corn offering to those of the smoke offering, illustrates the ritual identities.

The Smoke Offering:
Designation of the offerer
Filling the pipe
Receiving the pipe without hands touching

The Food Offering:
Designation of the offerer

Receiving the spoon with arm blessing
Filling the spoon, with inclusive gestures

The Smoke Offering Proper:
1. Offering tobacco
Lighting the Pipe
2. Offering smoke:
   a. To powers
   b. To sacred objects

   c. To men
3. Disposal of ashes
4. Sacramental motions:

   a. to Powers
   b. to objects

The Corn Offering Proper:
1. Offering corn

2. Offering by gestures:
   a. To powers
   b. With spoon to sacred objects
(Service of food, as below)
(1. Offering corn, as above)
(2. Offerings by gestures, as above)
(2a. to Powers, as above)
(2b. to objects, as above)

Self-Blessing:
Return of Pipe; received with arm blessing
(2a. Offering to men, as above)

Self-Blessing:
Return of spoon; received with arm blessing
Service of food

The significant differences of the two offerings are only that in the smoke offering rituals certain phases consist of the same ritual sequence repeated, as the offering of smoke, and the sacramental motions; while with the corn, that ritual sequence occurs only once.

Most significant to my mind, is the meaning which this comparison shows should be associated with the ritual forms of the service of the food. It is at this point that the people present are feasting together with the powers, in the same way that in handling the pipe, they join with the powers in smoking. This also explains why a definite formal sequence in the service of the food must be followed for all Pawnee ceremonies.

An interesting point is the physical equivalence of the quantities used in the offerings: a spoonful of corn in relation to buckets of corn, a pinch of tobacco in relation to a pipeful.

SPEECHES AT HAND GAMES

Speeches may be made at a number of places in the ritual order of hand game ceremonies. In some cases speeches are ritually prescribed. Thus the leader of the side which wins should make a few remarks before giving out the spoon for the food offering. This is never supposed to be a long speech. The rixkita merely refers to the fact that the food available has been provided by the powers above, to whom thanks should be accorded, that it is now to be eaten, that the offerer whom he has selected should look up to heaven in making the offering and ask for the well-being of the people, and that as a result of what the people are doing all sickness may be driven from the village.

At some games the rixkita of the winning side speaks after the feast, and before announcing that the assemblage should break up. On such an occasion, if any speech is made, it is usually a fairly long talk. It abounds in ritual forms, similar to those of old ceremonies, such as doctor dances. He tells the people that they have tried to follow the prescribed ways. He prays that the powers may continue to provide the people with what they need. He reminds the people that they have given everything to Mother Earth, and that it is she who should receive everything. Then he tells them that they have carried out what was intended and now it is the time for all to go.

Sometimes in making offerings, it is expected that the offerer pray aloud. Such occurs at Boychief's game in making the food offering. The offerer asks that the food be received, and that the well-being of the people be considered.

In practically all games speeches of a general import may be made in the intervals between games, after the singing of the Ghost Dance and society songs, and before play recommences. In such an interval Mrs. Goodeagle, at her own game, cried as she told the people that she knew there were many unbelievers among them, but that some also believed in what she was doing. She reminded them all that what she was doing was according to the way she had learned, and that it was serious, not to be taken lightly.

My informant, Mark Evarts, used a pause in one interval at a game to rise and talk to the people about their relations with the white people. He counseled them that they should not on the one hand be unfriendly to white people who came offering friendship, and on the other expect aid from the white people. He told them that the time had come when it was inevitable that they must adjust their ways to living with the white people, and that to do so, if they wished aid for their undertakings they should be friendly at all times. The immediate inspiration of his talk were some incidents involving myself. Some jealousies had developed over my study of the ceremonies and rituals, and in one case, in spite of the fact that I followed the ceremonial forms, some old men succeeded in getting a decision of a ritual owner reversed and having me ruled me out of the esoteric part of a ceremony. Later, when certain hand games were being put up, I was asked to help, and my offer to put up some food was accepted gladly. Mark wished to draw a moral from this, and used this occasion, reminding the people that I had helped, and that the same had been and occasionally would be true of other white folk.

In an interval of a game of Yellowhorse, Maggie Kasiya, the sister of Emmet Pierson, who had died ten days before, came forward crying to the altar. She told the people how she mourned because she had been away when her brother died and had not seen him before his death. She talked through her tears to the people about Pierson's ritual ways, of his share in the great events of the Ghost Dance times, of his ways of playing the hand games, and how these were gone. She could hardly control herself, and after her talk, Pierson's widow came forward to comfort her and lead her away. During her talk various individuals present uttered gutteral assents.

Hand game ceremonies do not differ essentially from others in the matter of speech-making. The speeches can bring to the people's attention matters considered worthy of serious consideration at a ceremonial occasion, and the ritual speeches carry the same figures and forms of speech as at the older ceremonies, with the same type of reference to the occasion in hand.

GHOST DANCE PRACTICES AT HAND GAMES

At recent hand games trances are not in evidence. The time has passed when the emotions can be aroused to such a pitch over the Ghost Dance doctrine. But when the Ghost Dance hand games arose the practices during the dancing at the games were the same as those at Ghost Dances proper. The same leaders rose and danced inside the circle, focusing the attention of dancers on special hypnotic objects, and inducing trances. Many fell in trance-fits that were self-induced. The trance visions at these Ghost Dances within hand game ceremonies had the same status as those occurring in Ghost Dance ceremonies proper.

Some particular game occasions of the past are especially recalled as played to great Ghost Dance excitement. It is said that in some cases individuals arose from their places even while play was going on, jumped into the center of the arena, and attempted to induce trances in themselves.

Hand game bundles occasionally bear mute witness to the former practices, containing objects whose known use was for inducing hypnotic trances. Leaders at the games and game owners were often prophets with great power over the people.

Although the excitement has long since waned, the owners of games continue to be affected at times by the play and its associations. Densmore refers to an incident at a game witnessed in 1919 at which the woman who owned the bundle (name unmentioned) "was afflicted with what was termed a 'Ghost Dance fit.' She staggered and moaned in a pitiful manner but did not fall to the ground. Several persons went to her aid and restored her in the manner peculiar to the Ghost Dance."[1] Densmore considers this an "unfortunate" occurrence. It should be remembered that this pre-trance state of self-pity was for the native mourning for the loved deceased ones, and a tearful hope that a reunion would be effected.

Mrs. Goodeagle, one of the chief survivors of the early days of excitement, uses a special starting song in which she says that she always has to cry when she plays the game, and at the game I witnessed she was more or less tearful and sad throughout. This is the same type of affect that Densmore refers to. Mrs. Goodeagle explained it in part herself in the speech to which reference has already been made.

---
[1] Densmore, Pawnee Music, p. 70.

IX

THE SOUTH BAND HAND GAMES[1]

JOSEPH CARRION

Ownership and Affiliation

Joseph Carrion, not a Pawnee by birth, was associated in his life among the Pawnee with the Kitkahaxki[x] band, and was affiliated with the Crow or north side. He secured his game in a Ghost Dance trance vision among the Arapaho, in part at an Arapaho Ghost Dance hand game. Upon his return he made a simple set and someone put up the hand game for him. He did not demonstrate the game more than a few years. Data on this game are meager; after a first visit to Carrion, other work delayed me in conferring with him again, and he died before I had another opportunity.

In a trance at the Arapaho Ghost Dance, Carrion saw a large circle of people above. In a vision on the fourth day he saw things whirling round in the sun, crows flying round the sun and flying over him, and an eagle feather in the whirling sun. Then he saw a black sun streaked with white coming toward him, and fell over. When he stood up he saw a buffalo bull stick his head out of the sun, and just before sundown Jesus standing in the western sun with one hand extended toward him.

These two part-visions combined were interpreted by the Arapaho prophets as a gift of the hand game. The circle of people were the players, and Christ held the set of sticks in his extended hand. As he held them extended downward toward Carrion, so in the inter-

---

[1] In the accounts of the individual games in this and the succeeding chapter, the form of presentation follows that of the formal analysis of Chapter VIII. In this way repetitions have been avoided as far as possible. The ritual structures of offerings, altars, etc., have been summarized in terms of the generic description of Chapter VIII; unique details of these and other aspects of the games are, however, given. Games witnessed of which an observation record was kept are given in narrative form within the formal structure. A few games require lengthy description. Wherever on a particular point of ritual, ceremonial order, and the like, no special comment is made, it should be understood that the generic forms described in the preceding chapter are used.

vals of Ghost Dance hand games the beneficiary must hold them
aloft toward the heavenly bestower.

At this late date, Carrion's memory cannot be trusted as to the
forms of the Arapaho Ghost Dance hand game; but it is of importance to note what Carrion thought he saw.

He said the Arapaho talked and prayed before playing the game,
but smoked no pipe. The game was held in a tipi, with the doorway
directed westward; the men sat at the east facing toward the
western door. The game sets consisted of 12 tally sticks. The men
painted face and body before conducting the hand game. One
drum used was set on the north side. Two sides played against
each other, on north and south respectively. There were no names
for the sides, so far as Joe knew, but he added that had there been
names he would not have known of it, as he understood no Arapaho.
A great many of those present wore Crow and Eagle feathers, but
as he observed these were not clustered on the respective sides,
but occurred miscellaneously. There were two guessers, one for a
side, each of whom wore in the hair as insignia a short stick ornamented with four crow feathers. Hand game songs were used for
the game play, Ghost Dance songs for Ghost Dancing in the
intervals between games. No rattle or other musical instrument
was used in the Ghost Dancing. It was a four-day ceremony; each
day seven rubber games were played. If one side won on any day
that side was considered luckier, and those who composed it were
given promise of good fortune. Before eating, after the game
play, a simple blessing with a bit of food was made.

The game was said to belong to a nephew of Sitting Bull, the
Arapaho, who had learned it in a Ghost Dance vision under
the leadership of Sitting Bull. Sitting Bull had interpreted it for
him. The play songs were hand game songs learned in Ghost
Dance experiences, not so far as Carrion knew the old hand game
songs.

Paraphernalia

When Carrion first demonstrated the game he had only a set
of 12 dogwood tally sticks, six painted red for Eagles, six blue for
Crows, counters, a pipe, and two crow clusters to be worn by the
guessers. Later he added other things; and it is probable that
among his later changes was a shift from 12 sticks to 8.

Altar

The altar arrangement was the generic form (see fig. 3) with the
pipe in the center, six red sticks south of it, six blue sticks north.
The two crow clusters were set upright in the ground before the

altar, until after the smoke offering, when they were given to the guessers.

Official Arrangements

He had four rixkita behind the altar. He placed one drum on the south side, and asked anyone who wanted to sing for the people. Carrion remembers asking Sunchief (the father) to be main rixkita of the south eagle side, and Tsaka'ª to take charge of the north. Both were chiefs; they died many years ago. Walter Sunchief (son of the above) was guesser for the south and Goodfox for the north.

Smoke Offering

A simple unadorned form.

First phase:
West of fireplace, offering: Heaven and earth combined. Pipe lit at northeast.

Second phase:
First mode:
West of fireplace, offerings: Heaven (4), Earth (4), West (4).
Second mode:
(? At altar, one offering over each side ?) To the drum (4).
Third mode:
To S 1, N 1. (Unusual order, does not agree with game emphasis.)

Third Phase:
West of fireplace, offerings: West, heaven and earth.

Fourth Phase:
Probably as first and second modes of second phase.
Self-Blessing.

Play of the Game

I have no notes on his game play, save that it is probable from his account of Arapaho play that Carrion followed the same form and played for seven games straight.

The Game Intervals

The singers used old time hand game songs for the game play; the Ghost Dancing was done in intervals led by the winning side, and the leader of the winning side held the game set aloft.

Food Offering

Carrion said that he made the corn offering himself. He used his hand as he had no spoon in his set. He said that it was ritually the same to use hand or spoon, but that spoon was preferred.

I have no details of the offering, except that he offered corn to the west. I believe he intended by this reference that the offerings included, heaven, earth, and west, the former being considered so generic and essential as not to require mention.

Special Notes

During the four days and nights of a Ghost Dance, or of an old Ghost Dance hand game, Carrion says that sexual intercourse on the part of the participants was banned.

Carrion considers himself responsible for the first definite demarcation of the two sides in the games as Crows and Eagles. Crows and Eagles were general in the Pawnee Ghost Dance, but unorganized; similarly he says they were general among the Arapaho, in both Ghost Dancing and hand games, but unorganized. Frank White, the Pawnee prophet, had seven Eagles to do the singing, unaided by any of the Crows, while the Crows unorganized were supposed to take charge of the dancing.

The symbolic references of the sides, according to Carrion, are the black crow for the north and the gray eagle for the south, (not the bald eagle, which is associated with the north).

When he first made and painted his twelve dogwood sticks, Carrion said that he consecrated them with a smoke offering.

TOM MORGAN

Ownership and Affiliation

Tom Morgan is a member of the Pitahawirat[a] band, and is affiliated with the south or Eagle side.

This game, organized at the time of the first Ghost Dancing, was not derived from a Ghost Dance vision. Nevertheless Tom Morgan is himself responsible for it, and has himself instituted the changes in its form which make it today identical ritually with a Ghost Dance hand game. Informants will say, "Afterwards the other people learned. But Tom Morgan had no trance, but just started it," or again, "Tom Morgan just made it up." One informant explained that as he recalled Tom Morgan's explanation, "when the people were camped at Seminole they had nothing to do but sit around and somebody said, 'we ought to do something to pass the time,' so Tom Morgan thought he'd better get sticks and have a game instead of just killing time, so he went and made the set of sticks. When he first made it it was just for fun, but as years passed and all these different people found things out and made hand games, it got so that they wouldn't look at his old set of sticks, and so he put them away, and only recently when someone asked him that was what he said, but when urged he brought them out for a game for fun. Probably when he first made the game at Seminole he played it the old way without a drum and without smoking." Thus it seems that Morgan's game was a play revival antedating the ritualized Ghost Dance forms, and was then altered with the changing fashion.

Paraphernalia

The bundle includes the fundamentals of eight tally sticks, counters, horn spoon, pipe and cloth spread. It is not possible to be certain what the game paraphernalia included earlier and later.

Altar Arrangements

As played in recent years, the altar accords with the generic pattern, as illustrated by fig. 3 of the White Elk and Eustace altars. The bowl opening of the pipe is, however, directed southward instead of northward.

Official Arrangements

Four rixkita behind altar; one drum placed on the south side, with Crow singers around the north half, Eagle singers around the south half[1]; fireplace, usually with fire; usually played indoors unless too hot. No watchers or old men stations. Morgan always selected a chief to be in charge on each side. He often selected old man Curlychief for the Eagles and Goodchief for the Crows.

The Smoke Offering

S 1 prepares pipe and selects offerer.
First Phase:
Clockwise circuit; offerings at west of fireplace: Heaven, earth. To northeast where pipe is lit by anyone with brand.
Second Phase:
First Mode:
Clockwise to west of fireplace. Offerings: Heaven (4), earth (4).
Second Mode:
To altar, offerings: one over south or left side, one over north or right side. To north drum (2), to south drum (2).
Third Mode:
To S 1, S 2, to N 1, N 2. To 1 and 2 Crow drummers. To 1 and 2 Eagle drummers.
Optional: Crow men west to east, Eagle men east to west.

---

[1] Not the Seven Brothers or Seven Crows. One informant believed that at times Morgan used two drums.

Third Phase:
    West of fireplace, offerings: Heaven (2), earth (2).
Fourth Phase:
    First and second modes, as first and second modes of second phase above.
    Self-Blessing. Returns pipe to S 1.

Play of the Game

The game is played straight, never even up, for five games with two additional games optional. There is no aftermath of play with this game. The game is said to have often been played by all the men against all the women. Morgan often played it in Ghost Dance times with the stake that whoever lost had to put up the food for the next day.

The Game Intervals

The usual pattern of the intervals is followed, Ghost Dancing to Ghost Dance dance songs, followed by the singing of one or two old songs by the winning side. Here the winning side usually used Young Dog Dance songs, Big Horse society songs, or Old War Dance songs. For starting the game, Tom was said to use regularly two special hand game songs that go back many generations. For this game the set is not held aloft in the intermissions; without a vision derivation the gesture would be meaningless.

No instruments are used for the Ghost Dancing.

The Food Offering and Service

The food is brought in by those who cooked it, and received by the game owner, set out at the east, the corn buckets in an arc.

The leader of the winning side speaks: In substance:

"God has provided us with this food. I don't want to talk too long. Now we're going to eat. Now I want—(mentioning the name of the selected offerer) to look up to heaven, and whatever he asks God may provide us. Wherever there is sickness in the village, God may drive it out so that we can live right."

The offerer receives the spoon, fills it and makes the inclusive gestures.

Corn Offering

Extended Method:
First phase as first phase of smoke-offering; second phase, first and second modes as first and second modes of second phase of smoke-offering; self-blessing, and return of the spoon.

Shorter Method:

(At suggestion of game owner). (Phases are reversed in order).
First Phase:

(As usual second mode of second phase). Carrying spoonful
to altar. Offerings: one over south or left side, one over north or
right side. To north drum (2), to south drum (2).

Second phase:

First Mode: (as usual first phase).

West of fireplace, depositing corn, offerings: Heaven, earth.
Second Mode: (as usual first mode of second phase).

West of fireplace, motions pressing corn. Offerings: Heaven
(4), earth (4). Clockwise circuit carrying empty spoon. Self-
blessing, spoon returned to S 1.

Service

Four servers for each side, selected by rixkita. Dishes are all
given out. Order: S 1, S 2 and N 1, N 2; 1 and 2 Crow drummers
and 1 and 2 Eagle drummers. Laymen.

No one leaves until after the feast the rixkita of the winning
side announces, "Now we have eaten, now all can go."

WHITE ELK
Ownership and Affiliation

White Elk belongs to the Kitkahaxki^x band and is affiliated
with the Crow or north side. White Elk derived his game in a
Ghost Dance vision of his own. The game is played in the South
Round House or outdoors near it, afternoon or evening.

White Elk often played his bundle against that of John Brown,
using half of his set against half of Brown's.[1]

Paraphernalia

The bundle contents are not entirely known. The set was a
simple one; it contained the 8 dogwood tally sticks, the pipe, two
white bone counters and the horn spoon, and a cloth spread; and
probably other objects.

Altar Arrangements
See figure 3.

Official Arrangements

Four rixkita behind altar; two drums with Crow and Eagle
singers, respectively *(not* Seven Brothers and Seven Crows);

---

[1] Joe Carrion considered the original form of play of the games of White
Elk and Brown as following his procedure closely; according to Carrion
these games were developed very soon after his own.

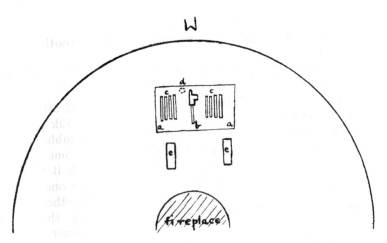

Figure 3. Altar Plan of White Elk and Annie Eustace

a - altar spread   d - position of concealed
b - pipe   horn spoon
c - game sticks   e - drums

fireplace, with fire if weather requires. No watchers and no old men stations near doorway. Probably an official tarutsius or two. White Elk may be rixkita N 1 for his own game.

Smoke Offering

N 1 prepares the pipe and selects the offerer; thereafter the outline of the phases is:

First Phase:

Clockwise circuit to west of fireplace. Offerings: Heaven, Earth. Clockwise to northeast; pipe lit, by tarutsius.

Second Phase:

First Mode:

Clockwise to west of fireplace. Offerings: Heaven (4), Earth (4), Westward (4).

Second Mode:

To altar. Offerings: one over north or right side; one over south or left side. To north drum (2). To south drum (2).

Third Mode:

To N 1, N 2; to S 1, S 2. To 1 and 2 Crow singers; clockwise, to 1 and 2 Eagle singers. Optional: To Crow men west to east; to Eagle men east to west.

Third Phase:

To west of fireplace; offerings: Heaven (2), Earth (2), West (2).

Fourth Phase:
First and second modes, as those of second phase; no third mode.
Self-Blessing.
Returns pipe.

Play of the Game

The game was played straight, for five games. If after these, any further rubber-games were called for, White Elk generally organized a special aftermath for two-out-of three rubber games. As an informant remarked, "After the five games, some one may call out, 'Let all the sticks come together.' He calls it that, but the sticks still lie four on each side." The leaders select one man and one woman for each side. These sit opposite each other, on the north and south sides of the fireplace, respectively, the woman toward the west, the man toward the east. One guesser is chosen for each side; the winning guesser of the previous game is not retained. The two players do all the hiding of the counters for their respective sides. In giving out the counters and taking them when lost, the guessers make clockwise circuits of the fireplace. "Everyone shouts because this is a tight game, and whichever side wins this, wins regardless of the outcome of the previous five games. That's because they selected good hiders and good guessers." In the aftermath, when a rubber-game is lost, the guesser of the losing side, as well as that of the winning side, is retained, but two other players are selected to play for the side which has just lost.

The Game Intervals

Young Dog Dance songs are used for this game when old society songs are called for. The Young Dog Dance was the principal society of the Kitkahaxki[x] in the old days. These songs are used to start off, and in the intervals after the three Ghost Dance dancing songs. For putting the counters in play, and the actual play, old hand game songs, or hand game play songs learned in the Ghost Dance times, were used.

After the five straight games, if an aftermath is played, the side winning the last of the five, leads only three Ghost Dance circuits. The ten Ghost Dance songs and circuits are led in that case by the side which wins the aftermath. No instruments are used in the Ghost Dancing. The winning leader holds the game set aloft.

The Food Offering and Service

The speeches by the winning leader are made, if an aftermath is played, by the leader of the side which wins the aftermath; otherwise by the side which wins three or more games of the five.

The corn buckets are set east of the fireplace in an arc.

The designated offerer receives the horn spoon, fills it, and makes inclusive motions east of the food.

The Corn Offering:

First Phase:

As first phase of smoke-offering; he may include west.

Second Phase:

First and second modes, as the first and second modes of the second phase of the smoke-offering.

Self-blessing, returns spoon.

The service. Four servers for each side. Order: N 1 and N 2; S 1 and S 2. 1 and 2 Crow drummers; 1 and 2 Eagle drummers. Laymen. A speech by the leader of the winning side closes the occasion.

JOHN BROWN

I have no information on this game other than that it was probably an Eagle game, and was often pitted against that of White Elk.

ANNIE EUSTACE

Ownership and Affiliation

Annie Eustace, a Crow, belongs to the Kitkahaxki[x] band. She secured her game herself in a Ghost Dance vision. In former times she played her game in an earth lodge, in recent times in the South Round House or nearby, usually in the afternoon.

Paraphernalia

Bundle contains game set of eight dogwood sticks, white bone counters, spoon and pipe, and associated cloth spread. There may have been additional objects.

Altar

See figure 3.

Official Arrangements

Four rixkita behind altar; two drums with Crow and Eagle singers (not Seven Brothers or Seven Crows); fireplace, usually with fire burning; at doorway, one tarutsius on each side; on north side next to tarutsius, an old man, and doctors, seated east to west respectively; on south side next to tarutsius, an old man and chiefs, seated west to east respectively. Annie Eustace herself takes a place anywhere on the north side, to direct activities. In 1930—31, informants recalled that the last time the game was played, White Elk was N 1 for the Crows, St. Elmo Jim S 1 for the

Eagles. Both of these have chief status and are members of the Kitkahaxki[x] band. For the full seating plan see figure 4.

Smoke offering.

N 1 prepares pipe, selects offerer.

First Phase:

Clockwise circuit; offerings, west of fireplace: Heaven, earth. Clockwise to northeast, pipe lit by north tarutsius.

Second Phase:

First mode:

Offerings west fireplace: Heaven (4), earth (4), west (4).

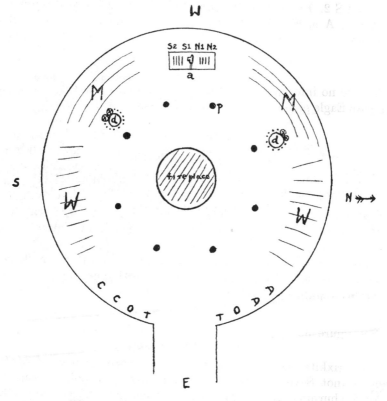

Figure 4. Plan of Arrangements of Annie Eustace

a - altar	T - tarutsius
p - houseposts	O - Old men
d - drums	C - Chiefs
N, S - rixkita	D - Doctors
x - drummers	M - Men
[x] - main drummers	W - Women

Second mode:
To altar, offerings: one over north objects, one over south objects. To north drum (2), to south drum (2).

Third mode:
Offerings: To N 1, N 2; to S 1, S 2. To 1 and 2 Crow drummers; clockwise, to 1 and 2 Eagle drummers. Clockwise to north old man, crossing past doorway to south old man. Clockwise: to all Crow men west to east; to Eagle men east to west.

Third Phase:
West of fireplace, offerings: Heaven (2), earth (2), west (2).

Fourth Phase:
First and second modes, as first and second modes of second phase, above; no third mode.

Self-blessing, returns pipe.

Play of the Game

Played straight, never even up, for five games, with two additional games optional. It is probable that the aftermath of play, as used at White Elk's game, could be played with this.

The Game Intervals

The Crow side for this game always uses, or always begins by using, Young Dog dance songs for the old society songs prior to putting the counters in play, and after the Ghost Dancing in the intervals. The Eagle side uses such also, or old war dance songs. Choice of songs rests with main singer, or with another singer of the side to whom the main singer may delegate his leadership.

Three Ghost Dance songs usually in intervals; after completed play, ten Ghost Dance songs concluding with finishing song. In intervals rixkita of winning side holds set aloft. No rattle used.

Food Offering and Service

Food received by game owner, set out east of fireplace, buckets of corn in an arc.

Offerer, designated by winning leader, receives spoon, fills it, and makes inclusive motions standing east of food.

Corn Offering.

First Phase:
As first phase of smoke-offering; may include west.

Second Phase:
First and second modes, as first and second modes of second phase of smoke-offering.

Self-Blessing, returns spoon.

Service:

Four servers for each side. Order: N 1, N 2 and S 1, S 2; 1 and 2 Crow drummers and 1 and 2 Eagle drummers: old men (and tarutsius) at doorway; north doctors and south chiefs near doorway; laymen, west to east down each side.

After the feast, the leader of the side which won the majority of rubber games makes a long speech. In substance:

"Now we are here. We give thanks to Tirawahat^n. We try to follow the way of Tirawahat^n, that he may provide for us. And the birds in the air too, and the animals upon earth, may they provide for us, and take pity upon us. We gave this to Mother Earth. She receives everything... Now that is all. Now we've finished the hand game. Now we've eaten. Now we'll cease. Now we'll go out of the doorway."

All depart. This ends the occasion.

X
THE SKIRI HAND GAMES

MRS. GOODEAGLE

Ownership and Affiliation

Mrs. Goodeagle herself is by birth of the Tcawi band, but after her marriage to Goodeagle was associated consistently with the Skiri, and particularly in Ghost Dance times. Her own game she derived in Ghost Dance visions. At the same time Goodeagle obtained a game, and in some respects the two games are similar. After Goodeagle's death, his game passed into the possession of Mrs. Goodeagle, so that she had two games. In strict theory, Mrs. Goodeagle's own game might be considered Tcawi, but in form and content it was determined by the Skiri Ghost Dance, and follows the structure of Skiri games.

Mrs. Goodeagle was one of the main Skiri Ghost Dance prophets. She was in part responsible for the organization of the Seven Eagle Brothers, and was affiliated with the Eagles. Her game is considered the most important ceremonially of Skiri Eagle games. In recent years, it was played in the North Round House, afternoon or evening. Densmore witnessed the demonstration of Mrs. Goodeagle's game on April 16, 1921, at the North Round House.[1] December 28, 1930, I was present at another demonstration by her at the same place. On both occasions the games were in the afternoon.

Densmore reports of Mrs. Goodeagle, "This was said to be her hand game, not only because she gave the invitations and provided the feast, but because certain features of the game, as played that day, had been revealed to her in a dream. The symbolism of certain articles used in that game was not made known to the singers and perhaps is known only to herself."[2]

When near Christmas 1930 it was announced that Mrs. Goodeagle would demonstrate her hand game, it was said she had not demonstrated it in many years. There was no official "putter-up", but relatives and friends urged her to demonstrate the game. At that time, games were fairly frequent, but were either those of Moses or

---

[1] Densmore, Pawnee Music, p. 70.
[2] Ibid.

Allen, or that of Tom Yellowhorse. The latter had been put up
frequently, and some Pawnee thought it had been overemphasized.
Without a putter-up, the burden fell on Mrs. Goodeagle and her
family, and when I spoke of attending I was asked to help. I supplied
about ten pounds of beef.

Mrs. Goodeagle had aged considerably by 1930, and her memory
was not what it had been. Her game was familiar to many old
people, and her children. My informant criticised things she did
as not correct according to her previous performances, and in
conversation with members of her family, I found that they also
felt she had made mistakes. This is an aspect of primitive ritualism
and ceremony that cannot be overlooked. Where all is oral,
memory and habit are the only records, and these must in time
falter.

Paraphernalia

As witnessed: 8 eagle feathers; three soft white eagle feathers;
four special eagle feather insignia; pipe; counters (soft buffalo
hair with piece of buffalo hoof); horn spoon; braided sweetgrass;
two drums.

This was not the complete original set, parts of which were said
to be missing. The eight eagle feathers were four black eagle tail
feathers for the north, four bald eagle tail feathers for the south.
These were set upright before the altar spread, four on each side
(see altar arrangements). As play proceeded they were used as
tally sticks, being removed one by one until all were in play.
Thereafter they lay on the altar spread. The original set included
these eight feathers as tally sticks, and in addition seven bald eagle
feathers (representing the Seven Eagle Brothers) which were set
upright in a row before the altar, and left there during the game.
This form is used by Yellowhorse, and is also reported for the
unidentified game witnessed by Densmore in 1919.[1]

The three white eagle feathers are left standing before the altar.
The four special eagle feathers are hair ornaments for watchers
and guessers; two are bald eagle (white), two black eagle. Each
guesser gets a white one, each watcher a black one.

In the original bundle were two bunches of eagle tail feathers, one
black for the north, one white for the south, which lay on the altar
spread until the game began. Then these were distributed to
players of the two sides, who wore them in the hair.

Field Museum 59538, a pendant of one crow and three eagle
feathers on a thong, is said to have formerly been worn by Mrs.
Goodeagle.

---

[1] Densmore, Pawnee Music, p. 69.

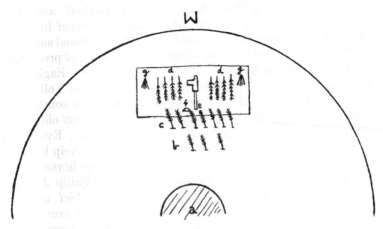

Figure 5. Altar Plan of Mrs. Goodeagle

a - fireplace
b - upright bald eagle feathers
c - upright bald eagle tail feathers
d - bald eagle tail feather tally sticks

e - pipe
f - spoon
g - bunched feather ornaments

Altar Arrangements

(See fig. 5). The figure represents the old form. At the game witnessed the eight feather tally sticks were not on the altar cloth but erect before it, instead of the seven which were missing; the bunches of feather ornaments were also missing; and during the smoke offering only the four feather ornaments and the spoon were on the altar spread.

Official Arrangements

Five rixkita behind altar, a main ceremonial official, who does not play, a rixkita in charge of each side (N 1 and S 1), and an assistant rixkita for each side (N 2 and S 2). One watcher for each side, who sits before the game just to north or south of the altar spread. Drums at northwest and southwest, presided over by the Seven Crows and the Seven Brothers or their successors. An old man should be placed on each side of the entrance; this Mrs. Goodeagle neglected to do.

Mrs. Goodeagle chose Suneagle to take ceremonial charge, Rush Roberts as rixkita of the Crow side (N 1), and John Moses of the Eagle (S 1). John Moses is, nevertheless, one of the original Seven Crows.

Only two or three were seated at each drum, because so far as possible members of the two singing organizations or their official successors must preside. Only Charley Knifechief and Mark Evarts were at first at the Crow drum, with Knifechief in charge. Evarts claims rights of seniority as one of the first official successors of the Seven Crows, but Mrs. Goodeagle gave Knifechief precedence. Yellowhorse and Ezra Tilden were at first at the Eagle drum (both members of the original Seven Brothers). When Yellowhorse became guesser for the Eagles, two others joined the south drummers who were not members of the organization, but older men. On the Crow side, when Knifechief became guesser, Evarts was left alone, and Henry Shooter sat down alongside to help him sing.

Mrs. Goodeagle selected as first guessers Yellowhorse for the Eagles and Knifechief for the Crows; she chose Philip Jim, her grandson, as Crow watcher and Hughey Horsechief as Eagle watcher. Suneagle selected the smoke-offerer and corn-offerer, in both cases choosing Knifechief. Knifechief is known as one skilled in the ritual lore of the pipe, and the like, although he is not the owner of a bundle or ritual, and is not a medicine man.

Densmore records more than two hundred people present at each hand game she attended.[1] There were large crowds present at outdoor games of Yellowhorse which I attended, and at games of Allen's and Moses', but for this game of Mrs. Goodeagle's the attendance was small. Between Christmas and New Year the Pawnee assemble for two separate series of social festivities, the South Bands at the South Round House, the Skiri at the North Round House. Mrs. Goodeagle's demonstration conflicted with dances at the South Round House. The Pawnee today number about seven hundred, and with many eliminated by church membership and lack of interest, and many young people avoiding older type ceremonial occasions, when the two band groups are divided by conflict of dates, the assemblage for either affair is small. There is no feeling that one must attend the gathering of one's own band. Shooter and Suneagle of the South Band came to the Skiri hand game. Convenience and personal choice seem to be the determinants.

For this hand game a fire must be burning in the fireplace.

Smoke Offering

In Densmore's account Mrs. Goodeagle made James Murie the ceremonial official and Murie himself made the smoke offering. I am not sure that this is possible. The official presiding prepares the pipe, selects the offerer, gives and receives the pipe, but does not ordinarily smoke himself.

---

[1] Densmore, p. 69.

Charley Knifechief left his place at the Crow drum and went to the altar where he received the pipe from Suneagle.

First Phase:

Clockwise through north to the east, where facing east Knifechief offered tobacco slantwise eastward, and placed it on the ground. At this point, Knifechief walked out of the ceremonial pathway to Mrs. Goodeagle who sat at the doorway on the Eagle side. He asked for instructions, and she whispered and motioned to him. Leaving the pathway in this way is not considered correct. Mrs. Goodeagle should have come to Knifechief. After instruction, Knifechief walked back into the ceremonial pathway at the point at which he had left it and continued clockwise to west of the fireplace, where facing east, he prayed silently as he offered tobacco aloft to heaven and placed it on the ground. Then he turned to face west, offered tobacco slantwise west, turned back and placed it on the ground. Then he proceeded clockwise to the northeast, where he squatted for the pipe to be lit.

Philip Jim, watcher for Knifechief's side, came with braided sweetgrass from the bundle. He lit this with a brand from the fire, then held the burning sweetgrass to the bowl while Knifechief puffed.

Second Phase:

First Mode:

Clockwise to west of fireplace, facing east. Offerings: Heaven (4), earth (4), slanteast (2), south, by turning the head only, (2), slantwest, turning the body to face west (2), north, by turning the head only (2).

Second Mode:

Directly to altar down sacred pathway. Offerings: One each to each of the three soft feathers, central, north or right, south or left (emphasis here is that of side making smoke offering); three to the eight upright feathers, middle, north side of row, south side of row (emphasis as for the three feathers; note also that he smoked as if there were an odd number, such as seven, which should have been there; for an even number, once for each side, or the two middle and two ends, or each individually, are the proper forms); to altar proper, three puffs, one down the center, one over the north side, one over the south side. (This indicates that there may have been a rattle or similar object in the center of the altar spread, otherwise smoking over the two sides would be sufficient.) To the Crow drum (2); clockwise to the Eagle drum (2).

Third mode:

At the altar to Suneagle. He then offered the pipe to Roberts (N 1), who refused it, telling him to give it first to Moses (S 1), which Knifechief did. This was an error, as the pattern of this smoke offering emphasizes and should emphasize the Crow or non-game side throughout; it is spoken of as a game that works backwards, or the reverse of what is expected. Roberts was ignorant of this apparently; he was correct in his advice from generic standpoints, but wrong in interfering with the procedure that Mrs. Goodeagle had told Knifechief to carry out. After offering the pipe to Moses, Knifechief offered it to Roberts. Knifechief then went to the Crow drum, and offered the pipe to Evarts and Shooter; then clockwise to the Eagle drum, and offered the pipe to Yellowhorse and Tilden. (At this point, if Mrs. Goodeagle had put old men at their official stations on each side of the doorway, Knifechief would have gone clockwise to offer the pipe to the north old man, then offered it to the south old man; with the stations vacant, he proceeded at once with the third phase).

Third Phase:

Offerings, as he deposited the ashes at the west of the fireplace, Heaven, earth. (Correct synchronism with first phase would be up, west.)

Fourth Phase:

First Mode:

Knifechief made the sacramental motions with the pipe, in the same order and the same number of times as puffs of smoke, in the first mode of the second phase above: Heaven (4), slanteast (2), south, merely turning body, feet constant in position (2), slantwest, turning to face west (2), north, merely turning body (2).

Second mode:

To altar. Sequence of motions follows exactly the sequence of puffs of second mode of second phase. To drums, each (2).

Self-Blessing:

Knifechief stood between fireplace and altar, facing west, standing just to the north of the sacred pathway, and made the self-blessing. Each time he ran his hand up the pipe he held it aloft a moment before putting it on his head to rub down his body, a gesture which according to my informant is not sound, since "it is like giving oneself away." He returned the pipe to Suneagle who took it with an arm-blessing.

Play of the Game

Distribution of Insignia:

After the smoke offering, Mrs. Goodeagle rose. She took in each hand one white eagle feather (for the guesser) and one counter. With these she went to the west of the fireplace, where facing

east she held both hands aloft; then proceeded clockwise to the
east where facing east she held counters and feathers slanteastward
aloft; then clockwise to the south where she faced south and held
them aloft toward the south; to the west where facing west she
held them aloft toward the west; and finally to the north where
facing north she held the objects aloft toward the north.

It will be noted that the form and order of these gestures follows
the pattern of the first mode of the second phase of the smoke
offering, save that a gesture toward the earth is omitted. This
pattern of five points in the order of zenith, east, south, west,
north, which is followed also in filling the horn spoon for the corn
offering (see below), is considered to constitute a five-pointed
star, and to be characteristic of Mrs. Goodeagle's game. The
pattern also demarcates a cross, by referring to the crossing and
the four extremities, each associated with a cardinal direction.
This is objectified in the arrangement of the corn buckets at Mrs.
Goodeagle's game, and the food offering. As a cross, however,
it differs from the order in which an actual cross is smoked.[1]

Mrs. Goodeagle, leaving the north, proceeded clockwise until
she reached the Eagle drum at the southwest, where she gave one
feather and one counter to Yellowhorse; then continuing clockwise
through the west to the Crow drum at the northwest she gave the
other feather and counter to Knifechief. Thus these two were
ceremonially inducted into office as guessers for the first game.

It was agreed by various people present that Mrs. Goodeagle
was at this point guilty of a slip of memory. She should have now
taken the two black eagle feathers, one in each hand, offered them
in each of the directions of the five-pointed star pattern, and then
given one to Hughey Horsechief, seated just south of the altar,
and one to Philip Jim, seated just north of the altar. This Mrs.
Goodeagle neglected. After giving feathers and counters to the
guessers, Mrs. Goodeagle went clockwise to her seat on the south
side at the extreme east (nearest the doorway). As the game was
about to begin, each watcher, when he rose, merely picked up one
of the black feathers from the altar and put it in his hair.

Putting the Counters in Play:

After the distribution of the insignia, the guessers arose to con-
front each other, and the watchers took their places beside the
guessers. As this was an Eagle game, and Mrs. Goodeagle (essentially) had put it up herself, the Eagles were hosts, hence the Eagle
guesser hid the counter first, the Crow guesser guessed first.

---

[1] See Mark Rudder's game; the smoke offering.

Play:

The objective of Mrs. Goodeagle's game is for one side to win five rubber games. On this occasion the play went: I. Eagles; II. Crows; III. Crows; IV. Eagles; V. Eagles; VI. Crows; VII. Crows. Here the score stood: Crows 4, Eagles 3. Then a special aftermath of play was used (see below).

While the guessers who lost a game yielded their office for the next game to another player of that side, the watchers were permanent for the whole occasion of game play. The watchers followed the guessers about, standing beside them. Often the guesser, when puzzled, would turn to his watcher and ask him for help. Sometimes the guesser asked his watcher to guess for him. The watcher signalled or called out the scoring for his side to the rixkita who did the tallying. When the counters were won, the watcher came forward and took them and then gave them to the guesser of his side. The guesser in turn carried them across the arena and gave them out to the two players whose turn it was.

The turns were on the north side from west to east, beginning with Rush Roberts and N 2; on the south side from east to west, beginning with two women who sat just to the left or west of Mrs. Goodeagle's place at the door.

Note on Songs:

For starting this game (putting the counters in play), Mrs. Goodeagle has a special song, which was not used, however, at the game I attended. This song says in substance:

"When I start this game I always cry...
When I think of how I got this game I cry...
When my father gave it to me then I cried..."

The song refers to the vision experience upon which the game is based. On the occasion of the vision Mrs. Goodeagle cried a good deal. Actually she cried all through the game occasion I attended. The reference to "father" implies the Christ concept of the Ghost Dance, and Mrs. Goodeagle's own father.

The Game Intervals

When a rubber game was won, the watcher of the winning side took the counters from the two players who had run out the game points and returned them to the rixkita of his side. Watchers and guessers of both sides kept their hair ornaments during the interval.

The usual Ghost Dancing was carried out. Three songs and circuits were led by the singers of the winning side, beginning at the west. No rattle was used.

Mark Evarts led the Ghost Dancing after the second rubber game (won by Crows), and although he himself led three circuits, he claims that four are preferable.

The rixkita did not arise with the game set and pipe and hold them aloft durting the Ghost Dancing. I was assured, however, that they should have. Apparently this is not done unless the game owner specifically directs the leaders to do so, and Mrs. Goodeagle forgot (so it was said) to tell them. If the set were held aloft, the rixkita carrying it would probably have to follow out the five-pointed-star pattern.

After the dancers returned to their seats, the rixkita of the side which had won rose and returned the counters to the former guessers.

Then the singers of the winning side sang one "society" song. Mark Evarts when he led used the Young Dog Dance. After the song the guesser who lost the previous rubber game rose and gave his feather and counter to another player of his side, who thus became guesser for the next game. Knifechief, who lost the first game, did this before the second; Yellowhorse functioned for two games, but as he lost the second to the Crows, selected another Eagle guesser for the third game.

Mrs. Goodeagle spoke in one of the intervals. She called attention first of all to the fact that Philip Jim and Horsechief should take places at the east on their respective sides of the doorway during the intervals, instead of keeping their places beside the altar. The positions at the east would be "tarutsius" positions. After she spoke Evarts rose at his place beside the Crow drum and addressed the gathering.[1]

The Aftermath of Play

When the score stood Crows 4, Eagles 3, the guesser for the Eagle side (which had just lost the seventh game) chose as his successor, Hughey Horsechief, the regular watcher of the Eagle side. This caused confusion, for if play continued regularly there would be a guesser and watcher on the Crow side against one individual on the Eagle side who was both watcher and guesser. The Crow rixkita told Phillip Jim to get the feather and counter from the woman who had been Crow guesser in the previous game. In the next game Horsechief and Phillip Jim each functioned in a dual role; each wore two feathers in his hair, a light and a dark one.

With these two as guessers, turns continued in regular order. The eighth game was won by the Eagles, tying the score at 4—4.

---

[1] The content of these speeches is described in Chapter VIII: Speeches at Hand Games.

Phillip Jim however, continued as Crow guesser for the ninth game, which was won by the Crows, so that the final score was 5—4 in favor of the Crows.

It was said that this procedure was begun in error. It was a procedure to be followed only when the score reached a tie at 4—4. The Eagle guesser after the seventh game either misunderstood the practice or thought that the score was then 4—4. Interesting in this aftermath is the fact that special hiders are not chosen; turns continue as before, but the permanent watchers become the guessers.[1]

After the play, the Eagle drum was returned to a position before the altar on the south side of the midline. The Crow drum was left with the Crow singers.

The final circuits of Ghost Dancing were led by the Crow singers. Only three circuits and songs were used. After the last circuits, the Crow singers led one final "society" song. Then the Crow drum was returned to a place before the altar.

Food Offering and Service

The food was brought in and received at the doorway for Mrs. Goodeagle by the two watchers. Mrs. Goodeagle had them set it between fireplace and doorway, with the buckets of corn just east of the fireplace. There were nine buckets, set in a "five-pointed star" arrangement, actually a "cross": With one bucket at center, four radial arms composed of two buckets each were set toward the cardinal directions. The meat was just behind (east of) the corn.

While this was being done, plates and utensils were distributed by the women folk who had provided these for the members of their families.[2]

Suneagle again selected Knifechief to make the offering. Knifechief came to the altar and received the horn spoon from Suneagle. He then came clockwise through the north to Mrs. Goodeagle's place at the eastern doorway, and asked her for directions. Mrs. Goodeagle said only a few words to him, which I understand were merely to instruct him to follow the smoke offering in everything.

Knifechief went to the buckets of corn and standing north of them facing south dipped some corn from the central bucket.

---

[1] This differs from the form which in former times was used by Mrs. Goodeagle, in which two special players would be selected for each side to do the hiding. See Chapter VIII: The Play of the Game.

[2] Densmore observes, "According to Indian custom, each person provided his own utensils and the food was served in large containers." *Pawnee Music*, p. 70.

Moving clockwise to the east, facing west he dipped corn from the outer or extreme eastern bucket; continuing clockwise, at the south facing north he dipped from the extreme outer southern bucket, then at the west facing east from the extreme western bucket, and finally completed the first round of the buckets standing at the north facing south and dipping corn from the extreme northern bucket. Now he repeated his circuit of the four directions, beginning at east facing west, and ending at north facing south, in each position dipping corn from the inner buckets. After he had taken corn from each of the nine buckets, he moved clockwise to the east of all the food, where he made two inclusive motions, right arm directed northward and swept over all the food, left arm southward analogously. Then, carrying the spoonful of corn he proceeded with the corn offering proper.

Food Offering Proper:

First Phase:

Clockwise through south to west of fireplace, where he faced east. Offerings, as he held the spoonful in each direction, and then pushed some off with his left hand onto the ground at his feet: Eastward, Heaven (and earth), Westward. (This was Knifechief's actual procedure, and agrees with the sequence of offerings of the first phase of the smoke ritual (see above) save that the offering eastward is here made while west of the fireplace but in the smoke ritual is made at the east).

Second Phase:

Knifechief carried out no second phase at all; he turned toward the altar with the empty spoon, made the self-blessing and returned it to Suneagle. According to informants this was ritually incorrect, and this phase of the corn offering should have a full two modes: First mode: putting spoon down at left, pressing corn into the earth, rubbing the hands together, and making motions for each puff of smoke in the offering to the directions of the "five-pointed star" pattern of the first mode of the second phase of the smoke offering. (Taking corn from bowls oriented for these directions is not the conceptual equivalent, since it has not been symbolically "offered.")

Second Mode:

A second mode should include a series of motions, one for each offering of the second mode of the second phase of the smoke offering.

Self-Blessing:

Knifechief stood before the altar, just to the north of the midline, facing Suneagle diagonally, made the full self-blessing, and returned the spoon to Suneagle who took it with an arm blessing.

The Service:

Phillip Jim for the north side and Hughey Horsechief for the south side, the respective watchers, served the corn. Together they took the central bucket of the "cross" and carried it clockwise through the south to the altar, where from it they filled the plates of Suneagle, then Moses (S 1), then Roberts (N 1). (This is the same error of order precipitated by Roberts in the smoke-offering; correct would be Suneagle, N 1, S 1.) From the altar they proceeded with the same bucket to the Crow drummers, where they served corn to Knifechief, then continuing clockwise around to the Eagle drummers, they served Yellowhorse. (If old men were stationed on each side of the doorway they would now be served from this bucket.) Having emptied the bucket in the above service the two servers brought it back to the east and set it down empty near the doorway (no special position). The two then served meat to the same individuals as above in that order, then prepared foods.

After all the special officials had been served, Phillip Jim served corn, meat, and other foods to the other Crow drummers, while Horsechief simultaneously served these to the other Eagle drummers.

For the service of the layfolk and visitors, four men were chosen on each side, and these served as rapidly as possible. The form, so far as it was maintained, was apparently to serve on each side from west to east and east to west, and from the middle eastward and westward.

After the feast the occasion closed when Suneagle made the appropriate closing remarks, "Now we've eaten... Now we go out..."

GOODEAGLE

Ownership and Affiliation

Goodeagle was associated with the Eagles. He secured his game in visions of his own. After his death it passed into Mrs. Goodeagle's possession. A set in the Field Museum was identified as probably the original Goodeagle set. Goodeagle's hand game is considered a Pipe Dance (Hako) hand game. This association is implied by the altar and paraphernalia.

The Skiri Pipe Dance prior to the Ghost Dance was in charge of Thief and Spotted Horsechief. Thief died before 1890, while Spotted Horsechief lived through the Ghost Dance period. Thief's son was taught by Thief, and should have taken over Thief's functions. He did not, but taught Sam Cover, and in later times Sam Cover and Yellowhorse took charge together.

Goodeagle learned something of the Pipe Dance prior to his Ghost Dance experiences, and later sat with Sam Cover (Sam Cover called Goodeagle atías, "father," a classificatory fatherhood relationship) and learned more. The Ghost Dance visions with their revival prerogatives gave Goodeagle an opportunity to display his Pipe Dance knowledge. In the visions in which he derived his game it was associated with Pipe Dance concepts. His game demonstration was a sign to the people that he knew the Pipe Dance and later anyone seeking Pipe Dance information went to him. Once he made a set of calumets for a regular Pipe Dance ceremony — those used with his hand game are somewhat smaller, and merely symbolic. It is also said that after his Ghost Dance visions, Goodeagle was responsible for carrying out a Pipe Dance ceremony.

Paraphernalia

The Goodeagle hand game set on exhibit in the Field Museum of Natural History is numbered 59547 to 59559.

The set includes a forked stick, two calumets, eight long black eagle tail feathers, three shorter black eagle feathers, three shorter white eagle feathers, two corn tassels, twelve tally sticks, braided sweetgrass, Indian tobacco, a blackbird, and bunched eagle feathers. In addition there are a bow and arrow, a pipe stem, a string of braided horsehair, and a black horse tail.

The eight black eagle feathers and the twelve tally sticks (59551) are alternative sets for tallying. If one is used the other is put away. Of the twelve sticks six are green for the north, six yellow for the south; all are notched like arrows.

The forked stick is used as an upright, against which the two calumets lean before the altar (59550). The calumet for the south side has a white stick, that for the north a green stick; the south calumet has a fan-spread of bald eagle feathers, a cluster of the same along the stem, and wing-like attachments of these feathers at the end, like an arrow, while the north calumet has similarly placed black eagle feathers. The south calumet has a small pendant of fur or wool; both calumets have two bindings of otter fur and three pendant bunches of died horsehair.

The two corn tassels, which lie on the altar spread, are one for the north, one for the south. The north has a stick inside it marked with an incised cross near the top end, and tassel and the concealed end of the stick are bound round with black buffalo hair rope. This is intended to represent the corn used in the Pipe Dance. The south tassel is a plain corn tassel.

The shorter white and dark eagle feathers (59555) are hair ornaments. It is not certain by whom these were worn. As for this game there are watchers and guessers as at Mrs. Goodeagle's game, it is probable that each guesser receives a white feather, each watcher a dark one. My informant believed one main white feather used to be worn by the central rixkita and the other two by N 1 and S 1, while the darker feathers were for guessers.

The braided sweetgrass is scorched black at one end; it was used for pipe lighting as in Mrs. Goodeagle's game.

F M 59557, according to the catalog Indian "medicine," wrapped in a small piece of calico, was identified as Indian tobacco, a bit of which was placed on top of the bowl full of kinnikinnick for an offering.

The blackbird (59556), a crow ornament, is according to the catalog, "worn in the hair." Similarly the bunch of eagle feathers for the south side. Both of these may be left on the altar during a game, not actually worn.

Additional objects include three which are associated with the game set because they were used by Goodeagle at Ghost Dance occasions proper. These are the bow and arrow (59547), the braided horsehair (59554), and the pipe stem (59548). The bow is trimmed with crow feathers and bells. In Ghost Dancing it was used by Crows to aid in putting dancers into hypnotic trances. It could be used similarly at a Goodeagle ceremonial game in Ghost Dance days. When the Crows were dancing, a Crow Ghost Dance leader could take this bow from its place on the altar spread and hold it before the eyes of a dancer, etc. An arrow trimmed with an eagle feather accompanies the drum.

The string of braided horsehair is trimmed with chicken hawk and woodpecker feathers. For the game proper it rests on the altar spread. At Ghost Dances it was worn by Goodeagle.

The pipe stem was carried in Ghost Dancing; it was not used at the game, but left on the altar spread. It is trimmed with three pendant bunches of eagle feathers.

There is finally in the case a black horse tail with a small trimming of white crow feathers and a concealed arrowhead. These belonged to Goodeagle, and were used by him when he participated in the Doctor Dance. They had been kept in his hand game bundle.

Paraphernalia not included in the exhibit which would be essential to the demonstration of the game include two pipes, a horn spoon, and counters. The original game set when complete also included two leather rattles, one for each side, used in the Ghost Dancing in the intervals. The counters were white bone made to represent moon and sun.

Altar Arrangements

Upright before the altar is the forked stick, against which lean the two calumets, each from its associated side. Behind these the eight feather tally sticks are set erect before the altar spread, as at Mrs. Goodeagle's game, until they are put into play. Pipes and all other objects are placed on the altar spread, each on that side of the midline with which it is associated.

Official Arrangements

Five rixkita behind altar, a central ceremonial official and N 1 and N 2 for the Crows, S 1 and S 2 for the Eagles. Watchers are appointed by game owner for the entire game, one for each side; these function as at Mrs. Goodeagle's game. Guessers appointed by N 1 and S 1. An old man and a chief are stationed on each side of the eastern doorway. Two drums, at northwest and southwest, presided over by Seven Brothers and Seven Crows. Generally a fireplace with a fire burning in it. The game was played inside a lodge.

Smoke Offering

For this game there are two pipes, and two simultaneous offerings are made. It is not clear whether both smokers are chosen by the central rixkita or one by the rixkita of each side. Probably the latter is the case. According to informant, N 1 probably selected the north side smoker, prepared the pipe for him and gave it to him for the offering, while similarly S 1 officiated for the south side smoker. Wherever in the procedure the movements of the smokers may bring them into conflict, the south smoker has precedence, in terms of the Eagle emphasis of this game.

Both smokers rise simultaneously and proceed to the altar where each receives a pipe.

First Phase: Each makes a circuit of the fireplace, coming to west of the fireplace, facing east. The Eagle smoker arrives first and takes up the offerings at once, while the Crow smoker stands a few paces behind him and to one side (the south) out of his way. Offerings: Heaven, east (slantwise), south (slantwise), north (slantwise), west (by reaching right arm backward, or turning to face west), earth. (The pattern here is exactly like that of first phase of the smoke ritual of Beaver's hand game; both Beaver and Goodeagle were medicine men). After making these offerings of tobacco, the Eagle smoker moves away from the fireplace a few paces toward the north and waits there while the Crow smoker comes forward to the fireplace and makes the same series of offerings.

After both have made these offerings they proceed to positions for the pipe lighting. The Eagle smoker who stepped aside from the north continues clockwise to the northeast, where he squats for the pipe to be lit. At the same time the Crow smoker proceeds counter-clockwise through the south to the southeast, where he squats facing east. The two watchers do the pipe lighting, using braided sweetgrass from the bundle which must first be ignited with a brand from the fire. The north watcher lights the pipe at the northeast (thus, the pipe of the Eagle or south side smoker), and the south watcher lights the pipe at the southeast (the pipe of the north side smoker).[1]

The two smokers puff to get the pipes going, then both rise and proceed toward the east, the Eagle smoker clockwise, the Crow smoker counter-clockwise. As they come face to face at the east, each smoker offers the other his pipe. In so doing the smoke-offerer retains hold of the pipe, merely placing the mouthpiece to the other's lips. The manner is identical with that used in the third mode of the second phase of a smoke-offering when the pipe is offered by a ritual smoker to ceremonial officials. After this exchange of smoke from the pipes, both smokers proceed with the second phase.

Second Phase: First mode: The Eagle smoker (whose pipe was lit at northeast) now passes inside the Crow smoker (between fireplace and Crow) and proceeds clockwise through the south to a position west of the fireplace, facing east. After being passed, the Crow smoker follows him, waiting a few paces behind and to the south of the fireplace position while the Eagle smoker makes the offerings of this mode. Offerings: Puffs of smoke to each orientation to which a gift of tobacco was made in the first phase; usually four for heaven and four for earth, two for each of the other four orientations (but four for each of the six is correct); the order is as the first phase. As the Eagle smoker concludes the first mode and turns down the sacred pathway directly to the altar, the Crow smoker moves in to take his place at the fireplace facing east, and makes the same series of offerings.

Second mode: At the altar, Eagle smoker offers smoke to each of the leaning calumets (first the south or left, then the north or right), then moving forward offers puffs to the upright eagle feathers (in the usual way, giving a south emphasis, he can puff each one individually, puff the middle two and the outer two feathers, or simply puff once over the south four from center out and once over the north four from center out). Over the altar

[1] A type of intercrossing ritual symmetry which occurs in Doctor Dances.

proper, the smoker offers a puff over the south side and one over the north side; he may add individual puffs to such objects as rattles, special feather clusters, and the like. As the Eagle smoker leaves the altar to proceed clockwise to the Crow drum at the northwest, the Crow smoker comes from the fireplace to the altar and makes the same series of offerings. The Eagle smoker offers two puffs to the Crow drum, then making a clockwise circuit *(or turning the body clockwise and crossing between altar and fireplace)* to the Eagle drum, offers two puffs to that. The Crow smoker follows him around and makes similar offerings.

Third mode: Eagle smoker leaving Eagle drum proceeds to the altar, and offers the pipe to central rixkita, to S 1 and to N 1; Crow smoker follows him to altar and offers the other pipe to the same three. Eagle smoker proceeds clockwise to main two Crow drummers, offering them pipe; Crow smoker follows. Eagle smoker proceeds clockwise to main two Eagle drummers, giving them pipe; Crow smoker follows. Now Eagle smoker makes a clockwise circuit to the old man and chief at the doorway on the north side, and offers them the pipe, then crosses to the old man and chief south of the doorway and offers the pipe to them, the Crow smoker following suit. From here it is optional if the pipes are to be handed down the Crow side west to east, and the Eagle side east to west.

Third Phase: Full ritual form would include offerings of the pipe as ashes are emptied to the series followed in the first phase.

Fourth Phase: Two modes, following the form of the first and second modes of the second phase, as above, a motion for each puff of smoke.

Self-Blessing: Each smoker stands to his side of the sacred pathway between altar and fireplace, makes the self-blessing facing the rixkita who gave him the pipe, and returns it to that individual, who receives it with an arm-blessing and replaces it in altar position.

Play of the Game

The game was played for five or seven straight. In taking turns the counters were handed down both sides from west to east. The watchers retrieve counters when won, the guesser gives them out on his side.

The Game Intervals

The main singer of the winning side, who leads the Ghost Dancing of the intervals carries a leather rattle. The rixkita of the winning side holds game set and pipes aloft outside the circle of dancers. The winning singers sing one society song before the guessers are changed. Young Dog Dance songs were preferred by the Eagles, Horn Dance songs by the Crows.

Food Offering and Service

Details were not obtained. It is doubtful if a double offering was carried out, since at Doctor Dances where such a simultaneous double smoke offering occurs only one man makes a food offering.

The food was as usual set out at the east, buckets of corn being closest to the fireplace. The watchers received the food for the game owner, as at Mrs. Goodeagle's game, and set it out according to instructions.

The order of service was: main rixkita, S 1 and N 1 (all food first), 1 and 2 Crow and 1 and 2 Eagle drummers (all food next), old men and chiefs at doorway (all food third), then laymen. The watchers served the officials, servers were selected to serve the people.

MRS. WASHINGTON

One of the earliest of the Skiri hand games, developed by the main Skiri Ghost Dance prophet, little is recalled by Pawnee of this game except that in essentials it was as played later by Barclay White, Mrs. Washington's son, to whom she taught her ritual, and to whom she turned the game bundle over when she retired. It was one of the principal Eagle games of the Skiri.

The sacred corn tassels in the altar arrangement (see fig. 11) were probably part of Mrs. Washington's original bundle. It is said that at her game in the early days, corn seed for planting was ritually given out, suggesting a revival by Mrs. Washington of aspects of the corn planting ritual.

SKIRI JAKE

No information was secured about this game. It was merely recalled that in the Ghost Dance days Skiri Jake originated a ceremonial game which had disappeared with his death.

GEORGE BEAVER

Ownership and Affiliation

George Beaver, one of the famous medicine men of the last generation of great doctors, was affiliated with the Crow. He secured his game in visions, partly in the Ghost Dance. His game shows interrelations with old medicine men's concepts and ideology.

Originally the game was played in a special tent made by Beaver. The tent was dark blue with white spots all over it, representing hail. Storm concepts also appeared on his drum. This game was played either afternoon or night, a different face of the drum being used in each case. The demonstration was believed to be efficacious in bringing rain, and was often put up by someone who wanted rain.

Paraphernalia

Field Museum Nos. 71850—71858 were identified as the original Beaver hand game set. Included are a game drum, four forked sticks on which the drum is suspended when in use, two sets of bow and arrow, eight tally sticks, two leather rattles, and a bunch of feathers as a hair ornament. In use a pipe and spoon were also required, but it is possible that one of Beaver's doctor pipes was associated with this game set, though not kept in the game bundle.

Sticks, rattles and bows and arrows are decorated to show their game side affiliation. Of the eight tally sticks four are decorated with bald eagle feathers for south affiliation, four with black eagle feathers for north affiliation. In each case two feathers are attached by thongs to the top of the stick. The leather rattle, gourd shaped, for the south side is decorated with a soft light feather and a dark string, while the north rattle is trimmed with otter fur and has also a light feather attached. The bow and arrow for the south side are trimmed with bald eagle feathers, those for the north with black eagle feathers. The south bow has a circlet of fur at the top end, possibly otter or wildcat, to which the feather is attached. The north bow has a band of otter fur at the grasp.

The bunch of feathers, used as hair ornaments should be accompanied by one of opposite affiliation, but this is not present.

All of these objects including the drum are on exhibit. Only one side of the drum can be seen, and it was impossible at the time to have the case opened. The side seen has storm birds painted upon it in black. These are probably for the scissor-tailed red-breasted swallow, which is said to fly southward in flocks before the storm. The other half of the face has a representation of dark storm-clouds streaked with lightning. The storm half should be northward, the bird half southward when the drum is set in position at the center west. It is this storm face that is used for the game if played in the daytime, the other face being uppermost for a game demonstration at night.

Previous to our visit to the Museum, my informant had decribed one face of the drum as follows; and he felt sure that his description was accurate for the face not seen in the case. There was a picture of a black eagle, with streaks of lightning coming out at each side from under the wings, and from the eyes. The bird presents the clouds coming, and hitting the drum symbolizes thunder.

Interesting as regards this set, besides its storm connotation, is the dominant eagle symbolism, although Beaver is reliably said to have been affiliated with the Crow side. The extensive use of bird and animal emblems, and the avowed effect of a demonstration (to produce rain) indicates the content was determined by Beaver's functions as a medicine man. An individual who had Ghost Dance visions generally experienced in the content of the visions aspects of culture with which he was familiar, particularly because the visionary had to make an effort to recapture some aspect of the dying culture.

The pipe for this game set would be one with smooth pipestone bowl and smooth dogwood stem, the regular type of doctor pipe.

Altar

See fig. 6.

Official Arrangements

Four rixkita behind altar; one drum set between fireplace and altar at west, singers for each side congregated on that side; fireplace, usually with fire; probably, one or two tarutsius, but no watchers. Some Owls mixed with the Eagles of the south side. The owl is supposed to have the same power at night that the eagle has in daylight.

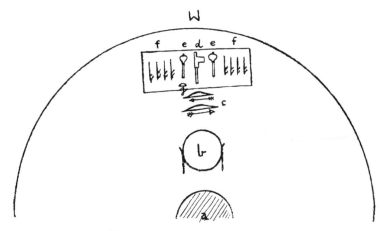

Figure 6. Altar Plan of Beaver

a - fireplace   e - rattles
b - drum   f - tally sticks
c - bows and arrows   g - spoon
d - pipe

Smoke Offering

N 1 prepares the pipe, selects offerer, gives and receives pipe.

First Phase: Clockwise circuit, west of fireplace, offerings: Heaven, east (slantwise), south (slantwise), north (slantwise), west (slantwise by reaching right arm backward), Earth. Clockwise to northeast where pipe is lit, probably by north tarutsius.

Second Phase: First Mode: Clockwise circuit to west of fireplace; offerings: Four puffs to each orientation to which a pinch of tobacco was offered in the first phase, *or* four puffs to Heaven, two to east, south, north and west, and four to Earth.

Second mode: To altar; offerings: One at head end of each set of bow and arrow (right or north, then left or south); one to each rattle (right, left); one over right or north side altar objects, one over left. To the drum. (2).

Third mode: To N 1, S 1, N 2, S 2. (This order, alternating from side in offering the main officials behind the altar, is definitely the order of smoking rituals for medicine men's ceremonies.) To main drummers. Optionally, to Crow men west to east, to Eagle men east to west.

Third Phase: A complete ritual form requires that offerings as ashes are deposited be made to the full series and order of orientations to which tobacco was offered in the first phase, and smoke in the first mode of the second phase.

Fourth Phase: First and second modes, as first and second modes of second phase above.

Self Blessing; return of pipe.

Play of the Game

When first played years ago Beaver asked Leadingfox, the putter-up, to decide the objective. He himself determined that the game was to be played even-up. Leadingfox chose twelve as the number of rubber-games. The game went on all night and part of the next day before one side won twelve games more than the other. Thereafter the game was played for four games even up, twelve being considered too long. The game was also played for seven games straight.

The turns are from west to east down both sides.

The guesser for each side carries the bow and arrow set of his side, returning these to the rixkita, along with the counters, in the intervals.

In this game, when the counters are being put in play by the guessers, there was no change of guessers for four misses by both, but guessing continued until the counters were in play.

The Game Intervals

The winning side singers lead three Ghost Dance circuits, the main singer carrying the leather rattle of his side. The dancing is inside the tent. The rixkita of the winning side holds game set aloft. Society songs were usually Young Dog Dance.

Food Offering and Service

The food is received and put at east of fireplace. The winning leader selects the corn offerer and gives him the spoon. The offerer fills spoon, and makes inclusive motions behind food.

First Phase: West of fireplace; offerings: as first phase of smoke offering.

Second Phase: First and second modes as first and second modes of second phase of smoke offering.

Self-Blessing; returns spoon.

The order of service: N 1, S 1, N 2, S 2, the main drummers, laymen usually west to east.

Closing remarks by winning leader usually conclude the occasion.

Special Note

This game is recalled as played to great excitement; many attempted during the game play as well as the interval Ghost Dancing, to induce visions in themselves.

Revival drums and lances of the Crow Society (raris kaka) may have been Beaver's and may have been used at his game. In that case the Crow lance would dominate the altar.[1]

MARK RUDDER

Ownership and Affiliation

Mark Rudder, a Skiri Ghost Dance leader, was affiliated with the Crows, and was in part responsible for the organization of the Seven Crow brothers.[2] Rudder derived his game in a vision. It was played in a tipi or lodge, or outdoors, afternoon or evening.

Paraphernalia

Pipe, eight tally sticks, white bones for counters, horn spoon, a cedar-wood cross topped with a soft eagle feather, three cedar sticks topped with four red-painted crow feathers, two sets of bow and arrow.

Several hand game objects in the Field Museum were identified as belonging to Rudder's set, although the game set was not present as a unit:

---

[1] See Chapter III: Revivals of the Societies.
[2] See Chapter II.

71649—1, 2.   Two crow feathered cedar sticks for watchers or guessers.

71653—   A crow feathered stick worn by Rudder himself.

These three are made as follows: a sharp pointed stick, knobby at one end, has set around the knob end four crow feathers. The quill tips are bound down to the stick below the knob by wrapping fine sinews around tightly. All are about the same length. That used by Rudder has the stick painted red. This one of Rudder's and one of the other two agree in that they are bound with a short wrapping of otter fur, and have a cross or x incised into the top of the knob. The third is plain. The otter fur and cross associate Rudder's and the one stick with the Crow side, while the plain stick ornament was used by the watcher or guesser of the Eagle side.

71603—   This is a whistle decorated with a leather sheath and pendant feathers, which was used by Rudder in starting his game.

71603 (apparently same number). This is a revival lance, made by Rudder for the Hatuxka society lance of former times. The reed? is covered with hide. Thongs are inserted in cuts down the side, and each end of each thong has a short crow feather attached; there are about 75 crow feather attachments. At the top end of the hollow staff are two eagle feathers.

Altar

See fig. 7.

Official Arrangements

Four rixkita behind altar; two tarutsius prescribed, both must be of Crow side; two watchers; fireplace, usually with fire; two drums, one for each side, presided over after the formation of the organizations by the Seven Eagles and Seven Crows.

Rudder costumes for his demonstration: He wears a shirt which is black on the left side (for the north horizon), yellow on the right side (for the south horizon), representing the darkness of the north, the brightness of the south, respectively. He paints his face left cheek black, right cheek red. In his hair he wears the central crow feathered stick, which is first placed at the altar. He paints the faces of two watchers like his own.

Special arrangements are involved in relation to the watchers, and pre-play dancing. These occur after the smoke offering.

Smoke Offering

N 1 prepares pipe, selects offerer, and gives and receives pipe.

First Phase:

Circuit, west of fireplace, offerings: Heaven, Earth, West. Pipe lit at northeast by tarutsius.

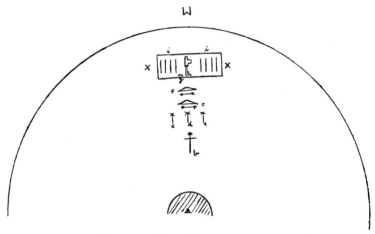

Figure 7. Altar Plan of Rudder

a - fireplace   g - spoon
b - cedar cross   h - pipe
c - ornaments for guessers   i - tally sticks
d - ornament of owner   x - positions of watchers
e - f - bows and arrows

Second Phase:
First Mode:
West of fireplace, offerings: Heaven (4), Earth (4), West (4).
Second Mode:
To altar, offerings: cross (5) (Top, crossing, right extremity of horizontal, left extremity of horizontal, base); one for each erect feathered stick (central, right, left); one at head end of each set of bow and arrow (right, left); one over each side of altar proper (right, left). To Crow drum (2); to Eagle drum (2).
Third Mode:
To N 1, N 2; to S 1, S 2; to 1 and 2 of Seven Crows; to 1 and 2 of Seven Eagles; to Rudder possibly, wherever he stands. Optionally, Crows west to east, Eagles east to west.
Third Phase:
West of fireplace. Offerings as first phase above.
Fourth Phase:
First and second modes as first and second modes of second phase above.
Self-Blessing. Returns pipe.

Play of the game
The game was played for five or seven games straight; possibly also even up.

During the smoke-offering, the two watchers sit in special places, each on his side alongside the altar-cloth, which puts each diagonally in front of the assistant rixkita of his side. After the smoke-offering, these arise, and each takes one bow and arrow and a counter, and puts his feathered stick in the hair.

Mark Rudder rises, and calls on the two groups of singers to join in singing one song. This was a Ghost Dance revival song of the Crow Lance society. Everyone begins to yell. Mark Rudder leads, dancing like a crow, with the north or Crow-man watcher just behind him and the south or Eagle Crow-man watcher, bringing up the rear. Making a clockwise circuit they dance clear around the fireplace close to the people. The step is a fast running step, with the arms bent sidewise like wings. The movement and posture are intended to imitate the crow, and to be at about the requisite speed. The watchers carry bow and arrow in left hand, and the white bone counter in the right. Rudder has nothing in his hands but has the whistle in his mouth. They stop when the song is finished, their position being immaterial.

According to informants, "Rudder danced this Crow performance to enliven the spirits of the people. One's mind may be wandering; the performance is intended to concentrate the people's attention on the game in hand."

After the Crow dance, the north watcher makes a complete clockwise circuit, then goes to someone on the Crow side and gives him the counter (thus constituting him guesser for the first game; the choice is made earlier by the N 1 rixkita). Similarly, the south watcher, after a half circuit gives the counter to one on the Eagle side who is to be guesser. Informant was not sure whether the watchers retained the bows and arrows and crow feathered sticks or replaced them on altar.

Now the Crow side singers sing two songs of some old society, usually for this game, the Horn Dance. Then the guessers arise and put the counters in play.

The Game Intervals

During the usual Ghost Dancing of the intervals, the winning leader holds the set aloft at west and east. For society songs *raris arusa* songs (Horse Society) were preferred.

Food Offering and Service

The cooking for this game was done in the game tipi or lodge or outside, usually by the two official tarutsius (who for this game differ from the watchers). They bring the food in. It is received and placed in the usual position east of the fireplace.

The winning leader selects the corn offerer, and gives him the horn spoon. The offerer fills the spoon and makes the inclusive motions behind all the food.

Food Offering proper:

First Phase:

West of fireplace as first phase of smoke-offering.

Second Phase:

First and second modes, as first and second modes of second phase of smoke-offering.

Self-Blessing, return of spoon.

Service, by tarutsius and others. Order: N 1 and N 2; S 1 and S 2; 1 and 2 Crow drummers; 1 and 2 Eagle drummers. Laymen, usually west to east down both sides, the other drummers being served as their position is reached.

The closing remarks by winning leader, and all disband.

JOHN MOSES I

Ownership and Affiliation

John Moses, a Crow, secured his older game in a Ghost Dance vision. The game was second in ceremonial importance to Rudder's among the Skiri Crow Ghost Dance hand games. It was usually played in the North Round House (earlier a lodge), afternoon or evening. After Moses' conversion to the Baptist faith, he discarded his older game and made a church game. A set in the Field Musum of Natural History purchased by George Dorsey was identified as the old Moses set.

Paraphernalia

The bundle objects belonging to this game[1] are F. M. 59383—1 to 15. These include eight dogwood tally sticks, two large crosses, two forked uprights and a cross bar, two pointed uprights, and two small wooden crosses used as counters associated with these pieces but unnumbered. There was no pipe of this serial number; probably the pipe was not sold with the set. Nor was there a horn spoon.

The 8 tally sticks (59383—5, 6, 10—15) are 20¼ in. long.

The two small crosses, identical (no number) are 1¼ by ¾ in.

The tall crosses for uprights (59383—1,2) are 34½ in. long, with a 7 in. crossbar.

---

[1] These and other identifications were made at the Museum by Mark Evarts.

Forked uprights (59383—3, 4) 24 in. long.

The cross-bar (59383—9) 28 in. long.

Two pointed uprights (59383—7, 8) 25 in. long.

In addition, John Moses had in the old days a red painted cedar stick, ornamented at the top with four crow feathers set radially. This was before the altar until the game, then worn by Moses.

A set of four small wooden counters, two and two, Field Museum numbers 71654—1, 2, and 71654—3,4, probably belonged to John Moses, and were used alternatively to the two crosses above. They are illustrated by Culin, p. 274, fig. 355, who describes them as "set of four sticks, 1¾ inches in length, marked in pairs alike, one pair with six notches on one side and one notch on the other, and the other with incised crosses, one on each side of each end of the stick." The meaning of the markings was unknown to my informant, but he observed of the alternative sets of counters that one set or the other involved a stricter game.

Altar Arrangements

See figure 8.

This game refers to the human sacrifice of the Morning Star bundle. It should be considered in the light of the identification of the Crucifixion with the scaffold sacrifice.[1]

The two upright crosses are symbols of the two Morning Star bundles of the Skiri Pawnee as well as of the Christian cross; the forked uprights with the cross-bar represent the scaffold used in the ceremonial sacrifice.[2]

Official Arrangements

Four rixkita behind altar; two drums presided over by the Seven Brothers and the Seven Crows; fireplace in which a fire must be burning. Probably tarutsius.

Smoke Offering

N 1 prepared the pipe and selected the offerer.

Probable structure of the offering proper:

First Phase:

West of fireplace, Heaven, Earth, East, West. Pipe lit at northeast by tarutsius.

Second Phase:

First Mode:

Heaven (4), Earth (4), East (4), West (4).

Second Mode:

---

[1] See Chapter II.

[2] It does not, however, reproduce the scaffold structure.

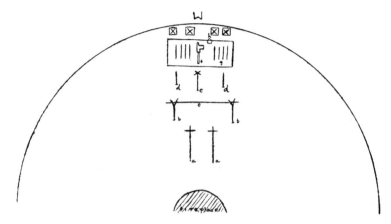

Figure 8. Altar Plan of John Moses I

a - tall crosses   f - pipe
b - forked uprights   g - tally sticks
c - cross-bar   h - spoon
d - straight uprights   x - rixkita
e - crow-feathered stick

North cross (1, or 5), south cross (1 or 5), middle of cross-bar, north forked upright, south forked upright; if other erect objects, crow-feathered stick, north vertical, south vertical. Over altar proper, one over north half, one over south half. To North drum (2), to south drum (2).

Third Mode:

To N 1 and N 2, to S 1 and S 2; to 1 and 2 of the Seven Crows; to 1 and 2 of the Seven Eagles. To Crow men on north from west to east; to Eagle men on south from east to west.

Third Phase:

West of fireplace; offerings with ashes two for each offering of tobacco in First Phase above.

Fourth Phase:

First and Second modes as first and second modes of the Second Phase.

Self-Blessing, return of pipe.

Play of the Game

The game was played for five straight. No aftermaths or special complications of play are remembered. The turns were from west to east on both sides.

The Game Intervals

Usual interval Ghost Dancing, unaccompanied by instruments. Rixkita of winning side holds set aloft. Old society songs of any of the old Skiri societies were sung; Crazy Dog Dance songs and Old War Dance songs were favorites.

The Food Offering and Service

I do not have details on the corn offering; it would have to be consonant with the smoke-offering. The service was: N 1 and N 2, S 1 and S 2, two main Crow singers, two main Eagle singers, laymen.

BOYCHIEF'S MOTHER

No details could be secured on the Crow game of Boychief as it was played by his mother, before it was turned over to him. In essentials few changes were introduced by Boychief. The original bundle and set were derived by his mother in Ghost Dance visions. Hers was one of the earliest Skiri games.

EMMETT PIERSON I

Ownership and Affiliation

Emmett Pierson, a chief of the Skiri, who died in 1930, was affiliated with the Eagles and in visions obtained two ritual hand games. Information was secured on only one of these. It is the most complicated ritual of all the hand games. In it all the Ghost Dance hand games were merged, and along with these bundles and paraphernalia of revived societies were brought together. The game was demonstrated by Pierson only in the spring. In intention, said an informant, "it was like an opening up of all bundles ceremony."

Paraphernalia

Pierson's game set included eight unfeathered dogwood sticks, two tubular bone counters, a whole eagle skin, two leather rattles (one white for south, one black for north), a red pipe with smooth stem, a horn spoon, a long eagle tail feather, two sets of bow and arrows, and a sack of crumbled cedar leaves. The miniature bows are stringed; each bow is accompanied by two arrows; bows and arrows are trimmed with eagle feathers, black for north, bald for south.

In bringing all the games together, the paraphernalia of each game set was brought into the lodge in which Pierson's game was played. Such sets were identically the same as used at games demonstrated by their owners.

In addition a number of the revived societies or dances were represented by their sacred objects.

Altar Arrangements

The altar of Emmett Pierson's own game set is indicated in chart figure 9. The whole altar was set in a position equivalent to N 1. See chart, figure 10.

At each of the numbered stations, 1 to 9, indicated in figure 10, the game owner of the individual game set has the altar for his game arranged exactly as it would be for demonstration of that individual game.

The altar arrangements of the sacred objects of revived societies and dances, stationed at points A to F on figure 10, are similar to generic patterns.

Official Arrangements

The formal positions or stations in relation to each other of the games and societies brought together was decided by Pierson. An exception limiting his control was that the Horn Dance had to be on the north side, but its station in reference to other games and societies on the north was determined by Pierson. My informant described from memory a systematic orientation of the games and societies which would be ritually sound. This is indicated in

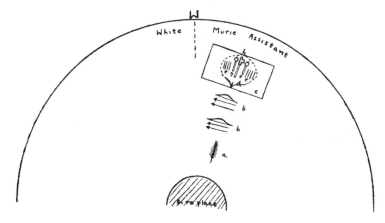

Figure 9. Altar Plan of Emmett Pierson I

a - eagle feather   e - tally sticks
b - bows and arrows   f - g - black rattles
c - spread   h - pipe
d - eagle-skin

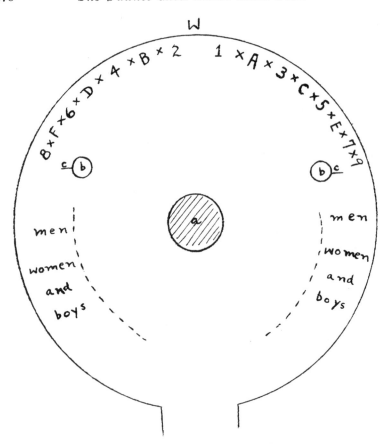

Figure 10. Plan of Pierson I Game

a - fireplace
b - drums
c - main drummers' positions

x - men seated between ceremonial
stations

Game Altars:
1 - Pierson (Eagle)
2 - White (Eagle)
3 - Moses I (Crow)
4 - Yellowhorse (Eagle)
5 - White Elk (Crow)
6 - Goodeagle (Eagle)
7 - Eustace (Crow)
8 - Morgan (Eagle)
9 - Allen (Crow)

Dance Society Altars:
A - Horn Dance
B - Old War Dance
C - Young Dog Dance
D - Crazy Dog Dance
E - Roached Heads
F - Big Horses

figure 10. The idea here is that the games are divided into groups
pitted against each other. The games placed on one side were

through their owners affiliated with that side. In this way a group of Crow games opposed a group of Eagle games. Between the games on each side the societies and dances were stationed, so that on each side there was an alternation of altars: game, society or dance, game, society or dance, etc.

The game owners, if men, generally presided over their own altars. If women owned a game set, and this game participated, a male relative was selected by the game owner to take charge of the altar.

Pierson did not, however, sit behind his own altar. He generally chose James Murie to preside for him; and in later times, after Murie's death, Charley Allen. Pierson himself stood or sat anywhere about, in order to direct proceedings.

Similarly for the altars of the society and dance revivals, men presided, chosen by the owners. Those recalled for the stations A to F of the chart are:

		Owner or Controller	In charge usually
A	Horn Dance	Mrs. Cover	Willy Wood
B	Old War Dance	Mrs. Washington	John Box
C	Young Dog Dance	Emmett Pierson	Moses, or Pratt
D	Crazy Dog Dance	White Feather, Skidi Tom	various men
E	Roached Heads	Knifechief's grandmother	Charley Knifechief
F	Big Horses	Mrs. Sodwell	Eli Sodwell

Those called owners or controllers in these cases are not individuals in possession by inheritance of the ancient bundles of these Pawnee societies and dances, but individuals who through Ghost Dance experiences secured a sanction to revive the memory of these activities.

Behind each of these altars, in addition to the man in charge, there was a man as assistant. Whenever the one in charge leaves the altar for any purpose, such as to smoke the pipe of the bundle, or for a game to play at the west, the assistant moves into place behind the altar. On the north side, assistants sit to the left (east) of those in charge, on the south side to the right (east).

My informant laid no stress on band affiliations of the game owners. He felt that at any time when Pierson demonstrated the game he would bring together all the available Ghost Dance hand games (of all bands) and all available revivals.

Those games which were considered more important ceremonially were placed nearer the west. This is indicated for example by the position given the games of Allen and Morgan, as opposed to the others. The Moses game indicated is the early orthodox hand game of Moses, Moses I.

Naturally at no two occasions when Pierson carried out his ritual was the exact arrangement duplicated. Games became extinct from time to time through the deaths of their owners, and revivals also died out. Games and revivals could be added by invitation of Pierson as they were developed in Ghost Dance visions, and came to be recognized.

Between the stations of the game and dance altars (save at the west between White and Pierson) one man was stationed to demarcate the "booths" or positions. A small space was left between the main two bundles, White's and Pierson's at the west, for the regular tally keeping. Here a cloth spread was laid out.

Pierson's game presided from a position equivalent to N 1, that is, to the main position on the Crow side, although it was an Eagle game. Hence in this game arrangement, the two bundles or game sets which led, were both Eagle games.

Two drums are required at this game, set at the eastern extremities of the arc of altars. The drums are in charge of the Seven Brothers and the Seven Crows. For a demonstration there are two official tarutsius.

All others present, men, women and children, occupy the remaining space between the eastern extremity of the altars, and the doorway, on both sides.

Preparations

Emmett Piersons fasts for the day before the game demonstration. He has had the lodge cleaned out and prepared. Before any others are present he remains alone with the rixkita who is to be in charge of his bundle (Murie) inside the lodge. At Pierson's direction, Murie takes a shovel full of coals from a fire (usually brought in) and puts these on the ground east of the fireplace (between fireplace and doorway). Murie then takes crumbled cedar leaves from the sack kept in the bundle, and proceeding clockwise through the north to the coals, offers a handful of the leaves aloft and places them on the coals. Then he suffuses himself in the smoke. Pierson does likewise. Should anyone else happen to come in as this procedure is taking place, he must also suffuse himself.

The coals and ashes of the leaves are then put into the fireplace where a fire is to be made and maintained during the game. After this, the Pierson bundle is opened and while it is arranged at the west, all the game bundle and society bundle custodians enter with their bundles, and take the positions to which they are directed by Pierson.

After all the bundles have been opened and are in order, the occasion is ceremonially opened by the ritual smoke offering.

Smoke Offering

When all are officially assembled, and the bundles lie open in their altar arrangements, Pierson speaks:

"Now is the time to smoke. Now I want you all to fill your pipes." By this he means that each man in charge of an altar should fill the pipe which lies on that altar. For this smoke offering ritual a pipe from every bundle present is smoked. It is prepared by the one in charge of the bundle, and smoked by him.

The order in which these smoke is not material except that Murie, that is, the man in charge of Pierson's altar, arises and smokes first, and that Barclay White, in charge of the main Eagle side altar, follows Murie. When each pipe has been filled, it is left on its altar. As each smoker arises his assistant moves over into the vacated main seat, and then hands the filled pipe to the smoker.

Murie makes the smoke offering according to Pierson's ritual. Each of the smokers who follows him smokes in the same way. That is, regardless of how the pipe of any game set bundle or society-dance bundle, would be smoked on an occasion dominated by that bundle, here it is smoked in the ritual manner of Pierson. To this there is one exception, a second pipe of the Horn Dance, which requires a separate individual ritual (see below).

Murie smokes in the following way:

First Phase:

Clockwise circuit coming back to west of fireplace facing east. Offerings: Heaven, turning to face west, westward; facing east again, Earth. Clockwise to northeast where tarutsius lights pipe with brand from fire (probably there was braided sweetgrass in this bundle).

Second Phase:

Clockwise to west of fireplace, facing east.

First Mode:

Offerings: Heaven (4); slantwise west (4), facing west; Earth (4); around southern horizon east to west (2), once for Sun, once for Moon; due north (1), by turning head, for the North Star.

Second Mode:

To altar of Pierson, by complete circuit, or turning and proceeding down sacred pathway. Offerings: Once to erect feather; once to each end of bows and arrows, tail end at right or north, then head end at left or south; once to eagle's nose; once over north side of altar objects (rixkita say "nawa"), once over south side (rixkita say "nawa"). To Crow drum (2) (drummers say "nawa"); to Eagle drum (2) (drummers say "nawa").

At this point the usual second mode would end, but for this ritual a complete form requires that the second mode include the altar objects of all altars. The smoker now proceeds through a complete clockwise circuit of the fireplace, and goes to altar A (Horn Dance), where he offers a puff to the Crow lance standing before the altar, and once over each side of the altar, first north side then south (or individually to objects on the altar); as he does this the man in charge of the altar says "nawa." The smoker now proceeds directly to altar 3, then to the other altars in the following order: C, 5, E, 7, 9 (that is, down the north side altars, west to east), clockwise through the east and to 8, F, 6, D, 4, B, 2 (that is, up the south side altars, east to west). The offerings to altar objects of the games would be exactly as this mode of the smoke offering of a game dominated by that game bundle, since most of the details of offerings for altar objects are generic.

The form of this mode is of course ritually very lengthy, and while I am in some doubt that the offerer would carry out all the detail, in theory this is the correct form. I am not certain what formal manner of telescoping the mode would be used, but it is probable that standing back from the Pierson altar, the smoker could offer puffs of smoke around both horizons from west to east or from west to the point at which the arc of altars ends on south and north. This he would do by directing his mouth toward the west and puffing out smoke around the horizon as he turned his head eastward through north, and eastward through south. These would be inclusive offerings, "everything on this side, and everything on that side."

Third Mode:

The smoker now proceeds to offer the pipe to individuals as follows: N 1 (this will be the assistant who has taken Murie's place while he makes the offering); the 1 and 2 Crow drummers, the 1 and 2 Eagle drummers; and those in charge of the altars in the order: north side, from west to east, south side from east to west. Those in charge will be the assistants who have taken the places of those making smoke offerings.

For such a lengthy second phase, it is more than probable that the pipes are smoked out before the third mode can be completed; if it is carried out, however, the pipe is handled by all as if it were burning.

Third Phase:

To west of fireplace. Offerings as ashes are loosened: Heaven (2); west (2), turning to face west for offering and turning back to deposit ashes on rim of fireplace: earth (2).

Fourth Phase:

First Mode:

Heaven (4), west (4), earth (4); slant east (2), around southern horizon (2), once for sun, once for moon; north (2).

Second Mode:

A complete ritual performance would involve carrying out the form of the second mode of the second phase, as above, a sacramental motion replacing each puff of smoke.

Self-Blessing:

Murie stands before the Pierson altar, just to north of the sacred pathway, facing the assistant who has taken his place. He returns the pipe to the latter, who receives it with an arm blessing and replaces it on the altar. The other smokers stand in each case before the altar to which the pipe belongs, a little to the east of directly in front, make the self-blessing and return the pipe to the one who is temporarily in charge.

The smoker for each of the altars follows the Murie offering in detail. First in the procession of smokers, is Murie, then White, then Wood. The order of the other smokers is not material. It more or less followed the arrangement in which the bundle altars were placed by Pierson, alternating from side to side.

The divergence of the smoke offerings of many of the games from the form they must follow here, is not great, since for most games the ritual includes Heaven, Earth and West as basic.

Special Smoke Offering

When all the smokers have finished, Pierson announces, "There's one more thing. He's (indicating Willy Wood in charge of the Horn Dance) got to smoke here yet." There are two ritual smoke offerings for the Horn Dance. The first has been carried out with the main pipe, following the Pierson ritual pattern. Now the smoker rises again to smoke alone. He uses another pipe belonging to the bundle. He does not have a regular pipe tamper, but uses anything that is considered "dead," such as a dead sunflower stalk. According to informant, "this is because everything is dead (in Horn Dance ideology). The idea is that the smoker is a priest and his ritual must carry out the bible ways."

First Phase:

Wood proceeds through a circuit clockwise until he reaches the northwest of the fireplace (the fireplace is said, however, to be conceptually unrelated to the offering). Facing north, Wood offers a pinch of tobacco northward and casts it northward on the ground. He moves clockwise to northeast where pipe is lit with a brand from the fire.

Second Phase:

Clockwise circuit to northwest, where facing north Wood puffs four times to the north.

Third Phase:

Wood then immediately loosens the ashes, making two offers toward the north as he does so, and deposits the ashes on the ground before him, as he faces north.

Fourth Phase:

Wood makes four sacramental motions over the empty pipe toward the north, touching the ashes at his feet each time.

No self-blessing. Wood proceeds through a clockwise circuit until he stands before the Horn Dance altar. He hands the pipe back to his assistant, who receives it without arm blessing (their hands must not touch). Wood takes his place. The dead stick used as a pipe tamper is now cast away.

Reference:

The Horn Dance is associated with the concept of Pahukatawa. My informant remarked about this smoke offering, "This smoke is for the Holy Ghost. Pahukatawa is the Holy Ghost. The Holy Ghost is placed in the North, the same way as the North Star. Everything is supposed to go around him. The Holy Ghost is also thought to be the Morning Star in the East because God sent Christ in the East." He pointed out that this Holy Ghost (Pahukatawa) was a Pawnee conception strictly. "He was a man who appeared several times to the Pawnee; he didn't like their ways and went east."

This and several other remarks indicated an attempt to assimilate the conception of the Holy Ghost to Pahukatawa. The attempt was inconsistent, at times merging the Pahukatawa conception with the Crucifixion, and at times straying into further amplification of the identification of the Morning Star with Christ and Christian ideas, as in the following:

"This man was once alive on earth among the Pawnee. When a young man, he was killed among the Sioux. Every little child stuck a stick into his body. He was killed in spite of his good ways, even as Christ was killed, in spite of the fact that he knew everything that happened and would happen on earth and in heaven. After they killed him, the spirits raised him up to heaven (that is, some kind of bird carried his body away), and he came to life again.

Afterwards he was around among the Pawnee and would tell them what was going to happen, and when he went away he became the Morning Star. While he was here they used to smoke to the North; that's why they keep on doing it for him even though he is in the East."

Play of the Game

The object of game play for Pierson's game is for one side to win seven rubber games. At the start, Pierson plays against White. Four tally sticks belonging to each set are used, being placed on their respective sides on a special spread between the Pierson and White altars; one counter of each game set is used.

In putting the counters in play, the game is officially opened by the south side. Thus the guesser of the Eagle side hides first, the Crow guesser guesses first. Meanwhile the singers of the Eagle side (around White's drum) begin the singing. Murie selects the Crow guesser giving him a white bone, White selects the Eagle guesser giving him a tuft of hair. The turns are from west to east on both sides.

At the conclusion of a rubber game, the losing game set is withdrawn from play, and the next set of that side is used for the second rubber game against the set which won in the first. With the arrangements

South Eagles	North Crows
White	Pierson
Yellowhorse	Moses
Goodeagle	White Elk
Morgan	Eustace
	Allen

if the first game is won by the Eagles, in the second White's set opposes that of Moses; if by the Crows, then in the second game Pierson's set opposes that of Yellowhorse. If one side continues to win in such a manner that Pierson opposes Morgan and the Eagles again lose, Pierson will again oppose White.

When Pierson's set opposes that of White, at the start, Murie and White keep the tally. The four sticks used from Pierson's set and the counter are those which would normally lie on the south side of his altar spread; those from White's the sticks which would normally be on the north side of his altar spread. In changing game sets, the four sticks and counter of the losing side are retired, being returned to their place on the altar to which they belong. Should White lose the first game, he replaces his sticks on his altar, and moves slightly southward. Tom Yellowhorse now comes from his game altar, bringing four sticks and a counter, and takes the place made vacant by White. For this next game Yellowhorse and Murie, sitting at central west, keep tally. At the altar of Yellowhorse's game the assistant takes charge. A game set, such as that of Allen, which normally uses 12 tally sticks, uses here only four, as the others.

If it comes to a 6—6 tie score, "the last game is played very hard by both sides as it will decide who is strongest in belief. If one wins it is said, 'God has taken pity on you'." I do not know of any aftermath for tie play.

The Game Intervals

When a rubber game is won, the main singers of the winning side, to the number of two, three or four, arise and lead several circuits of Ghost Dancing. The main singer gets the two rattles from Pierson. If the Crows have won, the main singer must use the black (Crow side rattle) himself, and give the lighter one to any other of the leading singers; if the Eagles win, the main Eagle singer carries the white rattle, and gives the black to another. The rixkita in charge of the altar of the winning side, arises and takes the game set which has been in play (viz. the four sticks of his altar used, the four sticks of the opposing set used, and the counters used) and holds this aloft at west and east of the circle of Ghost Dancers.

The change of game sets is made after the Ghost Dancing.

When the dancers are all seated again, the singers of the side which has just won and led the Ghost Dance, lead in the singing of a song associated with any one of the society or dance altars represented on that side: for Crows, in the diagram arrangement, Horn Dance, Young Dog Dance, or Roached Heads; for Eagles, Old War Dance, Crazy Dog Dance, Big Horses.

In singing one of these society dances, the paraphernalia of the dance represented at the altar is used. For example, should the Horn Dance be sung by the Crows after winning a rubber game: Murie would tell Willy Wood, in charge of the Horn Dance, "Take your drum over there for the Horn Dance." Wood would take the Horn Dance drum and the five drumsticks from before the Horn Dance altar, and go over to the position in which the Crow singers have been placed. The hand game drum in use there would be moved aside, and the Horn Dance drum put in its place. The five drumsticks belonging to this drum must be used with it. After the Horn Dance song, Wood would return drum and sticks to the Horn Dance altar, and the hand game drum would be replaced in its position.

A regular Horn Dance song would be sung, and some present familiar with the old dance would arise and dance.

At the end of the game play, the old form was for the winning side (that which had won seven games, which would also be the side which had won the last rubber game played) to lead ten ghost dance circuits, closing with the finishing song.

In the intervals after the singing, speeches could be made by those desiring to address the gathering.

Food Offering and Service

The tarutsius for each side is responsible for bringing in the food and placing it in accordance with directions of Pierson at the east between fireplace and doorway. The main cooking is likely to be done at a nearby house, and eight boys carry the food down, delivering it to the two tarutsius. The buckets of corn form an arc between the rest of the food and the fireplace. The number of buckets does not matter, twenty or even more being remembered. When the food is placed, and the tarutsius have taken their places, the rixkita in charge of the winning side, Murie or White, speaks:

"Now here we are. We won the hand game today. We worship God. Now here's the food before us. Now we must have one to look up to Heaven with the food. Whatever he asks God to provide for us, God may give us. This year we had a poor crop, that's why we offer to God very often, maybe next year we may have more crops, we may raise good food. Now we're going to eat the food before us."

Then he calls someone, usually one of the leaders or main singers, from the winning side (his own side), to make the offering. The offerer, for example Moses, for the Crow side, receives the spoon from Murie with an arm blessing. As he is taking the spoon, Murie may say in substance, "May God spare us living here together a while longer. Now take this spoon."

Moses proceeds with the offering. Pierson may go along and stand beside him to tell him what to do.

Filling the Spoon:

Offerer proceeds clockwise from the altar to the east, and going between corn buckets and fireplace, fills spoon by taking from each bucket individually, from north to south (left to right, as he moves between buckets and fireplace), *or* by taking corn from the middle bucket, the one at the south end, and after a body turn, the one at the north end. Offerer should, if he has taken from each bucket, now make a complete clockwise circuit of fireplace coming back to east behind all the food to make two inclusive gestures over the assembled food; if he has taken from middle and end buckets he finishes at north end of the arc of buckets and proceeds directly around the food to east of it, facing west for the gestures.

Food Offering Proper:

First Phase:

Clockwise to west of fireplace, facing east. Offerings: Heaven, west, earth. For the offering to earth, he merely places on the ground whatever corn is left on the spoon after the other offerings. "That is for Mother Earth. That's why we say, Mother Earth received everything."

Second Phase:

First Mode:

Spoon placed on ground at left; touching corn, pressing it into ground, rubbing hands, etc. Offerings: Heaven (4), West (4)—facing west, touching the corn only before the first motion—, earth (4), then slantwise east (1) for Morning Star, around the Southern horizon (2)—once for Sun, once for Moon, due north (1) for North Star.

Second Mode:

Picks up spoon, proceeds through clockwise circuit and to Pierson's altar. Offerings: As in second mode of second phase of smoke offering; a motion with spoon for each puff of smoke; also as in second mode of fourth phase of smoke offering: a motion over spoon for each motion along empty pipe. Similarly, motions at drums: Crow drum (2), Eagle drum (2).

At this point, the offerer telescopes the form, avoids the ritual need of going to each altar and making sacramental blessings over each and every sacred object, by coming clockwise to the west, standing midway between fireplace and altar, and as he faces west, making two inclusive motions around over all the altars. With right arm, he sweeps his hand from west around symbolically over the north altar, with left hand from west over the south altars. All say "nawa."

Self-Blessing, standing before Murie. Returns pipe to Murie who receives it with an arm-blessing.

Service:

Murie selects four from the Crow side to serve on that side, and tells White to select four for the Eagle side. Dishes are given out first when everything is quiet; these are dishes brought by the individuals present for their own use. Ceremonial officials would be served their food in sacred or ceremonial plates if Pierson's bundle had a special set of wooden plates to be so used.

The Order of Service is:

Murie and his assistant; White and his assistant (these four simultaneously). The Crow drummers and the Eagle drummers (simultaneously). The rest of the altars simultaneously down the two sides from west to east; while other servers on each side serve laymen from east to west.

When all have eaten the affair is at an end. Some may speak before the assemblage breaks up. The winning leader usually offers the closing remarks before all go out.

Note on Special Food Offering

Emmett Pierson sometimes made the food offering himself at his game. He had a special way. He took the erect feather from before the altar and put it in his hair. He told everyone to watch him. The drums are kept going a little. After Pierson fills the horn spoon in the usual way, he comes clockwise to the west of the fireplace. Facing east, he raises the spoonful of corn aloft. As he does so, all are quiet, and the drums are silent. Emmett begins to yell in a high-pitched voice "heeee..." and as he lowers the pitch he lowers the corn toward the ground. When he puts it on the ground, all present yell loudly and the drums beat. He repeats this motion and sound four times, and each time the solo and chorus are repeated. This completes the first phase of the corn offering when Pierson does it himself; there are just these four motions upward, rather than special motions upward, westward and earthward.

EMMET PIERSON II

Details were not secured on this game. It was a simpler hand game, more like the others, than is the main Pierson game. Usually Pierson played it collaboratively with his brother, Lonechief. Whoever won was supposed to have greater faith.

This was one of two or three collaborative or bundle-opposition games. This second game of Pierson's was played at any season, was considered less hazardous than Pierson's principal game, and less difficult.

LONECHIEF

Lonechief is said not only to have used his game bundle in collaborative opposition to Pierson's second game set, but also to have demonstrated with his bundle alone. I have no detailed information. It was probably a Crow game.

BARCLAY WHITE

Ownership and Affiliation

Barclay White, an Eagle, received his bundle from his mother, Mrs. Washington. She turned over the bundle to White some time before her death. She was still living when Barclay had a vision, in terms of which he altered the game ritual a little, and added conceptual implications.

One time he fell asleep, and in his dream vision he saw many children playing with corn tassels, and someone spoke to him and said, "This that you have is for the children." When he plays they try to select young people to do the guessing. Informants could not say what other changes had been made. The five corn tassels of the altar were almost certainly part of the original bundle and its ritual.

The game was played in a lodge, later in the North Round House, afternoon or evening.

Paraphernalia

The bundle included a wild cat hide, eight unfeathered cedar tally sticks, two soft pieces of hair for counters, five corn tassels, a pipe, a spoon, and probably a round rattle.

The five corn tassels are said to represent the five members of a family: father, mother, son, son's wife and child.

Altar

See fig. 11.

Official Arrangements

Four rixkita behind altar; two drums presided over by the Seven Eagles and Seven Crows for the respective sides; usually two tarutsius, one for each side; fireplace, with fire only when the cooking is done in the game lodge (originally it was).

Smoke Offering

S 1 prepares the pipe, selects offerer.

First Phase: Clockwise circuit, west of fireplace, offerings: Heaven, Earth. To northeast where pipe is lit by tarutsius.

Second Phase: First mode: Clockwise to west of fireplace; offerings: Heaven (4), Earth (4), probably west (4).

Second mode: To altar. Puffs to five corn tassels, once to each (middle, s—1, n—1, s—2, n—2). To nose of wildcat (2), over rattle (2). Once over left, south side; once over right, north side. To north Crow drum (2); to south Eagle drum (2).

Third mode: To S 1, N 1, S 2, N 2. To 1 and 2 of Seven Crows;

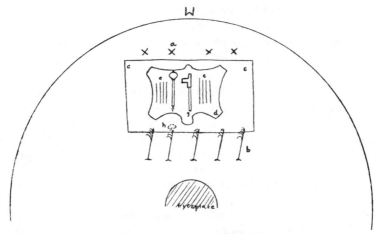

Figure 11. Altar Plan of Barclay White

(a x) - rixkita	e - tally sticks
b - upright corn tassels	f - rattle
c - spread	g - pipe
d - wild cat hide	h - spoon

to 1 and 2 of Seven Eagle Brothers. Optional: to Crow men west to east; to Eagle men east to west.

Third Phase: West of rim, offerings as ashes are disposed of: Heaven (2), earth (2), probably west (2).

Fourth Phase: Motions, first mode: West of fireplace: Heaven (4), earth (4), west (4).

Second mode: To altar; offering motions: One to each tassel, order as above (right hand, left, right, left, right). Two to wildcat nose (right, left). Two to rattle (right, left). One over each side (left over south; right over north). Crow drum (2) (right, left); Eagle drum (2) (right, left).

Self-Blessing, diagonally before S 1. Returns pipe.

Play of the Game

The game was always played straight, for five games or seven, or for five with an optional addition of two games if those assembled wished to continue. Turns were west to east on both sides.

The Game Intervals

Ghost Dancing as usual, while the leading singer of the winners carries the rattle. Rixkita of winning side holds game set aloft at *north* and at *south.* For the society songs Crazy Dog Dance or Young Dog Dance songs were preferred.

Speeches or short talks occurred in the intervals. It is mentioned also for this game that there used to be giving away in the intervals—generally to the altar powers, or to the game owner for them. The gifts were in turn redistributed by the game owner, as at Doctor Dances.

The Food Offering and Service

The food was generally prepared in the game owner's house, and brought over when it was time to make the offering and eat. Occasionally it was prepared after the game was over in the game lodge, while the assemblage waited. If the food is prepared outside the game lodge it is received when brought by the game owner who has it all set out east of the fireplace, the buckets of corn in an arc.

Food offering: Rixkita of winning side selects offerer, gives him spoon. Offerer fills spoon, makes inclusive motions behind all the food.

Extended form: First Phase: As first phase of smoke offering, probably including west.

Second Phase: First and second modes, as first and second modes of the second phase of the smoke-offering.

Self-blessing before rixkita who gave the spoon; return of spoon to that rixkita.

Shorter form: First phase is as second mode of second phase of the extended form. Namely, the motions over altar objects are made with the spoonful in hand.

Second phase in two parts west of fireplace. First part is as first phase of extended form, depositing corn. Second part is as first mode of second phase of extended form, motions with empty spoon to the powers.

Self-blessing; return of spoon.

Order of food service: S 1, N 1, S 2, N 2; 1 and 2 of Seven Crows, 1 and 2 of Seven Eagles; north tarutsius, south tarutsius; laymen, usually west to east down both sides, but with four servers for each side, this is altered to speed up the food service.

Closing remarks by winning leader. Assemblage departs.

BOYCHIEF

Ownership and Affiliation

Boychief, a Crow, inherited his game from his mother who secured it in a Ghost Dance vision.

The game was first played at a Ghost Dance. At this dance three main tents were set up, the sacred Ghost Dance tent for the leaders at the west facing east, one at the south facing north for the Seven Eagle Brothers, and one at the north facing south for the Seven Crows. The game was played in the north or Crow tipi. Hence it was customary to play the game in a tipi or tent, oriented north-south, with the altar at the north facing a southern doorway.

Paraphernalia

The bundle contained the pipe, horn spoon, eight tally sticks, white bones for counters, soft eagle feathers, red paint, blue paint, and a number of ornaments to be worn in the hair by guessers, watchers and rixkita. A small cedar tree about three feet high was used with this bundle. Old rituals which used cedar trees as part of ceremonial altars, such as Bear Dances and Doctor Performances, cut a special tree for each occasion, and it is probable this was done for Boychief's game. A large picture of Christ was part of this set. There was no rattle.

Several objects in the Field Museum were identified as probably used in Boychief's game.

F M 71650 — 1,2, and 71652 — 1,2, are soft white eagle feathers with fine wooden tips. These were probably used by the guessers and watchers, but may have been worn by four rixkita.

F M 71651 is a larger feather, bound around at the stem with soft fur. Today it appears yellowish, but informant thought it was originally red. This was probably worn by the central rixkita.

F M 71600 similar to the four plain feathers as above, but with a longer wooden stem. Use uncertain. Informant denied that it was worn by the game owner.

Altar

See fig. 12.

Official arrangements

Five chiefs as rixkita, of which the central one is in ceremonial charge. Boychief occasionally filled the office of principal ceremonial rixkita himself. Guessers selected by N 1 and S 1 respectively; and two watchers, one for each side, permanent for the game occasion, are selected by the game owner. Two drums are presided over respectively by Seven Crows and Seven Eagles. Three or four old men are stationed at the south doorway on the west side.

Bravechief is remembered to have officiated as the main rixkita for this game, Tom Yellowhorse as watcher for the Crows (although an Eagle), Jasper Hadley as watcher for the Eagles. Chiefs were always chosen as rixkita. Five rixkita were the usual number, but for this game, exceptionally, there could also be seven, in which

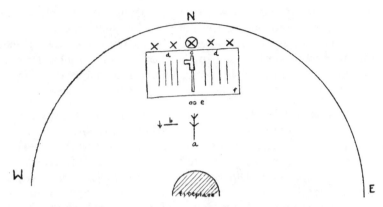

Figure 12. Altar Plan of Boychief (North Orientation)

a - cedar tree   e - paints and feathers
b - Christ's picture facing south   f - spread
c - pipe   x - rixkita
d - tally sticks

case the pattern would be the same, a central rixkita in charge, and three on each side of him, associated with the respective sides.

After the altar has been arranged and the officials are in their places, Boychief himself painted the rixkita. He asks the main Crow rixkita (normally N 1, with the north altar orientation E 1) to arise, and leads him through a clockwise circuit of east, south, to a position due west of the fireplace, where he seats him on a blanket, facing the south doorway. The paints, kept behind the cedar tree, are now called for. Boychief asks Yellowhorse, the watcher for the Crow (now eastern) side, (note that this is an additional function in which the watcher's office is consonant with tarutsius) to bring the paints. Yellowhorse brings them through the same circuit, puts them down at the right (west) side of the seated rixkita, and then retraces his path, counter-clockwise to his position on the east side, just before the altar. Rixkita sits with arms folded while Boychief paints his face all over with red, then makes two marks with blue, one down each side of the face. These are thick blue lines drawn with the finger from the mid-forehead, down each cheek to the level of the mouth. The right side is painted with the finger of Boychief's left hand, the left side with that of the right. Boychief then takes a soft white feather and puts it on the rixkita's head. Now he asks the rixkita to arise, and calls Hadley, watcher for the west Eagle side. Hadley comes from his position on the west side before the altar counter-clockwise through the west to the position in which the painting was done, and conducts the rixkita clockwise back to his seat at the altar. Yellowhorse is now told to bring the rixkita, the leader for the west or Eagle side. He conducts the rixkita through a clockwise circuit of east and south to the same position west of the fireplace. The rixkita is seated in the same way, and painted in the same way. Meanwhile Yellowhorse returns counter-clockwise to his position. In this manner all the rixkita for the game are painted by Boychief, after which the paints are returned to their position behind the cedar tree.

The painting is the face painting of chiefs. Blue is for the rainbow, red for the earth in fall.

The movements to and from the position west of the fireplace are determined by the sanctity of the west and the sacred pathway from fireplace to west, which is not crossed. The Pawnee theologian would consider the movements of the watchers and the rixkita as following the ceremonial circuit, but avoiding a crossing of the sacred pathway.

The Smoke Offering

A Crow is selected to make the smoke offering, by the ceremonial rixkita. After receiving the pipe:

First Phase: Clockwise circuit, returning to *north* of fireplace facing south. Offerings: Heaven, Earth. To *southeast* where pipe was lit by Crow watcher.

Second Phase: First mode: To north of fireplace; offerings: Heaven (4), Earth (4).

Second mode: To Christ's picture (2), to cedar tree (3) (top, middle and base). To the altar; offerings: one over right Crow side, one over left Eagle side. To the east Crow drum (2), to the west Eagle drum (2).

Third mode: To N 2 (rixkita 2 of Crow side, now actually E 2 — the smoke offering was described by informant as made by rixkita 1 of the Crow side, in which case the pipe is offered to the assistant rixkita of that side for the positions of both the offerer and the assistant); to S 1, S 2 (rixkita of Eagle side, now actually W 1 and W 2). (A further note is necessary here: It is not certain that this smoke was correctly described. A later discussion of the game with informants made it clear that there would be five rixkita behind the altar, in which case the generic pattern prescribes that the pipe be offered to the central official, then the main rixkita of the Crow side—or the assistant if the main rixkita is offerer—then the main 1 (and 2) rixkita of the Eagle side.) To 1 and 2 of the Seven Crow drummers, to 1 and 2 of the Seven Eagle drummers. Probably to old men on the west side near doorway. Optionally to Crow men from north to south, to Eagle men from south to north.

Third Phase: To north of fireplace. Offerings as first phase.
Fourth Phase: First and second modes as first and second modes
of second phase.

Self-Blessing; returns pipe.

Play of the Game

The game was played for five rubber games straight, to which
two could be added. In putting the counters in play, the guesser
for the Eagle side hides first, the guesser for the Crow side guesses
first. This although the Crow side own the game, and Crows are
likely to be putters up, hence hosts, because the Eagles are here
in complete control of the west, where all the sacred powers are
clustered. There "the powers watch over the people, and from
there everything begins."

Activities of Intervals

The first society songs before counters are put in play are sung
by the Seven Eagle Brothers for the Eagle side. This is determined
as the putting of counters in play, by the Eagle control of the west.

In the intervals as usual the winning singers lead Ghost Dance
circuits. These circuits now begin and end north of the fireplace
facing the south door of the tipi. "This," said informant, "is to let
the voice go out. One cannot sing into the wall." The game set is
held aloft by the winning leader, probably at west and east.

Society songs are led by winning singers before counters are
again put in play.

Food Offering and Service

The food is brought in and placed between fireplace and the
south doorway, the buckets of corn in an arc.

Boychief himself selected the offerer. He says a few words.
On one occasion he chose Yellowhorse, his brother, who was also
Crow watcher, to make the offering. He said, in substance:

"Chiefs, old men, and people, I choose my brother Tom Yellowhorse to look up to Heaven. Whatever he says, God may provide for
us."

The ceremonial rixkita in charge at the occasion was Bravechief.
He held the spoon while Boychief talked. Then Yellowhorse received
the spoon from Bravechief. Bravechief may also say a few words
quietly while Yellowhorse takes the spoon with an arm blessing:
"May we live long together."

The following corn offering by Yellowhorse, as witnessed by
informants, departs somewhat from the generic form. In part this
is due to the changed orientation, in part to special references of
the offering itself.

Yellowhorse left the altar with the spoon, proceeding clockwise through the east to the south, where he passed between food and doorway, until he reached the bucket at the extreme west of the arc. Beginning with this one, walking eastward between the buckets of corn and the fireplace, he took corn from each bucket down the row from west to east. Without motions behind the food, he proceeded at once clockwise between food and doorway through south and west until he came to Christ's picture. Here he made two motions, one with right and one with left hand, to the picture, touching the spoonful of corn each time before the gesture; then three motions to the cedar tree; then one motion over each side of the altar; then two motions for the Crow drum and two for the Eagle drum.

(Up to this point, the procedure from the time the offerer leaves the food at the south, is equivalent to a First Phase of the shorter form of the offering: in other words, it is analogous to the second mode of the second phase of the smoke offering).

When the offerer leaves the west Eagle drum, he proceeds to a position halfway between the point west of the fireplace at which the painting was done and the picture of Christ. Here he stops facing the doorway. The corn is still in the spoon. He says in substance:

"Now chiefs, Seven Brothers and Seven Crows and old men sitting around there, and people of the tribe, I'm going to do what I learned. I'm going to sing." All are quiet. He turns and faces Christ. Holding the corn aloft, he says, "Father, we're going to eat together this food that you have provided for us to eat. Take pity on me." Bringing the corn down to waist level as he holds it outstretched toward the picture, he turns to the fireplace, where at the north of the fireplace rim, he deposits all the corn with one motion.

This completes the offering proper. He makes no offerings of corn to the orientation of powers to which tobacco was given, and he makes no sacramental motions with the empty spoon. In other words, in this offering, as a shorter form, the first part of the second phase differs from the analogous part of the smoke offering (instead of Heaven and Earth, there is one offering to Christ's picture), and there is no second part, such as would be analogous to the first mode of the second phase of the smoke offering.

After depositing the corn, the offerer proceeds to the altar, where standing just to the right (east) and facing the main rixkita who gave him the spoon, he makes the self-blessing and returns the spoon. All say "nawa."

The Service: The two watchers serve respectively corn, meat and bread to the main rixkita of each side. (Note: In this game the watchers function more fully as tarutsius than in any other.) Then the watchers serve the two principal singers of their respective sides. Then the old men near the doorway are served, and finally the watchers serve from north to south on their respective sides. The game owner himself serves the two watchers, Yellowhorse and Hadley. He also speaks at that time and says, "Now people (if some one is sick) we must give him to eat; it may help him to recover," and special portions of food are sent out to the sick one.

After all have eaten, Boychief, the game owner, himself speaks. He uses the ritual form for closing, "Now we've eaten... etc. Now it's all over. Now we go out." All leave.

TOM YELLOWHORSE

Ownership and Affiliation

Tom Yellowhorse, an Eagle, derived his game ritual in Ghost Dance visions. It is still demonstrated by him, essentially in the old forms; in fact, it is the most used game of the old orthodox Ghost Dance hand games. I participated at hand games of Yellowhorse several times. In these cases it was played outside the North or Skiri Round House in the afternoon. It can also be played in the Round House. The narrative comments below refer to events at one of the afternoon demonstrations witnessed.

Paraphernalia

Fifteen dogwood sticks trimmed with eagle feathers, one large eagle feather, two small bells for counters, a red pipestone pipe with smooth dogwood stem, a horn spoon, two drums (neither of which with certainty belongs to the set of Yellowhorse; in these games of recent years any game drum can be borrowed for use, but its side affiliation must agree with that which puts it to use).

Of the fifteen feathered sticks, seven are uprights before the altar, eight are tally sticks. All have eagle feathers upright at the top end, and soft red feathers attached to the end with sinew. Of the eight tally sticks four are trimmed with bald eagle feathers for the south side, four with black eagle feathers for the north. The seven upright feathered sticks are symbolic of the Seven Eagle Brothers. The single upright feather is for Yellowhorse himself, and after the smoke may be worn by him if he chooses.

Altar

See figure 13.

Official Arrangements

Four rixkita behind altar; two drums at about northwest and southwest respectively, with the drummers grouped around them; tarutsius.

At the game recorded, the following officials were noted:

S 1 William Mathews
S 2 Hiram Goodchief
N 1 Rush Roberts
N 2 Shooter.

Of these only Roberts is Skiri. All have chief status, Shooter (since deceased) and Mathews being also medicine men. The neglect of band affiliation is due mainly to the necessity of selecting chiefs, and the small number of these now available.

Bob Hopkins sat at Shooter's left and when Shooter made the smoke offering, he should have received the pipe as substitute representative of the N 2 position behind the altar.

Main Crow drummer— Jesse Peters.
Main Eagle drummers— Tom Morgan, Willy Lewis.

Peters and Lewis are Skiri. None of these are surviving members of the two old organizations of singers. Tom Yellowhorse, himself one of the original Seven Eagles, sat on a camp stool next to the

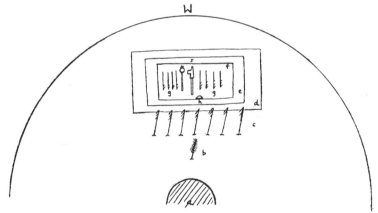

Figure 13. Altar Plan of Yellowhorse

a - fireplace
b - feather
c - feathered sticks (upright)
d - canvas
e - blanket

f - flag
g - tally sticks
h - spoon
i - leather rattle
j - pipe

Eagle singers, but did not actively participate with them. Recent games have tended to abandon the attempt to retain the remaining members of the two organizations as the leading drummers and singers, or their official successors, on account of their advanced age. In earlier times their control of the drums was prescribed.

Hughey Horsechief was tarutsius on the Eagle side.

The drums were not suspended from forked sticks, but placed on the ground, the drummers squatting around them, the main drummer for each side sitting on his side of the drum and facing the opponents across drum and arena.

The men present seated themselves on mats from about southwest and northwest to the western altar. The women sat from these points eastward on each side.

No fire was made in the fireplace which was indicated symbolically.

The Smoke Offering

Rush Roberts, main rixkita of the Crows, chose the smoker and prepared the pipe. This office belonged to N 1, although this was an Eagle game, because Roberts had supplied the money to purchase the food for the occasion: he was the putter-up.

Roberts chose Shooter, N 2, to make the offering. Shooter received the pipe from him, across the altar, without their hands touching. Shooter did not know what to do and waited for specific instructions from Yellowhorse. This is the more indicative of the personal and exclusive ownership of a ritual smoke offering, because Shooter was one of the most learned Pawnee in matters ritual and ceremonial, the chief medicine man of his band.

Throughout the offering the pipe was held so that the mouthpiece was directed upward. Shooter carried the pipe through a clockwise circuit.

First Phase: He stopped west of the fireplace rim, and made offerings of pinches of tobacco to Heaven and Earth (combined; he merely raised one pinch aloft and placed it on the ground); turning clockwise he faced west, offered a pinch slantwise westward, and turning back placed it on the fireplace rim. Shooter then proceeded clockwise through the north until he reached the eastern doorway, where standing between fireplace and doorway and facing east he offered a pinch slantwise east, throwing it eastward, not placing it on the ground. From here he turned clockwise and proceeded counter-clockwise to the northeast, where he squatted facing east while Hughey Horsechief brought a brand from a fire (burning elsewhere) and put it to the bowl while Shooter puffed.

Second phase: First mode: Shooter puffed the pipe as he walked clockwise around the fireplace until he reached west of the fireplace, where he stopped facing east and offered four puffs to Heaven and four puffs slantwise to the west. As he moved toward the altar, the pipe, which had not been burning well, went out. Shooter removed the stem from the bowl and blew through it to clean it out. After replacing it, Yellowhorse relit the pipe with a match. All of this was irregular. The pipe should have been so prepared before the offering that it would draw well and burn properly; separating stem and bowl in the middle of a smoke offering, and relighting the pipe after it has gone out, not to mention using a match, are sacreligious and court supernatural disaster. Tom Yellowhorse is perhaps not as orthodox a believer as he once was, and as other old Pawnee still are, but Shooter until his death clung to the old ways.

Second mode: Shooter came to the altar, where he offered one puff to the erect feather in front; then of the seven standing sticks he gave a puff to the left side, center toward end, and one to the right side, center toward right end (shorter form; he could have puffed the central, and then alternating left and right, each one individually). As he puffed these uprights the rixkita at the altar said "nawa." Then he gave one puff over the left and one puff over the right side of the altar spread itself, at each of which the rixkita said "nawa." He made no special puff for the rattle. Shooter now proceeded to the Crow drum at the northwest, and puffed twice to its upper face, the Crow drummers saying "nawa." Then he went clear around the fireplace clockwise until he reached the Eagle drum at the southwest, to which he puffed twice, the Eagle drummers saying "nawa."

Third mode: Shooter carried out no third mode. This was not correct ritualism, but inasmuch as there had been trouble with the pipe, the explanation seems to lie in the fact that Yellowhorse wished the smoke to end as quickly as it possibly could, in order to avoid further difficulties. The carrying out of the first two modes indicates the ritual part that must be finished.

A correct third mode would have been: To N 1 (although an Eagle, the Crow side is smoking, hence the emphasis in offering the pipe is first to rixkita of Crow side who prepared the pipe) Rush Roberts; circuit or pipe turn, and to S 1 Mathews, then pipe turn, etc., to S 2 Goodchief (since N 2 is smoking, his substitute yields seniority to the regular S 2 rixkita), then to Bob Hopkins, who takes the pipe for the N 2 station made vacant by Shooter, the offerer. The pipe should now go to Jesse Peters and his assistant at the Crow drum, then to Tom Morgan and Willy Lewis at the Eagle drum. Thereafter a complete form would take the pipe to John Tatum, a Wichita chief visiting the Pawnee on this occasion, who sat to Hopkins' left on the Crow side. From Tatum it should pass down the Crow men from west to east, then up the Eagle side men from east to west until it reaches the man at the right of Hiram Goodchief, S 2.

Third Phase: Shooter went to the west of the fireplace from the altar, loosened the ashes with the tamper, and emptied twice on the ground for offerings aloft to Heaven (and earth), and twice for offerings slantwise westward as he faced west.

Fourth phase: First mode: Facing east, standing west of the fireplace, Shooter made motions of blessing with the pipe, touching the ashes each time, four times upward, then turning and facing west, four motions slantwise westward (touching the ashes only before the first, before he turns to face west).

Second mode: He walked directly to the altar, where he made two motions, one with the right hand over all altar objects from south of west toward north, one left hand motion similarly from north of west toward south. (Here he has telescoped all motions into these two inclusive motions, meaning "everything on this side, and everything on that side," the side to which he belongs determining his emphasis.) Rixkita at the altar said "nawa." Shooter then went to the Crow drum, where he made two motions, right, left; Crow drummers said "nawa." Then he went clockwise to the Eagle drum for two similar motions; Eagle drummers said "nawa."

Self-Blessing: Shooter then proceeded clockwise until he reached a position north of the sacred pathway, where facing Rush Roberts diagonally across the altar, he made the motions of self-blessing, and returned the pipe to Roberts, who took it with an arm-blessing. As he received it all present said "nawa." Roberts returned the pipe to its proper altar position, and Shooter meanwhile went back to his seat.

Play of the Game

Mathews, S 1, now rose and gave out the two bells, the first one to a woman on the Crow side, the second to a woman on the Eagle side.

The Eagle drummers now began to drum and sing a hand game song, while the two guessers arose and faced each other to put the counters in play. The Eagle woman hid first, the Crow woman guessed first (following the game emphasis, rather than the side which put up the demonstration). After the counters were in play, the drummers of the two sides alternated, each set singing hand game songs while their side was in possession of the counters.

The turns to hide the counters were on the north side, first Rush Roberts and Shooter (N 1 and N 2), then to two women who sat at the extreme east on the Crow side, then to Hopkins and Tatum at the left of Shooter, then to two women to the right of the two at the east end of the Crows, and so on, alternating until the middle was reached, when the serial order was repeated.

On the Eagle side the first two to play were two women at the extreme east, then Mathews and Goodchief (S 1 and S 2), then two women to the left of the two at the extreme east, then two men to the right of Goodchief, and so on until the middle was reached after which the sequence was repeated.

The Eagles won the first game. The woman guesser of the Eagle side recovered the counters from the last two to play on that side (who had run out the game points) and returned them to Mathews (S 1).

The Game Intervals

Tom Morgan, the leading drummer of the Eagles, rose and went to the altar, where he received the rattle from Mathews. Morgan took his place with the rattle at the west of the fireplace, facing east. Here he was joined by Willie Lewis, number 2 singer of the Eagle side, who stood at his right, and Hiram Goodchief (S 2), who took the position next right. A moment later Frank Leader stepped up from the Eagle side and stood to Goodchief's right. Morgan led off the singing of a Ghost Dance song, standing in his place. As he began to repeat it he started dancing, circling clockwise, and women (and some men) of both sides came forward and completed a circle of people around the fireplace. All held hands. The step was the usual Ghost Dance side step, to the left. Morgan used the rattle as he sang, the other singers with him joining in, and continued until he had completed a circuit and again reached the west where he stopped. Standing in one place he sang another song, and then as he began to repeat it, he started circling leftward again. When he reached the west again, he stopped. This completed the Ghost Dancing in the first interval.

After Morgan took the rattle from Mathews, Mathews rose with the bells, the eight tally sticks and the pipe in his right hand. The tally sticks were held with the feathered ends forward and up, the pipe with mouthpiece up. Mathews came around the south side of the altar and forward to a position at the west between the fireplace and the altar, outside the circle of dancers (between dancers and altar). Here he stood silently a few moments, facing eastward, holding the game set and pipe aloft. Then he walked clockwise to the east, where facing west standing outside the circle of dancers, he again raised the set aloft a few moments. Then he walked clockwise back to the west where he repeated his first motion. Finally he turned so that he faced west, standing at the west between dancers and altar, and briefly held the set aloft. Then he walked to the altar and gave the objects back to Rush Roberts (N 1) who was sitting quietly in his place, and Roberts replaced them on the altar. Mathews returned to his seat around the south side of the altar spread.

When the Ghost Dancing was over, all the dancers returned to their places. Tom Morgan brought the rattle back to the altar and handed it to Mathews who replaced it in its position.

Mathews rose and returned the two counters to the same two women who had been guessers for the first game.

Then the Eagle drummers led the singing of a Young Dog Dance song, and Hiram Goodchief (S 2) rose in his place and danced, merely rising and falling on the balls of his feet. Any man present could have arisen and danced if he wished. Goodchief's step was not the Young Dog Dance step, which should be done in a posture bent forward and alternating on both feet, and should proceed around a circuit of the fireplace.

The guesser of the Crow side, who had lost the previous game, rose, after the singing was over, went to another Crow player and gave him the counter. He was now to act as guesser for the Crows.

Notes on Game Play

Five games in a row were won by the Eagles. This was the number of games straight which had originally been decided upon for the occasion. As the Eagles were consistently the winners, the activities of the intervals were exactly as they had been after the winning of the first game, save that on two occasions Willy Lewis, the number 2 Eagle singer, led the circuits of Ghost Dancing, instead of Morgan.

In one of the intervals between the first five rubber games Maggie Kasiya got up and came forward until she stood before the altar. She spoke for a few moments, crying all the while and backing away from the altar.

"I'm not very good (meaning feeling good) because my brother (Emmett Pierson) died. I'm sorry I didn't see him (she had been away for several weeks, and it was near the end of her absence that Emmet died suddenly), that makes me feel sick. He used to do all these things (meaning the hand games) and he used to push these things, telling the people to dance. Now he's gone, there are just two left here (Emmet was one of the Seven Brothers, of which only two were now left: Tom Yellowhorse and Ezra Tilden. She repeated this last remark several times). Now I'm going to buy food for Mrs. Pierson to eat."

At this everyone present expressed sympathy and pleasure. Mrs. Pierson got up and came to Maggie, blessed her with her hands (placing them on the head and running them down over the shoulders, sides, etc. to the ground) and they both cried. Then she led Maggie away.

The Crows were greatly dissatisfied at losing five games straight, and petitioned Rush Roberts to put on two more games. The decision rested with him as putter-up; he was the one who had decided on five games before play began. Roberts now agreed to have two more.

Both of these additional games were won by the Eagles so that again the procedure of the intervals was repeated.

The Crows were now still more dissatisfied, and there was much discussion as to whether play should continue. In theory more than seven games straight was a very bad number. After some discussion, it was agreed between the rixkita and Yellowhorse to play two more games (as if they belonged to another occasion) and then quit, in order to appease the Crows who felt it was unlucky to leave after losing seven straight games. Many of the Crow women contended the games had been lost so rapidly that they had had no turns, and that in any case bad guessers had been chosen for their side.

The two extra games were won by the Crows.

The procedure of the two intervals then was: The bells were returned to Rush Roberts (N 1) by the guesser of the Crow side; Jesse Peters, leading singer of the Crows, took the rattle from Roberts, and led the Ghost Dance circuits, accompanied by two other Crow singers and Shooter (N 2). The dancing proceeded in the same way as when led by Eagles. Rush Roberts now arose while the Ghost Dancing went on, came out around the north side of the altar, and held the game set and pipe aloft in the same way that Mathews had, after which he returned them to Mathews and took his seat again. After the Ghost Dance circuits the Crow singers sang a special society song, and Rush Roberts rose and gave out the counters.

Of the play of Tom Yellowhorse's game I was told that in former times he played more often even up than straight, and that in recent times his was one of the few games to be played even up. Even up play means that "should one be sick, as the other side gets ahead, he gets worse, then as his side catches up he improves and gets well."

Said my informant of the occasion we witnessed, "Sometimes bad luck comes right from the first. The smoke was wrong, that's why the Crows lost seven straight. (Note that it was the Crows who were responsible for the smoke offering.) Right at the beginning the smoke went out and the pipe wouldn't light. It has to be lit and warm like our bellies inside; when they get cold we are gone ... When the smoke is done it should be puffed rapidly to keep the pipe lit, just as with a sick person, he must be treated rapidly so that he doesn't get worse."

The Food Offering and Service

After the nine games, the food was brought in and set at the east, between fireplace and doorway position. Seven bowls of corn formed an arc in front of (west of) the other food.

Tom Yellowhorse chose the food offerer, selecting Hiram Goodchief (S 2; the offerer must be of the winning side). Tom went with him to direct him. Goodchief got the spoon from Mathews.

Goodchief proceeded clockwise through the north until he reached the food at the east. There he walked between the arc of bowls and the fireplace, and one by one from left to right (north to south) he dipped corn from each of the seven buckets until at the seventh he had a full spoon. He then made a complete clockwise circuit, coming again to the east outside the food (that is, between food and east), where standing behind all the food and facing west, he made the usual two inclusive gestures over the food.

First Phase: Continuing clockwise he came to the west of the fireplace where he stopped at the rim facing east. Here he offered the spoonful upward, then put half on the ground before him (for Heaven and Earth); then turned and facing westward offered the balance to the west slantwise, then turned back to the fireplace and pushed off all the rest of the corn onto the ground. He then put the empty spoon down at his left.

Second Phase: First mode: Bending and touching the corn on the ground and rubbing his hands together before each motion, Goodchief made four motions upward. (Apparently omitted in my notes: He makes four motions westward, without touching the corn each time, merely touching it before the first motion, before he turns to face westward.)

Second Mode: Goodchief picked the spoon up, turned round and walked straight to the altar. Here he rubbed his right hand over the spoon, and made one motion over the north side of the altar and objects, then with left hand a similar motion over the south side. The rixkita at the altar said "nawa" for each motion. Then Goodchief went to the Crow drum, and made two motions, right, left, over the drum face, the Crow drummers saying "nawa." From here Goodchief proceeded clockwise around the fireplace to the Eagle drum where he made two similar motions, the Eagle drummers saying "nawa."

Self-Blessing: Goodchief now went to the altar, where, standing to the south of the pathway from fireplace to altar and facing Mathews diagonally, he made the self-blessing and returned the spoon to Mathews who received it with an arm blessing. All present said "nawa."

The food was now served. Each woman had brought dishes and utensils for her family, so that there was no official giving out of plates. The women merely moved around and saw that their men folks had them.

The four rixkita were served first, then both sets of drummers, then the rest of the gathering. No clear cut formal order was preserved in serving the laymen and visitors.

After the feast the gathering broke up.

Note on Corn Offering

Sometimes for his hand game, Yellowhorse makes the corn offering himself, and if he does so, he has a special way of carrying out the First Phase of the offering.

He stands at the west of the fireplace, facing east, and as he holds the spoonful of corn he says:

"Now I am going to do what I know." Then as he holds the spoonful aloft, he sings:

"God has taken pity on me..."

and again:

"Mother Earth has taken pity on me..."

After his song, he puts all the corn at once on the ground. His song has indicated the essentials of the offering, and he makes no other gestures of offering before depositing the corn, save to hold it aloft.

Following this, Yellowhorse's procedure for the two modes of the second phase are the same as that carried out by Goodchief under his direction.

JOHN MOSES II

Ownership and Affiliation

This is considered a Crow game, after Moses' affiliation. It was made by Moses, not in accordance with a vision experience, but according to the general patterns of hand games, with much of the old religious reference and Ghost Dance significations eliminated. Moses had been converted to the Baptist faith, and dropped his old game. Usually played in open, or in open tipi shelter.

Paraphernalia
A cloth spread, four sticks for each side, counters. No pipe.

Altar Arrangements
The simple generic form, four sticks on each side.

Official Arrangements
Moses selects leaders for each side, not necessarily chiefs. Usually he uses only one drum, set in the center. Fireplace unnecessary. The singers for each side cluster on that side of the drum. They are usually young men. The game originated after death had partially disintegrated the Seven Brothers and Seven Crows organizations. Conceptually it does not prescribe the presence of either the survivors or the successors of these organizations.

Smoke Offering
None. Moses asks a fellow-Baptist to make a Baptist prayer and blessing before the game. I have not seen this performed.

Play of the Game
Seven games straight; more if desired. There is no prescribed limitation of number. The game cannot be played even up, a form which has definite Ghost Dance meaning. The turns are west to east down both sides.

The Game Intervals
Before counters are put in play the drummers usually sing a Crazy Dog Dance song.

After a rubber game is won, the drummers arise with the drum and take it outside the shelter, where they stand holding it and sing Forty-Nine or Soldier songs (a recent, and conceptually profane development); they are said sometimes to use Ghost Dance songs, but the attendant young people do not like these and as the occasion is a social one the singers are governed by the desires of those present. The young people, boys and girls, are those who join in the dancing. There is of course no holding aloft of the game set.

Food Service
There is no food offering. Someone is asked to say a Baptist grace before eating. The service is likely to be to leaders first, then others, but this formal phase is here not of primary significance.

CHARLEY ALLEN

Ownership and Affiliation

Charley Allen is affiliated with the Crows. He made his game set himself. It is not supposed to go back to a vision experience, but to have been in accord with his Baptist faith, and the general plan of the hand games.

Paraphernalia

Twelve tally sticks and two bone counters. The twelve sticks are said to symbolize the twelve disciples.

Altar

Generic form, a cloth spread, six sticks on each side.

Official Arrangements

Leaders selected by game owner, not necessarily chiefs, with singers on each side for the respective sides. Two drums at owner's option. The singers are not representative of Seven Brothers and Seven Crows. It is said of this game that when there is one drum all the singers sing together regardless of who has the counters, instead of the singers of a side accompanying the play for their side.

There is no fireplace or indication of fireplace. The game is played outside in the shade, or in a tent. This tent, as that for John Moses II game is a long arbor built of branches with a canvas cover over it. It is oriented eastward.

Allen is recalled as having put Charley Moses in charge of the Crows, or Mark Evarts, his uncle, and Tom Yellowhorse in charge of the Eagles. Moses is a Baptist.

Smoke Offering

None. A Baptist makes a Baptist blessing.

Play of the Game

For this game, as probably also for the John Moses II game, either side may begin the hiding, either side the guessing.

The game is played straight always, usually for seven games, but there can be more. It cannot be played even up. The turns are on the Crow side from west to east, on the Eagle side from east to west. To win a rubber game, twelve counters must be scored, in the same manner as eight in other games.

The Game Intervals

In intervals, the drummers take the drum outside, where they stand holding it and singing Forty-Nine Dances to which the young folks dance. Ghost Dance hand game play songs are used for the play of the game.

Sticks are not held aloft.

Food Service

No food offering. It is immaterial which side wins the game play as the old signification has been dropped. A Baptist is asked to say grace. Service pattern probably leaders, then others, but not significant.

IRENE GOODEAGLE

This game is considered the least ceremonial of the genuine Ghost Dance hand games. It is said that Irene Goodeagle often wanted to play at times and places when it was impossible to put up and put on the hand game of her grandmother because its ritual required so much formality that could not be hurriedly arranged. Mrs. Goodeagle heeded her granddaughter's wishes (in Pawnee kinship behavior patterns the grandparent generally does take particular cognizance of the grandchild's needs and desires), and made a special game set for Irene to play with. The sanction of this game set is derived from that of Mrs. Goodeagle's game set bundle, not directly from visions. Hence while the game is not considered complicated in ritualization, it is felt to have a religious meaning associated with the Ghost Dance. Nevertheless it is spoken of as a set "just to play with." It was made in quite recent years.

An indication of what is meant by saying that Irene can use this set to play with at any time, is offered by the fact that at a "pow-wow" held by Pawnee Bill, a white man, many white people who gathered from neighboring cities wanted to play the Indian hand game. The Pawnee agreed and asked Irene Goodeagle to get her set of sticks and this was used. Apparently to use this set no preliminary formalities and preparations, no ritual preparation of food and "putting-up" are required.

XI

COMPARISON OF
THE OLD HAND GAME AND
THE GHOST DANCE HAND GAME

The general character of the transformation of the Pawnee hand game can be summarized by the statement that a gambling game was transformed into a Ghost Dance hand game ceremony. But it is in the detail of this change that the significance lies. What from the native standpoint constitutes the new form a ceremony? What has been carried over? What are the sources of the new aspects and elements of the hand game ceremony?

In a detailed contrast of the changes which came about, three aspects of change must be considered: the persistence of traits, the loss of traits, and the addition of traits.

PERSISTENCE OF TRAITS

The persistence of traits constitutes that body of cultural elements without which no identification of the two forms would be possible. There are first of all those traits which persist from the old game into the new form identically; these form the base. In addition there are persistences of phases of the pattern or form, into which similar but not identical cultural material has been filled.

The persistences of the old hand game into the new are for the most part those traits which are associated with the actual play of the game. Let us see what these are. The basic content of play is that counters are hid by two players, one by each, and an opponent guesses in which hands they are concealed. This is identical in the two forms. These two players represent a side, composed of many players, who are in opposition to another side composed of many players; and the two sides are seated as opposing moieties of an incomplete circle, open at what is conceived the exit or doorway point. These aspects are retained. In the tallying of the score, eight sticks are used. In the old form these are heaped together until in play, in the Ghost Dance form four are associated with each side; but the tallying remains the same. The tallyers are the leaders of the respective sides, in the new game as in the old.

The points are scored in the play of the game identically for both the old and new forms. The guessing is done in both types of the game by official guessers chosen to represent a side for a specific rubber game. In both cases the attempt is to choose lucky and clever guessers, but the stress upon ability is not as strong in the Ghost Dance game as in the gambling game. In the Ghost Dance game the emphasis has shifted so that the conception is more that the luck of the individual is a sign of his faith and belief. In both games as a rule, the losing guessers are changed, in order to bring a change of luck, and the winning guessers retained; but while this is a definite rule in the Ghost Dance hand game, it was not prescribed for the old game. The motions used in guessing are the same for the old game and the new. Many of the play songs sung are still the old hand game songs, where these are remembered, and in both types of game the singing is done by the side which holds the counters, and ceases as soon as the counters have been lost. Many of the motions with the hands, which are done in time to the singing by the players hiding the counters, are the same as motions used in the old game, but a number of the old motions imitating animals, have been dropped.

Some phases of the ghost dance hand game recall similar but not identical aspects of the old game. In the Ghost Dance hand games the altar end is the head end, and this is either at the west, or for one game, at the north. Both of these positions for the head end where the leaders or tallyers sit with the tally sticks are present in the old form, but there the location of the sides is determined for each game occasion by the direction from which the attackers or visitors come. If it be from the north or south, the head end is at the west, the visitors occupy either the north or the south; while if it be from east or west, the head end is at the north, and the visitors occupy either east or west. In the Ghost Dance games the position of altar is fixed for the game ritual. Two determinants have made this position west and north. One of these factors is the same as that which determined that in the old game the head end was either west or north, never east or south, viz. that these two cardinal directions are natural head ends or altar ends to the Pawnee because of orientations in ancient ceremonies. The west is, however, the more basic, and with the association of the sacred conceptions of the Ghost Dance religion with the western altar place, Ghost Dance ceremony, such as the hand game, must be oriented from such an altar position. The determination of the altar position by the chance orientations of a particular game occasion, which was the usual mode in the old method of play, is, however, responsible for the north altar in one Ghost Dance hand game, but as a result, this became a fixed rule for that hand game ritual, which could not have happened in connection with the old game.

In relation to the head end, the sides form two semi-circular arcs around the arena of play. Between them is built a fire. In the old game this was a long narrow fire, while in the Ghost Dance game it is a round fire. The long fire is perhaps to be more associated with the warparty tactics of former days, while a round fire is the one and only form of a fire in Pawnee ceremony.

In the organization of the sides, there is at once a retention of older ideas and a change. The sides in the old game were all of one band affiliation, of one tribe affiliation, or of a group (as in children's play) chosen to form a side. In the Ghost Dance play the sides are of one religious Ghost Dance affiliation in the usual form of play, Crows against Eagles, and such affiliation is permanent for any individual. In other forms of play of the Ghost Dance hand game, however, such as men against women, visionaries against innocents, etc., we have the old tendency cropping out to vary the organization of sides and to choose a particular formal structure for a particular occasion. An important difference, not to be disregarded, is that a Ghost Dance hand game was never played by band against band or tribe against tribe.

While the side in possession of the counters is the side which does the singing, it is a specially delegated group of singers who represent the side in the Ghost Dance hand game, while in the old game any or all players of the side sang as they wished.

In the old game the gambling was for definite stakes bet by individual members. In the Ghost Dance game there are as a rule no material stakes, but there is nevertheless a definite feeling about the value of winning and losing. It is now a matter of greater faith, and a sign of greater fortune. Some Ghost Dance rituals allow play to be for the avoidance of some special burdensome task, such as rising the next morning early to lead the Ghost Dance, or doing the cooking the next day (most usual with men against women). Here we may say that the feeling is in part that those who lose should strive more strongly than the winners to establish a successful rapport with the spiritual powers of the Ghost Dance. One game, that of Tom Morgan, in form a Ghost Dance hand game, but apparently not derived in a vision, retains the possibility of an actual material stake in the form of playing that the losing side should supply the food for the next day of Ghost Dancing or play. In connection with stakes, conceptual or actual, a major difference between the two forms is that losing or winning was an individual matter in the old game (although the play was side against side) while in the Ghost Dance game it is always a loss by an entire side as a group, or a gain by an entire side as a group.

In the old game, winning a rubber game gave the winners the prerogative of counting a coup, and dancing an old display war dance. This aspect is retained in the Ghost Dance hand game in two forms. The winners have demonstrated their prior right to lead the Ghost Dance, as a celebration of victory, and in addition to sing songs of one of the old societies. Inasmuch as these societies were all in one form or another associated with war, this is almost the equivalent of the old coup and dance.

Fainter suggestions of the old form occur in the Crow-Eagle symbolism of the players which suggests the old animal imitations of men playing; in the use of permanent watchers in some games, selected primarily for game ability and luck, as well as faith, who dominate the play in an aftermath when the score is tied and fate hangs in the balance on one game; and in such aftermaths the choice of special players to represent the sides, which recalls the fact that there were no turns in the old game, but players were given the counters to hide according to the belief in their luck and deceptive sleight of hand ability. While deception has been eliminated as a factor in play, it appears that if it happened unconsciously it was a miraculous sign of good fortune.

LOSS OF TRAITS

The traits which have been lost in the transformation of the old game into a Ghost Dance ceremony are to be associated with two aspects of the old game: gambling, and the warparty simulation. In connection with gambling we have the material stakes now eliminated with conceptual values substituted, the elimination of the use of all manner of deceptive motions by the players, and of actual fighting over the correctness or incorrectness of the guess and the possession of the counters. We have the shift from merely choosing any player to hide, in order to win, to an insistence upon giving every participant his opportunity. Associated with the loss of warparty symbolism, the manner of the party's approach, the carrying of a pipe by the leader of the party, the announcement of arrival, the long fire, the orientation of the sides according to the directions from which they have come together, the animal imitations of the players, the dramatization by the guesser of seeking the lost trail of an enemy warparty, the dramatization by the side holding the counters of concealing the trail of a warparty, the counting of coup by the winners, and the dancing of war society dances are gone. For some of these we have substitutions of a peaceful nature, the round ceremonial fire, the Ghost Dancing instead of war dancing, the smoking of a ceremonial pipe on behalf of all present.

Some few of the animal associations, beside the Crow-Eagle symbolism of sides and players, reappear in a few games which are associated with revivals of societies that have animal affiliations, and in some cases animal or bird dances are performed at hand games.

ACCRETION OF TRAITS

In the transformation of the old gambling hand game into a Ghost Dance ceremony, many traits appear which were foreign to the old form. These can be traced to two general sources: ceremonialism, and the Ghost Dance.

Ceremonialism as a source is a manner of saying that when the Pawnee made a ceremony out of a gambling game, they superimposed upon the game the patterns and forms to which they were accustomed in ceremonial and ritual behavior, and so integrated the combination that what was alien to a ritual or ceremony was eliminated.

From Pawnee ceremonialism comes first of all the fact that each hand game is an individual ritual. The hand game set and its associated objects form a bundle which is kept by the individual owner and opened only for a demonstration of the bundle ritual. The ritual forms and the ritual or sacred objects are derived through vision experiences or taken over from a former owner. Certain very general traits now cluster around the ritual demonstrations. Prayer is used associated with offerings, prayers for the sick and the general well-being of the tribe, official speeches about matters of general importance are made, and many of the necessary phases of the ritual are introduced by formal types of statement, such as the smoke offering, the selection of the food offering, or the closing speech before the gathering breaks up. Thurification is used in some game rituals. The important units of the ritual sequence of events must not be disrupted by exits and entrances, and it is for this reason that when the demonstration takes place within a lodge, the door may be closed at certain times. Those who have not as yet entered must wait until the event is past, such as an offering, and those who wish to leave must similarly retain their places quietly until the event is over. In distributing food, it must not be forgotten that the sick must share the feast, and special dishes of food are sent to them. In the earlier time when the game was a four-day Ghost Dance ceremony, sexual intercourse is said to have been unethical during the period of the ceremony. All of these traits come from the general character of the old Pawnee ceremonies, whether medicine men's rituals, or the rituals of priests.

In arranging for the occasion of a Ghost Dance hand game, the old forms of planning a ritual demonstration have been carried over. Two forms are possible: Either the bundle owner, with the aid of relatives, puts up the demonstration himself, or some other individual offers to put it up for the owner. Both of these methods are derived from the code of the older ceremonies. When an individual has put the demonstration up, certain prerogatives devolve upon him, in the hand game ceremony as in other ceremonies. Not all of the old formality in putting up a ceremonial demonstration has however been adopted. In the older form there was a whole series of events prior to the ceremony proper, which could be summarized as "preparation." These begin with the calling together of the few who have the main offices in relation to the bundle and its ritual. These set a day for a preliminary feast. The preliminary feast is a formal occasion, at which what preparations have been made and what are still be made are discussed and made generally known. Further gifts necessary to supply the occasion are forthcoming at the affair, and finally someone, usually a chief, is asked to set the day for the event proper. He is already aware of what needs to be done before that time, and how long it will take, and he also knows the time which must be allowed for the people to assemble. In terms of these facts, he sets a date a few days off, allowing ample time.

These detailed formalities were not so far as I am aware followed in arranging for a hand game demonstration, but I have no doubt that they could have been, and some simpler form of preliminary was probably followed when the hand game ceremonies were matters of intensive belief and faith. Certainly such a formal manner was followed for the game of Pierson, which required the cooperation of so many bundle owners.

As a ritual the hand game ceremony involves formal seating arrangements and a formal layout of the interior of the lodge or the outdoor arena. There is first of all the orientation of the altar, basically at the west, which is the fundamental of all Pawnee ritual and ceremony. Here the bundle is opened and its contents arranged on a spread which may be the bundle covering. Sacred objects may stand before the altar proper, and behind it are seated the officials in charge of the demonstration. These are either four or five, both arrangements being ancient ones, and the order of their ceremonial importance follows old forms, the central officials (those closest to due west) having ceremonial seniority over others, the others being essentially assistants. It is also significant, in terms of old sacred bundle ceremonies, that the owners do not preside, but others preside for them.

In the center of the arena is a round fireplace, in which for games ceremonially important, a fire must be burning. The game ground or lodge floor must be prepared for the game as for a ceremony. It is cleared and mats spread for participants to sit on around the circumference.

Special hand game rituals involve the presence of tarutsius or their equivalent, of old men, chiefs and braves in specified positions. Such seating plans involve old ceremonial ideas and the positions in which such individuals are placed by ritual owners are traditional stations. These individuals, and all other officials at the hand game demonstration are and must be men (save guessers and bundle owner), a predominance of the male element in the control of ceremony which comes from the ancient ritual code. The emphasis is followed out into the seating plan of the usual form of play, Crows against Eagles, and men cluster toward the altar end.

The general structure of the hand game ceremony, as a ritual, introduces the formal order of events of older ceremonies. The general arrangements are completed prior to the opening of the demonstration proper, and the occasion officially opens with a smoke offering. After the performance of the main body of activity of the ceremony (the game itself with its intervals of dancing) comes a feast, before which a ceremonial food offering must be made.

In following out a ritual sequence of events that is ancient, each formal ceremonial event is carried out according to the old code. The smoke offering involves the handling of the bundle pipe according to traditional ritual pipe lore; it is filled the same way, received the same way, handled with the same motions, and returned with the same motions. The choice of the offerer follows the old form, the type of individual selected also. In the smoke offering itself the structure of the offering is composed of four phases with subordinate modes, and each of these detailed aspects can be identified with a similar part of the smoke offering of an old ceremony. In carrying out this offering as other offerings, the rules of the ceremonial circuit are retained, and the special aspects of a ritual which cause a break in the ceremonial are of the same type as those which affect the strict adherence to the ceremonial circuit in old ceremonies. In lighting the pipe, the traditional station for lighting is maintained, and it is lit in the same way with braided sweetgrass from the bundle or a brand from the fire.

In the details of the offering the basic orientations of powers addressed are carried over from old ceremony. These are Tirawahat^n (the expanse of the heavens), Mother Earth, the Morning Star in the East, the Evening Star in the West, the Sun in its passage across the southern horizon, the Moon in its passage across the southern horizon, and in some rituals special orientations of ancient meaning, such as the North Star, and the South Star. There are in addition orientations with new meanings which come from the Ghost Dance doctrine itself (see below).

In the smoke offering, the pipe is offered to objects at or on the altar and to men present. In these offerings not only are the traditional modes retained, but the ceremonial order in which the offerings are made are correlated with the ritual significance of the objects present and the stations represented by men, as in the older forms.

The food when it is brought in at a hand game ritual is placed at the east between fireplace and doorway. In these rituals the general clustering of the food is subordinated to the buckets of corn, and the position in which all is placed is the old position in which corn brought in is placed. In older rituals there is also an offering with meat, which is absent in the game rituals. Ceremonial meat would be placed at the southeast, cut up there, cooked in the fire at the ceremony, and taken out at the northeast. Then portions would be arranged again at the southeast. All this is absent in the game rituals, since ceremonial meat is not used, and what meat is eaten is considered relatively "profane." Hence the corn used dominates the food ceremonialism, and it is the ancient manner and lore of corn offerings which determines the mode and detail of the food offering at a hand game ceremony. In detail the phases and modes of the offering with corn, the use of the horn spoon, the motions and gestures, and most of the orientations, are identical with analogous aspects of the corn rituals of old ceremonies, and the congruence of the corn offering of a hand game ritual with the smoke offering of that same ritual is true to traditional thought.

Following the offering there is a ritual service of food which again brings to bear old ceremonial patterns, and the structure of this order of service is integrated with the ritual offerings of a hand game in the same way that this is done in an old bundle ritual.

In the hand games the basic division into north and south moieties and the associated color symbolism—light colors for the south, (red, yellow, white), dark colors for the north (black, green, blue), are derived from older ceremonial belief and thought and old society forms, and the meaning of these associations of color and horizons is the same. In terms of these color associations, and specific associations of species with horizons or directions, most of the paraphernalia is so painted, decorated and ornamented, as to indicate its affiliation.

A number of specific game rituals, in addition to the many generic phases of old ritualism which they involve, have also carried into the present specific aspects of an old ritual form. These are particularly the game rituals which involve revivals of special ritualisms, such as the Pipe Dance, definite societies, medicine men's ways, and the like. In addition there is the complicated thought involved in Pierson's manner of reproducing in a game a mergence of all bundles and their ways, a sacred opening of bundles; and the report that Mrs. Washington in early Ghost Dance days, used game demonstrations as ceremonial occasions on which to distribute sacred corn seed.

I have said that in addition to Pawnee ceremonialism as a source, we must look to the Ghost Dance religion for many traits that have been added to the hand game in the course of its transformation. Practically all new traits which cannot be traced to the generic old ceremonialism of the Pawnee come from the Ghost Dance.

Perhaps most fundamental are the conceptual changes. The Pawnee Ghost Dance is associated with the Arapaho center of the Ghost Dance. In this area the movement never took on a warlike aspect. Whatever was to be in the coming time, with the destruction of the white man, and the rehabilitation of the old Indian life, was to come about through faith and belief, through a faithful return to ancient codes and manners, and through Ghost Dancing as an active mode of fortifying belief and faith. This permeates the whole movement among the Pawnee, and the ceremonial ways which are associated with it. The hand game played in a Ghost Dance hand game ceremony has no longer warparty aspects. The absence of war ideology occured first of all perhaps at the Arapaho center from which the Pawnee Ghost Dance hand game inspiration came, but is consistent also for the Pawnee. It has been pointed out that among certain Plains tribes gambling is conceived generally as warfare and warfare as gambling[1] but the distribution

---

[1] Wissler, Blackfoot, p. 59.

of gambling games of the same form as those found associated with war ideology is far wider, indicating that the associated ideas are not necessary, and do not together form one historical complex. The association in fact remains to be explained. This being the case we may consider the two aspects both in their association and apart. Both gambling and warparty ideas are eliminated from the Pawnee hand game in the course of its transformation into a ceremony. It seems to be the peaceful nature of the Ghost Dance faith which demands that forms of play involving struggle and fighting be abandoned.

The conceptual change comes out clearly in the new idea of the significance of winning and losing. It is said the winners are the faithful, the losers the sinners; the winners are the honest folk (meaning doubtless honest in their profession of faith), the losers the liars; the winners are the good people, the losers the evil. Beyond that come the ideas of good fortune, for not only have the winners established their faith more securely, but they have secured a promise of the beneficent interest of the powers in them, and have proved their established rapport with the powers is sure and will issue in protection for them when the earth turns and they are reunited with their loved deceased ones. They have also proved the greater power of their intermediaries, such as the bird messengers, the crow and eagle, and the deeper penetration of their vision experiences into the other world.

The vision experiences are in the Ghost Dance mandates to continue faithfully the religious activity, and to establish specific forms of its expression. These visions are of the free individual type of the Plains, a form which while it must have been basic, ultimately, to Pawnee religion, was not functioning actively for several generations prior to the Ghost Dance. The religion of the Pawnee had already attained a stable structural form, and involved intensive and manifold ritual activities and complex theology. Hence the Pawnee found adequate religious outlet in their established and traditional forms, and for the most part the dream and trance vision was subordinated to the carrying out and transfer by learning of the many formalized ritual activities. As suggested in Chapter III, the old forms had established themselves strongly along with the doctrine that a ritual could only be transferred by the process of learning it from its owner and controller. In this way the old forms were gradually dying out. The free visions of the Ghost Dance were not only sanctions to the visionaries for their own behavior, but mandates to revive old cultural forms, and to this aspect we must trace the many revivals of societies, dances, ceremonies, and ideas which are associated with the hand game ceremonies.

The hand game ceremony is so much a gift of the powers in the west that when it is a vision derivation the thankfulness of the receiver must be indicated by holding aloft the game set in the intervals toward the powers who gave it, in the same way that in the vision these powers offered it to the one below.

The visions are free and individual in so far that there is no restriction in the matter of sex, and so for the first time in Pawnee ceremony we have women owning and controlling rituals. Their participation goes even further. While it seems to be true that among many tribes who play the hand game, both men and women play it (although there is usually the restriction that at any specific game only one sex participates), among the Pawnee the women never played the game. This would be consistent, furthermore, with its warparty ideology, since the women did not participate in the war societies and war activities. Thus the entrance of the women into the play of the game, and as the actual owners of game rituals, is a phase of these game ceremonies which must be traced to the type and significance of the religious experiences of the Ghost Dance. That significance manifests itself in other ways in these ceremonies. The Ghost Dance promise of a renewed aboriginal life was a promise to all the people of the tribe and surrounding tribes, without restriction of sex, involving only the limitation that the faithful alone would survive. This mood is part of the Christian ideas which appear in the Ghost Dance. The Father who is looking after the welfare of the deceased is none other than Christ. He is the Chief in the Western sky. In short, while the Evening Star and her priests are still there and still functioning, it is this Father who is to be the chief instrument of the change. It is usually he who looks down upon the people and tells them to dance, and reminds them that above in the west they are all dancing and looking down, and who hands individuals the game sets. This is reflected in the altars and game rituals, even to the presence of a picture of Christ and cross symbols. The association of both the Christ conception and the old significance of the west with the same orientation brings about a relation of the two to each other, such as we have seen in the identification of the Crucifixion with the Morning Star Sacrifice ceremony, of the star symbol with the cross, etc. But the Christian conception of the Father of his people which now dominates the west is too clearly the old Pawnee idea of the function and office of a chief not to have its effects, and for the first time in Pawnee ceremony we find that chiefs, sitting in the traditional places and stations of priests, are the ceremonial officials and leaders in ritual demonstrations. Apparently the thought is that the activity in hand is one which requires the offices of a chief, even as the Chief who is the Father is leading the dancing and playing in the west above. Again, it is a new thought that chiefs participate in the hand game play at all. When it was a gambling game they might look on but they did not play, because a chief was supposed to have attained a more serious and stable mood and frame of mind. The elimination of the gambling element opens the game to their participation, and the needs of Ghost Dance doctrine makes them the natural leaders.

In the hand game ceremonies many of the structural aspects are taken over directly from the forms of Pawnee Ghost Dancing. Thus we have the Crow and Eagle symbolism, finally eventuating in the recognition of two organized moieties, the symbolism which attaches to much of the paraphernalia, the significance of its decoration, and the like. The hand game being a Ghost Dance ceremony, we have Ghost Dancing in the intervals between games. The position in the order of events is consonant with dancing at the old gambling game and the counting of coup, but the content is here the Ghost Dance. At this dancing, visions are sought, many crying for them, and trance visions are induced by Ghost Dance leaders in the usual hypnotic ways. The songs used are the regular Ghost Dance songs, and at the close of the hand game ceremony the form required when it was carried out fully was to conclude with ten Ghost Dance songs ending with the closing song of the Ghost Dance. This was the manner in which a Ghost Dance dance proper would be finished off. From the Ghost Dance forms come the organizations of singers who are employed in the hand game ceremonies to sing for their respective sides. Many of the play songs used at the Ghost Dance hand game ceremonies for the play of the game are songs of a revival nature learned in Ghost Dance visions. The emphasis upon seven games especially in playing "straight" is from the Ghost Dance stressing of seven, even as the numbers of the two singing organizations are seven. From the Ghost Dance doctrine of a coming blessing for all the people comes the need of general participation of all in the forms of religious expression; this is what prescribes the necessity of turns in the play, so that all present have their opportunity. The formal order in which turns are taken at any game demonstration, while defined by the original vision teachings of the bundle, follows old forms of ritual order, being determined particularly by the requirements of carrying out the ceremonial circuit, and of ritual symmetry.

The use of musical instruments, such as drums and rattles, was unknown to the old gambling handgame, in which clapping hands was the only accompaniment of the singing. Nor can the use of these instruments be traced altogether to generic ceremonialism; the drums are not the old wooden, waterfilled drums used in sacred ceremonies. Furthermore the use of these instruments does not come from the Ghost Dance, which was unaccompanied by instruments. Instead the use of drums derives from the forms of the old societies, so much revived at the time of the Ghost Dance and the beginning of the hand games; and the use of rattles in a few games seems to be primarily associated with the requirements of the visions of those games and the cultural content of those visions.

SUMMARY

The preceding discussion has gathered together the loose strands of details and considered them under generic heads: the persistences, losses and accretions. These facts throw into a clear light the summary statement that: The change in the aspect of culture we have been considering was a transformation of a gambling hand game into a Ghost Dance hand game ceremony. What persisted was the game itself, with its forms of play and of arranging for play; what were eliminated were the gambling aspects, and the associated war party simulations; what was added to make the new form was the generic type of ceremonialism and ritualism of the Pawnee, and the concepts and suggestions of the Ghost Dance religion and the Ghost Dance ceremonial forms.

In the lengthy analysis which has brought us to this conclusion, each detail of the old and the new and the associated cultural sources have been considered. There is to my knowledge no residue. In a typical case of controlled cultural transformation, the method of exhaustive analysis supported by historical background has demonstrated with exactitude the origins and influences of change. It remains to consider briefly the perspective of the history of the game rituals and their significance as the major outcome of the Ghost Dance period.

XII
HISTORY AND
SIGNIFICANCE OF
THE GHOST DANCE HAND GAME

DISTRIBUTION OF THE GHOST DANCE HAND GAME

The Ghost Dance hand game was not a development of the Pawnee alone. We have already noted that the Arapaho Ghost Dance hand game probably preceded the Pawnee in time, and was the immediate source of inspiration of the Pawnee development. Available material has revealed only four other tribes which developed Ghost Dance hand games: Wichita, Oto, probably Assiniboine, and possibly Cheyenne.

Kroeber visited the Arapaho in 1899 and 1900. At that time he found the Ghost Dance guessing games already elaborately developed. Kroeber states, "Rather elaborate sets of a form of guessing game were made in considerable numbers at the time of the ghost-dance movement. These sets consist of buttons hidden in the hand, of sticks used as counters, and usually of other sticks and feathers which are used as pointers, as symbols of gifts of food, and in other semi-ceremonial ways."[1] Again, "A full set of objects for the game would seem to consist of hiding-buttons in pairs, a pair of feathers for pointers, ornamented sticks as food sticks, a pair of specially ornamented sticks for two singers, and a single longer stick for the host, besides accessory head-dresses. Most of the objects would be in two sets of colors, sometimes red and yellow, but usually red and black."[2] "The players using the black sticks are called "magpies"; those with the red sticks "crows." The number of such stick counters seems to be most frequently ten. In one set there are twenty; but the ten sticks used by each side are of two kinds. There is a secondary tendency toward twelve sticks."[3] Kroeber has detailed an exhaustive description of the game sets and the meaning of their symbolic decoration.[4]

While Kroeber has not recorded the play of the Arapaho Ghost Dance hand game, we may be sure from the type of these sets that

---

[1] Kroeber, Arapaho, part 4: p. 368.
[2] Ibid., 371.
[3] Ibid., 369.
[4] Ibid., 368—382.

these Arapaho games were ceremonialized hand games, not the old gambling games. The counters never number eight, which is the basic number in the Pawnee form, indicating that although the Pawnee probably took their inspiration from the Arapaho, the form of play continued to be that of the Pawnee game of earlier days.

Mooney's last visits to the Arapaho Ghost Dance center brought his evidence down to 1892—3. Up to that time, Mooney had apparently observed only the gambling hand game among the Arapaho.[1] Thus we can date the development of the Arapaho Ghost Dance hand game as having occurred between 1892—3 and 1899.

The Cheyenne were closely associated with the Arapaho Ghost Dance developments (see Chapter II). Nevertheless, we cannot be sure that the ritual hand game Ghost Dance ceremony was developed by the Cheyenne. Curtis specifically denies that the Cheyenne hand game was a ceremony, while she describes it in the following way:

"The game is held in a tipi, which is lit by a central fire replenished with fresh logs. The company sit on the ground, with four or five leaders of the singing grouped around a drum and the rest lined about the circular wall. The game opens with a prayer, delivered by one who may be, for the night, the leader in a game. In some tribes the hand game is itself a religious ceremony, but this is not the case among the Cheyennes. With the Cheyennes, the details of the game may change with each night of the playing, so there is always a leader to direct the game. This leader has usually beheld in a dream the arrangement of the game— the placing of the tally-sticks, and other details— or he has been taught by some spirit how the game is to be played on the night of his leadership...

"The opening hand game prayer asks that the games may be played as divinely revealed, and that to the people may be given happiness, good luck, health, welfare and old age. With simple dignity the leader tells of his dream, and gives his directions for the game...."[2]

These remarks indicate that individual forms of play follow vision sanctions and revelations. No gambling is suggested, but as well no ghost dancing at the game. Nevertheless the patterns are not those of the old gambling game and in view of comparative data imply the influence of the Ghost Dance. Curtis wrote in 1906—7.

---

[1] Mooney, Ghost Dance, 1008—1009; also quoted by Culin, Games, p. 268.

[2] Curtis, Indians' Book, pp. 161—162.

The Wichita developed the Ghost Dance hand game, probably, like the Pawnee, under the stimulation of the Arapaho. Dorsey visited the Wichita in 1901, and wrote a description of a Ghost Dance hand game as he witnessed it, which is printed by Culin. Culin also illustrates hand game sets of the Wichita Ghost Dance hand game. Counters are either eight or twelve, symbolism of colors and decoration of drums similar to what is found among the Pawnee.[1] My own experience among the Wichita shows that the ceremonialized hand game still follows early Ghost Dance forms; no complicated structuralization like the Pawnee has taken place.

The sets secured by Dorsey the same year (1901) from the Pawnee are all sets of the Ghost Dance hand game.[2] The earliest recorded mention of the ceremonial hand game among the Pawnee occurs in the agent's annual report for the same period.

"They have frequent and protracted dances and hand games. While the ghost dance is the most popular with them, they do not hold the same views respecting this as were originally held by the Indians. It has come to be a semi-religious affair, its leaders claiming to be students of the Bible and under inspiration from and communion with the Deity. It is accompanied by a feast paid for by some ambitious Indian, and lasts usually about five days. A large number of the tribe remains in camp from one to two months—in fact, as long as some one can be found with the necessary funds to furnish refreshments for recurring dances. The demoralization and loss of time resulting is great."[3]

This reference suggests that the games were four day affairs in 1901. This late date must not be accepted as the date of origin among the Pawnee. The sets collected show that the games were numerous and well developed. The general similarity between the Ghost Dance proper and the ceremonial hand game would tend to confuse the government observers, who, in reporting the prevalence of ghost dancing among the Pawnee in the years from 1892 on, were undoubtedly referring to all its forms under the one term. We have the recorded date for the Oto ceremonial hand game as 1894 or earlier. The Oto were closely associated with the Pawnee in Ghost Dance developments. Informants not only recall as early a date for the first Pawnee games, but also recall early games played together with the Oto.

---

[1] Culin, Games, 276—281.

[2] Ibid., 264—276.

[3] School Supt. Harvey, writing Sept. 1, 1902, Annual Report, 1901/02.

On the game among the Oto we have the remarks of a local agent writing in 1894:

"The greatest evil we have had to contend with at Otoe is the insatiable desire of nearly every member of the tribe for dancing. It would not be so bad if they would indulge in harmless dances, but they have what they term the "Hand Game," and claim it to be their worship of the "Great Spirit," which in reality is a form of the "ghost dance." We have worked hard to suppress this evil and have had partial success."[1]

The evidence of agents' reports during the years 1893 to 1900, while not conclusive, indicates that the ceremonial hand game did not develop among the Ponca, who lived close to the Pawnee and Oto, or for that matter among other southern Siouans.[2]

The only other reference to a hand game development which may be the ceremonial Ghost Dance hand game occurs in Lowie's account of the Assiniboine, whom he visited in 1907. "Hanbetcumbino, the handgame. This game has been recently revived by the Ft. Belknap people, and is played by a society, generally on Friday evenings. The buttons are two pairs of bones, or pieces of cherry-wood. Instead of indicating the guesses with the fingers, the players use a ceremonial wand...From 7 to 12 tally sticks are employed. Before the game the owner of the pointer gives a feast to his fellow members. Admission to the society is free, and both men and women may join. There are four players at a time, men alternating with women, but apparently never pitted against women. It is a rule of the game that all spectators within the lodge must take turns at playing...He (a member) was emphatic in stating that there was no gambling in the modern form of the game. The evening is concluded with a dance, in which the performers either move in a circle, or lift their feet without change of place. The set of objects used for the game is wrapped up in a bundle, and is not exposed on ordinary occasions. As played today this game seems to be a simplified form of the modern Arapaho (but apparently not Gros Ventre) guessing-game."[3]

That this ceremonialized form of the Assiniboine game is a modern development is substantiated by the earlier information of Denig, who described the hand game play as that of a gambling game.[4]

Tribes neighboring on the Assiniboine, so far as information goes, did not develop the Ghost Dance hand game. Kroeber,

[1] Agent Woolsey, August 15, 1894, Annual Report 1893/94.
[2] See the Annual Reports for these years.
[3] Lowie, Assiniboine, p. 17.　　　　[4] Denig, Indian Tribes, p. 569.

during the same years that he visited the Arapaho and found them playing the ceremonial hand game, was witness to the Gros Ventre game, which he found like the Arapaho in form of play, but altogether different from the Arapaho game in the absence of symbolism and ceremonialism.[1] It is not clear whether gambling was allowed or not.

Similarly the Blackfeet played a non-ceremonialized gambling hand game as late as 1903 to 1906.[2]

The evidence on dating among the six tribes known to have played the ceremonial hand game may be summarized as follows: Arapaho, between 1892—3 and 1899; Cheyenne, before 1906; Pawnee and Wichita, before 1901; Oto, by 1894; Assiniboine, by 1907. The earliest date is that for the Oto. This must be considered a matter of chance in our records. There can be little doubt that the degree of ceremonialization among the Arapaho, as well as the intensive development of the Ghost Dance proper by tribe, in association with the specific memory of living informants, establishes the priority in time of the Arapaho. The Oto, as well as the Pawnee and Wichita, must have developed the ceremonialized game along the general lines laid down by the Arapaho developments. How we are to account for the occurrence of the ceremonial hand game among the Assiniboine can for the present be only a matter of conjecture.

THE PAWNEE HAND GAME DEVELOPMENT

While this distribution of the ceremonial hand game may well not be complete, it indicates that the ceremonial game developed only among tribes who participated in a major way in the Ghost Dance, and primarily among tribes associated with the Arapaho Ghost Dance center. The occurrence of the ceremonial game suggests that each of the five tribes may have experienced a cultural renaissance under the stimulus of Ghost Dance doctrine, but only in the case of the Pawnee and Arapaho can we be sure of this. The hand game developments of the Pawnee and Arapaho, while stemming from a common inspiration which must be localized among the Arapaho, nevertheless developed along independent lines in the two tribes.

The first Pawnee development of hand games in the Ghost Dance years seems to have begun with the bringing out of old forms of play, as indicated by Tom Morgan's game, and the suggestion

[1] Kroeber, Gros Ventre, p. 186.
[2] Wissler, Blackfoot, p. 59.

of ceremonial game play, which Joe Carrion claims to have brought from the Arapaho in the fall of 1892. Tom Morgan's game, for play purposes alone, used the old form of Pawnee game play with eight counters; while Carrion claims to have first used twelve, as the Arapaho did, later changing to eight.

With the freeing of the Pawnee dancing from the control of White, individually revealed ceremonial games began to appear. These first games, it is said, employed only one drum, and were not at first organized into sides with definite designation as Crows and Eagles. The tendency of the visionaries to associate with one or the other, along with the side against side form of play of the older gambling game, and/or the Arapaho forms of ceremonial play, magpies against crows, may have been responsible for the organization of the sides. One drum was at first used, the singers for each side sitting to that side of the centrally placed drum.

The form of ceremonialization of the Pawnee game must be credited to the fact that the derivation of any individual game in an individual's vision followed the old theory of bundle derivation. The game set and associated objects becoming a bundle, its ceremonial treatment was in terms of old bundle ritual and ceremony.

The institution of seven singers was an Arapaho contribution to the Ghost Dance proper in the southern Ghost Dance area, and was directly instituted by Arapaho prophets among the Wichita and other tribes. This institution, begun by White among the South Band Pawnee, was elaborated and defined by the Skiri, who in terms of the institutionalization of the Seven Eagle Brothers and the demands of ritual symmetry, developed the complementary and analogous organization of the Seven Crows. As each step of this development took place, whether in the Ghost Dances or the ceremonial hand game, the forms were adopted as generic to both. Along with this development went the institutionalization of the use of two drums, one associated with each side and used by singers of that side.

The order of events at a ceremonial hand game was determined by the combination of the ritual order demanded of a bundle function, and the formal order of events of an old hand game. As the ceremonial games developed along the revival lines, the ceremonial associations of the games with old aspects of rituals and societies became apparent. The games, as the Ghost Dances themselves, were cultural instruments for revivals. The ceremonial associations, because of the theology of the Ghost Dance, included Christian ideas, which still later became more predominant.

The hand game ceremonies followed the time patterns of the

Ghost Dances. After the authoritative version of the Ghost Dance reached the Arapaho from Wovoka, the dances became four day ceremonies, the dancing on the last night continuing until the morning of the fifth day. The ceremonial games among the Arapaho, such as the one witnessed by Carrion, were also four day affairs, play occurring on each of the days at the time which in dances proper would be taken up by continuous ghost dancing. Similarly the Pawnee games were four-day affairs. The form seems to have been to play the game, interspersed with dancing, during the afternoons of four days, and the fifth night. The game forms may even have been preferred to a continuous routine of ghost dancing; they possessed the same associations and meanings and in addition satisfied the zest for play and gambling and called for a less strenuous dance routine.

As time passed the games disintegrated into one day affairs, as they are today. This occurred some time between 1902 and 1919, the year of Densmore's visit. Along with this disintegration came the change to church games, as in those of Moses and Allen; while finally, in recent years, the more ceremonial games which still exist are less and less played, and those games which are demonstrated are attended by many primarily as a form of social amusement. The game of Irene Goodeagle is specifically for non-ceremonial play.

SIGNIFICANCE OF THE HAND GAME DEVELOPMENT

The primary significance of this development of the Ghost Dance years has been considered already. We have seen how barren Pawnee life had become by 1892, how empty of cultural value. The Ghost Dance renaissance expressed a desire for the joys and pleasures attendant upon the native life of former years; it was a dramatic effort to recapture the old life. But a word needs to be added. Why was the transformation of a gambling game into a ceremony so predominant an expression of this effort?

First and foremost, because it brought back into activity forms of play, enjoyable on their own account. Revivals of play were among the most important of the cultural revivals, because play was missing from the life of the Pawnee in 1892. Secondly, the creation of the individualized forms of hand games replaced the old forms of creative intellectual effort. Carrying out most of the rituals was impossible; developing new ritual forms based on the vision and associated with the old life of planting, hunting and war was also impossible. The old ritual ceremonies were not only occasions of sanctity to the Pawnee, but also affairs of dramatic beauty. The ritual movements and gestures, the symmetry and order of the performance, the complexity of associations and acts to be remembered and performed, constituted an intellectual and aesthetic experience for the participant and the observer. All this was missed by the people. The ceremonial hand game became at once a mode for creative intellectual effort on the part of some, and aesthetically satisfying experiences on the part of the others. All who joined in the games succeeded in renewing the experiences and pleasures which had attended the old rituals and ceremonies.

For these reasons I have argued that the hand games were the chief intellectual product of Pawnee culture in the last forty years. They called upon the originators for intensive creative effort within a formal style; they were reasoned and symmetrical "dances" of a high order. Beside such a development, the peyote cult seems a religion of sleep and forgetfulness, an inactive and slothful attempt to avoid the issues of life.

Along with the redevelopment of forms which satisfied the desire for play and for creative effort, it must also be remembered that game ceremonies were occasions for large-scale social gatherings. The number present at a hand game in the early days was limited only by the ability of the people to get to the place at which it was held. Continuing over four days, during which the whole gathering was camped at one place, there were many hours of the day for social intercourse. The scattering of the tribe on allotments made this a real need, which the hand games could satisfy.

CONCLUSION

Culin, after an exhaustive survey of American Indian games, came to the following conclusions, among others:

"(3) That as they (the games of the North American Indians) now exist, they are either instruments of rites or have descended from ceremonial observances of a religious character...

"(5) That while their common and secular object appears to be purely a manifestation of the desire for amusement or gain, they are performed also as religious ceremonies, as rites pleasing to the gods to secure their favor, or as processes of sympathetic magic, to drive away sickness, avert other evil, or produce rain and the fertilization and reproduction of plants and animals, or other beneficial results.

"(6) That in part they agree in general and in particular with certain widespread ceremonial observances found on the other continents, which observances, in what appear to be their oldest and most primitive manifestations, are almost exclusively divinatory."[1]

Elsewhere Culin states that his earlier belief was that these games in origin went back to divinatory rites, a belief which he based upon Cushing's information that "the gaming implements which are sacrificed upon the Zuni altar were symbols of divination with which the ceremonies were originally connected." The absence of corroborative information from other tribes apparently led Culin to abandon this view.[2]

In considering these games as having been in origin of a religious or ceremonial nature, Culin did not postulate an origin for games as such, but considered rather the specific origin of the games of the North American Indians. This attitude referred not only to the guessing games and dice games, but as well to many of the games of "skill and dexterity."

Nevertheless, such explanatory attempts must be considered in the light of the specific history of Pawnee guessing games as it has been developed in this treatment. We know, beyond reasonable doubt, that the Pawnee hand game prior to 1890 was a gambling game. While its associations with war party patterns may be cited as evidence that the meanings of the gambling play transcended the mere chance of winning and losing, and that hence we have evidence in the early Pawnee game itself of ultimate origins in rite or ceremony, these contentions are at best hypothetical and do not affect the main argument here. They are hypothetical because, as is shown by the processes of change which we know to have gone on in relation to these games among the Pawnee, it is just as possible that the war associations of the Pawnee gambling hand game were attached to a mere gambling game which existed apart from them, as that the relation is intrinsic and indicates an original base. The arguments do not affect the points raised here, because what we are concerned with is the description and understanding of processes of change. When we can understand one basic form and follow it through a series of transformations, we have a foundation for statements of the character of processes of change, and what these indicate as to the identity of the institution or complex considered through its changing phases.

In the history of the Pawnee hand game we have the transformation of a gambling game into a complex ritual. As the doctrine which called these rituals into being weakens, the rituals tend to

[1] Culin, Games, p. 809.
[2] Ibid., pp. 34—35.

relapse once more into mere games. On this basis, as a preliminary statement, it can be said that games may become rites, as well as rites games.

In the transformation of the game into a ritual, as shown in the preceding chapter, there is persistence, loss and accretion. The persistences, in this particular case the game play, constitute cognitively the identity under discussion. They are, as it were, the nucleus or core of meaning in terms of which we are able to consider processes of change. These processes are then seen to be the dissociation from and association to the nuclear core or constant of other variables. In our particular case, the difference between the core of game play and the old gambling game involves the dual aspects of gambling and war party simulations. These are readily seen to be detachable, since they were dissociated from the play of the game in the course of its transformation. On the other hand, the difference between our constant of game play and the ceremonial hand game consists of ceremonialism and Ghost Dance ideology. These are associated to the core of game play, from which fact we know that the relation is relatively extrinsic. The transformation of the Ghost Dance hand games proper into the later Baptist hand games, or mere games, could be considered in a like manner. In such a case we need a different base. What is common to the games of Allen and Moses on the one hand, and the older ceremonial games on the other? It is the play of the game plus some ceremonial arrangements. Some of the ceremonial arrangements which come to be associated with hand game play when the game is ritualized persist into the later forms. Thus Moses and Allen use altar arrangements, the division into sides with names, some form of blessing before starting the game, etc., but specifically eliminate smoke offerings and food offerings, ceremonial singing groups, etc. What they have eliminated are definitely those aspects which carry the meaning of old Pawnee religion. Some are replaced by Christian meanings of a similar sort, such as asking for a blessing in the Baptist manner instead of making a smoke offering. Here again we are dealing with types of association and dissociation of extrinsically related themes to and from a certain analytic core or constant. If we further consider the most recent tendencies of the game we find that the sets are still considered to require a certain sanction, and to necessitate the altar arrangement of leaders (who are chiefs) at the head end, the order of taking turns (which must include everyone), the division of the players into named moieties with associated half sets of tally sticks, etc. These aspects are all in addition to the core of game play which is the analytic constant throughout the transformations from gambling game to ritual to church game to social game. They might be called "survivals" from the ceremonial Ghost Dance hand games, because in those games their existence was significant, viz., their connotation and denotation was bound up with the whole complex ideology of the ritual games in a systematic manner. In the game type of recent tendency their presence needs explanation, and that explanation requires the use of the historical background. That background is not necessary to an explanation of why they are retained, but it is unavoidable if we are to know that they are something retained, and why they are associated with the games at all.

An illustration may make this methodological point clear. The ritualization of the game in terms of Ghost Dance doctrines called for the participation of men, women and children. The gambling hand game was limited to men, or boys. This general participation of all filled a great need for social intercourse in Pawnee life. With the wane of the doctrinal meaning of general participation in the game, the social function of these game gatherings is preserved by retaining the requirement that men, women and children join in and that everyone present must take a turn to play. All that explanation in terms of the contemporary could offer here would be a statement that the gatherings to play the hand game fill a social need, serve a social function. The contrast between the Pawnee game and the still widely distributed gambling hand game in which the two sexes never participate would remain unexplained. The historical background indicates here that a pattern which had doctrinal meaning has survived its religious sources because it serves a genuine social function; and at the same time it explains why general participation of all the people in playing the hand game is among the Pawnee associated with a form of play which elsewhere is a gambling game excluding the participation of both sexes.

I have sketched the significant transformations in this way to indicate a general method or plan which applies, not only to this treatment of a game, but to a treatment of any aspect of human culture when we are interested in the processes of change and their character. Over a period of time through which changes can be traced and controlled, and their meaning, sources and stimuli disclosed, we plot a cultural institution or complex. The persistent core constitutes an analytic unit or constant against which the changes can be visualized. This method makes clear that the total institution at any one time, viz., the core plus its analytically revealed associations, is a manifold which is not a unit system. The argument can be pushed further. If we were to consider on its own account that which in the present discussion I am calling the nuclear core, viz., the play of the game, it could be shown that this in turn is not a connected system of intrinsically related aspects, but also a combination of meanings which have tended to become associated. We have only to refer to Chapter IV, herein, in which some of the varieties of the hand game are considered, as well as related variables, the other guessing games, to realize that the hand game is not an indivisible unit. For example, there is no a priori necessary relation between the principle of guessing between two or four alternatives, and the manner of scoring by the use of eight tally sticks: the tally sticks could theoretically be any number, and could be used in various manners. In short, the play of the hand game itself, here considered for analytical or methodological purposes a core or unit, has itself a history in terms of processes of change. This indicates that the analytic constant is such in relation to a definite inquiry. Analysis of that constant may indicate that it is itself a manifold, as in this case. On the other hand, it does not follow from what has been said that that which is discovered to be an analytic constant in one given inquiry need necessarily prove to be itself composed of themes which are merely associated together. This latter fact is important. It leaves open the possibility of discovering systemic relations within culture which have the character of necessary or causal connection.

The implication herein then, is that it is for the purpose of a definite inquiry that it is methodologically possible and useful to determine analytically a relative unit of culture. My intention is also to show that developmental or transformational changes come about by processes of associating and dissociating meanings to and from that which in the particular inquiry is analytically determined as a nucleus. The next question concerns the character of the meanings which are added or taken away. We have considered a game, and the particular additions to it were of a ritual or ceremonial nature, hence we may say a game became a ceremony, or, as the process is tending to reverse itself, a ceremony is becoming a game. We can also say that the end result being achieved is that a gambling game has finally become a cultural institution for social gatherings. If we were still to consider a game, rather than any other institution, it would nevertheless be possible to show in other cases that artistic or aesthetic meanings can and do become associated with a game. An illustration of this is offered by the carved sets of sticks used in the stick game on the

Northwest Coast. Nor are mythologic or literary associations necessarily to be eliminated as possible accretions to a game core. In short, the particular associations which become attached to some particular persisting cultural core cannot be predicted or predetermined. On the other hand, a consideration of the processes of change which have gone on can show not only what the character of the added associations are, but that they have been added, to what they have been added, and in terms of conditions and influences, why they have been added. These generalizations apply not only to this discussion of a game, but, using it as an illustration of a controlled case of cultural change, to all cultural aspects and institutions.

I add a word lest these remarks be misinterpreted. In speaking of a cultural institution at any time as a manifold which is not a unit system, but a combination of meanings which have tended to become associated, I do not want to prejudge the question of necessary or what is usually called "causal" relationship. That is another problem and concerns the question of in how far given analytic units or sets of relations can be shown to reoccur repeatedly under similar conditions. What is meant here is that in relation to a career in time, an institution is a combination of cultural aspects or themes of different degrees of interrelationship; the linkages are not all of equal strength. Some aspects taken together form an analytic unit which can be shown to have persisted as such through a temporal career which is longer than that of others, or longer than the connection of the given unit with others. As an illustration let us consider two aspects of the hand games: first, the play of the game, which I have been calling the analytic core or constant, and second, the ceremonialism which was combined with it in the Ghost Dance hand game. The play of the game, as a constant, has had a longer career than the association between it and Pawnee ceremonialism, which, in relation to an analysis of the Ghost Dance hand game, indicates that the link between the play and the ceremonialism is not of the same strength as those between the internal aspects of the play of the game which have persisted as a unit complex. Pawnee ceremonialism, when taken on its own account, can be shown to have had a very long career in time as an integrated set of ritual patterns and ideas; and again, the indication is that the relation between separable aspects of the ceremonialism is closer than that between the ceremonialism as such and the play of the game. From the standpoint of an analysis of the Ghost Dance hand game, the institution is composed of at least two "systems" which are associated or combined. The systematic character of the separable complexes is, however, (subject to special independent consideration) *relative* to the consideration of the combined form. On a deeper level of analysis, within either of these "systems" we may find linkages between themes or aspects to be either of different or the same weights. If of the same weights, we may be dealing with a system of "necessary" relations.[1]

Latterly, social anthropologists have tended to emphasize the psychological aspects of the interplay between cultural phases or items and their cultural context. We have had this tendency in interpretations upon a variety of bases, such as psychological functions, sentiments, functional cultural disorders, psychological cultural types, and especially motivations and purposes. I have emphasized the importance of discriminating within a culture the types and degrees of cultural interconnection between aspects or elements. In the first place this seems to be an essential of modern scientific method. We know nothing of things save in so far as we can define and control their interrelations or interconnections with other things, and it is an inevitable part of such investigation to note the different modes and intensities of these functional interrelations. The understanding which comes with such analysis is not only more useful than vague conceptions of tendencies and hypothetical connections but to a great extent makes them superfluous. In the second place if we wish to consider psychological concomitants (I prefer "concomitants" to deductively derived "purposes" or motivational determinants) of cultural aspects, controlled investigation of cultural interrelationships is an inescapable preliminary. If differences of sentiments, feelings, emotions, etc. exist, and if they be at all correlated with the temporal duration of the association of some psychological content with some cultural institution, aspect, belief, etc., then it is obvious that we cannot understand the place of sentiments in a culture without making such discrimination of their depth or intensity. It is highly questionable whether this can be done on a pure psychological level in a primitive culture. On the other hand the cultural background with which such psychological aspects are associated can be analytically controlled. It is then possible to weight correlatively and to check this weighting.

---

[1] A method by which such a possibility can be checked has been indicated in reference to kinship and social organization in my Kinship Origins in the Light of Some Distributions.

In this sense then, the present study can be considered an illustrative case. In terms of it I would contend that methodologically time perspective or historicity is essential to an understanding of culture whatever special approach is undertaken.[1] Culture is not a static content but a dynamic continuum like the rest of the universe. Its state at any moment, as the condition of any element within it, has multitudinous associations, affects and effects, and has been determined by many factors of which the greater part have not determinately but accidentally come to play a part. It is impossible to substitute intuitional interpretation for the more lengthy and difficult attempt to control actual connections as they happen without sacrificing truth on the altar of preconceptions. The failure of many to realize that there are not two roads in anthropology, the historical and the psychological, but one method which is no different from analytical methods in other disciplines is probably to be traced to the judgment that history per se (viz., the theoretical absolute record) or psychological awareness are each ends in themselves, and that in each case our whole effort is directed toward attaining the one particular end. This attitude is I think in error. If in the course of this study I have conveyed an idea which has been in the background throughout, that cultural understanding is a manifold and that the more content we put into it the profounder it becomes, this study may prove of heuristic value. The historical record is instrumental, and so too is any psychological record which can be validated. But, and here I think the primary principle of our methodology must lie, the fact of historicity is neither an end nor by itself a means but a condition which must be recognized at every step. Lip-service alone will not do.

In this study historicity has, I hope, been used instrumentally. With its guidance the treatment offers, in relation to a limited case, the mechanics of continuing change in culture. Light has been thrown on many incidental points, both methodological and factual, but the main purpose has been to offer comprehension of an institution in terms of change. The severe limitation to the hand

---

[1] From the standpoint taken herein functionalism in social anthropology which is divorced from time perspective is metaphysically false. A spatial, static description of observed cultural interrelationships offers no technique by which the variability of the strength of connections which tie cultural aspects together meaningfully or functionally can be comprehended. If a chemist classed mixtures, solutions, compounds and free elements together in his experimental work the intellectual obstructionism in such an analogous case would be readily perceived.

game and its associated material, while it may eliminate from consideration more spectacular aspects of cultural breakdown among the American Indians, nevertheless is a methodological essential which results substantiate. It permits an integration of related materials around a central theme. This theme is the story of the development among the Pawnee of an institution which in part filled their intellectual and social needs in the midst of cultural barrenness — a cultural barrenness produced by uncontrolled assimilation.

BIBLIOGRAPHY

Berlin, Nathalie Carter, ed. *The Indians' Book.* New York: Harper, 1923.
Buckstaff, Ralph N. "Stars and Constellations of a Pawnee Sky Map." *American Anthropologist,* new series, 29:279-85.
Culin, Stewart. *Games of the North American Indians.* Bureau of American Ethnology, Annual Report 24, pp. 1-809. Washington, D.C.: Government Printing Office, 1907.
Denig, Edwin T. *Indian Tribes of the Upper Missouri.* Bureau of American Ethnology, Annual Report 46, pp. 325-628. Washington, D.C.: Government Printing Office, 1930.
Densmore, Frances. *Pawnee Music.* Smithsonian Institution, Bureau of American Ethnology, Bulletin 93. Washington, D.C.: Government Printing Office, 1929.
Dorsey, George A. *Traditions of the Skidi Pawnee.* Memoirs of the American Folk-Lore Society, vol. 8, 1904.
Dunbar, John B. "The Pawnee Indians." *Magazine of American History* 4:241-81, 5:321-85, 8:734-56.
Grinnell, George B. *Pawnee Hero Stories and Folk Tales.* New York: Forest and Stream Publishing Co., 1889.
——. *Story of the Indian.* New York: D. Appleton and Co., 1895.
Gunther, Erna. *Klallam Ethnography.* University of Washington Publications in Anthropology, vol. 1, no. 5. Seattle: University of Washington Press, 1927.
Kappler, Charles J., ed. *Indian Affairs, Laws and Treaties.* 2 vols. 57th Cong., 1st sess., 1903, doc. 452.
Kroeber, Alfred L. *The Arapaho.* Part IV, "Religion." Bulletin of the American Museum of Natural History, vol. 18, part 4. New York: The Trustees, 1907. Pp. 279-454.
——. *Ethnology of the Gros Ventre.* Anthropological Papers of the American Museum of Natural History, vol. 1, part 4. New York: The Trustees, 1908.
——. *Handbook of the Indians of California.* Smithsonian Institution, Bureau of American Ethnology, Bulletin 78. Washington, D.C.: Government Printing Office, 1925.
Lesser, Alexander. "Cultural Significance of the Ghost Dance." *American Anthropologist* 35:108-15.
——. "Functionalism in Social Anthropology." *American Anthropologist* 37:386-93.
——. "Kinship Origins in the Light of Some Distributions." *American Anthropologist,* new series, 31:710-30.
——. "Levirate and Fraternal Polyandry among the Pawnee." *Man,* 1930, no. 78.
——. "The Right Not to Assimilate." Occasional Papers, Phelps-Stokes Fund, 1961, entitled "Education and the Future of Tribalism in the United States." Reprinted in the *Social Service Review,* June 1961. Reprinted in Morton H. Fried, *Readings in Anthropology,* 2d ed., 1968, vol. 2, pp. 583-93.
Levine, Stuart, and Nancy Lurie, eds. *The American Indian Today.* Deland, Fla.: Everett Edwards, 1968.
Lowie, Robert H. *The Assiniboine.* Anthropological Papers of the American Museum of Natural History, vol. 4, part 1. New York: The Trustees, 1909.
Mintz, Sidney W. "History and Anthropology: A Brief Reprise." In *Race and Slavery in the Western Hemisphere,* ed. Stanley L. Engerman and Eugene D. Genovese, pp. 477-94. Princeton: Princeton University Press, 1974.

Mooney, James. *The Ghost Dance Religion and the Sioux Outbreak of 1890.* Bureau of American Ethnology, Annual Report 14, part 2. Washington, D.C.: Government Printing Office, 1896.

Murie, James R. *Pawnee Indian Societies.* Anthropological Papers of the American Museum of Natural History, vol. 11, part 7. New York: The Trustees, 1914.

Murie, James R., and Clark Wissler. *Ceremonies of the Pawnee.* Smithsonian Institution, in press.

Royce, Charles C. *Indian Land Cessions in the United States.* Bureau of American Ethnology, Annual Report 18, part 2. Washington, D.C.: Government Printing Office, 1899.

Schifter, Richard "Trends in Federal Indian Administration. "*South Dakota Law Review 15* (Winter 1970).

Spier, Leslie. *Havasupai Ethnography.* Anthropological Papers of the American Museum of Natural History, vol. 29, part 3. New York: The Trustees, 1928.

Strong, William D. "Plains Culture in the Light of Archaeology." *American Anthropologist,* new series, 35:271-87.

————. "Review of the Pawnee Ghost Dance Hand Game." *American Anthropologist* 38:112-13.

United States, Indian Affairs Office. Annual Reports of the Commissioner of Indian Affairs. Washington, D.C., 1824 to date.

Williamson, John W. "The Battle of Massacre Canyon: The Unfortunate Ending of the Last Buffalo Hunt of the Pawnees." *Republican Leader,* Trenton, Nebraska, 1922.

Wissler, Clark. *Social Life of the Blackfoot Indian.* Anthropological Papers of the American Museum of Natural History, vol. 7, part 1. New York: The Trustees, 1911.